BIBLICAL COVENANTALISM

BIBLICAL COVENANTALISM

In Prophets, Psalms, Early
Judaism, Gospels, and Acts

Volume Two

Judaism, Covenant Nomism,
and Kingdom Hope

Douglas W. Kennard

WIPF & STOCK · Eugene, Oregon

BIBLICAL COVENANTALISM
in Prophets, Psalms, Early Judaism, Gospels, and Acts

Copyright © 2015 Douglas W. Kennard. All rights reserved. Except for brief quotations in critical publications or reviews, no part of this book may be reproduced in any manner without prior written permission from the publisher. Write: Permissions. Wipf and Stock Publishers, 199 W. 8th Ave., Suite 3, Eugene, OR 97401.

Wipf & Stock
An Imprint of Wipf and Stock Publishers
199 W. 8th Ave., Suite 3
Eugene, OR 97401

www.wipfandstock.com

ISBN 13: 978-1-66671-273-3

Dedicated to my son, Peter Kennard.
May he realize Christ's New Covenant benefits throughout his life.

CONTENTS

1 **Introduction** | 1

2 **A Deuteronomist Perspective in *Torah* and Covenant** | 8
   Torah Psalms | 10
   Covenant Renewal Psalms | 14
   Second Temple Development in Mosaic Covenant and Psalms | 17
   Conclusion | 23

3 **Davidic Covenant** | 25
   Davidic Covenant | 25
   Davidic Covenant Extended to Solomon and Beyond | 34
   New Covenant Embraces the Davidic Covenant | 38
   Royal Psalms | 39
   Daniel's Son of Man | 43
   Daniel's Messiah and the Seventy Weeks | 44
   Second Temple Jewish Expectations | 46
   Gospels | 54
   The Son of Man in the Synoptics | 63
   The Son of Man in the Gospel of John | 63
   Acts | 66
   Paul | 68
   Hebrews | 69
   Revelation | 70

4 **Jeremiah's Covenant Nomism and New Covenant** | 73
   Covenant Lawsuit | 73
   New Covenant | 79
   New Covenant in Second Temple Judaism | 87

CONTENTS

5 **Instances of Covenant Nomism in Second Temple Judaism** | 90

God Graciously Elects and Recovers Israel in Covenant | 96
Covenant Nomism Entails a Two Ways Strategy | 103
Works of the Law | 114
Covenant Nomism as Salvation with an Afterlife | 124
Spirit Empowerment unto New Covenant | 129
Gentiles | 131
Conclusion | 134

6 **Matthew's Jesus on the Law** | 136

Jesus as Teacher of the Law | 138
Sermon on the Mount and Plain (Matt. 5–7; Luke 6:20–49) | 140
Excursus on Righteousness in the Synoptics | 152
Matthew 5:17–20; The Law and the Kingdom Salvation Paradigm | 155
Matthew 5:21–48; Jesus Teaching of the Law | 164
Jewish Legal Controversies with Jesus | 182
Jesus as the Superior Jewish Scribe (Matthew 21–23) | 191
Excursus on Jesus' Death in the Synoptics: Service and Martyrdom | 197
Jewish-Christian Lineage | 208

7 **As a Gentile Gospel, Mark Eschews Mosaic Law and Jewish Tradition** | 214

8 **Luke and John: Spirit Extended Salvation to the Gentiles Without the Law** | 221

Gentile Recipients of Luke and John | 223
The Spirit in the Synoptics | 223
Synoptic Gospels: Israel Emphasis With Occasional Gentile Events | 225
Gospel of Luke's View of Law for Jews | 230
John's Promise of the Spirit | 233
The Great Commission | 235
Bestowal of the Spirit, Gentile Salvation and the Parting of the Ways | 235
Paul Called by Christ as Apostle to Gentiles | 239
Jerusalem Council Decision | 241

9 **Conclusion** | 248

Bibliography and Index will be in third volume: *Biblical Covenantalism in New Testament Epistles: Engagement of the New Perspective and New Covenant Atonement.*

1

Introduction

THIS BOOK IS ABOUT Biblical Covenantalism. Let me define these terms. "Biblical" because this book is a selected study of *biblical theology*. That is, the biblical text analyzed in its context will define the terms and agenda for how to approach covenantal material in the Bible and in Christianity.[1] Covenants are used to increase confidence in God's promise and to establish a lasting framework of hope and direction within the narrative. The previous volume, *Biblical Covenantalism in Torah* provides a basic orientation to this trilogy which this volume, *Biblical Covenantalism in Prophets, Psalms, Early Judaism, and Gospels, and Acts*, extends further. Explanations and defense are provided in the respective chapters explaining the covenants and issues. This volume extends the idea of Jewish concepts for salvation into an afterlife and into Christianity, even to such changes as to include Gentiles within salvation. The development in this volume will be further brought to an integrated Christian salvation, ethic and eschatological hope in the third volume: *Biblical Covenantalism in New Testament Epistles*.

Each of the biblical Covenants is initiated by God and continues forever. So instead of a multi-economy theology like Dispensationalism, or a Covenant Theology with a unified people of God for all time, or a supercession[2] program under which the subsequent peoples of God only reflect part of the Biblical material, each of the respective peoples of God benefit from their respective covenants with which they are associated. Each additional covenant adds to the previous revelation so that the covenant program builds upon itself. However, once each of these biblical covenants begins it continues as an everlasting covenant from

---

1. My methodology is explained in detail in: Kennard, *A Critical Realist's Theological Method* and *The Relationship Between Epistemology, Hermeneutics, Biblical Theology and Contextualization*.

2. Supercession replaces Israel's future with that of the Church.

God describing another layer of divine governance. That is, the blessing and obligation continues from these covenants forever. This progressive revelation program can be charted as follows:

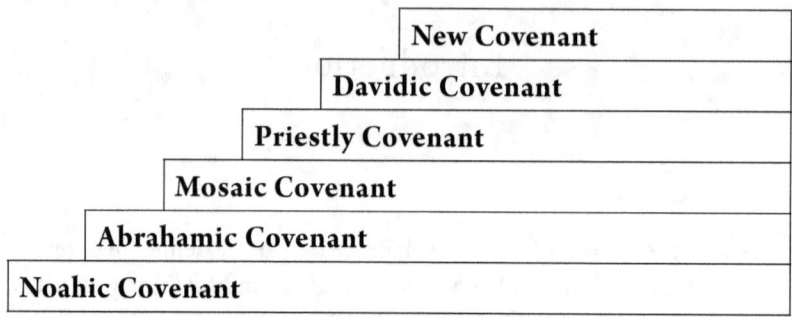

If aspects of these covenants challenge or contradict each other, then the subsequent covenantal revelation takes precedence for the intended audience. For example, the New Covenant governs the Christian, so that the Mosaic Covenant stipulations are not required for Gentile inclusion into Christianity (Acts 15:1–29).

The election covenants (Abrahamic, Mosaic, and New) especially telescope out of each other and govern much of the same blessing. My previous volume, *Biblical Covenantalism in Torah*, laid a foundation in the first two of these covenants briefly summarized in this introduction. The New Covenant was hinted at within the Mosaic Covenant. However, the New Covenant promises the divine Spirit to transform Israelites so that they might obey the Mosaic Covenant and continue with its covenant blessings even into an afterlife.

The Abrahamic Covenant is an everlasting unilateral covenant grant guaranteed by God for the nation of Israel, but each individual male is conditionally included within the covenant based on his involvement with its sign of circumcision (Gen 12; 15; 17). Presumably, females are included as daughter of or wife of a circumcised male. The covenant primarily promises Israel's blessing (honor, blessed, blesser, nation, land). This covenant is especially important in defining Israel as a divinely elect ethnic people and nation continuing the genetic, national, and covenantal heritage of Abraham. Israel's eschatological future is grounded in a land promise. Political alignment and blessing of Israel provides other nations and peoples with the opportunity to be blessed by God. Some Abrahamic Covenant benefits are extended to the Church by blessing believer's with repentance and broad salvific blessing, and thus making the Church Abraham's spiritual seed (Acts 3:25–26; Gal 3:16–18). The Abrahamic Covenant telescopes into the Mosaic Covenant, since both are everlasting covenants which elect the nation Israel and provide guidance for their relationship with Yahweh and His ethic, which Israel is to live.

The Mosaic Covenant is an everlasting suzerainty treaty that binds Israel in a distinct relationship which extends God's Abrahamic Covenant blessings and land for Israel. God has elected Israel everlastingly as a people but this covenant is worked out in a conditional manner dependent upon each generation of Israel obeying the covenant stipulations (Exod-Lev; Deut; Josh 24; Neh 8; Jas 2:8–12). The loyalty issues and the call to love God is more reflected in the form of a suzerainty treaty. The remaining stipulations have more in common with ancient Near Eastern law codes because they are more concerned with the welfare of all subjects rather than just the Suzerain's rights.[3] Thus in its very makeup the Mosaic Covenant is a fusion of covenant and law or *covenant nomism*. This involves covenant nomism for Israel in blessing; Jewish faithfulness to God through the Mosaic Covenant contributes toward Yahweh's gracious national blessing. Such a Law-governed life is one of profound benefit (Ps 119). Unfortunately, the Bible is a record of Israel's rebellion and unwillingness to zealously live the Mosaic Covenant, so they repeatedly obtain curse. Jeremiah especially is exampled to show this impending curse through covenant lawsuit and oracle of judgment. Currently, Israel (mostly in dispersion) is under Mosaic Covenant curse for being unfaithful to Yahweh and rejecting their Messiah. Currently, to politically bless and enable Israel while God has them under covenant curse is working at cross purposes with God's Deuteronmist and Messianic curses upon them. Those heading toward the Kingdom in a Jewish setting should live out the Mosaic Covenant in a zealous intrinsic manner (Deut 10:16; Matt 5:17–28). Eventually Israel will be re-gathered into the land in Kingdom blessing and intrinsic obedience to Yahweh through the Mosaic Covenant (Deut 30:1–16; Rom 11:26). Historically, many Jewish Christians expressed their love of God through many of the details of the

3. Cross, *From Epic*, 3–21.

Law as well.[4] Within this perspective the phrase "works of the Law" in these contexts is best taken as the center of Jewish obedience to the Law.[5]

This last paragraph identifies that I am an advocate for both deepening the Jewish perspective for Israel and the third quest for the historical Jesus, but I embrace only about one sixth of the New Perspective for Paul, while I deeply position myself in the wake of pre-new Paul Jewish affirming interpreters such as Albert Schweitzer and W. D. Davies. Such a position could also be characterized as a post-new perspective with more nuance than accomplished by Douglas Campbell. Specifics are best seen in the following individual chapters, in the current volume, *Biblical Covenantalism in Prophets, Psalms, Early Judaism, Gospels, and Acts* (especially chapter five: "Instances of Covenant Nomism in Second Temple

---

4. Epiphanius, *Pan.* 2.3–5; 9.3.6; 15.3; 18.7–19.4; 21.1–6; 22.1–11; 30.7.1–7; 30.9.4; Justin Martyr, *Dial.* 47–48; Irenaeus, *Haer.* 1.26.2; Hyppelytus, *Refut.*; Clement of Alex., *Strom.* 2.9.45.5; Tertullian, *Marc.* 4.8; Origen, *Princ.* 4.3.8; Celsus statement in Origen, *Cels.* 2.1 and *Hom. Gen.* 3.5; Eusebius, *Hist. eccl.* 3.27.1–6; Chrysostom, *Homily* 32; Ignatius, *Magn.* 8–11; *Phld.* 6–9; Jerome, *Comm. Isa.* 3.30 on Isa 9:1; Augustine, *Faust.* 19.7; Pseudo-*Clementines Recognitions* 1.28.1–2; 1.32.4; 1.37.1–4; Hippolytus, *Haer.* 8.18.1–2; *Ps.-Clementine Homilies* 7.8; 42.355–56; *Didascalia Apostolorum* 21; Rouwhorst, "Jewish Liturgical Traditions," 82; These polemics against the Jewish-Christians are essentially the same polemics made against the Jews (for example, Aphrahat of Persia, Syriac *Demonstrations* 12–16); Klijn, "The Study of Jewish Christianity," 419–31; Taylor, "The Phenomenon," 31334; Bagatti, *The Church from the Circumcision*; Velasco and Sabourin, "Jewish Christianity," 5–26; Klijn and Reinink, *Patristic Evidence*; Ray Pritz, *Nazarene Jewish Christianity*; Skarsaune and Hvalvik, *Jewish Believers in Jesus*.

5. Several different Hebrew phrases translate as "works of the Law" (ἔργων νόμου) from either "works" (מַעֲשֵׂה) or "faithfulness" (עוֹלָם חַסְדֵי): Neh 13:14; 1QS 5.21, 23–24; 6.18; 1QpHab 7.11; 8.1; 12.4–5; CD 13.11; 4Q171 frgs. 1–2 ii 14; 4Q174 frgs. 1–3 ii 2; 4Q176 frg. 17 line 7; 4Q394 frag. 3–7 col. 1–2.1–3; 4Q398=4QMMT frag. 14 col. 2.3; C.23–28; 4QFlor. 1.1–7; 4Q470 frg. 1 line 4; 4QpPsa 1–2.2.14, 22; 11QT 56.3; 2 Bar. 57.2; 4 Macc 7.9; Lohmeyer, *Probleme paulinischer*, 31–74; Christianson, *The Covenant*, 334–35; Evans, "Paul and 'Works of Law,'" 201–26; Hofius, "Werke des Gesetzes," 271–310; Dunn, *The New Perspective on Paul*, especially chapters 1, 8, 10, 14, 17, 19 which were articles from 1992–2008 on works of the Law which nicely provides a trajectory for how the view grew; de Roo, "The Concept of 'Works of the Law,'" 116–47; "*Works of the Law*," esp. 1–26; Cranfield, "The Works of the Law," 89–101; these contrast with Dunn, *Romans*, 1:159; Sanders, *Paul and Palestinian Judaism*, 118; for example, of reformation view: Moo, *Romans 1–8*, 216–17; "'Law', 'Works of the Law,'" 82; Bachmann, "Rechtfertigung" 1–33; "4QMMT," 91–113. In spite of Dunn's identification of the concept with the "palisades and iron walls to prevent mixing with any other peoples" *Letter of Aristeas* 139–42 (*The New Perspective on Paul*, 8–9), even though the phrase "works of the Law" is not in the *Letter of Aristeas*; Hogterp, "4QMMT," 359–379.

Judaism"), and especially chapter three: "Covenant Pneumaticism-Paul, the Law, and the Spirit: As Seen Through the Wider Net of Covenants, Spirit, Disputed Practices, and the Parting of the Ways" within the final volume: *Biblical Covenantalism in New Testament Epistles*.

Additionally, the Mosaic Covenant sets a two ways framework within which Israel's relationship with Yahweh is shown by their consistency to choose to live within the narrow way of loving God and neighbor. In the synoptic gospels and Acts, this narrow way is also following Christ's ethic and mimetic atonement.[6]

The Noahic Covenant is an everlasting universal, unconditional covenant grant through which God promises to benefit all life with protection from global flood, and blesses humankind again with fruitfulness within the modified mandates of: eating meat while abstaining from blood and preserving human life (Gen 9; Acts 15:20, 29). This covenant is helpful in contributing to a universal human ethic within creation theology and also informs the Gentile Christian ethic to make Gentile Christians more palatable for a unified Christian community with Jewish Christians already included in Christ.

Additionally, there are covenants that ground ministries of service, such as the Davidic and Priestly Covenants. The Davidic Covenant, developed in this volume, guarantees a continuing lineage for David's family being on the throne as kings of Israel forever. Unfortunately, the sin of Davidic kings meant that they lost the throne for generations, leaving Judaism with the hope of an ultimate Davidic King to come and reign in the future. Many of the Abrahamic and Mosaic Covenant blessings such as fame, national protection, continuing in the land, peace, rest, blessing, and discipline in sin are also enmeshed with the Davidic Covenant (2 Sam 7:4–17). This Davidic Covenant is an everlasting covenant that ultimately brings about the everlasting reign of the Messiah upon the earth (2 Sam 7:12–16; Pss 89:2, 4, 29, 36–37; 132:12, 14; Luke 1:32–33; Rev 1:5–6; 22:5).[7]

---

6. Pate and Kennard, *Deliverance Now and Not Yet*, 19–72, 301–334, 401–482.

7. 4Q504 1–2 iv 4–8; cf. 4Q252 5.2–5; Abegg, "The Covenant," 82; 4Q161 frag. 7–10.iii.22; 4Q174 frag. 1–3.i.11–12; 4QpIsa. frag. 7–10 iii 22; *4QCommentary on Genesis A* 5.3–4; 4Q252 frag. 1 v. 3–4; 4Q285 frag. 5.3–4; frag. 7 lines 3–4; 11Q14 lines 12–13; *Pss. Sol.* 17.4, 21, 27–36; 18.7; 4Q252 fragment 1, 5:1–5 translated by WAC, 277 but corrected VanderKam and Flint, *The Meaning of the Dead Sea Scrolls*, 266, and myself; a similar point is made by 4Q521 column 2, and 4Q521 frag. 7.3.

Jesus is honored by wise men, His disciples and God as this everlasting Messianic King of Israel (Matt 1–2:11; 3:17; 16:16–17).[8] Jesus dies as the King of the Jews (Matt 26:63–64; 27). However, as King, Jesus already has a growing Kingdom of disciples and the world as His Kingdom which will, after judgment, be combined to become an eschatological expression of Kingdom (Matt 5:3–11; 13:31–33, 38, 41–43). Jesus is proclaimed to be the Davidic King in the gospel on the basis that God raised him already from the dead and seated him at the right hand of God (Acts 2:29–36). On the basis of the Davidic Covenant, Jesus is already declared to be the Christ functioning in His reign by His titles, throne, anointing, place of honor, and Christ's pouring forth the New Covenant Holy Spirit for ministry in the Church (Acts 2:33; Heb 1:5–13). There is a grander eschatological expression of the Kingdom not yet realized in which Jesus Christ will reign forever (Matt 5:4–9; Luke 1:32–33; Heb 1:13; Rev 1:5–6; 19–22).

Furthermore, the Priestly Covenant developed in the earlier volume (*Biblical Covenantalism in Torah*) is a Covenant Grant of Peace resulting in the Levitical line being in perpetual everlasting service as priests (Num 25:12–13). This promise is affirmed in both the Davidic and New Covenants (Jer 33:14–22; Ezek 44:10, 15; 48:11).

The New Covenant emerges as an everlasting covenant grant to transform Israel into a responsive and *torah*-obedient community in intimate relationship with Yahweh (Deut 30:3–6; Jer 31:27–37). Early Judaism recognizes that the New Covenant and the Mosaic Covenant fuse as the divine Spirit enables Israelites to obey and continue within the covenant blessings made available by these two covenants. This New Covenant is extended to all Christians, including Gentiles, highlighting that the believer in Christ is mystically *in* Christ in a New Covenantal manner whereby the Holy Spirit is relationally present to transform the believer's life (Luke 22:20; Acts 2:16–21).

The Spirit's empowerment within the New Covenant will eschatologically transform the heart of Israel so that Israel will obey the Law intrinsically and possess all those Abrahamic, Mosaic, Priestly and Davidic promises like the land, kingship, peace, functioning Levitical priesthood, and atoning Mosaic sacrifices (Jer 31:27–32:22; Ezek 40–46). Additionally, the New Covenant everlastingly brings resolution and peace for Israel and animals in Kingdom (Isa 11:6–9; 54:9–10; Jer 32:40; Ezek 34:25–30; 37:26; Hos 2:18). As such, the New Covenant is already instituted for the

---

8. Kennard, *Messiah Jesus*, esp. 377–414.

Church by Christ's death in a weaker form than eschatological Kingdom (of intrinsic Spirit motivation, Spirit produced righteousness and fruit, everlasting forgiveness, and cleansed conscience) (Luke 22:20; 1 Cor 11:25; 2 Cor 3; Heb 9–10; Acts 2:17–21 as compared to Joel 2:28–29). In that eschatological day, the Spirit causes each believer in Christ to resurrect with an immortal bodily unto eschatological Kingdom.

2

A Deuteronomist Perspective in *Torah* and Covenant Renewal Psalms

THE MOSAIC COVENANT IS Yahweh's gracious means for Israel to retain itself in God's favored blessing, having been initiated previously by Yahweh's election of the nation.[1] Yahweh's gracious loyal love includes Israel in a Covenant community relationship with Him (Pss 25:10; 40:11; 61:7; 89:14; 138:2). *Torah* Psalms (Pss 19; 119) praise the *Torah* (or Mosaic Covenant instruction and accretions) as the highest good that should govern all of Israel's life. The Wisdom Psalms begin to fuse the creation-based "you reap what you sow" (retribution principle) wisdom program with this Mosaic Covenant *Torah* (Pss 1:2; 37:31; 78:1, 5), pioneering this fusion which will become so commonplace in second Temple Jewish literature. However, the *torah* perspective is a more active personal involvement of God in judgment, recovery and blessing than the secondary creation based retribution principle of wisdom literature. In this *torah* perspective the psalms provide an active response in prayer to Yahweh as the Covenant Lawgiver Who directly brings judgment curse upon the disobedient (Deut 28:15–29:28) and to Whom the appeal is made as the active Redeemer, Protector, and Blesser of those who obey Him (Deut 28:1-14). So, *torah* psalms join with the main Covenant-Prophetic program of the O.T., providing a pattern for Israel to respond to this program in liturgy, as covenant renewal texts like Deut have provided its base. Covenant Renewal Psalms (Pss 50; 81) emerge from this same covenant renewal base that Deut provides, perhaps aided by the wisdom-regret that Israel has not kept *torah* (Ps 78:10). In this Deuteronomist perspec-

---

1. Sanders, *Paul and Palestinian Judaism*, 75, 420, 544; Neusner while critical of Sanders methodology accepts Sanders understanding of covenant nomism for Judaism ("Comparing Judaisms," 177–91). Von Rad affirms essentially the same points in *Old Testament Theology*, 1:130, 147, 371.

tive, obedience begets blessing and disobedience begets curse from Yahweh. However, grounded upon Yahweh's election of Israel, Yahweh is forever faithful to Israel in Mosaic Covenant to protect her (Pss 105:8, 10; 106:45; 111:5, 9) and call her to renew her commitment with Yahweh in Mosaic Covenant relationship (Ps 78:37). If Israel is faithful to the Mosaic Covenant, then Yahweh will be faithful in the Deuteronomic blessings of protection and empowerment in covenantal privilege (Pss 25:10; 103:18; 111:5). Such renewal at times involves a cultic sacrificial expression of recovery, which by the way is *not* the emphasis in the Psalms. Instead, the Psalms emphasize *renewal of the heart attitude and verbal acknowledgement in the community of one's sin for forgiveness* (Pss 32:5; 50:5; 51:16–19; 119:108; 130:1–4, 8). Edward Cook summarizes this Deuteronomist perspective within the book of Psalms as *covenant nomism*.

> The book of Psalms would seem to be unusually hospitable to the development of themes drawn from covenant nomism, since its theology anticipates and (as part of Judaism's sacred book) supports the development of the pattern of religion. The election of Israel is presupposed, and often explicitly mentioned (MT Pss 33.12; 47.5; 135.4; etc.). God's gift of the law is cited (99.7; 148.6) and praised: 'How I love Your Torah!' (119.97; *et passim*). The psalmists stress the human obligation to keep the covenant (25.10; 132.12), as well as God's (74.20; 89.35; 106.45). There are blessings for those who keep the covenant (103.18), and punishment for those who do not (38.7; 78.10, 37). God is ready and willing to forgive (32.1; 25.11; 86.5; 103.3) and provides the means of atonement (65.4; 78.38; 79.9). Repentance is a way back into the favor of God (51 *passim*, 38.19; 106.6). God's grace (25.7; 21.8; 17.7; 6.5; 5.8, חֶסֶד; etc.) and his goodness (69.17; 65.5; 31.20; 27.13; 23.6; 21.4, טוֹב etc.) are constantly emphasized.[2]

Edward Cook extends this assessment of covenant nomism: "the Psalms Targum as a whole manifests a commitment to the pattern of covenant nomism."[3] However, he goes on to point out that some psalms (such as Ps 51) strain the pattern with forgiveness coming other than through the covenantally sacrificial means.

---

2. Cook, "Covenant Nomism," 203–220, especially 204–5.
3. Cook, "Covenant Nomism," 219.

Torah Psalms

There are two *torah* psalms. Ps 19 contrasts Yahweh's revelation through the creation (Ps 19:1–6) with the greater and more beneficial expression in the *torah* (Ps 19:7–14). Whereas, Ps 119 is an acrostic (A to Z or א to ת) composed of eight verse units in which each verse of the eight begins with the letter of its unit. Ps 119 structurally created a fullness of instruction on the subject of *torah*. These psalms combine to celebrate the Divine guidance of the *torah* in Israel's and the psalmist's life. They provide a liturgy to frame a worldview and prompt Israel's prayer response to Yahweh, reflective of the covenantal program that Yahweh has enveloped them within.

Torah Psalms praise the Mosaic Covenant through a variety of synonyms. *Torah* (תּוֹרָה) is Yahweh's Divine *command* and *instruction* (Lev 10:11; Deut 33:10; Josh 24:26; Pss 19:7; 119:29, 34, 44, 53, 55, 61, 70, 72, 77, 92, 97, 109, 113, 126, 136, 142, 153, 163, 165, 174). *Torah* is then the *Mosaic Covenant* and its expanded teaching by other agents of God like the prophets.[4] As a synonym to *torah* (Pss 19:8; 119:14, 22, 24, 31, 36, 69, 79, 88, 95, 99, 111, 119, 125, 129, 138, 144, 146, 157, 167), '*dut*/עֵדוּת identifies *covenant* declaration (2 Chr 34:31), at times in a context of tabernacle (Exod 25:16). The *mṣwt*/מִצְוֹת are the *commands* of Yahweh (Deut 4:2; Pss 11:9; 119:6, 19, 32, 35, 48, 60, 66, 73, 86, 115, 127, 143, 151, 172, 176). Yahweh's *Laws* (*mšppṭ*/מִשְׁפָּטֵי) are the *Divine pronouncements to be obeyed* (Lev 18:4–5; Pss 19:10; 119:7, 13, 20, 30, 39, 52, 62, 75, 106, 137, 164). Likewise, Yahweh's *word* ('*mrt*/אִמְרָתֶ: Ps 119:11, 38, 50, 67, 103, 140, 158, 162, 172 and its synonym *dbr*/דְּבָר: Exod 34:1, 28; Deut 4:13; Pss 119:9, 16–17, 25, 28, 42–43, 49, 57, 65, 74, 81, 89, 101, 105, 107, 130, 139, 147, 160–61, 169) is to be obeyed. The *precepts* (*ppiqqudě*/פִּקּוּדֶי) are the divisions of the Law (Pss 19:9; 119:4, 45, 56, 104, 128, 141) or the precise accounting of Israel (especially in Numbers). The *drštty*/דְּרָשְׁתֶּי are Yahweh's *precepts* (Ps 119:10, 45, 94). All of these words refer to the stipulations of the Mosaic Covenant and the way of life they call Israel to live.

Ultimately, the prayer is to Yahweh, Who is Creator (Ps 119:73), good (Ps 119:68), source for *torah* (Pss 19:14; 119:114) and *torah* Teacher (Ps 119:12; 18–19, 26, 33, 68, 102, 108). Yahweh is thus the Redeemer Who expresses His loyal love and faithfulness through *torah* (Pss 19:14; 119:64, 89–91, 114), which means that God teaches through/*torah* (Ps 119:24, 26–27, 66, 102, 124–125, 135, 144). This has the direct result that

---

4. dePinto, "The Torah and the Psalms," 154–174.

if the Israelite has greater intimacy in obedience with *torah* then he likewise has greater intimacy with Yahweh (Ps 119:8, 55–57). Yahweh's loyal love prompts reviving these obedient people in relationship with Him (Ps 119:88, 149, 159). This means that since Yahweh stands faithfully *forever* (*'lm*/עוֹלָם) then *torah* stands faithfully forever (*'lm*/עוֹלָם; Ps 119:52, 89–91, 152). Likewise, since Yahweh is Truth, so *torah* is truth (Ps 119:142, 151, 160). The Israelite's proper response is to join the psalmist and to recognize that *torah* is the essential lamp to his feet to guide him in all issues of life (Ps 119:105, 130). So the psalmist urges prayer for Yahweh to intimately respond to him after the pattern of *torah*, which he is trying to keep (Ps 119:58-9, 131–35, 169–74). Such an obedient life is presented as theoretically possible and a desirable lifestyle with divine blessings.

Furthermore, since Yahweh is righteous, so *torah* is righteous as well (Ps 119:40, 75, 86, 123, 128, 137–38, 142, 144, 160, 164, 172). This has the direct result that Israelites are righteous to the exact extent that they obey *torah* (Ps 119:1, 3, 7, 11, 30, 121).

The psalmist exemplifies and urges his readership to highly value *torah*. For example, *torah* is greater than wealth of gold, inheritance, and captured spoil (Pss 19:10; 119:11, 72, 127, 162). Internalizing the value to the senses, *torah* is sweeter than honey (Pss 19:10; 119:103).

This priceless value should prompt the Israelite to love *torah* (Ps 119:97, 113, 119, 127, 140, 159, 163, 167). Thus the proper response for those in the Mosaic Covenant is to deeply long to obey *torah* (Ps 119:11, 28, 31, 47–48, 81–82, 131, 139, 174). In fact, there should be an intimacy of obedience as is conveyed by the mixed metaphor of one's feet being intimate to obey *torah* (Ps 119:59, 151). This self-defining attitude of a *torah*-defining-self prompts the desire to lodge within and pilgrimage with God and *torah* as the primary definition of oneself as an Israelite (Ps 119:54–56, 94).

The underlying qualities or virtues of this *torah*-defined person are that one is: righteous or faithful (Ps 119:1, 3, 7, 11, 30, 121), perfect or blameless (Pss 19:7, 13; 119:80), pure (Ps 119:9, 140), seeking Yahweh (Ps 119:2, 10), and fearing Yahweh (Ps 119:63, 120). Such a person believes *torah* (Ps 119:66). Such a person has an enlarged heart to obey *torah* (Ps 119:32). This orientation results in such people being selfless toward others (Ps 119:36).

Involvement with *torah* draws the psalmist into prayer with Yahweh concerning *torah*. The psalmist expresses prayer that his meditation would be appropriate (Ps 19:14). The psalmist prays that his life might be righteous and kept from sin (Ps 119:29–40, 66, 88, 116, 133). Within a life framed by *torah*, the psalmist hopes in God and what *torah* promises (Ps 119:116, 166). The psalmist prays that, in this obedience to *torah*, that Yahweh would bless in His loyal love (Ps 119:17, 41, 58, 76, 86, 88, 94, 107, 116–117, 121–124, 132–135, 149, 153–156, 169–170, 173). The psalmist expresses his trust by promising to testify to others about the living veracity of *torah* in life (Ps 119:13, 42–43, 46). The psalmist further praises *torah* and Yahweh behind it (Ps 119:12, 38, 164, 171, 175). The psalmist, framed by covenant curse statements, even prays imprecatory prayers for Yahweh to shame the arrogant, who are those who disobey *torah* (Ps 119:78, 84–85).

Because Yahweh's commands are to be obeyed (Ps 119:4–5, 17), the psalmist urges his readers to:

1. Meditate on Yahweh's commands, which includes deeply considering *torah* and comparing it to one's life (Ps 119:15, 23, 27, 48, 59, 97, 148). In verse 59 the Hebrew "my ways" emphasizes the comparison to prompt obedience, while the LXX "Thy ways" focuses obedience upon *torah*.
2. Remember *torah*, so as to frame one's life by it (Ps 119:16, 109).
3. Obey *torah* (Ps 119:33–34, 44, 55, 60, 101–102, 129, 168).

Such a *torah*-framed life benefits people in every way of covenant blessing if *torah* is obeyed by them (Deut 28:1–14; Ps. 19:11). Covenant blessing such as peace, life, recovery, strength, and hope are realized in keeping *torah* (Ps 119:1–2, 17, 28, 41, 49, 77, 165). Yahweh restores the soul through *torah*'s commands (Pss 19:7; 119:25, 37, 50, 52, 88, 93). These commands enlighten the simple so that one can become wise in growing discernment and knowledge (Pss 19:7–8; 119:66). Such wisdom extends beyond one's years and training because it provides God's perspective on life (Ps 119:98–100). *Torah* also provides an answer to an accuser (Ps 119:42). Part of this discernment is to warn of sin in such a manner that the person will stop his own erroneous ways (Ps 19:11–13). Within this discernment there is also the means of obtaining forgiveness and removing Yahweh's contempt and judgment (Pss 19:12–13; 119:22, 39, 81). The goal of this discernment includes the practical removal of shame from one's life (Ps 119:6, 31, 46, 80, 116). Indeed, there is liberty in walking in the commands of *torah* (Ps 119:45).

Salvation in this pre-Pharisaic context is the recovery of those into the Covenant blessing to which they are elected. As such, the psalmist prays for salvation as a recovery from potential stumbling to faithful obedience to *torah* (Ps 119:41–43, 81–83, 123–24, 155–56, 165–66, 174–76). The psalmist acknowledges that these blessings are from God's gracious loyal love, not something he earns as his own right.

Such a life expresses gratitude for the direction that *torah* brings for righteous living (Pss 19:8; 119:7, 62). Such lives rejoice in God's commands; *torah* is their delight (Ps 119:14, 16, 24, 35, 47, 70, 77, 11, 143, 162, 172). Furthermore, since the *torah* life is a communal one, the psalmist celebrates the comradeship he has with all others who fear God and thus obey *torah* (Ps 119:63, 74, 79, 120).

The psalmist makes an everlasting commitment to obey *torah* even in the face of opposition (Ps 119:44, 51, 61, 69, 78, 83, 85–88, 95, 98, 106–107, 110, 112, 115, 121, 134, 139, 141, 145–158, 161). The disobedient are the arrogant, who do not submit to God (Ps 119:21, 118–119). Part of the underlying attitude is that of a fat or obese heart that is insensitive to Yahweh's commands (Ps 119:70). In Israel these are those who are double-minded, being *in* covenant but *not mindful of* covenant (Ps. 119:113, Hebrew: s'pym/סֵעֲפִים, whereas, LXX simply calls these "transgressors"). Yahweh rebukes the arrogant with covenant curses leading to their rejection and destruction (Deut 28:15–29:28; Ps 119:21, 118–119). The psalmist responds within himself and to God concerning these arrogant with indignation about their disobedient and false ways (Ps 119:53, 104, 113, 128, 158, 163). This attitude prompts the psalmist's imprecatory prayers for Yahweh to shame the arrogant (Ps 119:78, 84–85). However, since the psalmist remembers that Yahweh's afflictions had previously brought the psalmist back to God (Ps 119:67, 71, 75, 176), the psalmist also cries an irrigation channel full of tears because the arrogant do not keep the Law (Ps 119:136).

Hans-Joachim Kraus summarizes the *Torah* Psalms as the praise of powerful, personal healing in *torah*. Kraus maintains that *torah* is an active verbal engagement of Covenant in the psalmist's life, not a baseline standard for blessing or curse.

> God's revelation in word is found primarily in the Torah. It is worthy of the praise of all who pray (especially Psalm 19B and Psalm 119). For the singers of these Torah psalms the תּוֹרָה (*torah*) is the "highest good," more valuable than gold or silver (Ps 119:72). It is the epitome of what is reliable and abiding (Ps.

119:142). Wondrous thing proceed from it (Ps 119:18). In this connection three features should be noted. (1) in Psalm 119 the Torah is no fixed, static entity, but a power that is creative and life-giving. (2) Neither is the Torah an impersonal, absolute, given entity, but a דָּבָר ("word") that goes out from Yahweh's majestic person, an אִמְרָה ("utterance") that is addressed to humans. (3) All the healing, saving, creative powers of the Torah are contained in the fact that it is פִּיר דְּבָר instruction from the mouth of Yahweh, and that means spoken, purposive word (*viva vox*). A disjunction between "law and gospel" in the manner of Luther's theology does not do justice to the events and realities to which the Torah psalms bear witness.[5]

Kraus concludes that "Psalms 19 and 119 show with special clarity that men and women in Israel loved *torah* of their God and were faithful to it, that joy over the "instruction of Yahweh" filled their lives, and that they carried *Torah* in their hearts (Ps 40:7–8)."[6] All these *torah* celebrations are echoed by the Jewish festival of *Simchat Torah*, which includes the words of a medieval hymn:

> This Feast of the Law all your gladness display. Today all your homages render.
> What profit can lead one so pleasant way, what jewels can vie with its splendor?
> Then exult in the Law on its festival day, the Law is our Light and Defender.[7]

Covenant Renewal Psalms

The concept of covenant renewal does not require the abrogation and restoration of covenant but the vassal Israel admits failure within Mosaic Covenant and so the Divine Suzerain graciously extends the covenant relationship, blessings, and recovery for Israel. The Mosaic Covenant was repeatedly given within a context of such covenant renewal (Exod 32:11—34:1; Deut; Josh 24:2–27). The book of Judges presents this covenant renewal from the vantage point of Israel's desperate need for a military leader (a judge) to free them from the threat of the surrounding

---

5. Kraus, *Theology of the Psalms*, 34.
6. Kraus, *Theology of the Psalms*, 161.
7. Goodman, *The Sukkot*, 88.

powers. Sometimes Yahweh generously renews Covenant blessing with Israel without their repenting (Deut; Josh 24:2–27; Judg 3:28–31; 9:56–57; 13:2–25; 14:19; 15:7–19; 16:28–31). However, Israel cannot presume on such Divine generosity. More commonly, Yahweh has required Israel to repent and obey the Mosaic Covenant stipulations, namely, when Israel repents of their sins, Yahweh overthrows the oppressor and gives Israel rest and blessing (Judg 2:16; 3:9–15, 19–23; 4:3–6, 14–24; 5:31; 6:6–7, 34–8:28; 10:1–3, 10, 15–16; 2 Kgs 22:9–20; 2 Chr 29:5–31:21; 34:14–33; Neh 9:1–10:29). At times this repentance is prompted by a prophet communicating the word of Yahweh, while at other times it is Israel's appropriate response to the reading of *torah*. Even Qumran developed an annual covenant renewal ceremony with confession of repentance.[8] These narrative Qumran covenantal renewal texts identify possible *sitz im leben* for the covenant renewal psalms as Israeli community responses led by a political leader and the priest to liturgically renew Israel within the continuing Mosaic Covenant. When the sin violating covenant takes place the Mosaic Covenant is not rendered void but the people are at risk of covenant curse until the covenant is renewed. So the fact of covenant renewal does not require Israel to fail. Rather, Israel's history unfortunately indicates that they are *likely* to fail but they retain culpability before God and His covenant. Furthermore, the fact of covenant renewal indicates God's generosity in providing a way of recovery among the tools of the Mosaic Covenant.

The two covenant renewal psalms are Pss 50 and 81. Both are psalms of Asaph. Both include again rather generic language and thus are available for any Jews who need liturgical guidance as to how to recover within Mosaic Covenant.

Against the backdrop of God's heavenly courtroom, Asaph declares in Ps 50 Yahweh's indictments against His people Israel[9] as: 1) formalism in worship and 2) hypocrisy in living. Then he calls Israel to a proper response of: 1) proper sacrifice and 2) obedient living according to the Law. In the God of Gods or the One True God, Yahweh summons His people to appear before His presence for judgment (Ps 50:1–6). He has already communicated Himself perhaps through public Law reading (Ps 50:16) and the people have entered into this covenant relationship with sacrifice (Ps 50:5; Exod 24). So if He remains silent as the people appear

---

8. CD 9.13; 1QS 1.24–2.1 with possible introduction 4Q256 2.2 and possibly 4Q286 1.1.7–8?, 4–5?; Nitzar, "Repentance," 2:758–59.

9. Ibita, "O Israel I will Testify against you," 537–50.

before His presence, then He will bring judgment (Ps 50:3, 21). Yahweh summons the covenant witnesses to fulfill their role in the trial (Ps 50:4, 6). Yahweh's first indictment is to decry formalism in worship and calls Israel to sacrifice from a *heart of trust* (Ps 50:7–15). God does not reprove Israel for the fact of sacrificing for He even provides the sacrificial animals for these offerings. Qumran reflects the priority of obedience and purity in covenant over sacrifice.[10] However, God urges Israel to call upon Him in the day of trouble, promising to rescue them in this time of need. Yahweh's second indictment decries Israel's hypocrisy in disregarding Law and associating with sin which begets covenant curse (Ps 50:16–23). Specifically, they hate God's training and instead encourage stealing and deceit (Ps 50:17–19). In this neglecting of obedience they forget God, and He comes with vengeance (Ps 50:22). The solution for Israel is to both offer sacrifices with thanksgiving and to order their way according to God's covenant (Ps 50:23). In this situation, God will be faithful in covenant and deliver Israel with the salvation that God provides.

Through Ps 81, Asaph calls Israel to rejoice in the feast of Tabernacles, which Yahweh ordained as a reminder of: 1) His delivering exodus, 2) their allegiance and 3) Yahweh blesses them in obedience. This psalm is likely to be accompanied by the guitar, tambourine and *shopar* horn (Ps 81 superscription, 2, 3) with a rousing call to sing for joy (Ps 81:1 similar to Deut 32:43). The occasion is likely for the Feast of Tabernacles because it is a feast day with the theme of liberation and travel from Egypt to Mt. Sinai (the place of thunder), required by the Law to be celebrated on the full moon, the 15th of the month with *shopar* horn (Exod 19:16–19; Lev 23:34; Ps 81:3–7). Bernard Anderson calls the reader to recognize the similarity of this psalm with Josh 24 covenant renewal.

> Notice that Psalm 81 closely parallels the liturgy of covenant renewal found in Joshua 24. It begins with an invocation to praise "the God of Jacob" at the sanctuary" on the feast day" ... (vs. 1–5a). Then the cultic priest or prophet reminds the worshipper of what Yahweh has done for the people, beginning with the deliverance from Egyptian bondage (vs. 5b–10). The psalm reaches a climax with an appeal to the people to repent and reaffirm their loyalty to Yahweh, to "walk in my [Yahweh's] ways" (vs. 11–16), that is to accept anew the duties of the covenant law. The theological assumption of Psalm 81 is that of the Mosaic

---

10. 1QS 3.6–12; 9.3–6; Nitzar, "Repentance," 2:758–59.

Covenant: "*If* you will obey my voice and keep my covenant, you shall be my own possession among all peoples" (Exod 19:5).[11]

Echoing the center of the Decalogue, Asaph calls Israel to hear (šemaʿ/שְׁמַע Deut 6:4; Ps 81:8) and be completely loyal to Yahweh with no worship of foreign gods, because God brought them out of the land of Egypt and will continue to bless those loyal within covenant (Ps 81:8–10). This covenantal blessing is conditional because it requires Israel to open their mouth to receive covenantal blessings such as their rescue from Egypt (Ps 81:10b, 16). These blessings are those promised in the Song of Moses in anticipation of the Promised Land (Ps 81:16; Deut 32:13–14). However, Israel has a heritage of stubbornness of heart to walk in their own ways (Ps 81:12–13). Israel's failure at Meribah is merely one example of this rebellious nature (Ps 81:7; Exod 17:6–7; Num 20:13). God's desire is that the people would walk in His ways by keeping the Law (Ps 81:13). If Israel would walk in Yahweh's way, then He would wonderfully bless them with protection, sustenance and sweetness that would amply satisfy (Ps 81:16).

Second Temple Development in Mosaic Covenant and Psalms

Part of the results of new second Temple Jewish studies is to recognize that at least a segment of Judaism expressed a deep commitment to the Mosaic Law as the Covenant document from God, to be obeyed, if Israel was to be blessed. This sentiment continues the commitment indicated in the *Torah* and Covenant Renewal Ps. That is, Israel is already in covenant with God, so that they are not trying to obtain this initial blessing. N. T. Wright says it this way: "The Torah was the boundary-marker of the covenant people: those who kept it would share the life of the coming age."[12] Joining the faithful of the Qumran community entailed swearing allegiance "to return to the Torah of Moses."[13] Such *torah* living was not one of perfection as God is perfect but one of loyal relationship to Yahweh. While there is acknowledgement that no human is "righteous" as God is

---

11. Anderson, *Out of the Depths*, 172.
12. Wright, *Jesus and the Victory of God*, 301.
13. CD 15.9, 12(=4Q266 17 I 3); 16.2, 5 (=4Q271 2 ii 3–4).

righteous,[14] nevertheless God's people are still called to be righteous as God is righteous.[15]

Perhaps this is broadly parallel or inclusive of the Qumran annual ceremony celebrating the Festival of Weeks where a yearly covenant renewal ceremony was celebrated.[16] In this ceremony of *Šavuʿot*, the Qumran Community renewed the covenant, admitted new members, and cursed those who had quit the community.[17] The covenant renewal date locates this covenant renewal ceremony at Qumran as occurring upon the very traditional date in which Moses was to have initiated the Mosaic Covenant with Israel, which is also the same date claimed by traditions for Abraham's Covenant initiation (Gen 15), circumcision (Gen 17) and Noahic Covenant (Gen 9).[18]

Covenantal nomism was the means by which Israel maintained relationship with God, particularly in difficult times. For example, the *Testament of Moses* 9.6 expresses this Jewish attitude as: Mattathias against Antiochus IV to Bar Kokhba against Hadrian, "Let us die rather than transgress the commandments of the Lord of Lords, the God of our fathers." Such a death possibility might be contemplated by the Covenant Renewal Psalms only when Israel was unfaithful to Covenant (Pss 50:3, 15; 81:7, 11–15). However, in the dispersion, Daniel and his three friends, insisted on keeping kosher and not participating in idolatry even if it would cost their lives (Dan 1:1–21 and 3:1–20).

Israel interpreted God as establishing them in covenant nomism as within the Mosaic Covenant such that they must obey the Law or cease to have God's blessing as a people.[19] These Jews saw this passion for the Law as a realization of the New Covenant in which God was giving

---

14. Pss 25; 51; 79; 90; 105; 143:2; 11Q5 24.7; 1QH 1.25–27;7.28–29; 8.19; 9.14–17; 10.3–12; 12.19, 24–31; 15.28; 17.14–15; 11QPs 155.8; 1QS 11.9–11; *Pss. Sol.* 3.5,9; 9.7; *L.A.B.* 12; 13.9; 26.14; 19.9–10, 44; Philo, *Vit. Mos.* 2.147.

15. *Sifre Deut.* 49.

16. *Jub.* 6.17; 1QS 1.18–3.12 including a confession of sin 1.22–23.

17. *Damascus Document* in 4Q266 frag. 11, lines 17–18; 4Q267 18 v 16–18; 4Q270 11 ii 11–12 and the *Community Rule* in 1QS 2.19; *b. Šebu.* 88a; Evans, "Covenant in the Qumran," 55–80.

18. *Jub.* 6.10, 11, 17; 14.10, 17, 20; 15.1, 11; 4Q266 frag. 11, lines 16b–17; 4Q270 7 ii 11; 4Q275 frag. 1, line 3; Martin Abegg "The Covenant of the Qumran," 81–98, especially 89.

19. Jdt 5:17–21; 8:18–23; *Pr. Azar.* 6–14; CD 10.14–11.18; Cook, "Covenant Nomism," 203–20; Evans, "The Aramaic Psalter," esp. 51.

them a "new heart" and a "new spirit."[20] As a result, Israel insisted on circumcision, kosher, and Sabbath-keeping as expressions of this purity.[21] Likewise Tobit, captive in Ninevah, did not eat their food.[22] Furthermore, when Judith ingratiated herself to Nebuchadnezzer's general, Holofernes, so she could kill him, she took all the kosher food to eat through the fourth day when she carried out the deed.[23] In the LXX version of Esther 4:17 she reminds God that she has not eaten food from Haman's table or drunk wine of libations. Another instance is that seven brothers and their mother were tortured and executed on orders of Antiochus IV rather than eat pork.[24] Furthermore, the Egyptian Jews kept separate from Gentile food and worship which led to hostility between Jews and Gentiles.[25] Antiochus attempted to force cultural conformity by forbidding aspects of the Law that distinguished Israel from other people such as circumcision and ordering Jews to worship foreign gods.[26] While circumcision was practiced by some other groups, its practice was a strong affirmation of Jewish male identity.[27] Many of the Jews abhorred pagan sacrificial meat as evidenced when Antiochus ordered some Jews to eat pork and food sacrificed to idols but Eleazar and others refused and were tortured and killed.[28]

Covenant nomism informed national policy in Israel as well. For example, the Hasmonean John Hyreaus (135-104 B.C.) broke off an important siege because of the coming of the Sabbath year.[29] This theme of commitment to *torah* regarding the Sabbatical year is also reflected in psalms of his era.[30] Furthermore, in the *Letter of Aristeas* 139-42 it says

20. As in Jer 31:31-34 and Ezek 36:24-37:28 so too in: *Jub.* 1:22-25; 1Q3 4, 5; 1QH 4, 5, 18; 4Q Shir Shalb; CD 4Q266 frag. 2 1.6-8; B 19.12-13; 1QpHab 2.3; 11.13; 4Q434 frag. 1 1.4; 4Q437 frag. 1 1.14.

21. *Jub.* 2:17-33; 15:11-34; *Jdt.* 10:5; 12:2.

22. Tob 1.10-12; 4:12-13.

23. Jdt 10.5; 12:2, 9-19; 13:8.

24. 2 Macc 7.

25. 3 Macc 3.4-7; 7.11.

26. 1 Macc 1:48 and 2:15-28.

27. Philo, *Migr.* 89-93; Josephus, *Ant.* 1.10.5.

28. 2 Macc 6:18-31; 4 Macc 5:1-6:30 also *Joseph and Aseneth*.

29. Josephus, *J. W.* 1.157-60; Jews compliance with Sabbath law was well known in the ancient near East (Josephus, *Ant.* 14.10.12; *Ag. Ap.* 2.2, 39; Philo, *Mos.* 2.21; and even more so in sectarian Judaism [CD 10.14-11.18; *Songs of the Sabbath Sacrifice*; *Temple Scroll*=11Q19]).

30. *Songs of the Sabbath Sacrifice*.

"In his wisdom the legislator (Moses) . . . surrounded us with unbroken palisades and iron walls to prevent our mixing with any of the peoples in any matter . . . So, to prevent our being perverted by contact with others or by mixing with bad influences he hedged us in on all sides with strict observances connected with meat and drink and touch and hearing and sight, after the manner of the Law."[31] Additionally, in 63 B. C. when Pompey hemmed Jews in Jerusalem, he raised the earthworks on Sabbath without firing missiles but the Jews would not fight the Roman troops under their noses because the Jews would only defend themselves on the Sabbath if they were attacked.[32] In fact the Jews' strict observance of Sabbath kept Jews from service in imperial armies, for it became a characteristic feature that marked off Jewish communal life.[33]

The Jews risked their lives to be faithful to the Mosaic Covenant. For example, in 5 B.C. Herod had erected a golden eagle over the temple as a votive offering, and two learned teachers (Judas and Matthaias) inspired the young men to pull down the image.[34] Herod responded by having many of them arrested, tried and burned alive. Furthermore, Josephus describes instances such as that in 26 A. D. when Pilate introduced Roman standards as well as a bust of Caesar into Jerusalem. Here Jews were ready to die rather than transgress the Law.[35] A large group followed Pilate to his residence in Caesarea and sat outside his house for five days. When they were summoned to tribunal and troops surrounded them with drawn swords, the Jews fell to the ground extending their necks and exclaiming that they were ready to die rather than to transgress the Law. Pilate was impressed and withdrew the standards. Likewise, when in 41 A. D. Caligula ordered Petronius to set up his statue in the Temple, Josephus claims that the protestors said, "slay us first before you carry out these resolutions . . . we will sooner die than violate our laws."[36] Their hope was that God would intervene and prevail with blessing from the Mosaic Covenant.[37] These examples reflect merely a sample of Israel's commitment to Yahweh under the framework of corporate covenant

---

31. Particular translation quoted in Dunn and Suggate, *The Justice of God*.

32. Josephus, *J. W.* 1.145–47.

33. Horace, *Sat.* 1.9.69–70; Philo, *Somn.* 2.123–24; *Legat.* 158; Josephus, *Ant.* 13.252; 14.10.12; 14.237. 16.2.3; 16.6.2–4.

34. Josephus, *J. W.* 1.651–55; *Ant.* 17.149–67.

35. Josephus, *J. W.* 2.169–74; *Ant.* 18.55–59.

36. Josephus, *Ant.* 18.261–64 and 271.

37. Josephus, *Ant.* 18.267.

nomism.[38] It is in this framework of sectarian Judaism that the hope for a Messiah includes that He be a definitive teacher of the Law.[39]

In contrast to this sectarian covenant nomism, Israel repeatedly rebelled and brought Israel into covenant curse and Gentile dominance (Deut 9:7; 28:15–30:20; 2 Kgs 17:23; Neh 9:32; Isa 9:1–2; Ezek 21:3; 20:31; Mic 5:3–4).[40] Their precarious condition was confessed by Bar 1.18–19, much as the Covenant Renewal Psalms had confessed previously.

> We have disobeyed Him, and have not heeded the voice of the Lord our God, to walk in the statutes of the Lord that he set before us. From the time when the Lord brought our ancestors out of the land of Egypt to this day.[41]

This rebellion was due to Israel's unfamiliarity and disregard for the Mosaic covenant. Judaism's hope for the Kingdom was in part a divine work that would render Israel a transformed New Covenant people (Deut 30:1–6; Jer 31:33–34).[42] Furthermore, when Israel was dispersed in *Diaspora*,[43] a Divine re-gathering was the hope of the *Diaspora* Jews as they anticipated God's covenant blessing.[44] However, this hope did not

---

38. I realize that challenges to this view have been marshaled. Probably the most formidable challenge was raised by Elliott in *The Survivors of Israel*. However, the impact of this work on this question is in my opinion significantly diminished because of its high selectivity of sectarian documents surveyed and admits it surveys (13-26). At this point I believe Sanders and Dunn to be presenting a broader reflection of Judaisms of this era. Additionally, Biblical texts like James, Matthew and Acts indicate that Jews and Jewish Christians were zealous for the Law. See chapter on early Judaisms in this book.

39. 4Q174 (4QFlor) 1.11 (different from the "branch of David"); 4QpPs (4Q171) 3:13-16; 1QpHab 1.13; 2:2, 8-9; 5:10; 7:4-5; 11:5; CD 1.11; 6.7; 7:18 (identified with the star); 20.1, 28, 32.

40. *1 Esdr.* 8.73-74; *2 Esdr.* 9.7; Bar 1.13, 18-19; 2.6; *CD* 1.13-21; 1QS 2.4-5; 1QH 2.8-19; 1QpHab 2.1-4; 5.3-8.

41. Bar 1.18-19 within penitential prayer 1.15-3.8; similar to Dan 9:4-19; Ezra 9:6-15; Neh 1:5-11; 9:5-37; *1 Esd.* 8.74-90; *Prayer of Azariah*; *Pss. Sol.* 2; 8; 9; Jdt 9; 1 Macc 3.50-53; 4.30-33; 3 Macc 2.2-20; 6.2-15; *Jub.* 1.15-18, 22-25; 10.3-6; *2 Bar.* 48.2-24; 54.1-22; Tob 3.1-6; *Pr. of Man.*; 1QS 1.18-3.12; 4Q393; 4Q481c; 4Q504; 4Q506; Josephus, *Ant.* 2.334-37; 4.40-50; Boda, Falk, and Werline, *Seeking the Favor of God*, vols. 1-3.

42. CD 6.19; 8.21; 20.12; 1QpHab. 2.3.

43. Meaning: Jews living outside their home land of Israel.

44. *Pss. Sol.* 8.28; 11.1-4; 17.28; Falk considers the *Psalms of Solomon* and the *Prayer of Manassah* to be covenant nomist texts ("Psalms and Prayers," 1:15, 51); Winninge, *Sinners and the Righteous*, 9-180, esp. 125-136; *T. Mos.* 4.9; Philo, *Praem.*

remove Israel from their obligation to the Law, rather God would enable them to be faithful to the Deuteronomical framework present in the Mosaic covenant (Deut 30:8–18; Jer 31:29–30).[45] This means that there is no contradiction with the same Qumran hymns declaring humans to be both *unworthy* and as divinely made to be *righteous* (as a member of the covenant community).[46] With regard to the *Psalms of Solomon*, Franklyn describes the godly as "not free from sin, but are sinfully pious, unrighteously righteous. Their opponents are the sinners."[47] Bruce Longenecker describes it as follows.

> The antithetical status of these two groups (viz. the righteous and the sinners) is wholly determined by whether or not one is, and intends to remain, a member of the covenant community, for common to both groups is sin, but restricted to the covenant community is the grace of God which is efficacious for the repentant members of that community who seek his forgiveness.[48]

This hope of divine transformation, forgiveness, and blessing resonates with the *Torah* Psalms prayer and commitment.

Late in the O.T., Israel's faithfulness to *torah* began to include a personal resurrection in the afterlife, where the dead will awake from their sleep among the dust to either everlasting life or everlasting contempt (Dan 12:2–3).[49] This sort of resurrection hope is much more common in second Temple Judaism within the wake of developing Pharisaic theology.[50] That is, the faithful in the Mosaic Covenant when they die continue

---

162–63; 2 *Bar.* 78.7; *Tg. Isa.* 53.8; *Tg. Hos.* 14.8; *Tg. Mic.* 5.1-3.

45. Kennard, "Jeremiah and Hebrews."

46. Hymn 1 1.22, 25–27 with 1.36; Hymn 5 3.23–25 with 3.19–23; Hymn 7 4.29–30 with 4.31–33 1nd 4.35–37; Hymn 11 7.16–17 with 7.17–25; Hymn 12 7.28–29 with 7.29–31; Hymn 14 9.14–16 with 9.12–14; Hymn 17 11.3 with 11.9–12; Hymn 18 11.20 with 11.17–18 and 11.29–32; Hymn 19 12.19, 24–31 with 12.20–23, 32; Hymn 20 13.13–16 with 13.16–19; Hymn 25 alternating in 17.26–18.30; Vermes, *The Dead Sea Scrolls*; Longenecker, *Eschatology and the Covenant*, 26.

47. Franklyn, "The Cultic," 8.

48. Longenecker, *Eschatology and the Covenant*, 27.

49. Baldwin, *Daniel*, 204–206; Wright, *The Resurrection*, 108–110.

50. *1 En.* 58.3; 62.14–16; 91.10; 92.2; 108.11–14; *2 Bar.*[Syriac] 30.1–5; 2 Macc 7.9–14, 22–23; 14.43–46; 4 Macc 7.19; 16.25; *4 Ezra* 7.32; *Sib. Or.* 4.180; *T. Benj.* 10.6–8; *T. Levi* 18; *T. Jud.* 24; *T. Hos.* 6:2 interprets this text to be resurrection whereas the text speaks of the reviving of Israel on the third day; *Tg. Jon.* on Isa 27:12f describes salvation as being accomplished on the third day; *b. Sanh.* 90b where Gamaliel claims that God would give the resurrected patriarchs land, not merely their descendants and

to be blessed in the afterlife with bodily resurrection unto paradise. For example, some Qumran manuscripts speak of an afterlife as everlasting life,[51] and possibly others even intimate bodily resurrection for the faithful.[52] While this afterlife is an extension of salvation beyond the grave that the Torah and Covenant Renewal Psalms never developed, such a resurrection idea was seen by second Temple Jews as having basis in biblical and extra-biblical psalms.[53]

Conclusion

Covenant nomism or a Deuteronomist perspective is the norm in *Torah* and Covenant Renewal Psalms. That is, Israel views themselves as elect of God and blessed if they love God as indicated by being faithful to the Mosaic Covenant. *Torah* Pss provide hope that the righteous life of

---

Johanan Num 18:28 the portion of YHWH given to Aaron is taken that he will be alive again, likewise Num 15:31 is claimed that the remaining guilt of the offender will be accountable in the world to come; 91b–92a; *B. Ta'an.* 2a; *B. Ket.* 111; *m. Sanh.* 10.1, 3; *T. Mos.* 10.8–10; *Gen. Rab.* 14.5; 28.3; *Lev. Rab.* 14.9; *Messianic Apocalypse* adds resurrection to a modification of Ps 146:5–9 as a Messianic expectation to be done to others; *T. Jud.* 25.4 claims this Messianic resurrection would begin with Abraham, Isaac, and Jacob; *T. Ben.* claims that after these are raised the whole of Israel will be raised; *Ps. of Sol.* 3.11–12; 4Q521 frag. 2, col. 2.1–13; frags. 7 and 5, col. 2.1–7; 1QH 14.29–35; 19.10–14; *Tg. Songs* 8.5; the benediction in the *Amidah*, the *Shemoneh Esre*. However, Wis 3.1; 8.19–20; 9.15 and Josephus' description of the Pharisees (*Ant.* 17.152–154; 18.1.3–5; *J. W.* 2.151–153; 2.8.14; *Ag. Ap.* 2.217–18) follow more a Platonic immortality of the soul view, but even here the soul eventually is given a body to match (Wis 9.15; Josephus, *J. W.* 2.163). Also the Biblical authors (Matt 22:23–33; Mark 12:18–27; Acts 23:6–7) and the *Eighteen Benedictions* present the Pharisees as believing the bodily resurrection of the dead; cf. Neil Gillman, *The Death of Death*, 101–142; Wright, *The Resurrection*, 129–206 for the post-Biblical Jewish view. The early church from patristic through medieval eras embraced bodily resurrection instead of Platonic immortality of the soul with regard to personal eschatology (Bynum, *The Resurrection*, 200–1336; Wright, *Resurrection*, 480–552).

51. 1QS 4.6–8; CD 3.20; 4Q181 3–4; *1 En.* 37.4; 40.4; 58.3; 4 Macc 15.3; *Pss. Sol.* 3.12; *Sib. Or.* 3.49 frag. 3.

52. 1QH 3.10–22; 6.34; 11.12; 1QM 12.1–4.

53. Ps 16:1, 8–11 is taken by Peter and Luke in Acts 2:25 as fusing this psalm with 2 Sam 7:12 to proclaim the necessity that David's greatest Son, Jesus must have risen (Acts 2:25–32), which argument reflects a similar fusion of Ps 132 and 2 Sam 7:10–16, which *4QFlorilegium* takes to be messianic; *Messianic Apocalypse* adds resurrection to a modification of Ps 146:5–9 as a Messianic expectation to be done to others; *Pss. Sol.* 3.12; the *Eighteen Benedictions* present the Pharisees as believing the bodily resurrection of the dead.

torah-keeping is possible, and Covenant Renewal Pss provide a liturgical guide in recovering any who would wander and need recovery to the Mosaic Covenant. Furthermore, second Temple Judaism extends this Covenant blessing into an after-life salvation, grounded on a love of God as indicated by being faithful to the Mosaic Covenant.

3

Davidic Covenant[1]

THE DAVIDIC COVENANT IS where the primary focus of the human kingship in Israel lies. What had been promised in the Abrahamic Covenant as a lineage of kings (Gen 17:6, 16; 35:11; 49:10) was incorporated with governance restrictions in the Mosaic Covenant stipulations (Deut 17:14–20). It wasn't long before the people sought a king, asking Gideon to rule over them with multiple generation succession (Judg 8:22) but Gideon refused this role even though he took up many of the accouterments of royalty such as having an ephod, oracle, royal jewelry and raiment, as well as a royal harem (Judg 8:26, 27, 30). Gideon's son Abimelech is named by him with a name which means "my father is a king." It is this Abimelech who tries to succeed Gideon as king but rules only three years in a brief, impotent reign (Judg 8:31; 9:2, 16, 22). When Abimelech did evil in God's sight it was fostered by an evil spirit from God such that in his violence he might be destroyed (Judg 9:23–56). This same tale of unbelief, rebellion and abuse is told several times over in the life of Saul and subsequent kings.

Davidic Covenant

The Davidic Covenant is the grounding for Messianic Kingship. As a covenant foundation the Davidic Covenant has been moved to a high place in Old Testament theology. For example, G. E. Wright referred to the "problem of theological accommodation to the covenant faith" which arose when Israel adopted the monarchy and was confronted with a "royal theology which we know must have been fostered in the royal court of the Davidic dynasty in Jerusalem."[2] In light of this and the dramatic

---

1. This chapter is revised from Kennard, *Messiah Jesus*, 377–414.
2. Wright, *God Who Acts*, 79.

salvific place that the Davidic Covenant occupies, Gerhard von Rad devotes a whole chapter in his O.T. Theology to its development. In fact, he sees that the Davidic Covenant is one of the two main events in Israel's history that is unusually productive theologically.

> If we reduce the comprehensive accounts of her history which Israel wrote to what is basic theologically, that is, to those actions of Jahweh which were constitutive for Israel, the result is as follows: Jahweh twice intervened in Israel's history in a special way, to lay a basis of salvation for his people. The first was in the complex of acts which are gathered together in the avowal made by the canonical saving history (that is, from Abraham to Joshua), the other was in the confirmation of David and his throne for all time . . . On these two saving data rested the whole of Israel's existence before Jahweh. Even the prophets in their proclamation of the new creation of Israel cannot hark back to any other than them, the covenant at Sinai and the covenant with David.[3]

While most portray that the Sinai and Davidic covenants are two separate arrangements (of a suzerainty treaty and covenant grant respectively), not all maintain this distinction. Rost tried to merge these two covenants into one.[4] Additionally, popular Covenant Theology tries to maintain a unified covenantal strategy[5] rather than aspects of two covenants that telescope out of the previous covenants. P. J. Calderone argued that the Davidic Covenant was not configured as a suzerainty treaty but instead expressed itself as a dynastic oracle.[6] The inter-textual development of the Davidic Covenant takes precedence over what is conveyed by these appeals to potential genre.

While a few other books (like the book of Ruth) justify the legitimacy of David as king, the book of Samuel is primarily focused on Davidic legitimacy as a dynastic oracle. Likewise, 1 Chronicles explores much of the same material as Samuel but from the vantage point of a post-exilic chronicle, which then takes on more the emphasis of explaining Israel's

---

3. Von Rad, *Old Testament Theology*, 1:355.

4. Rost, "Sinaibund," 129–34; *The Succession*.

5. Kline, *Kingdom Prologue*, 6; Dumbrell, *Covenant & Creation*, 42; Hafemann, *The God of Promise*, 59.

6. Calderone, *Dynastic Oracle*; this dynastic oracle is really not of the same Egyptian kings story (königsnovelle) with the king's unique relationship to the gods (Gakuru, *An Inner-Biblical Exegetical*, 51; contra Hermann, "Die Königsnovelle," 51–62).

rebellious route to Babylonian captivity and Yahweh's repeated faithfulness climaxing in the re-gathering. Rising above these other works, Samuel appropriates the genre of an accession document explaining and defending the Davidic kingship through a book-long development. In this role, the book of Samuel has some parallels with annalistic documents of the ancient Near East. For example, in the fourteenth or thirteenth century B.C. from Hittite Anatolia *The Proclamation of Telepinu*[7] includes a decree with a long prologue justifying accession by recounting several generations of events including no hereditary legitimacy (like David) but the legitimate and successful predecessor's principles were betrayed by kings, leading to their removal. Another, the *Apology of Hattusilis*, justifies revolt that brought Hattusilis to the throne over an unworthy predecessor.[8] The book of Samuel functions in just this way explaining and justifying the legitimacy of David's kingship and the Davidic Covenant. So we will begin by briefly surveying the whole of the book of Samuel because by this sample the Davidic Covenant and Davidic kingship is demonstrated to be the thrust of this book. This is an approach that goes deeper than that of most evangelicals' proof-texting of a few verses about David's reign, because it follows the textual emphasis of Samuel to legitimate David as king. In this approach the literary feature of doublets in the book of Samuel probably indicates God's sovereign involvement strengthening the case for divine justification of the legitimacy of David's reign.[9]

Yahweh is the One who empowers and saves the humble, strengthens the king,[10] and reveals Himself to Samuel. Yahweh also destroys the proud such as: Eli and his house (1 Sam 2:27–36; 4:17–18), Israel in their sins, trying to manipulate success by treating the ark as a talisman (1 Sam 4:1–18; 6:19–21), and the Philistines who wished to do the same

---

7. *The Proclamation of Telipinu*, 175-200.

8. See these ancient documents in Herbert Wolf, *The Apology of Hattusilis*; McNeal and Sedlar, *The Ancient Near East*; Cohn-Haft, *Source Readings*, 179–85; Calderone, *Dynastic Oracle*.

9. Doublets are not to be taken as rival accounts of pro- and anti-king forces but greater divine involvement as in the Joseph narrative (Gen 37–50). Examples of these doublets include: Saul twice rejected as king for different reasons (1 Sam 13:13–14; 15:10–31), David twice meets Saul (1 Sam 16; 17), David joined Philistines twice (1 Sam 21:10–15; 27:1–4), David spared Saul's life twice (1 Sam 24; 26), Goliath or one like him is killed twice (1 Sam 17; 2 Sam 21:19). Additionally, the multiple callings of Samuel confirm the divine authenticity of his being chosen (1 Sam 3:1–18).

10. There is no king yet when in this hymn of salvation formulaic language is used to express the future expectation (1 Sam 2:10; Gen 17:6; Num 24:17; Deut 17:14–20).

by treating the ark as an idol (1 Sam 4:19–22; 7:1–2). Samuel called the people to repent before Yahweh and when the Philistines attacked they were subdued by Yahweh thundering[11] after them in battle (1 Sam 7:3–17). When Samuel was old and his children were not faithful to Yahweh as their Father, the people asked for a more permanent solution: they asked for a king so that they could be like the nations around them (1 Sam 8:1–5). This request was a rebellious rejection of Yahweh, Who in fact had been Israel's king (1 Sam 8:7–8). However, Yahweh granted their request as he had promised (Deut 17:14–20), but Samuel explained the justice[12] through which the king would reign including practices of: draft, seizure and royal tithe (1 Sam 8:9–18).

As a tall man, Saul looked the part of a would-be king (1 Sam 9:1–2). Saul seemed faithful in searching for the lost family donkeys and even seeking wisdom through the seer[13] or prophet with an appropriate payment.[14] Yahweh had told Samuel that He had designated Saul to rule[15] over the people. Saul was honored at a banquet, anointed king, given signs to authenticate divine choice, and enabled by the Spirit[16] to

---

11. In the ancient Near East, the gods fought for people by riding on the thunder clouds thundering in judgment with lightening as spears (1 Sam 7:10; *Sumerian Exaltation*). The victory was commemorated by raising a memorial stone, called Ebeneezer, which probably functioned as a boundary stone (such as a Babylonian *kudurru* stone).

12. Justice (מִשְׁפָּט) probably irony or satire in this context.

13. 1 Sam 9:9; prophets (נָבִא, *nabi*) called out for special duty to declare God's word from Akkadian *nabu* "to call to duty." Early prophets were called seer (רֹאֶה) or one who sees but later they are used interchangeably (1 Chr 9:22; 26:28; 29:29).

14. 1 Sam 9:8; one fourth shekel of silver is one week's wages for an ordinary laborer.

15. 1 Sam 9:17; this word for rule (עָצַר) is used only here and in 10:1 and means "keep in check."

16. The Spirit of Yahweh occurs 15 times in Samuel compared to 39 times in the O.T.: Eight times as an evil spirit from God (1 Sam 16:14, 15, 16, 22; 18:10; 19:19 parallel to Judg 9:23). Five times as bringing about prophecy (1 Sam 10:6, 10; 20:20, 23; 2 Sam 23:2 parallel to Num 24:2; 1 Kgs 22:24; 2 Chr 15:1; 18:23; 20:14; 24:20) and interpreting dreams (Gen 41:38; Dan 4:8). Two times enabling to be king (1 Sam 10:6, Saul; 16:13, David) parallel to establishing Joshua, Daniel and judges (Num 27:18; Dan 6:3; Judg 3:10; 6:34; 11:29; 13:25). One time as leaving Saul, which indicates his loosing kingship (1 Sam 16:14) parallel to when the Lord left Samson when his hair was cut. One instance as providing military might (1 Sam 11:6 parallel to 1 Chr 12:18). Such specialized ability is also enabling the craftsman to construct the tabernacle (Exod 31:3; 35:31). Notice that for Saul the Spirit of Yahweh brought profound ability as prophet, king and in battle but primarily indicated his loss of kingship by being tormented by Yahweh; if the enabled disobey it brings about enabled curse in their lives.

prophecy and to lead in battle, and chosen by lot (1 Sam 9:22–11:13). The people made Saul king but Samuel reminded them that Yahweh had been their salvation and king, and He would bring curse if they rebelled against Him (1 Sam 11:14–12:25).

Unfortunately, Saul's disobedience showed him to be unworthy to be king. Several instances show Saul's rebellious nature. Saul reigned for a number of years, but early Saul called Israel to gather at Gilgal and was unwilling to wait for Samuel to lead the sacrifice. Saul's disobedience meant forfeiture of his kingship (1 Sam 13:13–14). Twice Saul made a rash vow which hindered the people from doing their best in war and sentenced Jonathan to death (1 Sam 14). Additionally, Saul disobeyed Samuel's command to utterly destroy Amalek, so Yahweh rejected him from being Israel's king (1 Sam 15:3–11–12–35).[17]

Yahweh sought to replace Saul with a man after His own heart, responsive to God's perspective (1 Sam 13:14; 16:7). So Samuel anointed David to be king and the Spirit of Yahweh came upon him, departing from Saul (1 Sam 16:13–14). An evil spirit from Yahweh terrorized Saul. In Saul's turmoil, David is found to be a skillful harpist who was able to relieve Saul's terror by the spirit of Yahweh. Goliath challenges the champion of Israel (presumably Saul) to representative warfare but Saul is unwilling and thus unworthy. In contrast, stone-wielding David defeats the giant in the name of Yahweh of hosts (1 Sam 17). In recognition that God had empowered David, Jonathan made a unilateral parity treaty with David and presented him his armor (1 Sam 18:1–4). David gained a reputation as a conquering field commander but jealous Saul tried to kill him (1 Sam 18:5–16). Saul gave his daughter Michal to David in marriage (requiring a dowry of 100 dead Philistines) as an attempt to kill him but Yahweh was with David to obtain David's legitimacy to the throne (1 Sam 18:17–30). Saul rebelled against David and Yahweh, but David's life is preserved by Jonathan, Michal, Samuel, Ahimelech, Achish, and ultimately Yahweh (1 Sam 19–22; 27; 29). David inquired of Yahweh and defeated the Philistines at Keilah as a king would do but Saul pursued him there, so David fled to the wilderness (1 Sam 23). David twice spared Saul's life, repenting of raising his hand against him (by cutting off

---

17. In 1 Sam 15:27 Saul tried to seize the hem (an Akkadian gesture of supplication and submission) but tore Samuel's hem (which identified him as priest and prophet). In 1 Sam 24:4–5, 10 David cut off the edge of Saul's robe identifying him as king. A Mari text describes divorce as done by husband cutting off the hem of wife's robe. It is likely that these tearing of robes reject Samuel's and Saul's authority.

hem, and taking water and weapon[18]) (1 Sam 24; 26). However, David is kept within the good[19] by wise Abigail, whom David acquires as his wife (1 Sam 25).

In this context of oppressing David, Saul felt the pain of being excluded by means of divine silence, for Yahweh would not answer him by dreams, Urim, or prophets (1 Sam 28:6). So, Saul rebelled by seeking a medium, who conjured[20] up Samuel who pronounced swift death upon Saul (Lev 19:31; 1 Sam 28). God brought it about that while David (God's man) destroyed the Amalekites, the Philistines overwhelmed Saul to death (1 Sam 30–31).

The establishment of David's kingdom meant the defeat of all opposition. For example, an Amalekite claimed to have killed Saul, so David likewise had him killed and grieved the death of Saul and Jonathan (2 Sam 1). David inquired of Yahweh and went up to Hebron to be anointed as king over Judah for seven and a half years (2 Sam 2:1–7). In response, Abner (Saul's cousin) anointed Ish-bosheth (man of shame) king over northern tribes two years (2 Sam 2:8-11). However, Abner suggested a representative conflict, which was inconclusive, so that David's side won the war (2 Sam 2:12–32). In response, Abner defected to bring Israel to David (2 Sam 3:1–21). However, Abner and Ish-bosheth are murdered by rogue forces for blood vengeance but David grieves their deaths (2 Sam 3:22–4:12). Finally, all Israel came to David, who made a covenant with them as they anointed him king over all Israel for thirty three years (2 Sam 5:1–5).

Consolidation of David's reign meant that David could conquer for Israel and establish his own capital. David conquered the Jebusites making their stronghold, Jerusalem, his capital (2 Sam 5:7–21). In David's responsiveness to Yahweh, he inquired of Yahweh and Yahweh conquered the Philistines (2 Sam 5:22–25).

Further consolidation of David's reign meant that the tabernacle was drawn within David's royal context. After mishap and reassurance,

---

18. Depriving a man of water and weapon in the desert threatens Saul's life, which shows Saul's life was in David's hands.

19. Abigail was beautiful (טוב) and prevented the massacre at the festival (טוב or good day) which kept David doing good (טוב; 1 Sam 25:3, 8, 21).

20. Homer's *Odyssey*, Mesopotamia and Hittite literature provide details of conjuring practice. In general, it is done at night at a divined spot with a pit dug by a special tool. An invocation ritual calls the spirit's name. The pit is covered to prevent other spirits escaping after the ritual. In 1 Samuel 28:13, Samuel appears as an *elohim* coming up out of the earth.

ephod wearing David brought up the ark and sacrificed to God (thus fusing priestly roles with kingship; 2 Sam 6:23). In fact, with Yahweh giving David rest, the concern to build a permanent Temple for Yahweh fuses the priestly and kingly roles again (2 Sam 7:1–7). David also encourages worship like a priest in his composition of so many psalms. Yahweh had indeed wonderfully provided for David (2 Sam 7:8; 1 Chr 17:7). Yahweh had cut off David's enemies (2 Sam 7:9; 1 Chr 17:8). Yahweh had given David rest and a house so David wished to build a permanent Temple house for the ark of the covenant, but Yahweh forbade David to build a Temple house (2 Sam 7:1–5; 1 Chr 17:1, 4). However, Messianic expectations arose concerning the role of building the Temple that God granted to Solomon (2 Sam 7:13). This was reaffirmed again later after the Babylonian captivity by seeing Zerubbabel build the Temple after the pattern of Solomon (1 Chr 17:12; Zech 4:7–10; 6:12).[21]

Imbedded within the narrative is an event that Moshe Weinfeld identified as a covenant grant that described a unilaterally established Davidic dynasty and Covenant after the pattern of Assyrian and neo-Assyrian royal grants.[22] This analysis developed parallels of the Davidic Covenant with the royal grants of Ulmi-Tessub of Dattassa and Assurbanipal to Baltaya. These royal grants were contained within the broader narrative dynastic document (Samuel and Chronicles) in the same manner as Griphus Gakuru identified a dynastic oracle of salvation contained dynastic oracles for Esarhaddon.[23] So, as a covenant grant Yahweh elects David to an exclusive dynastic relationship. This dynastic oracle was established to support divine legitimacy for the Davidic dynasty. This

---

21. Second Temple Judaism continues the hope of the construction of the Temple as identified with the new creation at the end time (1 Chr 17:12–14; Ezek 40:1–43:5; *Jub.* 1.27–28; 1QS 8.6–7; 4Q174 3.10–13; *Tg. Zech.* 6.12), which Temple is indwelt by the presence of God (Pss 11:4; 79:1; Isa 6:1; 66:6; Ezek 43:2–5; 11QTa 29.7; 45.12–14; 46.3–4) and populated by functioning priests in a covenant relationship with God where sacrifices atone and forgive (Ezek 44:11–31; Sir 45.25; 47.11; 1QM 2.5; 11QT 25.10–27.10; *Shemoneh Esreh.* benediction 14). This central focus of Temple in eschatological Israel becomes a metaphor for the community of Israel (1QS 8.5–6; 9.6).

22. Weinfeld, "The Covenant Grant," 184–203; "Addenda to *JAOS*," 468–69; *Deuteronomy*, 79–80; "Covenant Terminology," 190–99; "Bond and Grace," 85–105; "Berît-Covenant," 120–28; "The Loyalty Oath," 379–414; *The Promise of the Land*, 222–64; Güterbock, "Siegel," 48, 190; Postgate, *Neo-Assyrian Royal Grants*, 28.

23. Gakuru, *An Inner-Biblical Exegetical*, 63–71, 231; British Museum # K410.V.26–VI.31; K2401.III.15–16; K4310.1–VI.

narrative reiterated and defended this continuing unique relationship through the Solomonic lineage.[24]

In the Davidic Covenant Yahweh promised David personally reassuring blessings. First, Yahweh promised David would be famous (2 Sam 7:9; 1 Chr 17:8). Then David is also promised a good death with his fathers (2 Sam 7:12).

Yahweh's promises in the Davidic Covenant merge the Davidic Covenant with that of the Abrahmic and Mosaic in that previous covenantal promises are now reiterated within this later Davidic Covenant.[25] For example, Israel will be planted in the land by Yahweh (2 Sam 7:9–10 and 1 Chr 17:8–9 with Gen 12:7; 15:18–21; Deut 28:3–11). Furthermore, reflecting the Mosaic Covenant blessings, David will have rest from his enemies (2 Sam 7:11 with Exod 3:20; 20:11–12; 33:14; Deut 5:14; 12:10; 25:19; Josh 1:5; 21:44; 22:4; 23:1). After Babylonian captivity, Chronicles promises this Mosaic Covenant blessing more forcefully with Israel's enemies being subdued (2 Sam 7: 11; 1 Chr 17:10). Additionally, the construction of the Temple by the Davidic king draws him into the pattern of Moses, who had given Israel the Tabernacle in the first place. David recognized that Yahweh had been faithful to him in the Mosaic Covenant (2 Sam 22; Ps. 18).

This transition from David and his lineage to a more ultimate Messiah can also be seen in the shift from 2 Sam 7 to 1 Chr 17. For example, after Babylonian captivity, Chronicles promises this Mosaic Covenant blessing more forcefully with a more ultimate Davidic King or Messiah Who will subdue Israel's enemies (2 Sam 7:11; 1 Chr 17:10). This Davidic son will have an everlasting Kingdom as God's Son, which serves as an adoption formula to establish dynastic relationship[26] in God's Kingdom enabling him to build the Temple house and not be rejected as was Saul (2 Sam 7:12–15; 1 Chr 17:11–14; 22:10; Pss 2:7; 89:3–4, 26–27, 34–37; 132:11–12).[27] For example, as a comfort, in 2 Sam 7:14, Yahweh promises

---

24. Sir 45.25; 47.11.

25. McCarter, *II Samuel*, 218, 224.

26. God is Father to king as Son, ancient Near East examples include from: Egypt: Pharaoh as son of Re, Ugarit and Mesopotamia: Keret is son of El, and Roman: Caesar as Son of God; von Martitz, *TDNT* 8:336–40; Hengel, *The Son of God*, 24; Dunn, *Christology in the Making*, 14–16; Deismann, *Light from the Ancient East*, 346.

27. The Messiah is predicted to be the builder of the Temple (2 Sam 7:13; 1 Chr 17:12; Zech 4:7–10; *Sib. Or.* 5.420–33). Additionally, God is portrayed to be the builder of the Temple (*1 En.* 90.28–29; *Jub.* 1.17; *2 Bar.* 4.3; 32.4; 11QTemple 29.8–10; 4QFlor. 1.3, 6; *Midr. Ps.* 90.17; *Mekilta* of R. Ishmael 3).

through an adoption formula[28] continued light to correct the Davidic son when he sins, "When he commits iniquity, I will correct him with the rod of men and the strokes of the sons of men" (2 Kgs 8:19; 2 Chr 21:7). So for the particular generation of Davidic king to live in peace and blessing requires each king's faithfulness. For example, the necessity of the Davidic king's compliance with human obligation (2 Sam 7:14; 2 Kgs 8:19; 2 Chr 21:7; Pss 89:30–32; 132:10; possibly 2 Kgs 11:17–18), does not put at risk the Davidic Covenant blessing for the Davidic lineage (2 Sam 7:15–16; 2 Kgs 8:19; 1 Chr 17:12, 14; Pss 89:33–36; 132:11).[29] Furthermore, this phrase about discipline is left out of 1 Chronicles 17 perhaps because the captivity removed the disobedient Davidic kings and probably because there was hope of a grander eschatological king. With the Davidic kings removed from office by the captivity, the promise of the Davidic king not being rejected like Saul becomes hollow without a return to a Davidic king on the throne. With the failures of the Davidic kings and their not being like David (1 Kgs 11:4–8, 33; 14:8; 15:3–5, 11; 2 Kgs 14:3; 16:2; 18:3; 22:2; 2 Chr 7:17; 11:17; 29:2, 25–30; 34:2–3; 35:4, 15), after the Babylonian captivity, the Chronicler looks for a more ultimate Davidic king, Who will subdue Israel's enemies (1 Chr 17:10). Furthermore, 2 Samuel 7:16 is more oriented to David: "*Your* house and *your* kingdom shall endure before Me forever; *your* throne shall be established forever" while Yahweh speaks in 1 Chr 17:14, "I will settle *him* in *My* house and in *My* kingdom forever and *his* throne shall be established forever."

The covenant from Yahweh to David is binding as a covenant grant *forever* (2 Sam 7:12–15; 1 Chr 17:11–14; Pss 89:3–4, 34–37; 132:11–12).[30] This theme of *foreverness* within the Davidic Covenant is especially developed in a few pages within the royal Ps 89. However, in the giving of the Davidic Covenant, this foreverness ('*lm*/עוֹלָם) of the Davidic Son's reign is promised and interpreted by His never being removed so that He could bring in the Kingdom with all opposition removed. Significant parallels develop between Ps 89 and the narrative formulations.[31] The permanent binding nature of the Davidic Covenant is further indicated

---

28. Adoption formula you are "my son" 2 Sam 7:14 parallel to 2 Kgs 16:7; Parallel to Hittite treaty between Šuppiluliuma and Šattiwazza as contained in Weidner, *Politische Dokumente aus Kleinasien*, 2:22–26; Weinfeld, "The Covenant Grant," 469; similar language is used in the "Testament," 2–7, 12; Kalluveettil, *Declaration*, 368–72.

29. Freedman and Miano, "People of the New Covenant," 13–16.

30. The Davidic Covenant is also declared to be everlasting in 4QSam 23.5.

31. Gakuru, *An Inner-Biblical Exegetical*, 124–27 develops many of these parallels.

in 2 Chr 13:5 as a "covenant of salt" to David and his sons (after the pattern of Num 18:19).[32]

David's response to Yahweh's covenant drew David into humble reverence before Yahweh in prayer (2 Sam 7:18–29; 1 Chr 17:16–27). David is amazed that Yahweh has brought him this far and has spoken of the distant future. David worships with praise, "Adonai Yahweh is great; there is no Elohim like You." Through the exodus, Yahweh established Israel as His people forever. David petitions in line with Yahweh's covenant promises that Yahweh might bless the Davidic house so that they might be established as Yahweh's servant forever. This divine blessing is seen in the conquests which Yahweh brings about for Israel over Philistia, Moab, Zobah, Syria, Edom, and Ammon (2 Sam 8:1–10:19). Furthermore, within such excess blessing David blesses Mephibosheth (crippled son of Jonathan), with regular hospitality (2 Sam 9:1–13). Finally, within the context of David's generosity, all throne-claims for Saul's lineage cease.

While the book of Samuel presents the grandeur of the Davidic Covenant, it is not a whitewash because unfortunately David himself rebelled and all Israel suffered consequences of his rebellion (2 Sam 11–24). Several chapters reverberate with the sins with Bathsheba, Amnon, Absalom, and David's over-confidence in the wake of his census of Israel. Delivered by Yahweh from all his enemies (especially these remainders from the sins of Saul), David praises Yahweh as his deliverer Who fought for him in earthquake, volcano, and thunderstorm, which shows forth Yahweh's blessing for David's faithfulness in the Mosaic Covenant (2 Sam 22; Ps 18). The royal psalm ends giving thanks to Yahweh for His deliverance and lovingkindness to King David and his descendants forever (2 Sam 22:50–51; Ps 18:49–50). David's last words are of praise to Yahweh Who anointed him to be king, and continued to enable him by wisdom from the Spirit to speak and rule in an everlasting covenant of salvation from enemies (2 Sam 23:1–7).

Davidic Covenant Extended to Solomon and Beyond

King Solomon is blessed as the one who will sit on the throne of David after him and this Davidic throne will be established forever (1 Kgs 2:45). However, within this covenant grant extension to the subsequent Davidic king, the conditional nature for each generation, which is present

---

32. Dillard, *2 Chronicles*, 107; Japhet, *I & II Chronicles*, 691.

within the Mosaic Covenant, is embedded within this statement of the Davidic Covenant. From the basis of Assyrian covenant grants, Gary Knoppers argues for the Davidic Covenant and all covenant grants being deeply conditional upon the continued faithfulness of the recipient, namely the Davidic kings, and since the kings were *not* faithful then the Davidic Covenant's conditionality means that the Davidic Covenant is forfeited.[33] Whereas, Moshe Weinfeld and H. G. Güterbock argue that the covenant grant establishes an unconditional adoption and dynasty grant dependent upon the character of the grantor.[34] Ultimately this defense is made inter-textually from within the biblical text. Biblically, the emphasis grounds the Davidic Covenant as unconditional for the dynasty ultimately grounded in the character of God, but each generation of David's dynastic lineage might conditionally be excluded from the unconditional dynastic benefits granted by God. So, the biblical pattern cuts a route between the extremes and while for each generation Davidic kings may lose benefits the realization of the Davidic Covenant ultimately is grounded in God's character and oath. This is realized in Yahweh's address to Solomon, extending the Davidic covenant, fused with Mosaic Covenant stipulations.

> If you will walk before Me as your father David walked, in integrity of heart and uprightness, doing according to all that I have commanded you and will keep My statutes and My ordinances, then I will establish the throne of your kingdom over Israel forever, just as I promised to your father David, saying "You shall not lack a man on the throne of Israel" but if you or your sons

---

33. Suzerainty treaty threat of removal of successors is more severe than that of this grant ("Treaty Between Mursili 2 of Hatti and Tuppi-Teshshup of Amurru" sect 5-6; "Treaty Between Tudhaliya 4 of Hatti and Shaushga-muwa of Amurru" sect 3-7 in Beckman, *Hittite Diplomatic* Texts, 60, 104-5; Roberts, "Davidic Covenant," 210. Knoppers, "Ancient Near Eastern Royal Grants," 670-97, esp. 691; Johns, *Assyrian*, 4:164-73 (#646, 647, 648); Postgate, *Neo-Assyrian*, 27-38 (#9, 10, 11). Knoppers (691) also claims that there is no border delineation in 2 Sam 7, nor Ps 132 so he questions whether the Davidic Covenant is a covenant grant in the first point. His argument would argue for dissimilarity and undermine his foundational point but since the Davidic Covenant operates within the wake of the Abrahamic and Mosaic covenants the land is probably best seen as implied within the Davidic Covenant when the place and continued protection of the Kingdom and people Israel is discussed.

34. Weinfeld, "The Covenant Grant," 468-69; *Deuteronomy*, 79-80; "Covenant Terminology," 190-99; "Bond and Grace," 85-105; "Berît-Covenant," 120-28; "The Loyalty Oath," 379-414; *The Promise of the Land*, 222-64; Güterbock, "Siegel," 48, 190; Postgate, *Neo-Assyrian*, 28.

shall indeed turn away from following Me, and shall not keep My commandments and My statutes which I have set before you and shall go and serve other gods and worship them, and the house which I have consecrated for My name, I will cast out of My sight, so Israel will become a proverb and a byword among all peoples. And this house will become a heap of ruins; everyone who passes by will be astonished and hiss and say, "Why has Yahweh done thus to this land and to this house?" And they will say "Because they forsook Yahweh their God, Who brought their fathers out of the land of Egypt, and adopted other gods and worshipped them and served them, therefore Yahweh has brought all this adversity on them." (1 Kgs 3:14; 9:4-9; 2 Chr 7:17-18).

So faithfulness to the Mosaic Covenant has implications on realizing the Davidic Covenant, and faithfulness to the Davidic Covenant has implications on realizing the blessings of the Abrahamic and Mosaic covenants.[35]

Subsequent kings are seated upon David's throne in David's house (1 Kgs 2:12, 24, 45; 12:11, 19, 20, 26; 2 Chr 8:11; 13:5). Solomon loved Yahweh and walked in the statutes of his father David, except in marrying Pharaoh's daughter Solomon's heart is turned away enough to also sacrifice and burn incense on the high places (1 Kgs 3:1-3; 2:3-4; Deut 17:17). So Solomon turned his heart toward idolatry, departing from David's pattern of full devotion to Yahweh (1 Kgs 11:4-8, 33). Thus, David becomes the standard for all subsequent kings (1 Kgs 11:4-8, 33; 14:8; 15:3-5, 11; 2 Kgs 14:3; 16:2; 18:3; 22:2; 2 Chr 7:17; 11:17; 29:2, 25-30; 34:2-3; 35:4, 15). The kingdom is split because of this idolatry and subsequent kings not following David's heart and way (1 Kgs 11:31-39). For example, Jeroboam follows Solomon in idolatry on the high places and thus the kingdom is split from him (1 Kgs 13:1-10; 14:8). In spite of these rebellious generations, Yahweh was unwilling to destroy Judah because the Davidic Covenant included the divine promise that He would always give David's sons a lamp of instruction and correction (2 Kgs 8:19; 2 Chr 21:7). In contrast to royal unfaithfulness, the Davidic character of the reigns of Hezekiah and Josiah preserved the kingdom for a time.

Covenantal language of being *in* a person and his respective covenant retains the established pattern of being both a beneficiary and inheritor "*in* David" (2 Sam 20:1 contrast with 19:44 MT; 1 Kgs 12:16). Perhaps even the election choice of God that retains the Hebrew phrase

---

35. Cogan, *1 Kings*, 296-97; Dillard, *2 Chronicles*, 58-59.

"*in* David" (*bdwd*/בְּדָוִד, 1 Kgs 8:16; Ps 78:70) also makes this covenantal inclusion point. This "in David" idea precedes and lays the groundwork for Paul's concept of being "*in* Christ."[36]

Eventually, Yahweh was compelled by the king's rebellion to tear Israel away from the house of David (2 Kgs 17:21). As captivity comes to Judah, the New Covenant is prophesied to encompass both David and the Davidic Covenant which includes a Davidic son on the throne and multiplied descendants of David (Jer 31:31-36; 33:14-26; Ezek 34:25-31). In fact, the fixed order of the Davidic Covenant is reaffirmed within the New Covenant with everlasting confidence on the pattern of the continuing order of creation. However, in contrast to the ravages of captivity experienced by Israel, the Davidic Covenant is identified as a covenant of peace because it ushers in the eschatological Kingdom (Ezek 34:25-31).

The prophets identify that as Israel goes into the Babylonian captivity, Israel will be without a Davidic king for many days (Hosea 3:4). However, in the last days, Yahweh will rebuild Israel including the re-establishment of the Davidic kingdom (1 Chron 17:24; Isa 11:1-2; Hosea 3:5; Amos 9:11-12).[37] This Davidic King will be born in Bethlehem (Mic 5:2). This King will shepherd and lead the remnant of Israel into peace which He Himself grounds (Isa 9:2-7; Mic 2:13; 5:3-4). His reign will be particularly characterized by righteousness (Isa 9:7; 16:5). His reign, with its abundant loyal love and blessings shall exist forever as a co-regency with the Sovereign God (Isa 55:1-5; 2 Sam 23:5; Ps 89:1-4, 28-29).[38] In this context His throne-names declare His and God's glory (Isa 9:6). The zeal of Yahweh will accomplish the full extent of the Messiah's Davidic Kingdom.[39]

The servant songs of Isaiah are often viewed as Messianic though they are nowhere specifically declared to be Davidic.[40] Isaiah's servant is identified with Israel (Isa 41:8; 49:3) but is also an individual who will establish justice within a world kingdom, as the Davidic King will

---

36. This is a point Wright makes in *Justification*, 104 after the pattern of "in Christ" in Schweitzer, *The Mysticism of Paul*, 225.

37. Watts, *Isaiah 1-33*, 172-175; eschatological Davidic King recipient of Davidic Covenant (*T. Jud.* 22.3; Sir 45.25; 47.11; *Ps. Sol.* 17.4; 4Q174 1 I.7-13; 4Q252 5.1-5; 4Q504 1-2, 4.6-8).

38. Mays, *Micah*, 117.

39. Eschatological Davidic King called "Messiah" or "Anointed One" (Ps 2:2; *2 Bar.* 70.10; 72.2; *1 En.* 48.10; 52.4; *4 Ezra* 7.28; 12.32; *Ps. Sol.* 17.32; 4Q252 5.3).

40. Clements, "The Davidic Covenant," 39-69.

accomplish (Isa 42:4; 61:1–3 in comparison to 11:1–10). This servant is described as a *covenant of the people* (*berit*/בְּרִית, διαθήκην) in Isaiah 42:6 probably in His roles of recovering Israel and the nations into the Kingdom. This sense of covenant could be seen as an expression of Kingdom which would fit this emphasis of the *everlasting Davidic covenant* elsewhere in Isaiah (*berit*/בְּרִית, διαθήκην; Isa 55:3).[41]

New Covenant Embraces the Davidic Covenant

In Jer 31–33 the New Covenant punctuates through the context of captivity and dispersion with an encouraging message of "Behold days are coming" of renewal, re-gathering, New Covenant, rebuilding, and of Davidic Covenant (Jer 23:5–6; 30:3, 9; 31:27, 31–34, 38; 33:14–16).[42] In those days a righteous branch of David will spring forth, enabled by the Spirit of Yahweh to be characterized by wisdom, understanding, counsel, strength, knowledge, and the fear of Yahweh (Isa 11:1–2). He will act wisely to execute justice and righteousness on the earth, especially for the poor and needy (Isa 11:3–5; Jer 33:15). The peace of His reign will extend even to undoing the curse of animosity between snakes and humans, as well as the fear animals have of each other from the Noahic Covenant, thus returning human and animals to a pre-fall condition of peace with the creation (Gen 1:30; 3:15; 9:2–3; Isa 9:7; 11:6–9). This Davidic reign will bring about Judah's deliverance to safety and righteousness. In the same way as Israel has been defined by the exodus from Egypt it will in that day be defined by gathering from dispersion (Isa 11:10–16; Jer 23:7–8; 30:9–24; 33:16). From this point on the Davidic throne of Israel will not lack a man to sit and reign (Jer 33:17). This is thought of as continuing the lineage of Davidic kings for continued generations (Jer 33:17). This "branch" will reign and rebuild the temple within which a continuing lineage of Levitical priests will function, yet He Himself will

---

41. Smith, "BĔRÎT 'AM/ BĔRÎT 'ÔLĀM," 241–43.

42. Jer 30:8–12 and 33:14–26 is absent from the LXX but present in the MT. Some conjecture that the difference is reflective of the Zadokite eclipse of the Davidic line (McKane, *Jeremiah*, 2:862) or the rise of the Hasmoneans (Duhm, *Jeremiah*, 276; Holladay, *Jeremiah*, 2:230). However, beyond these textual critical ellipses, the everlasting character of the Davidic Kingly reign is amply supported in LXX Jer 23:5–6 and among the other prophets in the MT and their LXX counterparts (Isa 55:3–5; Ezek 34:23–24; 37:24–25; Hos 3:5) and Qumran (4QJer c 33:16–21), so both source critical explanations are unlikely (Leuchter, *The Polemics of Exile*, 72). So there is support for Davidic Covenant in both MT and LXX.

be a king-priest on His throne (Zech 3:8; 6:12–15; Jer 33:1–8, 21–22). The certainty of this Davidic reign coming about is promised by God on the same degree of certainty as the continuance of day and night (Jer 33:20–21).

Royal Psalms

The royal psalms provide another angle on the commitment, hopes and benefits of the Davidic Covenant. In the royal psalms King Yahweh is praised and petitioned as enabling and providing the Davidic Covenant king with what he needs to conquer foes and remain faithful.

In Ps 101 David shows himself to be a man after God's heart as he resolves to follow Yahweh's way of loving-kindness and justice with integrity of heart, not letting any evil thought, sight or person dwell with him in the land. As a coronation vow it is the kind of commitment all Davidic kings should emulate. Unfortunately, David didn't live up to this commitment and his sons failed even more miserably.

David crafts a pair of Pss 20 and 21 petitioning and praising Yahweh for giving him his heart's desire (Pss 20:4; 21:2). In Ps 20, David petitions Yahweh in time of trouble to remember Israel's offerings to grant victory and his heart's desire. David confesses his trust that Yahweh overwhelms mere military confidence by saving His anointed by His right hand. When Yahweh answers this petition, David praises Yahweh for giving him his heart's desire, for he trusts in Yahweh's strength and preserving loving-kindness, which destroys all enemies (Ps 21). David's heart desire includes salvation, his kingship, blessing, long life forever and joy in Yahweh's presence.

Psalms 144 and 18 have greater verbal affinity though they are separated in the psalter. In Ps 144, David: l) praises Yahweh's loyal love and strength for equipping him for war and the defeating of a local rebellion, 2) then reflects on the brevity of human life, and 3) petitions for Yahweh to manifest His presence as at Sinai to deliver David from his enemies so that youths could mature, and blessing abound. Ps 18 answers this with the repeated verbal metaphors from Ps 144, of Yahweh as rock, fortress and storm to bring salvation for David. Delivered by Yahweh from all his enemies (especially the remainders from the sins of Saul), David praises Yahweh as his deliver Who fought for him in theophany (earthquake, volcano, and thunderstorm), which shows forth Yahweh's blessing for David's faithfulness in the Mosaic covenant (2 Sam 22; Ps 18). The psalm ends by giving thanks to Yahweh for His deliverance and loving-kindness to the anointed king, David, and his descendants forever (2 Sam 22:50–51; Ps 18:49–50).

Perhaps Psalm 45 emerges out of a context of a royal wedding. Each partner is addressed: 1) in a context of victorious battle, the divine king is blessed by God with: everlasting throne, scepter, virtue, and anointing to reign; 2) in the wedding, the queen should forget family allegiances and submit to the Davidic king and the marriage will be prosperous and remembered for generations. This psalm is a performative liturgy presumably available for all royal wedding partners within the Davidic lineage.

Solomon[43] prays that God would give him the divine judgments (familiar in the Mosaic Covenant) so that he could bring peace, righteousness and blessing to his people, victory over his enemies, and aid to the needy as an expression of God's glory (Ps 72). This noble aspiration which Solomon expressed early in his reign serves as a good guide for Davidic kings to follow.

In the song of ascent, Ps 132, Israel petitions Yahweh to remember the vow of David concerning a permanent dwelling for the ark, resolving to worship Him in the expectation that God will be in the temple in power and righteousness. Yahweh responds to Israel's prayer reiterating the Davidic Covenant with everlasting reign. Weinfeld argues that Ps 132:1 depicts that David is granted a dynasty by comparing this claim with grants from Ugarit, a deed from Elephantine and a letter from El Amarna.[44] The psalm addresses the issue of the establishment of Temple and the length of the reign for Davidic sons as *forever* because Yahweh commits to dwell in the land *forever* ('lm/עוֹלָם, Ps 132:12, 14).[45]

Psalm 89 develops the forever promise of the Davidic reign more than any other royal psalm. Weinfeld argues that the imagery of the deity grasping the rulers hand in Ps 89:21–22 indicates an adoption by the deity.[46] The inter-textual "forever" (עוֹלָם) promise of the Davidic son's reign

---

43. The MT text reflects Solomon as author (or collector) rather than LXX which declares that this text is intended for Solomon. *Ps. Sol.* 17 parallels Ps 72 in many Messianic points. Broyles has a good discussion of the psalm's contributions ("The Redeeming King," 23–40.

44. Weinfeld, "The Covenant Grant," 187–88.

45. Son of David will reign *forever* (2 *Bar.* 73.1; 1 *En.* 49.1–2; 1 Macc 2.57; *Pss. Sol.* 17.35–38; 4Q174 1 I, 1–5, 11; 4Q246 II, 5–9; 4Q252 5, 4).

46. Weinfeld, "The Covenant Grant," 190–92; similar language is used in the

indicates a boundless time with regard to the Davidic son's reign, which is designated to all generations (Ps 89:4, 29, 36). This same forever promise for Davidic covenant is confirmed because Yahweh has sworn it in covenant and He does not lie (Ps 89:3, 35). The everlasting Davidic reign is further described as continuing as long as sun and moon continue to shine (Ps 89:2, 36–37). "Forever" is also mentioned in the psalm as the length of time which Yahweh is loyal in love and thus is the length of time Yahweh is to be praised (Ps 89:2, 52). However, this strong everlastingness nature of the Davidic Covenant raises a problem for the psalmist because the Babylonian conquest has in fact destroyed the Davidic reign and Jerusalem. Ethan praises incomparable Yahweh's everlasting (*'lm*/ עוֹלָם) Davidic Covenant to all generations (in spite of his sinning sons) as Yahweh's means of destroying enemies and saving his own. Then Ethan petitions: so how long must we wait with Jerusalem destroyed and no Davidic king which you formerly swore in loving-kindness; please deliver us to the Davidic king promised. Ethan is still praising Yahweh for a forever Davidic Covenant that is not undone by the Babylonian captivity. That is, Ethan expects a Davidic king again as an expression of Yahweh's everlasting loyal love. This Davidic king will be exalted above what David and Solomon realized as sons of their Father Yahweh, for he will be the supreme earthly king (over all other earthly kings) and thus identified by the phrase "first born" and thus the rightful heir.[47] Yet even without this supreme king visibly on earth reigning, Ethan's petition is still appropriate: "Yahweh how long must we wait for your everlasting loyal love to renew the Davidic king in Your everlasting Davidic Covenant; please deliver us to the Davidic king promised."

David looks in Psalm 110 toward this eschatological end. After receiving an oracle of the exaltation of his Lord, David describes the holy army of the King-Priest as He comes to do battle with all the nations. Yahweh grounds the promise to Adonai (David's Lord) because Yahweh will bring about utter defeat of the enemies, rendering them to be a footstool with the king's feet on their neck (Ps 110:1). In this, Yahweh who fights for Adonai, the same Adonai who fights at Adonai's right hand (Ps 110: 1, 5). This merges kingship and divinity, elevating David's Lord above David

---

"Testament," 2–7, 12. So eschatological Messiah is God's Son (Ps 2:7; 4Q174 1 I.11; 4Q246II.1; 4Q369 1 II; *Sib. Or.* 5.261; *4 Ezra* 13.32, 52).

47. In Ps 89:27 "firstborn" is defined as "highest king" consistent with the ancient near East pattern. For example, Marduk is called "firstborn of gods" to identify his supreme kingship *(ANET, Babylonian Creation Epic,* 4:20).

and yet retaining Him as an earthly Davidic king. David's Lord is then vice-regent with Yahweh over all.[48] Yahweh will stretch forth His emblem of rule and call David's king to rule in the midst of his enemies which Yahweh also rules (Ps 110:2). The people serve in the Davidic King's army willingly, as holy, abundant, and fresh troops (Ps 110:3). Yahweh's oath identifies the Davidic king as a priest after the pattern of Melchizedek (Ps 110:4).[49] We have already seen that David blended the royal and priestly roles so it should come as no surprise that the greatest Davidic King will do the same (2 Sam 6:2; 7:1–7; Ps 110:4). The Davidic king is victorious at His coming by the help of Yahweh (Ps 110:5–7). This is expressed in a nice turn of a phrase: the heads of a broad country will be shattered but the Davidic king's head will be lifted up (Ps 110:6–7).

In light of the nations' eschatological utter defeat, Ps 2 counsels the nations to abandon rebellion against Yahweh and His anointed Davidic king. These nations must submit to the Son ordained to rule over them. Imbedded in this psalm is the turn away from exclusion of Gentiles in their rebellion, to a call of submission to the Davidic King to rule the whole world as well as Israel. Though, the resolve of the unrepentant is amazing, however, Yahweh scoffs and terrifies them by announcing that He has installed His Davidic anointed king in Zion (Ps 2:1–6). The installation of the Davidic king initiates an adopted Sonship relationship under God, which enables him to forcefully defeat all enemies (Ps 2:7–9). The statement of "begetting" is an adoption formula, probably of coronation,[50] which identifies the Davidic king to be the Son of God. Such a concept in itself does not deify the individual but rather speaks of the Son of God as God's heir to His realm.[51] Thus the warning: submit to the Son lest He utterly defeat you as enemies of His wrath (Ps 2:10–12). In this context, there is poetic assonance in the word-play made off the imagery: worship ('bd/עָבַד) Yahweh or perish ('bd/אָבַד). Blessed are all who take refuge in Him.

---

48. Anderson, *The Book of Psalms*, 2:769.

49. Kennard, *Messiah Jesus*, 353–76.

50. Based on the synonymous parallelism in Ps 2:7 and further indicated as God doing for the Messiah in the Qumran manuscript *Messianic Rule*.

51. Anderson, *The Book of Psalms*, 1:68; this phrase is alluded to in the Messiah reference in 1QSa 2.11–12.

Daniel's Son of Man

While not actually a Davidic king image, Jesus and second Temple Judaism merge the Davidic King with Daniel's Son of Man. Jesus blends Daniel's Son of Man with the Davidic king image of Psalm 110:1 at His trial (Matt 26:64; Mark 14:62; Luke 22:69).

Daniel 7 concludes the vision of four beasts with the divine Ancient of Days in His throne room, who will conquer all the Gentile nations which have stood against God. The MT and Theodotion's LXX present the Son of Man as a distinctive second divine power to the Ancient of Days fostering the Jewish two-powers heresy within monotheism.[52] That is, entering into the midst of this throne room is the Son of Man riding on the clouds (Dan 7:13–14). Some take this title to refer to the primordial man who will rule like Ps 8:4 mentions, but most recognize that the cloud-riding identifies the Son of Man as the king of the Gods,[53] like Marduk or Baal. Yet in Judaism's monotheism the Ancient of Days is clearly the presentation of God. Therefore, this divine one comes up to God and receives His dominion to rule the Kingdom. Second Temple Judaism retains the pre-existent Son of Man as a heavenly being with everlasting dominion on the earth.[54] An alternative reading in the Old Greek LXX identifies the Son of Man *as* (ὡς) the Ancient of Days, perhaps as a reaction to this Jewish two-powers heresy.[55] However, Zeigler and Munnich consider that a likely scribal ellipsis of an epsilon before the ὡς would bring the Old Greek in line with the MT and Theodotian's LXX, thus continuing to support two divine participants in the throne room as do the other Dan texts.[56]

In Dan the movement is *toward* God to receive the Kingdom, while early Jewish and New Testament texts describe the cloud riding Son of Man as coming *from* God to implement the Kingdom on earth. In the

---

52. Segal, *The Two Powers*; Schreuer, "Midrash, theology," 230–54; Boyarin, "Beyond Judaisms," 323–65.

53. Sabourin, "The Biblical Cloud," 290–311, especially 304; another option of Son of Man definitions is that of a prophet, following Ezekiel's use, however that is unlikely with the divine, conquest and king imagery with Daniel's Son of man; Casey, *Son of Man*; Burkett, *The Son of Man*; Tödt, *The Son of Man*; Slater, "One Like a Son of Man," 183–98; Moloney, *The Johannine Son*; "The Johannine Son,", 177–202.

54. *1 En.* 39.6; 40.5; 48.3, 6; 62.7; *4 Ezra* 13.26, 52; Syr. Bar 29.

55. Old Greek LXX Dan 7:13; H. Daniel Zacharias, "Old Greek Daniel," 454–55.

56. Ziegler and Munnich, *Susanna-Daniel-Bel*," note at Daniel 7:13; Zacharias, "Old Greek Daniel," 454–55.

N.T. sense, coupling this Dan text with Ps 110's conquest to reign makes perfect sense. This Danielic Son of Man is explicitly called "Messiah" in the *Similitudes of Enoch* 46.1; 47.3 and in *4 Ezra* 7.28–29; 12.11; 13.32. Furthermore, the DSS manuscript 4Q246 refers to "the Son of God" in profoundly Danielic language as before the throne of God, and then coming to earth to conquer his enemies and establish his everlasting Kingdom. Drawing upon the insights of John Collins (from 4Q246) and N. T. Wright (from Mark 13), Marvin Pate argues that the Danielic Son of Man is portrayed as fighting on behalf of the righteous (Essenes or the disciples of Jesus, respectively), whose enemies include the nation of Israel.[57] However, Judaism generally developed this Son of Man image to be Messianic in Israel's favor.[58] This meant that any resistant Gentile powers were generally crushed as the Son of Man rode the clouds to conquer and establish righteous Jews in the Messiah's Kingdom (Dan 7:17–27). Jewish tradition also developed a co-regency between God and this Son of Man to reign in the Kingdom.[59]

Daniel's Messiah and the Seventy Weeks

Daniel noticed in Jer the prophet that the Babylonian captivity had been predicted to be seventy years long for the purpose of recovering the sabbatical years lost from Israel's noncompliance over the last four hundred and ninety years (Dan 9:1–3; Lev 26:34–35, 43; Jer 25:11; 29:10; 2 Chr 36:21). This realization motivated Daniel to pray toward this recovery for Israel. God reassured Daniel by sending Gabriel to him to explain his vision (Dan 9:20–27). In this context the "seventy weeks determined" for Israel and for Jerusalem would likely identify another four hundred and ninety years (of 360 days each, to reflect the Jewish calendar) into the future for specific things to be realized for Israel that had not been realized as of yet.[60]

Within the seventy weeks, Israel will experience rehabilitation into Kingdom (Dan 9:24). Using synonymous Hebrew parallelism God will finish transgression and make an end of sins. This would likely be more

---

57. Pate, *Communities of the Last Days*, 127–132.

58. *1 En.* 37–71; *4 Ezra* 13; *Tg. 1 Chr.* 3.24; *b. Sanh.* 38b rabbi Akiva sees it as a messiah reference while rabbi Jose does not.

59. 11Q13; 4Q400–5; 11Q17.

60. Hoehner, *Chronological Aspects*, 115–139.

than an atonement for sins, for ending such conditions also describes the triumph of God's Kingdom in reality,[61] as is common in Dan so far (Dan 2:44–45; 7:9–14) and perhaps visualizes a revitalizing of a covenantal lifestyle as well. The next two lines may continue to be parallel, especially if they revolve around the restoration of covenant. Reconciliation for iniquity would in second Temple constructs identify covenant renewal, which is of course a condition that Israel needs as the Babylonian captivity continues to dominate their condition. Likewise, the condition of everlasting righteousness would be especially identified with the realization of the New Covenant condition that would usher in the eschatological Kingdom. The last pair of accomplishments within this seventy weeks consists of sealing up prophecy and anointing the Most Holy. This probably indicates either closing out prophetic ministry, or fulfilling what prophets have predicted to this point.[62] The anointing of the Most Holy would then either be realized by a Messianic person being anointed, or the Temple being anointed in Kingdom.

The seventy weeks begins with a decree to restore and rebuild Jerusalem, especially streets and wall, in a troublesome time (Dan 9:25). Artaxerxes' decree to rebuild Jerusalem's wall given to Nehemiah in 444 B.C. best fits this focus (Neh 2:1–8).[63] Harold Hoehner assumes that the decree was given on the first of Nisan (because the month is mentioned but no date is identified by Neh), which he calculates to be March 5. This era of the rebuilding is clearly in distressing times, for realization of the decree was even slowed and threatened by surrounding nations (Ezra 4:7–23; Neh 4–6).

The seventy weeks are artistically broken out into units of seven weeks, sixty-two weeks and a final single week. There is no development in the text that explains the separation of the first seven weeks from the following sixty-two weeks. Harold Hoehner computes that this sixty-two weeks is complete on Nisan 10 or March 30, 33 A.D., which he identifies as Jesus' triumphal entry into Jerusalem.[64] Daniel identifies that after the sixty-two weeks are complete, Messiah will be cut off by the people who will come to destroy the Temple (Dan 9:26). 11QMelchizedek 18 echoes

---

61. Baldwin, *Daniel*, 168–69.
62. Baldwin, *Daniel*, 169.
63. Hoehner, *Chronological Aspects*, 121–28.
64. Hoehner, *Chronological Aspects*, 135–39; historically Jesus dies within 30–34 A.D. based on the issues in Pilate's reign such as the last two years of his reign (35–36 A.D.) were taken up with a rebellion in Samaria (Josephus, *Ant.* 18.85).

Daniel's "sixty-two weeks" as an indicator for identifying when the King-Priest Melchizedek would arrive and as the Anointed would be cut off, showing further second Temple Messianic expectation. So this sixty-two weeks fits both expectations in that the King-Priest Jesus was present on March 30, 33 A.D. and after this date both: 1) Jesus was killed by the Romans, and then, 2) the Romans destroyed the Temple. The identification of these two events after the sixty-two weeks may indicate that the final seventieth week does not immediately follow until these events are realized. The seventieth week is identified by two features: 1) the coming prince of the people will make a covenant with Israel for one week, and 2) in the middle of this week the Temple will be destroyed (Dan 9:26–27). Antiochus Epiphanies defiled the Temple in these kind of "abomination of desolation" terms according to Daniel's prophecy but he did not destroy the Temple (Dan 11:31). The Romans both defiled and destroyed the Temple in 70 A.D. and did so again with the functioning Temple remains in 135 A.D., remaking the Temple into a temple for Jupiter. In none of these was there an apparent limited covenant of seven years, though the Jewish war lasted from 66 to 73 A.D. Additionally, Daniel writes of an end time that will not be understood until it is happening, in which a conquest of Israel and an "abomination of desolation" of the Temple will occur after a time, times and half a time (Dan 12:7–11). It is possible that this "time, times and half a time" refers to three and a half years, or the middle of a seven year period, especially since it is immediately followed by two designations of days that are themselves slightly longer than three and a half years (Dan 12:11–12). When these times conclude, Daniel describes the occupants as blessed, indicating that the eschatological Kingdom at the end of time has been realized (Dan 12:4, 13).

Second Temple Jewish Expectations

Second Temple Judaism is that period of Jewish thought and expectations from the fifth century B.C. through the Roman conquest of 70 and 135 A.D. John Collins argues that there are four messianic paradigms in the Jewish inter-testamental literature: Davidic Messiah (anointed king)[65] or

---

65. Davidic King references include: *2 Bar.* 70.10; 72.2; *1 En.* 48.10; 52.4; *4 Ez.* 7.28; 12.32; *Pss. of Sol.* 17.32; 18.57; *Shemoneh 'Esreh* 14; Sir 47.11, 22; 1 Macc 2.57; CD 7.20; 12.23–13.1; 14.19 (=4Q266 frag. 18, 3.12); 19.10–11; 20.1; 1QS 9.11; 1QSa 2.11–12, 14–15, 20–21; 1QSb 5.20; 1QM 5.1; 4Q161; 4Q252 frag. 1 5.3–4; 4Q381 frag. 15.7; 4Q382 frag. 16.2; 4Q458 frag. 2, 2.6; 4Q521 frag. 2 4, 2.1; 4Q521 frag. 7.3; 4QFlor.

Son of God[66], priest, prophet and Danielic Son of Man.[67] Only the first model, the Davidic Messianic King fits the Davidic Covenant material. Some texts just focus on the divine election of the Davidic Covenant hope.

> You have loved Israel more than all the peoples. You have chosen the tribe of Judah and have established your covenant with David that he might be a princely shepherd over your people and sit before you on the throne of Israel forever.[68]

However, the Davidic King and the Danielic Son of Man are often joined to develop the Messianic King imagery further. Combining these images, the Jewish apocalyptic writings of *1 En.* 37–71; *4 Ezra* 11–12 and *2 Bar.* 39–40 develop a coming deliverer who will defeat the enemies of Israel. Qumran joins in with this sentiment. For example, the Qumran *Florilegium* text 4Q174 interprets 2 Sam 7:11–14 as a promise that there will be a descendant of David who destroys the enemies of God and will reign on an everlasting throne. The text refers to a "shoot"[69] which is the Davidic Messiah from Isa 11:1; Jer 23:5; 33:15 and Zech 3:8 and 6:12.

> This passage refers to the Shoot of David, who is to arise with the Interpreter of the Law, and who will [arise] in Zi[on in the La]st Days, as it is written, "And I shall raise up the branch of David that is fallen" (Amos 9:11). This passage describes the fallen booth of David, [w]hom He shall raise up to deliver Israel.[70]

Appendix B to the *Rule of the Benediction* (1QSb 5:21) expresses a blessing on "the prince of the congregation,[71] that God will raise up for him

---

1.10–13; 4QPat. 3–4; *b. 'Erub.* 43a; *Yoma* 10a; *Sukk.* 52a; 52b; *Meg.* 17b; *Hagiga* 16a; *Yebam.* 62a; *Ketab* 112b; *Sotah.* 48b; *Sanh.* 38a; *Gen. Rab.* 97 on Gen 49:10; *Ex. Rab.* 25.12 on Exod 16:29; *Num. Rab.* 14.1 on Num 7:48.

66. Messianic Son of God references include: 1QSa (1Q28b); 4Q174 (4QFlor) 1.10–12; 4Q174 1 I.11; 4Q246 1.9; 2.1 and 4Q369 1 II; *Sib. Or.* 5.261; *1 En.* 105.2; *4 Ezra* 7.28–29; 13.32, 37, 52; 14.9.

67. Collins, *The Star and the Scepter*, 3–14, especially 12; Pate (*Communities of the Last Days*, 107–132) follows him in this analysis to an abbreviated fashion.

68. 4Q504 1–2 iv 4–8; 4Q252 5.2–5; Abegg, "The Covenant," 82; *Pss. Sol.* 17.4.

69. For branch of David texts Cf. 4Q161 frag. 7–10.iii.22; 4Q174 frag. 1–3.i.11–12; *4QpIsa.* frag. 7–10 iii 22; *4QCommentary on Genesis A* 5.3–4; 4Q252 frag. 1 v. 3–4; 4Q285 frag. 5.3–4; frag. 7 lines 3–4; 11Q14 lines 12–13; *Pss. Sol.* 17.4, 21, 27–36; 18.7.

70. 4Q174 3.11–13 translated VanderKam and Flint, *The Meaning*, 265 and 450 chapter 11, note 7.

71. Additional texts speak of this messiah as the prince of the congregation (CD 7.19–20; 1QSb 5.20; 1QM 3.16; 5.1; 4Q496 frag. 10.3–4 (1QM 3.11–15); 4Q161 frags.

the kingdom of His people," which Collins observes is heavily indebted to Isaiah 11:

> To dispense justice with [equity to the oppressed] of the land (Isa 11:4a). [May you smite the peoples] with the might of your hand and ravage the earth with your scepter; may you bring death to the ungodly with the breath of your lips! (Isa 11:4b) . . . and everlasting might, the spirit of knowledge and of the fear of God (Isa 11:2); may righteousness be the girdle [of your loins] and may your reins be girded [with faithfulness] (Isa 11:5).[72]

Such a reign of Messiah sometimes has Him referred to as "the scepter."[73]

> The scepter will not depart from the tribe of Judah . . . . Whenever Israel rules, there will not fail to be a descendant of David upon the throne. For the staff is the covenant of kingship, and the thousands of Israel are the standards . . . until the Messiah of Righteousness comes, the Branch of David. For to him and his seed is granted the covenant of kinship over his people for everlasting generations which he is to keep . . . the Law with the men of the Community.[74]

In fact, the sectarian perspective of Qumran means that the Davidic Messiah would destroy that portion of Israel that would not align themselves with the Qumran community.[75] This judgment to establish the Kingdom is also presented by *1 En.* as occurring by Daniel's Son of Man. Additionally, the Kingdom reign of the Messiah is more clearly a reign over the whole world.

> On that day all the kings and the mighty and the exalted, and those who possess the earth, will stand up; and they will see and recognize how he sits on the throne of his glory, and righteous are judged in righteousness before him, and no idle word is spoken before him. And pain will come upon them as upon a woman in labor . . . And pain will take hold of them, when they see that Son of Man sitting on the throne of his glory.[76]

2–6.ii.17; 4QTestim 9:13; 1QM 11:6; 4Q285 frag. 4.2, 6; 5.4; 6.2; 4Q376 frag. 1.iii.1, 3; 4QpIsa 2:6.2:15; *Jub.* 31.18; *Sib. Or.* 3.469) and the Davidic "Messiah of Israel" (CD 12:23–13:1; 14:19; 19:10–11; 20.1; 1QS 9:11, 16; 10:11; 1QSa 2:11–22).

72. Collins, *The Star and the Scepter*, 60–61.
73. CD 7.19–20=4Q266 frag. 3.iv.9; 1QSb 5.27–28; 4Q161 frags. 2–6.ii.17.
74. 4QCommGen. A 5.1–5; also 4Q252 col. 5.
75. 1QM with 1QS 1:23–24; 2:14–17; 9:16.
76. *1 En.* 62.4–5; and in 52.4 this messiah is called the Anointed One; also in 48.10;

This deliverance will entail a judgment and then a celebration of cleansing to prepare for the Kingdom. The Qumran text known as *The War of the Messiah* (4Q285 fragment 5) comments upon Isa 10:34-11:1 developing the effectiveness of the shoot of Jesse to begin the Kingdom.

> [This is the] Branch of David. Then [all forces of Belial] shall be judged, [and the king of the Kittim shall stand for judgment] and the Leader of the congregation-the Bra[nch of David]-will have him put to death. [Then all Israel shall come out with timbrel]s and dancers, and the [High] Priest shall order [them to cleanse their bodies from the guilty blood of the c]orpse[s of] the Kittim.[77]

The Qumran text 4Q252 fragment 1, 5:1-5, commenting on Gen 49:10, develops the Messiah as the Branch of David who reigns forever.

> A ruler shall [no]t depart from the tribe of Judah when Israel has dominion. [And] the one who sits on the throne of David [shall never] be cut off, because the "ruler's staff" is the covenant of the kingdom, [and the thous]ands of Israel are "the feet," until the Righteous Messiah, the Branch of David, has come. For to him and to his seed the covenant of the kingdom of His people has been given for the everlasting generations, because he has kept[. . .] the Law with the men of the *Yahad*.[78]

The Messiah's Kingdom lasts for everlasting generations with no end.[79]

The Qumran manuscript, *Messianic Apocalypse*, identifies these Jewish expectations for a kingly Messiah who will bring in a Kingdom program that meets real needs.[80]

52.4; 84.2 this messiah is ruler of the whole world; 4Q246; 4Q382 frag. 16 2; *4 Ezra* 13; *Sib. Or.* 5; Reynolds, "The 'One Like a Son of Man,'" 70-80; Collins, "The Son of Man," 448-66.

77. 4Q285 fragment 5 translated by VanderKam and Flint, *The Meaning*, 266, and 451, chapter 11, note 11; *Pss. Sol.* 17.4, 21-36; 18.5-7; 4QpIsa^a frags.7-10 iii 22-29 and echoed in 1QSb 5.21-26, *4 Ezra* 13.2-10; Matt 2:23; Acts 13:23; Rom 15:12; Heb 7:14; Rev 5:5; 22:16; Clement of Alexandria, *Strom.*5.6; *Paed.* 1.7; Justin Martyr, *Apol.* 1.32; *Dial. Tryph.* 87, Irenaeus, *Haer.* 3.17.1; 4.33.1 and probably 4Q285 5.1-6 and *Test. of Levi* 18.7.

78. 4Q252 fragment 1, 5:1-5 translated by VanderKam and Flint, *The Meaning*, 266, and myself; a similar point is made that the Son of David will reign *forever* (*2 Bar.* 73.1; *1 En.* 49.1-2; 1 Macc 2.57; *Pss. Sol.* 17.35-38; 4Q174 1 I, 1-5, 11; 4Q246 II, 5-9; 4Q521 column 2; 4Q252 5, 4; 4Q521 frag. 7.3).

79. 4Q252 fragment 1, 5:5; 4Q521; *2 Bar.* 73.1; *Sib. Or.* 3.767.

80. 4Q521 as quoted in Vermes, *Jesus the Jew*; "Qumran Forum Miscellanea I,"

> [the hea]vens and the earth will listen to His Messiah, and none
> therein will stray from the commandments of the holy ones.
> Seekers of the Lord, strengthen yourselves in his service!
> All you hopeful in (your) heart, will you not find the Lord in
> this?
> For the Lord will consider the pious, and call the righteous by
> name.
> Over the poor His spirit will hover and will renew the faithful
> with His power.
> And He will glorify the pious on the throne of the eternal
> Kingdom,
> He who liberates the captives, restores sight to the blind,
> straightens the b[ent].
> And the Lord will accomplish glorious things which have never
> been...
> For He will heal the wounded, and revive the dead and bring
> good news to the poor.

This reign of the Lord's anointed one will have heaven and earth obeying Him, benefited by Him in Kingdom and fellowshipping before Him forever.[81]

This left Israel with an expectancy for the coming Davidic king. With the failure of the Maccabeans and especially Judas Maccabeus in 164 B.C., another was expected. Pompey conquered Israel for Rome in 63 B.C. which fostered a sense that the Davidic king could come at any time, perhaps prompted by reflection on Daniel 2 and 7. For example, shortly after Pompey's capture of Jerusalem in 63 B.C. the *Pss. Sol.* celebrate the expected Davidic Messiah.

> Behold, O Lord, and raise up unto them their king, the son of
> David,
> At the time in which thou seest, O God, that he may reign over
> Israel thy servant.
> And gird him with strength, that he may shatter unrighteous
> rulers,
> And that he may purge Jerusalem from the nations that trample
> her down to destruction.[82]

JJS 43(1992): 303–4; Puech, "Une apocalypse messianique (4Q521)," *RQ* 15(1992): 475–522; Similar sentiments are echoed by Maimonides, *Thirteen Principles of the Faith*, no. 12; *Yad haHazaqa* contained in Patai, *The Messiah Texts*, 323–27.

  81. 4Q521 frag. 2, 4.ii.1; 1QSa 2.14–15, 20–21.
  82. *Pss. Sol.* 17.23ff.

Herod the Great tried to capitalize on this sentiment as he rose to power by killing Judas ben Hezekiah and destroying the Jewish resistance.[83] Despised though Herod the Great was, he tried to realize the expectancy of the Messiah as he built the Temple with his Temple construction project (37–34 B.C.), designed to present himself as the Davidic king. As Herod lay dying Judas ben Sariphaeus and Matthias ben Margalothus pulled down the ornamental eagle from the temple and a revolt was on, only to be crushed by Herod's son Archelaus.[84] Other would-be messiahs fostered peasant movements to bring in the Kingdom during this power vacuum before Archelaus put together his power block, namely, Judas son of Ezekias, Herod's servant Simon, and Athronges.[85] When Archelaus and Antipas each argued in Rome for succession, a Jewish delegation plead for autonomy. During the absence of the would-be rulers, another rebellion took place and twice had to be put down by Varus, king of Syria.[86] Such rebellions have at the core the hope that God would raise His Messiah to bring in the Kingdom.

N. T. Wright identifies that Pontus Pilate crushed seven rebellions during his procuratorship (A.D. 26-36).[87]

(1) Pilate tried to bring Roman standards into Jerusalem, but backed down after a mass protest.[88]

(2) He used money from the Temple treasury to build an aqueduct, and crushed the resistance that this action provoked.[89]

(3) He sent troops to kill some Galileans while they were offering sacrifices in the Temple, presumably because he feared a riot.[90]

(4) He captured and condemned to death the leader of an uprising that had taken place in Jerusalem, involving murder; he then

---

83. Josephus, *Ant.* 14.158-160, 420-430 which incurred the wrath and denouncement of the Jews (Josephus, *Ant.* 14.172-176; *J. W.* 1.208-215; and from Qumran [*T. Mos.* 6.2-6]).

84. Josephus, *Ant.* 17.149-166, 206-218; *J. W.* 1.648-655, 2.1-13.

85. Josephus, *Ant.* 17.7, 10.5-6; *J. W.* 2.4.1.

86. Josephus, *Ant.* 17.250-264; *J. W.* 2.39-50.

87. Wright, *The New Testament and the People of God*, 174.

88. Josephus, *Ant.* 18.55-59; *J. W.* 2.169-174. A similar incident occurred when Vitellius was sent to fight Aretas in A.D. 37: see *Ant.* 18.120-123.

89. Josephus, *Ant.* 18.60-62; *J. W.* 2.175-177; Eusebius, *Hist. eccl.* 2.6.6-7.

90. Luke 13:1.

released the man as a gesture of goodwill during the Passover feast.[91]

(5) At the same Passover, he faced a quasi-messianic movement, having some association with two ordinary revolutionaries.[92]

(6) He provoked public opinion by placing Roman votive shields, albeit without images, in the palace at Jerusalem, which according to Philo annoyed Tiberius almost as much as it did the Jews.[93]

(7) Finally, he suppressed with particular brutality a popular (and apparently non-revolutionary) prophetic movement in Samaria. For this he was accused before the Roman legate in Syria, who sent him sent back to Rome.[94]

Such frequency of rebellions show the fever-pitched hope for Kingdom of that era. Many of these had central figures viewed by their followers as being this Davidic Messiah.

A brief moment of quiet occurred during Herod Agrippa's reign (A.D. 41–44) due to his apparent piety and his care not to offend Jewish sensibilities. However, with the resumption of procurator rule, insurrectist messianic movements began again, with the subsequent Roman persecutions. In this era, Tholomaeus,[95] Theudas,[96] Judas the Galilean and

---

91. Luke 23:19–25. Luke's description of Barnabus' activities (committing murder during an insurrection in the city) reads just like a sentence from Josephus.

92. Wright (in *The New Testament and the People of God*) writes "On Jesus of Nazareth see vol. 2 Josephus' account in *Ant.* 18.63–64 is notoriously controversial (see the discussion in [bibliographic information added by Kennard]: Schürer, *The History of the Jewish*, 1.428–41; Baras, "The *Testimonium*," 338–48), but it seems to me that some parts of it at least are likely to be original. The crucial sentence *ho christos houtos en* does not mean, as is usually supposed, 'this man was the Messiah,' but, because of the position of the article, '"the Messiah" was this man.' The implication is that Josephus expects his readers to have heard of someone who bore, almost as a nickname, the title 'ho christos' (Suetonius, *Claudius* 25, *impulsore Chresto*), and is simply identifying this person with the one he is now describing. On Jesus' followers: it is highly likely that some at least of Jesus disciples believed themselves to be involved in a movement of national liberation. The title of one of them, Simon *ho Kananaios* (Mark 3:18) or Simon 'called *Zelotes*' (Luke 6:12) probably indicates known revolutionary tendencies."

93. Philo, *Leg.* 299–306. Wright suggests probably Josephus passed over many more of these events.

94. Josephus, *Ant.* 18.85–89.

95. Josephus, *Ant.* 20.5.

96. Josephus, *Ant.* 20.97–99; Acts 5:36 identifies this event in the company with movements led by Judas the Galilean and Jesus of Nazareth.

his two sons Jacob and Simon,[97] Eleazar ben Deinaeus and Alexander,[98] and an unnamed "imposter" who had promised his followers "salvation and rest from troubles"[99] were all executed for the separate rebellions that they led. Also, during this time, several other brigand bands fostered rebellion but were crushed. This revolutionary activity came to a fever pitch especially in the main Jewish War itself (A. D. 66–73). Within this Jewish revolt Josephus mentions two messianic movements, those of: Menahem, son of Judas, the Galilean and Simon bar Giora or "the proselyte."[100] Josephus writes during the Jewish Wars which shows that this expectancy of the Davidic King continued and is seen by him as actually being the major reason that the Jews rebelled.

> But what more than all else incited them to the war was an ambiguous oracle, likewise found in their sacred scriptures, to the effect that at the time one from their country would become ruler of the world. This they understood to mean someone of their own race, however, in reality signified the sovereignty of Vespasian, who was proclaimed Emperor on Jewish soil. For all that, it is impossible for men to escape their fate, even though they forsee it. Some of these portent, then, the Jews interpreted to please themselves, others they treated with contempt, until the ruin of their country and their own destruction convicted them of their folly.[101]

Obviously, Josephus identified the Roman emperor Vespasian as this Davidic king and claims that Israel would be released from their exile and would have their kingdom if they only would have submitted to him. N. T. Wright extends Josephus' view in claiming that Vespasion as Messiah is an expression of the second messianic coming of Jesus Christ to judge the Jews since they rebelled against Him, thus fulfilling the Olivet Discourse judgment on Israel.[102] In such a supercessionistic view, the church replaces Israel as the place where Christ's Kingdom resides. However, Josephus' and Wright's views do not reflect the O.T. and Jewish expectations of a Davidic King actually ruling the world by reigning in Israel. This novel perspective and the defeat by Rome did not quash the Jew-

---

97. Josephus, *Ant.* 18.1.1; 20.102.
98. Josephus, *J. W.* 2.253.
99. Josephus, *Ant.* 20.188.
100. Josephus, *J. W.* 2.17.8.
101. Josephus, *J. W.* 6.5.4.
102. Wright, *Jesus and the Victory of God*, 624–625.

ish Davidic expectation. Simon ben Kosiba of the Bar Kokhba rebellion (A. D. 132–135) was hailed by venerable Rabbi Akiba as the "Son of the Star" and the "Son of David," in his additional rebellion crushed by the Romans.[103] So the expectations were high for the Davidic King to arrive and free Israel, when Jesus turns up.

The "Blessing concerning David" in the *Eighteen Benedictions*, shows the Jewish expectation during the first century A.D. as they were regularly prayed by Jews.[104]

Palestinian recension

Be gracious, O Lord, our God, according to thy great mercies
To Israel thy people, and Jerusalem thy city,
And Zion, residence of thy glory;
And to thy Temple and dwelling-place;
And to the kingdom of the house of David, thy righteous Messiah.
Blessed art thou, O Lord, God of David, Builder of Jerusalem.

Babylonian recension

Make the Branch of David soon spring forth,
And let his horn be exalted by thy salvation,
[For we await thy salvation (always).]
Blessed art thou, O Lord, who makest salvation spring forth.

These Jewish prayers reflect the same expectation as the gospels present concerning the Messiah Jesus at His birth.

Gospels

"Jesus will be great and will be called the Son of the Most High; and the Lord God will give Him the throne of His father David." (Luke 1:32).

The titles "Davidic king," "Christ," and "Son of God" are all synonymous. For example, in the ancient near East, kings were called "son of God."[105] Usually this did not mean that people thought that the king was deity,

---

103. Dio Cassius, *Hist.* 59.13.3; *Y. Ta'an.* 68d.
104. Vermes, *Jesus the Jew*, 131–132.
105. Fohrer, "υἱός, υἱοθεσία," *TDNT*, 8:349–53.

but that he had a special relationship with the god so that he could call upon the god's favor to protect and bless the nation. In Jesus' situation the phrase "Son of God" becomes a synonym with "the anointed Davidic king" or "the Christ." In standard Hebrew parallel statement Peter declares, and the high priest asks Jesus if He is the Christ, the Son of the living God (Matt 16:16; 26:63–64; Mark 14:61–62; Luke 22:69–70). Jesus acknowledges that these titles describe Himself. Mark's gospel begins by identifying Jesus in parallel statements as "the Christ, the son of God" (Mark 1:1). Luke's commentary on the demons' declaring Jesus to be the son of God is that they knew Him to be the Christ (Luke 4:41). The term "Christ" or "Messiah" or "Anointed One" is most often identified with kingship, especially in the O.T. Such Davidic Messiah terminology is more focused in the birth narrative, healings, disciples identifying Who Jesus is as a climax of the gospels, and the passion week with triumphal entry unto death.

The angel Gabriel announced to Mary (a descendent of David engaged to Joseph, a descendent of David) that she would give birth to One called "the Son of God" (Matt 1:1, 6, 17, 20; Luke 1:27, 32, 35; 3:31, 38).[106] Though Mary will call Him Jesus, His title is the Son of God, for the Lord God will give Him the throne of His father David and He will reign over Israel forever and His Kingdom will have no end (Luke 1:32–33). With this statement the title elevates Jesus to be the King Who will reign in the everlasting Kingdom. When Mary asks how this can be, Gabriel explains that a deeply personal divine intimacy will impregnate her; the Holy Spirit will come upon her. In Lukan theology "upon" (ἐπισκιάσει) does not mean sexual intercourse but rather an empowerment event such as Pentecost (Luke 11:22; 21:26; Acts 8:24; 13:40; 14:19). The power of God will overshadow her (ἐπελεύσεται), which is imagery for "cloud" or "shadow" (Luke 9:34; Acts 5:15). In the O.T. this imagery was used of God's presence and blessing in the tabernacle and in protecting His people (Exod 40:35; Pss 91:4; 140:7). Here God's intimate presence on Mary creates a son born to the title, Son of God. The title "Son of God" reveals a unique conception and birthing relationship that identifies Jesus' biological father as God (Luke 1:35).

---

106. Hegesippus reports a tradition that Roman authorities interrogated Jesus' brothers' grandsons for Davidic descent (Eusebius, *Hist. eccl.* 3.20). Julius Africanus attests Jesus' relatives claimed Davidic descent (*Letter to Aristides*). No non-Christian Jewish polemicist bothers to refute this Davidic claim (Keener, *Matthew*, 75). Matthew opens and closes the genealogy with the title Jesus Christ.

John the Baptist's father, Zacharias blesses God at the birth of his son, concerning the unfolding events that will birth Jesus as the King of Israel, who he anticipates will conquer the Romans and bring in the Kingdom.

> Blessed be the Lord God of Israel,
> For He has visited us and accomplished redemption for
>   His people,
> And has raised up a horn of salvation for us
> In the house of David His servant-
> As He spoke by the mouth of His holy prophets from of old-
> Salvation from our enemies, and from the hand of all who
>   hate us;
> To show mercy toward our fathers, and to remember His
>   holy covenant,
> The oath which He swore to Abraham our father,
> To grant us that we being delivered from the hand of our
>   enemies (Luke 1:68-74).

Zacharias envisions that the Davidic King will realize the fusion of the Abrahamic, Mosaic and Davidic Covenants in removing Roman enemies and bringing Israel into a glorious reign of peace and covenant blessings.

Mary breaks out in praise with Elizabeth concerning the privilege she anticipates coming to her and other poor people in a personal way when her son Jesus is born to be King and brings eschatological reversal through His reign.

> For the Mighty One has done great things for me;
> And holy is His name.
> And His mercy is upon generation after generation
> Toward those who fear Him.
> He has done mighty deeds with His arm;
> He has scattered the proud in the thoughts of their heart.
> He has brought down rulers from their thrones,
> And has exalted those who were humble.
> He has filled the hungry with good things;
> And sent away the rich empty-handed.
> He has given help to Israel His servant,
> In remembrance of His mercy,
> As He spoke to our fathers,
> To Abraham and his offspring forever (Luke 1:49-55).

Mary anticipates that Jesus will meet real needs. Jesus' ministry meets the needy, the downtrodden, and the poor in the midst of their need and brings down the proud, powerful and rich in their resistance to God.

Matthew's birth narrative identifies Jesus as this King of the Jews, which in the context of his genealogy (with its repetition of David) identifies him as the Davidic King of the Jews (Matt 1:1, 6, 17, 20). The magi from the East identified to Herod that the king of the Jews had been born and that they would go to worship Him (Matt 2:2). Such *worship* (προσκυνῆσαι) is usually focused on deity but could be merely homage to a king. The magi fell down and *did homage* (προσεκύνησαν) before the child with royal gifts appropriate to be received by a superior like a king (Matt 2:11). Jesus is born the King of the Jews. Herod refers to the king of the Jews as the Christ or Messiah or anointed One (Matt 2:4). The magi are warned to return another way and Joseph flees to Egypt to avoid the persecution, and to fulfill the pattern that identifies Jesus Christ as the divine Son (Matt 2:15).

Jesus' baptism is the beginning of His ministry. John the Baptist announces that the Kingdom of God is at hand (Matt 3:2). In this, God declares to Jesus in the hearing of the crowd, "Thou art My beloved Son, in Thee I am well-pleased" (Matt 3:17; Mark 1:11; Luke 3:22). Since God is speaking the Sonship should be seen as Son of God. Thus, Jesus is declared to be the King of Israel in His baptism. In this event, the relationship which God has with His Son is declared to be one of special love and favor. This shows a special purposeful intimacy and unity of purpose which God has with His Son. Later God speaks in similar ways at the transfiguration of Jesus, revealing a glimpse of the Kingdom[107] among the glowing ones.[108] Matthew and Mark record the same phrases as at the baptism identifying Jesus as God's beloved Son with "When He is well pleased" (Matt 17:5; Mark 9:7). Luke adds that Jesus is God's Chosen One (Luke 9:35). All of these statements should be seen within a context that provides a glimpse of Jesus as the King in His Kingdom, which He occupies in co-regency with God where which Jesus is already the King of Israel (Matt 16:28; Mark 9:1; Luke 9:27). So the beloved Son title, which

---

107. Manns makes a compelling case that traditionally from the fourth century the transfiguration was viewed as having occurred on Mount Tabor ("Mount Tabor," 167–77).

108. Moses and Elijah are joined by Jesus as glowing ones in an appearance similar to heavenly beings (Dan 7:9; Matt 28:3; Mark 16:5; Luke 24:4; John 20:12; Acts 1:10; *1 En.* 14.20; *2 En.* 22.8–9; *3 En.* 12.1; *Test. Job.* 46.7–9).

highlights intimacy, also declares Jesus' Kingship. Luke's description of Chosen One should be seen as identifying Jesus' unique Kingship under God as well. Such a presentation from God clearly identifies Jesus as possessing special kingly authority. God's last words call the disciples to "listen to Him," implying obedience.

John's Gospel begins with repeated claims that Jesus is Messiah. For example, Andrew called his brother Peter to come to Jesus, because he claimed Jesus is the Messiah (John 1:41). Likewise, Nathanael identified Jesus as the Son of God, the King of Israel (John 1:49). Furthermore, the woman at the well declared to her village that Jesus is the Messiah, in response to Jesus making that specific claim (John 4:25–26, 29).

Jesus identified that His Kingdom has already begun in certain ways. For example, the disciples identify by their beatitude virtues that they are already in the Kingdom on the basis of the present tenses used in the context of Matthew 5:3, 10 and Luke 6:20.[109] Thus, Jesus' Kingdom is already established as the field of the world (Matt 13:38, 41). It is this Kingdom that is already growing and permeating the world (Matt 13:31–33). Jesus Christ must already be reigning if His Kingdom is present, and will reign even more pervasively after the judgment which will extend Jesus' Kingdom into that of the Kingdom of the Father (Matt 13:43). Furthermore, the blind call out to Jesus as the "son of David, have mercy upon us," and receive healing from Him as they requested (Matt 20:31–34; Mark 10:47–52; Luke 18:38–43). These healings are an expression of Jesus' Kingdom already present. Furthermore, in the first woe Jesus indicates that this Kingdom has begun when He speaks to the religious leaders (Matt 23:13). The use of present verbs "you do not enter" and "you do not permit" is action simultaneous with the speaker's words, so again, Kingdom has indeed begun.

Jesus' transfiguration is a momentary glimpse into Jesus' Kingdom (Matt 16:28—17:9; Mark 9:1–10; Luke 9:27–36; 2 Pet 1:11, 16–19). While Jesus warned the disciples of His and their impending deaths, He identified that some of the disciples would not die until they would see the Son of Man powerfully coming in His Kingdom. A week[110] later, Jesus

---

109. This is not an appeal to tense as absolute time but an appeal to this tense in the context, which applies the sermon in their present as applicable to them then.

110. Matt 17:1 identifies the transfiguration as occurring 6 days after Peter pronounced Jesus was the Christ (Matt 16:16), whereas, Luke records this span of time to be about 8 days (Luke 9:20, 28). This can be harmonized because Matthew uses Hebrew time and Peter could confess Jesus is the Christ in the beginning of the Hebrew

took Peter, James and John and led them to a high mountain where He was transfigured before them. Jesus' face and clothes shone as the sun, enabling these disciples to be eyewitnesses of His majesty. Moses and Elijah appeared talking with Jesus. Luke identified that the topic of their conversation is Jesus' exodus (Luke 9:31 ἔξοδον).[111] Such an exodus reference is quite appropriate to prefigure Kingdom (Isa 40:3-5). Out of fear, Peter blurted out that it was good for them to be there and that if Jesus wished, they could make three tabernacles, one each for Jesus, Moses and Elijah. Perhaps Peter was thinking that the Feast of Tabernacles which commemorates the exodus and might be appropriate as Kingdom is initiated, since as a festival, it will be celebrated in Kingdom (Zech 14:16), and perhaps it was that time of year. Instead, a bright cloud overshadowed them and the *bath qol*,[112] the voice of God (the Excellent Glory) spoke from the cloud, saying, "This is My beloved Son, in whom I am well pleased. Hear Him!" In giving a preview of the Kingdom, this voice reassured the disciples that the prophecies of Christ's Kingdom will be confirmed further in Christ's grander eschatological reign with our salvation (2 Pet 1:11, 16-19). Then, Jesus came alone and touched the disciples, asking them to rise and not be afraid but "Tell the vision to no one until the Son of Man is risen from the dead." The disciples kept quiet about what they had seen until later, but they questioned Jesus about what "rising from the dead" meant.

The synoptics record a number of understandings and responses to the title "Son of God" when they apply to Jesus, but the divine assessment is the standard by which all others are to be measured. It is interesting to explore the various individual expressions. It is never recorded that Jesus

---

day after sunset, while Luke uses Roman time (Acts 2:15), which would mean that Peter's statement would occur toward the end of the first day. With the days breaking at different points, the transfiguration could be six days later according to Matt (on the seventh day), which would be Luke's eighth day.

111. Philo and Josephus often take ἔξοδον as the exodus rather than merely a departure.

112. On the concept and instance of *bath qol*: Dan 4:31; Jos. *Ant.* 13.282-83; *Song Rab.* 8.9.3; b. *'Abot* 6.2; B. *Bat.* 73b; 85b; *Mak.* 23b; *'Erub.* 54b; *Shab.* 33b; 88a; *Soṭa* 33a; p. *Soṭa* 7.5.5; *Pesiq. Rab. Kah.* 11.16; 15.5; *Lev. Rab.* 19.5-6; *Deut. Rab.* 11.10; *Lam. Rab. Proem* 2, 23; *Lam. Rab.* 1.16.50; *Ruth Rab.* 6.4; *Qoh. Rab.* 7.12.1; *Sib. Or.* 1.127, 267, 275; Artapanus in Eusebius, *Praep. ev.* 9.27.36; Dion. Hal. 1.56.3; 5.16.2-3; 8.56.2-3; Arrian, *Alex.* 3.3.5; Lucian, *C.W.* 1.569-70; Plutarch, *Is. Os.* 12; *Mor.* 355E; *Mart. Pol.* 9. The *bath qol* was present in Israel before the spirit of prophecy departed (b. *Pesaḥ.* 94a; *Ḥag.* 13a; *Sanh.* 39b) and a few sources give it future ramifications as well (*Lev. Rab.* 27.2; *Pesiq. Rab. Kah.* 17.5).

described Himself as "Son of God" but there are a number of places where He refers to Himself ambiguously as "Son" in the context of referring to God as Father. In the context in which Jesus pronounces judgment upon unbelieving Galilean cities, Jesus also breaks into praise for God as Father. Jesus highlights that as Son, He has an intimate relationship with the Father and that the Father has granted Him all things (Matt 11:27; Luke 10:22). Perhaps this hints at Jesus' Kingship but it certainly acknowledged that Jesus as Son has an unusual intimate relationship with God in order to have knowledge of God and God's purposes. None know these things except those to whom the Son reveals them. The Son compassionately calls many to this freeing knowledge. Some things, such as when the Son would return, are known only by the Father for He has not even revealed them to His Son (Mark 13:32). Jesus declares that He has all authority on heaven and on earth in a context in which He identifies Himself as Son of the Father (Matt 28:18–19). Jesus understands and declares the divine assessment of Him as the Son of God from early in His ministry to His ascension.

The demonic opposition recognizes Jesus as the Son of God with authority, against whom demons rebel. The devil tries to tempt Jesus with the prefaced claim, "If You are the Son of God" (Matt 4:3, 6; Luke 4:3, 9). The kind of conditional used by the devil expects an affirmation that Jesus is the Son of God in order for Jesus to demonstrate it upon demand, thus submitting to the devil's authority. Demons recognize Jesus as the Son of God Who has the authority to judge and punish them under the eschatological judgment (Matt 8:29; Mark 5:7; Luke 8:28). These same demons recognize that as Son of God, Jesus has authority to limit where they can go. They rebel and try to thwart Him by going into swine to make Jesus repulsive to those who live there. The other tactic demons take in rebellion is to declare Jesus openly as the anointed king, Son of God, when they are cast out, perhaps to make Jesus' crowd unwieldy with messianic expectations and focused on miracles (Mark 3:11; Luke 4:41). Jesus responds by silencing the demons under His authority, keeping His ministry focused on Kingdom proclamation and calling a select band of disciples to accentuate understanding and accountability in His ministry.

The disciples acknowledge Jesus as the Son of God with divine authority and worship Him. Jesus walked on water of the stormy Sea of Galilee, which frightened the disciples (Matt 14:22–33). Peter was also enabled to walk on water as an attempt to alleviate their fear. When Jesus rescued Peter and they got into the boat the storm subsided. The amazed disciples worshipped Jesus as God's Son (Matt 14:33). To them the Son of God entailed deity in order for them to worship Him. Later, Peter declared his assessment that Jesus is the Christ, the Son of the living God (Matt 16:16). Jesus agreed with Peter's assessment that He is King with a Kingdom and blessed Peter for his pronouncement. This blessing included Peter as son of Jonah,[113] perhaps in identifying with the resurrection sign (Matt 16:4, 17) and maybe hinting that he will go to Gentiles like Jonah did.

The multitude see Jesus fulfill what they take to be a Messianic prophecy,[114] Zech 9:9, "Your King is coming to you, gentle, and mounted on a donkey" (Matt 21:5; John 12:15). This riding of a donkey identifies with a royal means of transport (Judg 5:10; 10:4; 12:13–14; 2 Sam 13:29; 18:9; 19:26)[115] but indicates that Jesus dismisses military aspirations because He was not on a war horse. The people praise Christ on His entry into Jerusalem as the King, the Son of David (Matt 21:15; Mark 11:10 'father' for king; Luke 19:38). Their use of palm branches alludes to the Maccabean triumphs, implying the crowd still saw Him in revolutionary Messianic terms.[116]

The religious leaders tested Jesus and He demonstrated superior scribal ability. Jesus turned the tables on the Pharisees gathered there and asked a *haggadic*[117] or contrary question (Matt 22:41–46; Mark 12:35–37; Luke 20:41–44). His question raised the real issue, the authority of the Messiah. "Whose son is the Christ?" The religious leaders answered, "The son of David."[118] While not denying their answer, Jesus then asked the contrary question, "Then how does David in the Spirit call him 'Lord,' saying, 'The Lord said to my Lord, Sit at My right hand, until I put Your enemies beneath Your feet?' If David calls Him 'Lord,' how is He his son?" This contrary question pressed the authority of Christ consistent with rabbinical reasoning[119] beyond the Davidic king idea to a One Who was more, perhaps to that of Daniel's Son of Man. No one was able to answer Him.

---

113. In contrast to Peter elsewhere being called son of John (John 1:42; 21:15–17; *Gos. Heb.* frag. 9).

114. *b. Sanh.* 98a; 99a; *Gen. Rab.* 75ab; Edgar, "The New Testament and Rabbinic," 48–49.

115. *ARM.* 6.76; *ANET* 1.44–47.

116. 1 Macc 13.51; 2 Macc 10.7; Rev 7:9; *Pesiq. R.* 51.8.

117. Owen-Ball, "Rabbinic Rhetoric," 4; Keener, *Matthew*, 532.

118. *Pss. Sol.* 17.21–25; 4QFlor. 1.11–13; Justin Martyr, *First Apology* 45.

119. None of the following sources is pre-Christian but they show Jesus to probably be unoriginal about the application of Psalm 110 to Messiah (Akiva, *b. Sanh.* 38b;

When the high priest put Jesus under oath to respond as to whether He is indeed the Christ, the Son of God, the Davidic King, Jesus says "Yes" and further identifies Himself as Daniel's Son of Man Who will come and judge the religious leaders for their rejection of Him. In response, the high priest has Him crucified for blasphemy (Matt 26:63–64; Mark 14:61–62; Luke 22:69–70). Whether the high priest thought Son of God referred to a divine One is not clear but the affirmation certainly includes a claim for kingship of Israel (Matt 27:11, 29, 37; Mark 15:2, 12, 18, 26; Luke 23:2–3, 38). Additionally, the title of Daniel's Son of Man as applied to Christ was taken by the high priest as an offense against God. The high priest rebelled by killing Jesus when Jesus identified Who He is. In response, Jesus identifies Himself as Daniel's Son of Man Who will come and judge the religious leaders for their rejection of Him.

Pilate questions Jesus as to whether He is the king of the Jews (Matt 15:2; Luke 23:2–3). Jesus responds that it is as Pilate says, which is a "Yes" reply (after the pattern of Matt 26:25 and 64). Jesus clarifies that His Kingdom is not of the pattern of the world, or His followers would take up weapons to fight. Herod rightly gets the point that Jesus is a King (John 18:33–37). The charge on the cross in the crucifixion clarified the issue, "This is Jesus the King of the Jews" (Matt 27:37; Mark 15:26; Luke 23:38). In response to this charge, part of the mob scoffed at him, "If you are the Son of God, the King of Israel, come down from the cross" (Matt 27:40, 43). This mob recognized that the title Son of God meant King of the Jews. However, they rebelled against Jesus, not wishing him to reign over them and actually expecting this crucifixion to be His demise.

With the drama of darkness in Jesus' death followed by miraculous opening of tombs and resurrection and tearing of the temple veil, the centurion guarding Jesus declared that Jesus was truly a Son of God (Matt 27:54; Mark 15:39). The centurion does not use an article so the meaning of Son of God in his declaration probably holds only the meaning in the context, that of being a king of the Jews.

The title, "Son of God" identifies Jesus as already the Davidic king over Israel and everyone forever. It also highlights an intimate biological and favored relationship which Jesus has with God. Some take it to mean that Jesus is God, though neither God nor Jesus identify that as its meaning.

Gen. Rab. 85.9; Num. Rab. 18.23; Tg. on Ps 110; echoed in Ep. Barn. 12.10–11; Davies and Allison, Matthew, 3:253–54).

The Son of Man in the Synoptics[120]

In the synoptics Jesus' favorite way of referring to Himself is as Son of Man. There is inherent ambiguity present in this name with the possibility of it being taken as "human" (Ps 8:4), or as a prophet (Ezek 2:1), or as authority (Matt 12:8; Mark 2:28; Luke 6:5), but at the apex of Jesus' ministry He clarifies to His disciples that He refers to Himself with the meaning of Daniel's quasi-divine Son of Man to come to the earth as Judge and reign as Davidic King (Dan 7:13–14; Matt 24:27, 30; Mark 13:26; Luke 17:24, 36; 21:27; Acts 7:56). Likewise, at the climax of Jesus' trial, Jesus identified to the religious leaders that the kind of Davidic king He meant by this self-attribution was that of Daniel's Son of Man (Matt 26:64; Mark 14:62; Luke 22:69). Jesus then coupled the Son of Man role with Ps 110's presentation of the Davidic King seated at the right hand of God to reign, and promised that these religious leaders will see Him operate in this role, judging all opposition, including them. This further underscores that Jesus is the Davidic King already in the judgment, and that He has already begun to mete out judgment in destroying Jerusalem and temple in A.D. 70 and 135, thereby judging the religious leaders who sentenced Him to death.[121] Jesus' Davidic Messiahship is implemented in judgment upon Israel as Daniel's Son of Man. Jesus will continue to show His Davidic Kingship when He returns to judge all rebellious nations and establish His Kingdom (Matt 24:30–31; Mark 13:26–27; Luke 21:27–28). For the disciples, who hear His Olivet message, such a second coming of Daniel's Son of Man is a comfort, "for your redemption is drawing near." This redemptive hope to enter into the Kingdom and be vindicated while Jesus' and the disciples' opponents are judged indicates the Kingdom will begin in its grand eschatological manner.

The Son of Man in the Gospel of John

In contrast to the synoptics where the Son of Man will in the future descend, in the Gospel of John Jesus identified Himself to Nicodemus as the Son of Man already descended from heaven to become the object of faith (John 3:13–18). Those who believe in Him in this glorified descended Son of Man role already have everlasting life. Likewise those who do not

---

120. Kennard, *Messiah Jesus*, 471–524.
121. Wright, *Jesus and the Victory of God*, 624–625.

believe that He is the glorified Son of Man are judged already. The Father has already given the Son authority to execute judgment, because He is the Son of Man (John 5:27).[122]

The multitude wants Jesus to be the Messiah for their benefit rather than the Son of Man come to challenge and judge them. The multitude sailed across the Sea of Galilee to Capernaum to seek Jesus as their Messiah. In response, Jesus presented them with difficult sayings in the synagogue, that forced them to weigh their commitment (John 6:22–71). People wanted to know when Jesus had arrived, since He had come across by walking on the water, whereas the disciples strained on the oars. He told the crowd that they were seeking signs like miraculously being fed in the wilderness, as Moses had done for Israel. The implication here is that they are seeking to make Him King to bring themselves into Kingdom by supernaturally exterminating the occupiers of the Land (the Rom; John 6:15). Part of the people's motivation is that some Jewish traditions emphasized that the final redeemer would in fact bring down manna as Moses had done.[123] Jesus tried to prompt the multitude to get beyond focusing on perishable food, earned by work,[124] but rather to seek everlasting life given by the Son of Man and the Father. In this sense of seeking nourishment, that is not everlasting, this multitude parallels the confusion of the Samaritan woman at the well (John 4:15; 6:34). The multitude responded Jewishly,[125] "What shall we do to work the works of God?" Jesus responded, "This is the work of God, that you believe in Him

---

122. This statement echoes with the sense of Dan 7:13–14 and *1 En.* 69.27.

123. Early Aramaic tradition in *Pesiq. Rab. Kah.* 5.8; *Num. Rab.* 11.2; *Ruth Rab.* 5.6; *Eccl. Rab.* 1.9; and a revivified Moses as eschatological leader of Israel (*Ex. Rab.* 2.6; *Deut. Rab.* 9.9).

124. Perhaps the phrase "earned by work" is nudging the multitude beyond the desire for the dole. Rome had a dole system against which the people rioted when the supply ran low (Dionysius of Halicarnassus, *R. A.* 9.25.2; Tacitus, *Ann.* 6.13; 12.43; Dio Cassius, *Hist.* 56.47.2; 62.18.5; Aristotle *Pol.* 5.1.6, 1301b).

125. Jews were concerned with Covenantal obedience and the ethical works of God's statutes and laws (Exod 18:20, the people's work [הַמַּעֲשֶׂה] has the plural LXX works [ἔργα] for statutes and laws; Wis 9.12; *Bar.* 2.9–10; CD 2.14–15; Jesus summons His disciples to His works in Rev 2:26; cf., John 14:12). However, such Covenantal faithfulness would have ramifications for divinely accomplished (plural) mighty deeds of deliverance from oppressors to bring in Mosaic Covenant blessing (Deut 32:4 [LXX: ἔργα]; Pss 92:5 [בְּמַעֲשֵׂי; LXX: 91:5, ἔργα]; 104:31 [בְּמַעֲשָׂיו; LXX: Ps 103:24, ἔργα, 31, ἔργοις]; 107:24 [מַעֲשֵׂי; LXX: 106:24, ἔργα]; and similar expressions in Pss 111 [LXX:110]:2, 6–7; 118 [LXX:117]:17; 139 [LXX:138]:14; 145 [LXX:144]:4, 9, 10, 17; Tob 12.6; 1QS 4.4; 1QM 13.9; CD 13.7–8; John 9:3; Rev 15:3).

whom He has sent." Jesus shifted the focus from Mosaic Covenant faithfulness and blessing to New Covenant internalization of faith continuing within this worldview, in order to believe that the divine origination of Jesus identifies Him as the Son of Man come from God already to provide them with everlasting life. In contrast to the manna that their fathers received and died, which this multitude seeks, *Jesus is the bread of life, come from heaven* so that those who internalize Him will not die but have everlasting life already. At this point the multitude grumbled even more about the cannibalistic metaphor of eating Jesus' flesh.[126] Jesus made the difficult statement acute.

> Listen up, this is important, unless you munch on the flesh of the Son of Man and drink His blood, you have no life in yourselves. He who munches My flesh and drinks My blood has everlasting life; and I will raise him up on the last day. For My flesh is true food, and My blood is true drink. He who eats My flesh and drinks My blood abides in Me, and I in him (John 6:53-56).

That is, to internalize Jesus as the mystical sustenance from God, transforms the person into a mystically interpenetrated covenantal relationship with the Son. "As the living Father sent Me, and I live because of the Father; so he who eats Me, he also shall live because of Me. This is the bread which came down out of heaven; not as the manna the fathers ate, and died; he who eats this bread shall live forever" (John 6:57-58). Many of the disciples who heard this cannibalistic statement grumbled at the revolting description. Conscious of the disciples grumbling, Jesus asked them, "Does this cause you to stumble into damnation?" Pressing the origination issue acutely, Jesus said, "What if you should see the Son of Man ascending to heaven where He was before?" This raises the Dan 7:13 vision and identifies that Jesus is this divine Son of Man come to judge the wicked and establish His Kingdom. Life is sourced in the Spirit and Jesus' words, when believed include His New Covenant people in the Spirit and everlasting life. Jesus said these difficult words because He knew some of the people there did not believe, including the one who would betray Him. So He said, "No one can come to Me, unless the Father chooses him" (John 6:44, 65). These issues (of: divine origination

---

126. This metaphor should not be taken as encouraging the Jews to bring Jesus to His death on the basis of parallels with *1 En.* 90.2-4, the nations as wild animals devouring sheep, since those involved in Jesus' metaphoric cannibalism are gaining everlasting life in contrast to those involved in the killing of Christ who instead are judged (Kennard, *Messiah Jesus*, 415-438).

of Jesus, the cannibalistic internalistic metaphors and strong sovereign election) caused many who were Jesus disciples to withdraw from Him and to not continue to walk with Him (John 6:66).

Turning to the twelve, Jesus asked, "You do not want to go away also, do you?" Peter answered Him, "Lord, to whom shall we go? You have words of everlasting life. And we have believed and have come to know that You are the Holy One of God" (John 6:67–68). Jesus responds even to the twelve with a difficult saying to make them weigh their commitment, "Did I Myself not choose you, the twelve, and one of you is a devil?" (John 6:70). He meant Judas who was to betray Him. However the statement, unexplained stops each of the twelve to ask himself, am I the opponent of Christ?

Jesus repeatedly tried to move believers into a deeper level of personal engagement. In the previous passage the issue for the twelve is whether or not they identify with Jesus as Messiah, the Son of Man come from God (John 6:67–71).

Acts

After Christ's resurrection He continued teaching about the Kingdom so that His disciples asked, "Is this the time when You are restoring the Kingdom to Israel?" (Acts 1:3, 6). Christ merely corrected them about the time and not about the fact of His reign and restoration of Kingdom for Israel. Then, leaving them with the task of being witnesses, He ascended into heaven.

Peter proclaims the gospel that Jesus is the Christ and thus must have been raised because of God's empowerment and the ultimate realization of Psalm 16, which entombed David had not received (Acts 2:24–29). The Davidic Covenant promised to seat (καθίσαι) one of David's descendants upon David's throne (τὸν θρόνον αὐτοῦ; 2 Sam 7:12–14; Acts 2:30). Jesus' resurrection identifies that He is the one Davidic King to be seated on David's throne (Acts 2:30–32). This resurrection ushers in Christ's exaltation to the right hand of God which is identified with royal Ps 110:1, "The Lord said to my Lord sit at My right hand until I make thine enemies a footstool for thy feet" (Acts 2:33–35). The right hand is the place of honor or equality. To sit (Κάθου) at God's right hand as said by God is to be identified as accomplished in the exaltation to be at God's right hand. So Christ is already seated (Κάθου) at God's right hand which is reminiscent of the promise to seat (καθίσαι)[127] Christ on the Davidic throne (Acts 2:30, 33–34). It is on these bases that Peter declares that the house of Israel should know for certain that God has already made (γινωσκέτω) Jesus both Lord and Christ. The declaration that He is already Lord (κύριον) identifies Him as the Lord (κυρίῳ) to whom the Lord (κύριος) God addresses to sit Christ at God's right hand. This use of the same root for Lord does two things: 1) it shows that Christ is God, since the psalmist's distinctions of Yahweh and Adonai are combined in the same "lord" term (κύριος) and 2) in the ascended recognition that Christ is God there is a parallel recognition that Jesus is already the anointed Davidic King over Israel (Acts 2:30, 34, 36).[128] While in this context "Lord" (κύριος) stands for Davidic king and deity. As a term it was also appropriated by the Caesars (Augustus, Tiberius, Caligua, Nero and Domitian) and the Jewish rulers (Herod the Great, Agrippa I and Agrippa II).[129] So, as a title, more than position is at stake since "Jesus as Lord" includes allegiance and loyalty. The Davidic kingship of Christ is further developed by the parallel confidence that Jesus is made Lord and Christ. Such a declaration of being made Christ (Χριστὸν) reminds one of the basic meaning of Christ as "anointed one," usually meaning "King." This means that Jesus should be honored as Israel's king in this near context which contains a Davidic covenant declaration. Since Jesus is already the Davidic king seated at God's right hand, Christ is already effectively operating from His kingship role. For example, as ascended King, Christ receives the promise of the Holy Spirit from the Father and has poured forth the associated phenomena of wind sound, fire above heads, tongues, prophecy and gospel proclamation all of which Peter's audience both sees and hears (Acts 2:33). This means that the bestowal of the Spirit identifies Christ as *already functioning* as Davidic King. Obviously, Christ also

---

127. The verbs for seating from N.T. citing LXX (καθίσαι, aorist infinitive indicating Davidic covenant of future [2 Sam 7:12]) and Davidic king (Κάθου, present imperative from Ps 110:1 indicating from this royal psalm that a Davidic king should sit at God's right hand). The first is a future occurrence in covenant prediction and the second is a past accomplishment in Christ's ascension.

128. This author recognizes that κύριον can mean sir (Matt 27:63), teacher (Matt 8:25), master or owner (Luke 10:42; 19:33), husband (1 Pet 3:6), King (Acts 25:26) and god (1 Cor 8:5), but in the context of Acts 2:30–36 divine and Davidic covenant king are the contextual emphases (Acts 2:30, 34, 36); O'Toole, "Acts 2:30," 245–58.

129. Bietenhard, "Lord, Master" in *DNTT*, 2:511; Cullmann, *The Christology*, 197–99; Suetonius, *De Vita Caesarum* 13.2; the title was also used to describe gods (1 Cor 8:5); Deismann, *Light from the Ancient East*, 352–53.

waits God's reducing of his enemies to be utterly defeated under His feet, showing that there is a greater expression of Christ's reign to come when God metes out eschatological judgment.

Luke records two instances where Paul refers to Jesus as the Son of God which, as developed means "king." Paul's gospel message is summed up as declaring Jesus to be the Son of God (Acts 9:20). This concept of Son of God is built from O.T. references such as Paul's citation of Ps 2:7 (Acts 13:33) which acknowledges Jesus to be the Davidic king who will reign forever.

Paul

Paul alludes to the same Ps 110:1 text in identifying how Christ must reign until God renders all His enemies a footstool for Christ's feet (1 Cor 15:25). In this N.T. allusion, Paul utilizes the present infinitive (βασιλεύειν) to likely describe the present continuous action of Jesus *reigning* as the Davidic King *already* so that when God subjects the whole of creation to the final stage of Christ's rule, this subjection of the enemy to death will be accomplished in the midst of the continuing reign of Christ from now until then.[130] As such, Christ begins to reign as the Davidic King before the resurrection of the elect and final stages of His Kingdom begin, such as death being abolished. So, Christ reigns even now, before our resurrection.

The center of Paul's gospel statement is to identify Jesus as Lord (Rom 10:9). To facilitate this, Paul regularly identifies Jesus as our Lord and Christ (Rom 1:4 Ἰησοῦ Χριστοῦ τοῦ κυρίου ἡμῶν). In a few of these instances, Paul affirms Jesus is Davidic and Lord in close proximity (Rom 1:3; 2 Tim 2:8), which affirms the present realization of the Davidic Covenant. However, usually Paul's affirmation that Jesus is Lord is more of a divine affirmation for Jesus' divinity and our submission to Him, especially in instances of letter form short blessings where one expect prayers to be made to a divine One called God (θεοῦ) or Lord (κυρίου)[131] (Rom 1:7; 1 Cor 1:3; 2 Cor 1:2; Gal 1:3; Eph 1:2; Phil 1:2; 1 Thess 1:1; 2 Thess 1:2; 1 Tim 1:2; 2 Tim 1:2) or when Paul reworks the Jewish *shema* (from Deut 6:4) in 1 Cor 8:4–6 to affirm the divinity of the Son with the Father.[132]

---

130. Bock, "Exegetical Insight," 298.

131. O'Brien, "Letters, Letter Forms," 551; Deismann, *Light from the Ancient East*, 214; Francis, "The Form," 117.

132. Kennard, *Messiah Jesus*, 491–92; Wright, *What Saint Paul Really Said*, 66–67.

Hebrews

The author of Heb declares the Son as the divine Davidic King. With the recipients being tempted to leave off following Christ and to return to Judaism and the following of the Mosaic Law, the Son is shown to be superior over all those associated with the Mosaic Covenant. For example, Christ is the superior revelation to that of fathers and prophets since He is the exact representation of God (Heb 1:1–4). Christ is also superior to Moses in that Moses is a faithful servant in the house but Christ is faithful as Son over the house of God (Heb 3:1–6). In this context this Sonship over the house is the divine Davidic kingship that shows Christ as superior to angels (the avenue through whom the Law was given, Heb. 2:2). No angel has ever had the divine declarations which Jesus Christ has *already had declared of Him*. That is, the royal Ps 2:7 identifies that "Thou art My Son, today I have begotten Thee" (Heb 1:5). This "today" of announcing this Davidic Covenantal authority has already been realized for Jesus Christ. This identifies Jesus as the divinely authorized Davidic King or Son. This begetting includes the adoption right and possibly an incarnation right by which He reigns already. This Sonship is informed by quoting 2 Sam 7:14 which identifies Jesus as already the Davidic covenant King-Son of God. As metaphorically first born, (meaning: supreme King)[133] He has the right to reign and He reigns as God to be worshipped (Heb 1:6, 8). In a contrast of things already declared, Psalm 45:6–7 leaves the marriage feast context to declare some of the extent to which Christ reigns already as Davidic King. He has the throne, which should be seen as the Davidic throne following this Davidic covenant statement by a mere three verses (Heb 1:5, 8). Jesus is addressed as God on that Davidic throne. His throne will last forever so the everlasting continuance of His reign has already begun. He has the Davidic covenant kingship motifs which began at His coronation (Heb 1:8–9). He is anointed (Christed or ἔχρισέν) by God to be King. The anointing includes the oil of gladness identifying Him as above His co-sharers. Along with having the Davidic throne already, He has the Davidic scepter of His own righteous kingdom. This imagery of the scepter is even a Messianic title in Qumran.[134] These motifs, which

---

133. In Ps 89:27 "firstborn" is defined as highest king consistent with the ancient near East pattern. For example, Marduk is called firstborn of gods to identify his supreme kingship (*ANET, Babylonian Creation Epic* 4:20). In the same manner, 4Q458 frag. 15 refers to the messianic Davidic king as apocalyptically, God's "first born."

134. CD 7.19–20=4Q266 frag. 3.iv.9; 1QSb 5.27–28; 4Q161 frags. 2–6.ii.17.

are already possessed, identify that He has already begun to reign, and of course Christ has perfect right to reign since He created everything (Heb 1:10–12). Psalm 110:1 already declares from God that Christ is to "sit at My right hand until I make Thine enemies a footstool for thy feet" (Heb 1:13). The footstool metaphor is the ancient near East way of indicating that though Jesus is already the Davidic King there will be a time in the future when He will put His foot on their necks as evidence of their utter defeat. So the Kingdom has begun already, but there will be a greater era of eschatological Kingdom. The place of seating in this context is the Davidic throne which Christ already has (Heb 1:5, 8). Christ is already sitting on this throne at the right hand of God (Heb 1:3), showing He has already begun to reign. The fact that Christ awaits God's climactic judgment to subdue His enemies shows that there is a grander phase of Christ's kingdom yet to occur when no opponent will try to thwart His reign. This Davidic kingly reign realizes the aspirations of God for all mankind ruling over the creation, for Christ as King (appointed by God) rules over all the creation already (Ps 8:4–6; Heb 2:6–8). God has already subjected everything to Christ in His reign. Christ's reign makes Him the Prince and author of life (ἀρχηγὸν; Heb 2:10; 12:2).[135] Another part of the effectiveness in His kingly reign identifies Him in the fused King-Priest role (Pss 2:7; 110:1–4; Heb 1:5, 13; 5:5–6; 7:17, 21). That is, in the begetting of Christ as King, He is simultaneously begotten as Priest. The extensive priestly ministry developed in Hebrews as before, during and after His death shows Him to be King as well. And since the kingly and priestly ministries are fused in One begetting and role, He has effectively functioned as King-Priest in an extended Davidic covenant way to provide atonement for His brethren.

Revelation

John included Jesus the Sovereign King among his co-authors:

> Jesus Christ the faithful witness, the firstborn of the dead, and the ruler of the Kings of the earth. To Him who loves us and releases us from our sins by His blood, and He has made us to be

---

135. The same word ἀρχηγὸν in Acts 3:15 and 5:31 stands for the ascended glorified role of royalty that Jesus is as He grants Israel repentance and forgiveness, and comes to establish the Kingdom period of restoration. This idea in Lukan thought forms would identify Him with the Davidic King (Acts 2:30, 33; 3:20–21).

a kingdom, priests to His God and Father; to Him be the glory and the dominion forever and ever. Amen (Rev 1:5-6).

Jesus Christ (the Anointed One) is seen by John as already the faithful witness and continuing to be such through His visions recorded in the book. Jesus Christ is already resurrected and guarantees our resurrection with new life in His blood. Jesus Christ is already the Ruler (ὁ ἄρχων) of the kings of the earth having already made believers into a Kingdom that includes His glory and dominion forever. Jesus Christ is then functioning as the reigning King in His Kingdom already and forever. Jesus Christ presents Himself glorified in a vision in the midst of the churches and with the power over the destinies of the churches (Rev 1:12-20).

One aspect of Jesus' reign will be a millennial Kingdom. The only biblical description of this is in Rev 20:2-7 when Satan is bound and the Kingdom can develop. This limited temporal Kingdom has some prior Jewish development in 2 *En.* 32:1-33:2 text J which describes the climax to a 6000 year earth to be a 1000 year Kingdom followed by an everlasting Kingdom.[136] This chiliasm is also evident in two Arabic manuscripts of the 2 *Bar* 27:1-15. After these expressions of time limited Kingdom, the Kingdom ushers into an everlasting grand phase, as the prophets and gospels portrayed.

When the earthly forces of the beast and "Babylon the great" rebel, then Jesus Christ will lead an army of called, chosen and faithful with throne names written on His robe and thigh: "King of kings" and "Lord of lords" (Rev 17:14; 19:16). These phrases are a Hebraism for the supreme King. In the midst of these descriptions, God Almighty is reigning as well, probably in a co-regency (Rev 19:6). Then, in the removing of Satan, Christ and His faithful will reign for a thousand years (Rev 20:4).

Christ's Kingdom continues and includes Christ reigning forever. When the new heavens and earth are made, God Almighty and the Lamb

---

136. 2 *En.* 32:1-33:2, text J includes this, while text A does not. 4 *Ezra* or 2 *Esdras* 7:26-44 describe a temporary Messiah Kingdom of 400 years, where most Arabic and Syrian manuscripts of this describe a Kingdom of 30 years, and two Arabic manuscripts describe this Kingdom as 1000 years. Perhaps after the book of Revelation, the 2 *Bar.* 27:1-15 describes alternating dark and light weeks with a tribulation preceding the Kingdom. The second century Christian *Ep. Barn.* 15:4-9 also includes a 1000 year Kingdom. Post N.T. Jewish tradition is not uniform with Messianic Kingdom of all the following: 40, 70, 365, 400, 1000, 2000, 7000 years (Eleazar ben Hyrcanus, Joshua, Eleazar ben Azariah, Jose ben Galilee, Akiva, *Pes.* 68a, *Ber.* 34b, *Sanh.* 91b, 97a-b; 99a, *Shab.* 63a, 113b, *Abod. Zar.* 9a, *Sifre* [Deut 310], *Tanch.* 'Ekeb 7, *Pesiq. Rab.* 1.7.1-3). Strack and Billerbeck, 3:826; Helyer, "The Necessity," 606-9.

(Jesus Christ having been sacrificed) shall be the Temple within which we the priests will function (Rev 21:22). New Jerusalem will be the capital and center of this reign of God and Christ (Rev 21:2–22:5).[137] Their co-regency is conveyed by the single throne that God and the Lamb share (Rev 22:1, 3).[138] Jesus Christ's bond-servants share this co-regency with Him to reign forever and ever (Rev 22:5).

Lest the reader miss it, Jesus Himself declares that presently and in the context of His everlasting reign, He is "the root and the offspring of David" (Rev 22:16). The character of Jesus Christ's reign today, in millennium and forever should be seen as fulfilling aspects of the Davidic Covenant.

---

137. *4 Ez.* 7.26–27; *B. Bab. Bath.* 75a-b; *Pesiqta. diR. Kahana* ed. Mandelbaum, 299, 466; *Sefer Eliahu, BhM* 3.67–68; *Pirqe Mashiah, BhM* 3.69, 74–75; *Milhamot Melekh haMashiah, BhM* 6.118.

138. The parallel construction in the genitive of throne of God and of Lamb draws the throne into being described as both God's and the Lamb's.

4

Jeremiah's Covenant Nomism and New Covenant

JEREMIAH REPEATEDLY UTILIZED COVENANT formula reminiscent of Exod 19, "I will be your God and you will be my people" and then Yahweh called Israel to be faithful in obedience (Jer 7:23; 11:4).[1] Yahweh called Jeremiah to proclaim the words of the "covenant" (*berit*/בְּרִית, διαθήκην), offering Israel blessings reminiscent of Deuteronomic blessings if they would obey the Mosaic Covenant and warning them of Deuteronomic curses if Israel was unfaithful (Jer 11:2 in context). Such Deuteronomism places Jeremiah within the preceding covenant nomism.[2] As repeated disobedience of Israel is discussed by the prophet, the covenant formula phrase was reduced to a covenant warning, "cling to Me that you might remain My people," followed by the regret that Israel did not listen (Jer 13:11).

Covenant Lawsuit

With further rebellion, Jeremiah reflects a covenant lawsuit Yahweh enacts against Judah and Israel on the basis of the Mosaic Covenant. The Mosaic covenant is a suzerainty treaty which Yahweh bound upon Jewish forefathers elected by God when He brought them out of Egypt (Jer 11:2–4). Under this arrangement the Jews are already in Mosaic Covenant which means that they need to obey in order to be blessed, for if they disobey they will be cursed (Jer 11:3; 18:6–10). This Mosaic Covenant served as a covenant nomist arrangement within which Yahweh graciously folded Israel into His plans. The Mosaic covenant continued to bind the generation of Jews in Jeremiah's day under this same Mosaic covenant curse

---

1. Rendtorff, *The Covenant Formula*, 31–32.
2. Carroll, *From Chaos*, 13–15; Kennard, *Biblical Covenantalism in Torah*.

(Jer 11:6). Unfortunately, Judah and Israel stubbornly did evil in breaking God's covenant commands; Yahweh then brought disaster upon them with no preventative option (Jer 11:8–11). They were swept away into captivity and death for their violation of the Mosaic Covenant.

Such a prophetic exhortation responds to the suzerainty treaty stipulations as did the diplomatic correspondence which follows a disobedience to the treaty stipulations, threatening devastation for the vassal from the Great King if the vassal does not quickly comply with what the suzerainty treaty demanded in the stipulations section. For example, the "Letter from Hattusili 3 of Hatti to Kadashman-Enlil 2 of Babylon" threatens Babylon with a severe military campaign if they do not swiftly submit to the terms of the suzerainty treaty.[3] The analog for such diplomatic correspondence in the O.T. is that of the prophets, calling Israel back on the basis of the suzerainty treaty of Deuteronomy. To the extent that the Great King is powerful, the vassal should fear and comply with the terms of the suzerainty treaty. To the extent that the vassal's disobedience is answered by diplomatic correspondence (or prophets), the vassal should immediately and fully submit to the stipulations of the suzerainty treaty. To not comply would bring the experience of covenant curse.

The covenant lawsuit or complaint pattern (רִיב/rîb) is as follows in the prophets and illustrated by Jer 2:4–3:1.[4] First, there is a call of witnesses to hear and testify (Jer 2:4). The heavens and the earth are often part of this testimony against the indicted, as they are here (Jer 2:6–7, 12). In such a situation, the frequent use of "say" followed by quoted speech (Jer 2:6, 8, 20, 23, 25, 27, 31, 35) as well as the use of interrogative particles (Jer 2:6, 8, 14, 28, 31) indicate a lawsuit context.[5] Second, there is

---

3. An example is the "Letter from Hattusili III of Hatti to Kadashman-Enlil II of Babylon," see no. 23 in Beckman, *Hittite Diplomatic Texts*, 138–139; Thompson, *Jeremiah*, 169.

4. Gemser, "The *rîb*-controversy-Pattern;" Huffman, "The Covenant Lawsuit," 285–95; Gunzel and Begrich, *Einlietung*, 329; Harvey, "Le Riv-Pattern," 172–96; *Le plaidoyer*, 54, 80–81; Wright, "The Lawsuit of God," 53; Bright, *Jeremiah*, 89; Limberg, "The Root רִיב," 291–304, esp. 297 and 301; Martin, "The Forensic Background," 82–92; Boyle, "The Covenant Lawsuit," 338–62; Suganuma, "The Covenant Rib," 121–54; Harrison, *Jeremiah and Lamentations*, 24; Ramsey, "Speech Forms," 45–58; Nielsen, *Yahweh*, 15–17, 27–32, 62–83; Owens, "Jeremiah," 372; deRoche overreacts against a legal *sitz im leben* for one of confrontation in covenant but it is helpful to remember Suzerainty warnings of covenant violation are not modern law courts for the great king is prosecutor, judge and general all in one to do as he pleases ("Yahweh's *rib*," 563–74); Fensham, "Common Trends in Curses," 157; Williamson, "Isaiah 1," 392–406.

5. Craigie, Kelley, and Drinkard, *Jeremiah 1–25*, 21.

an introduction to the case at issue, that is, Israel walked away from God and became empty (Jer 2:5). Third, there is a historical indictment which develops the benevolence of Yahweh and indicts the people in their sins (Jer 2:6–10). Yahweh's generosity brought Israel out of Egypt and planted them in the fruitful Promised Land. In response, Israel walked away from God and defiled the land. The leadership of priests, kings (literally "shepherds") and prophets walked away from Yahweh in not correcting the people but instead encouraging their departure to Baal all the more (Jer 2:8). Such a rebellious response drew Yahweh to *contend* against Israel in trial (Jer 2:9, two times אָרִיב/'rîb). This rebellion is truly outrageous with no near parallels elucidated. Fourth, the covenant lawsuit declared the peoples' guilt, namely, Israel left their God for an impotent strategy that will not hold water (Jer 2:11–13). Fifth, the sentence of the people's condemnation is declared to follow their guilt; Israel left their glory for an impotent strategy that will not profit, so Yahweh floods them with covenant curses which: stains, kills, divorces, destroys, and dishonors them into captivity (Jer 2:11–3:1).

Yahweh accused Judah and Israel of a host of sins all of which can be found set out in the stipulations of the Mosaic covenant. Because Israel has done the *evil* (e.g., רָע; Jer 1:16; 2:13, 19; 2:33) of rebellion Yahweh will bring on them *calamity-evil* (e.g., רָע; Jer 1:14; 2:27–28) of covenant curse. Violating the first and second commands, they worship false gods instead of Yahweh (Jer 2:8, 11, 28; 7:9; 8:19; 10:8, 11, 14; 11:12, 17; 16:18, 20; 18:15; 32:35). Disregarding Yahweh's authority, they persecuted the prophets and established their own false prophets (Jer 2:8; 18:18–23; 20; 23:9–40; 27:9–18; 28; 29:8–9, 26–27; 37:14–16). Violating the fourth command they work on the Sabbath and ignore the sabbatical release of slaves for sabbatical year (Jer 17:21–24, 27; 34:8–18).[6] In fact, disregarding sabbatical release involves them in violating the vow they made under King Zedekiah in an attempt to turn away God's wrath. Violating commandments six through nine of the Decalogue, Israel was deceptive,

---

6. Commemorating sabbatical years meant: Judas Maccabeus yielded fortress Beth-zur to Syrians in 135 B.C. (1 Macc 6.49, 53–54), prevented John Hyrcanus to avenge his father's death (Josephus, *Ant*. 13.8.1), facilitated Herod's capture of Jerusalem 37 B.C. (Josephus, *Ant*. 14.16.2), Agrippa 1 mentioned 41 A.D. began a new sabbatical cycle (*M. Soṭ*. 7.8), Sabbatical year as Nero's second year of reign (55 A.D.; *Discoveries in the Judean Desert*. ed. Benoit, Milik, and deVaux, 2:101), and during Bar Kochba rebellion (132 A.D.; *M. Šeb*. 10.3; *Discoveries in the Judean Desert*, 2:121–32). Also Alexander the Great and Julius Caesar did not require taxes during the Sabbatical years (Wacholder, "Sabbatical Year," 763).

stole, murdered, committed adultery, and swore falsely (Jer 3:6–11; 7:8–9; 8:5, 8, 10; 9:2–6; 13:26–27). They refused to serve Yahweh because their leadership ruled them without regard to Yahweh's commands (Jer 2:8; 5:31; 23:1–2). The people have spurned Yahweh in an adulterous harlotry of rebellion ignoring their marriage to Yahweh (Jer 3:1–10). The people selfishly and unjustly amassed wealth not caring for the needy (Jer 5:27–28; 7:5–6; 8:10; 17:11). It is on account of all these sins in Yahweh's Mosaic Covenant relation with them that Israel is swept away into captivity, calamity, and death.

Dilbert Hillers made an extensive study of treaty-curses in the ancient Near East in which he noticed many of the following parallels to ancient Near Eastern curses within the book of Jeremiah.[7] Kennard has added updated support for Hillers' covenant-curse categories.

1. The people and the land are destroyed (Jer 2:12, 30; 4:6, 13, 20, 26; 5:10; 6:19; 7:33; 8:16; 9:11; 10:18; 11:22; 12:11–12; 13:14; 14:18; 15:8, 11, 14; 16:4; 17:18; 18:7, 16, 21; 19:8; 26:10–15; 34:22; 41:3; 45:5; 46:22–23; 50:26; 51:1–4, 55–56).[8]

2. War and captivity will come against you (Jer 4:5–6, 13, 29; 5:15–17; 6:23; 11:22; 15:2; 18:17, 21; 19:9; 21:4–7; 41:4–18; 46:3–5; 49:37; 50:13–15; 51:1–4; 52:4–16).[9]

3. The land will be a dwelling for devouring animals (Jer 2:14–15; 4:7; 5:6; 8:17; 10:22; 12:9; 48:40; 49:19, 22, 33; 50:44; 51:37; Lam 3:10–11).[10]

---

7. Hillers, *Treaty-Curses*, 29, 44–71, 76, 88; list modified by Kennard's own study of Jer and ancient Near Eastern sources. Some metaphors are not duplicated in Jer such as becoming malt from husks (Beckman, *Hittite Diplomatic Texts*, 48, 52).

8. Beckman, *Hittite Diplomatic Texts*, 17, 29, 33, 40, 48, 52, 58, 64, 69, 86, 92, 112, 122; also other futility curses: Sefire I.4.19; Hos 4:10; 5:6; 8:7; 9:12, 16; Amos 4:4; 5:11; 8:12; Mic 3:4; 6:14–15; Zeph 1:13; Hag 1:6; Mal 1:4; CD 1.16–18; 3.10–11; 8.1; 4Q463 1 1; 4 Bar. 1.1–12; Josephus, *Ant.* 10.78–158; Hillers, *Treaty Curses*, 28–29. This destruction entails the covenant curse of death, which is the point of Isa 28:15 covenant with death rather than Hays explanation selling out in pagan worship to the Egyptian god of death ("The Covenant," 212–40).

9. Beckman, *Hittite Diplomatic Texts*, 139.

10. Sefire I.A.31; II.A.9, 30–32; Aramaic "Treaty Between Bar-Ga'yah and the King of Arpad," Sephire 1.27; Fitzmyer, *The Aramaic Inscriptions of Sefire*, 44–45; "The Aramaic Inscriptions of Sefire I and II," *JAOS* 81(1961): 181, 185; *Gilgamesh Epic* 12.93–94; Deut 28:38–42; 32:24; Lev 26:22; Isa 5:29–30; 7:18; 35:9; 51:8; 56:9; Hos 2:20; 5:12, 14; Hillers, *Treaty Curses*, 28–29, 54–56.

4. Removal of joyful sounds (Jer 7:34; 9:10, 17–19; 14:2; 16:5, 9; 25:10; 33:11; Lam 5:14–15).[11]

5. Removal of Peace (Jer 6:14; 8:11, 15; 12:12; 14:19; 16:5; Lam 3:17).[12]

6. Removal of the sound of millstones (Jer 25:10).[13]

7. To be stripped like a prostitute (Jer 13:22, 26–27; Lam 1:8).[14]

8. Breaking of weapons (Jer 49:35; 51:56).[15]

9. Breaking the scepter (Jer 48:17).[16]

10. To eat the flesh of sons and daughters (Jer 19:9; Lam 4:10).[17]

11. Ravish wives (Jer 8:10).[18]

11. *Sefire* I.A.29; *Ashurnirari treaty* 4.19; *Rassam Cylinder* 6.101–3; *Ludlul bēl nēmeqi* I.101–2; *Era Epic* I.2; Ezek. 26:13; Lam 5:14–15; Amos 8:10; Hillers, *Treaty Curses*, 57–58; Lambert, *Babylonian Wisdom*, 36; Borger and Lambert, "Ein neuer," 137–49 esp. 141. Jer personifies this in his own weeping over Jerusalem's destruction (Lam; 1 Esd 1.32; 2 Bar. 5.5–7; 9.1–2; 3 Bar. 1.1–3; Josephus, *Ant.* 10.5.1).

12. Beckman, *Hittite Diplomatic Texts*, 139.

13. *Esar* 443–45; Delbert Hillers, *Treaty Curses*, 58.

14. Hillers (*Treaty Curses*, 58–60) develops two curses together: 1) Becoming a prostitute: *AshN* rev. 5.9–11; *Gilgamest epic* 7.3.6–22; Isa 23:15–18; Amos 7:17; and 2) Being stripped like a prostitute: *Sefire* I.A.40–41; Isa 3:17; 47:3; Ezek 16:37–38; 23:10, 29; Hos 2:5, 12; Nah 3:5.

15. *Sefire* I.A.38–39; *Baal* rev. 4.18; *Esarhaddon* 543, 573–75; *Code of Hammurabi* rev. 28.3–4; *Hittite Soldier's Oath ANET* 354; King, *Babylonian Boundary Stones*, 23 text 3.16, p. 47 text 4.21–22 (boundary stones); Kupper, *Correspondence*, # 15, lines 7–8; Wiseman, *The Alalakh Tablets*, p. 25 #1 line 17; Budge and King, *Annals*, 1:107, line 80 (Inscription of Tiglath-pileser 1), p. 172 lines 19–21 (Inscription of Ashurnasirpal); *AfOB* 9, p. 44 line 75 (Inscription of Esarhaddon); *VAB* 7:322–23 line 5, 7:194–95: line 25 (Inscriptions of Ashurbanipal); Hirsch, "Die Incriften der Könige von Agade," *AfO* 10(1963): 43 lines 36–44 (Inscription of Sargon of Akkad), p. 45, lines 47–55; p. 46 lines 22–30; Hillers, *Treaty Curses*, 60–61; 1 Sam 2:4; Ezek 39:3; Hos 1:5; 2:20; Zech 9:10; Pss 46:10; 76:4.

16. Curse from *Shsmshi-Adad treaty* 22; *Code of Hammurabi*, rev. 26. 45–51; Pritchard, *Ancient Near Eastern Texts*, 179; *Code of Hammurabi* rev. 26.45–51; Hillers, *Treaty Curses*, 61; Isa 9:3; 14:5, 29; Zech 10:11; Ps 89:45; Sir 32.23.

17. *AshN* rev. 4.10–11; Openheim, "Siege-Documents," 69–89 esp. 79 note 34, *Esarhaddon treaty* lines 448–572; Hillers, *Treaty Curses*, 62–63; Deut 28:53–57; Isa 9:19–20; 49:26; Ezek 5:10; Zech 11:9.

18. *Esar* 521–22; Hillers, *Treaty Curses*, 63; Deut 28:30; 2 Sam 12:11; 16:20–22.

12. Divorced from God (Jer 3:8).[19]

13. Contaminated water (Jer 8:14; 9:14; 23:15).[20]

14. Incurable wound (Jer 8:22; 10:19; 14:17, 19; 15:18; 30:12–15; 46:11; 51:8–9).[21]

15. Warriors become like women, loosing strength and virility (Jer 22:23; 50:35–38; 51:30).[22]

16. No burial (Jer 7:33; 8:2; 9:21; 14:16; 16:4, 6; 15:33; 22:19; 25:33; 34:20; 36:30).[23]

17. Like a bird in a trap (Jer 5:26; 48:43–44; 50:24).[24]

18. Judged by cooking (Jer 1:13).[25]

19. Storm (Jer 4:13).

20. Wildfire (Jer 7:20; 15:14; 17:4, 27; 20:9; 43:12–13; 44:6; 49:27; 51:58).

21. Flood (Jer 46:7–8; 47:2).[26]

19. Hosea graphically illustrates the marriage and divorce by God of prostituting Israel. Hos 2:19–20 English, 21–22 Hebrew resolves this divorce, though many Jews consider this statement as a reflection of the Exod Mosaic Covenant. A curse of prostitution is recorded in *Ashur-Nerari 5 Treaty with king of Arad* rev. 5.9, 12–13; Parpola and Watanabe, *Neo-Assyrian Treaties*, 12, rev. 5.9.

20. *Esar* 521–22; Hillers, *Treaty Curses*, 63–64.

21. *Baal* rev. 4.3–4; *Esar* 643–45; *Code of Hammurabi* rev. 28.50–69; *AfOB* 9, 99, lines 40–41; Hillers, *Treaty Curses*, 64–66; Isa 1:5–6; Ezek 30:21; Hos 5:13; Mic 1:9; Nah 3:19; the theme is reversed to prophecy renewal: Jer 30:17; 33:6; Isa 58:8.

22. *Ashur-Nerari*, 12–13; Parpola and Watanabe, *Neo-Assyrian*, 12, rev. 5.9; an old Babylonian prayer *CAD* ed. Ignace Gelb, Z:110b; Hittite prayer to Ishtar, lines 25–29 in F. Sommer, "Ein hethitisches," 98; Hittite soldiers oath in Pritchard, *Ancient Near Eastern Texts*, 354, obv. 2.48–49, 51–53, rev. 3.1; *Era Epic* 4.55–56 in *AfOB* 9, 99; Hillers, *Treaty Curses*, 66–68; Isa 13:8; 19:16; Mic 4:10; 2 Sam 3:29; Ps 48:7.

23. Esarhaddon treaty 426–27, 483–84; *Maqlû* 4.42–44 and 8.85–89 in King, *Babylonian Boundary-Stones*, 47 #4.19–20; p. 62 #2.14–19, 24–25; p. 127 #6.54–55; *AfOB* 9, p. 58, line 6; Hillers, *Treaty Curses and the Old Testament Prophets*, 68–69; 1 Kgs 14:11; 2 Kgs 9:10, 36; Isa 5:25; Ezek 39:17–20; Pss 79:2–3; 83:11.

24. *Esar* 582–84; *Annals of Assyrian Kings* describes Hezekiah surrounded in Jerusalem "like a bird in a cage" in *AfOB* 9, p. 58, lines 12–18; *Era Epic* 4.18–19; Hillers, *Treaty Curses*, 69–70; Ezek 17:15–21; Hos 7:12; similar to: Isa 8:14; 28:13; Josh 23:13.

25. Beckman, *Hittite Diplomatic Texts*, 17.

26. Beckman, *Hittite Diplomatic Texts*, 52; *Esarhaddon Treaty* 488–89; 442; *Esarhaddon Annals* episode 5 and 7 in *AfOB* 9, p. 13–14; p. 32 line 12, p. 48 line 69, p. 65 line 10; Hillers, *Treaty Curses*, 70–71; Isa 8:7; Amos 8:8.

22. Earthquake (Jer 4:24; 8:16).

This multitude of covenant-curse metaphors is coupled with other devastating descriptions of demise for Israel or other people as they violate the terms of covenant. The destruction and warfare emphasis is present in covenant curses as within the prophets. However, the biblical prophets write and speak with more metaphors to render vivid the imagery to motivate Israel's repentance. To the extent that this ancient Near East covenant language for curse is appropriated by Jeremiah further confirms that the overarching framework is that of covenant, even though the stipulations being violated are more like law. This further draws the imagery of prophetic curse toward covenant nomism.

In the midst of Judah and Israel's experience of the devastation of covenant curse, Jeremiah prays for Yahweh's faithfulness to bless them on the basis of the Mosaic covenant (Jer 14:21). Jeremiah's prayer involves other appeals to Yahweh, but he is confident that the Mosaic covenant is still binding upon them with the possibility of future blessing. In the midst of this closure of the seventy year captivity for Israel, curse is extended upon Babylon and the host of Gentile nations that surrounded and took advantage of Israel (Jer 25:12–31).

New Covenant

Within the context of devastating covenant curse the book of consolation (Jer 30:1–33:26) provides hope of restoration and a New Covenant.[27] Yahweh declares that His plans change from calamity (רָעָה/rʿh) to peace (שָׁלוֹם) to provide a future hope of reconciliation (Jer 29:11). The section coheres with its restoration emphasis and sometimes expresses this restoration in the extreme as a "new creation" (Jer 31:22 [LXX 38:22]; Isa 65:17; 66:22). The ingredients of the message further cohere since the restoration will be realized at a set time as indicated by the phrase, "Behold days are coming" which serves as a temporal refrain throughout the section (Jer 30:3; 31:1, 27, 31, 38; 33:14).

Part of the restoration of Israel is that the covenant lawsuit (רִיב/rîb) shifts from against Israel to against the nations which violated Israel in Yahweh's judgment (Jer 25:31; 50:34, 36). In this context Yahweh defends Israel. Such a context of no peace in covenant curse is turned

---

27. Raitt, *A Theology of Exile*, 178–80; Robinson, "Jeremiah's New Covenant," 181–204.

to realize abundant peace and truth from God (Jer 14:13; 23:17; 28:9; 33:6, 9). Therefore, in pleading Israel's cause, Yahweh provides Israel with great Kingdom hope.

Yahweh responds to Israel in the genre of salvation oracles, initiating the return of covenant-formula. For example, Jer 24 recounts a vision in a two ways tradition of good and bad figs. The good figs image envisions Yahweh rescuing those Jews sent into Babylonian captivity and establishing them again in a reaffirmed covenant election and blessing: "For I will set My eyes on them for good, and I will bring them again to this land; and I will build them up and not overthrow them, and I will plant them and not pluck up" (Jer 24:6). However, the New Covenant blessing from Yahweh will transform Jews from within, so that they will be deeply and relationally responsive to Yahweh from the core of their being: "I will give them a heart to know Me, for I am Yahweh; and they will be My people, and I will be their God, for they will return to Me, with their whole heart" (Jer 24:7). Such a covenant formula strongly reaffirms the reconfirmation of Yahweh's covenant relationship with Israel,[28] also recovering them to be responsive in love of Yahweh (Deut 6:5; 10:12, 16). In the midst of these salvation oracles, covenant formulae resound repeatedly tolling a chorus of hope. For example, in the midst of Yahweh's re-gathering Israel to Himself, blessed in the land, Yahweh reconfirms Israel's covenant relationship, "You shall be My people, and I will be your God" (Jer 30:22; 31:1, 31–34; 32:36–44).

This adoption hope for Israel as son anticipates that they would be blessed in the Mosaic Covenant blessings unto Kingdom (Jer 3:19). But the unfortunate reality is that as sons Israel was destroyed under covenant curse of the Babylonian captivity (Jer 10:20) only to be re-gathered by God from the dispersion for Kingdom blessing (Isa 43:6; 45:11).

Within this context of restoration there is a leitmotif of terror and grief in captivity which contrasts against the major theme of restoration. In fear of the time of Jacob's distress, men behave as a women in childbirth (Jer 30:5–7). Yahweh has wounded Israel as punishment for their sins causing others to devour and plunder her in her great pain (Jer 30:12–16). Bitter weeping reflects the crush the captives feel as they are assembled at Ramah for captivity in Babylon (Jer 31:15). Yahweh expresses His anger against Judah by flooding them into Babylonian captivity because of their worshipping of other gods, defiling the Temple (Jer

---

28. Rendtorff, *The Covenant Formula*, 32–35.

32:26-35, 42-43; 33:4-5). This destruction leaves Judah as dead, waste, and without inhabitant or beast because of Judah's sin (Jer 33:4-5, 10, 12).

The New Covenant prophecy breaks in with an internal transformation for Israel's remnant heart condition (Jer 31:33). In such a bleak devastation as the Babylonian captivity, Yahweh's hope brings redemption for Israel's remnant. However, some Christian interpreters understand it as a supercessionistic replacing Israel with Christianity.[29] Instead, the text speaks of Israel as transformed internally, having the Mosaic Law applied to Israel's heart in a covenant renewal.[30] Some commentators extend this internalism to Christianity through an Augustinian reading of regeneration by the Spirit.[31] In this, John Calvin advocated that this regeneration retains the Law for Christian life while abrogating ceremonial laws.[32] Francis Watson went further, using this text to reapply Jewish festival celebrations within the Church today.[33]

"Behold days are coming" when this terror and grief are transformed to restorational blessings and joy. Yahweh will restore the fortunes of Israel and Judah (Jer 30:3; 31:23; 33:7). Their bondage is broken; they will be joyfully re-gathered into the land which Yahweh gave to their forefathers through Mosaic covenant (Num 34; Joshua 13–21; Jer 30:3; 31:8-11, 16-17, 21, 23-24). They will possess (יְרֻשָּׁה/yršh) the land as an inheritance in peace, without fear (Jer 30:3, 10). They will buy and sell land again, and redemption of land will be valued (Jer 32:7-15, 44). Jerusalem will be rebuilt and enlarged (Jer 31:38-40). Their dwelling places will be rebuilt (Jer 30:18). Judah will again dwell in its cities and farms, because Yahweh will satisfy the weary and refresh any who languish (Jer 31:24-25; 33:13). The vineyards will be replanted in such

---

29. Supercessionism and a change of sacraments are advocated by: Jerome, *In Hieremiam Prophetam litri*, 6. 26.5-6; 6.250.74; Justin, *Dial.* sect. 11; Aquinas, *Hebrews*, 152; Peter Lombard, *Sententiae in IV libris distinctae*, 5.iii.d40.c.3; Bullinger, "A Brief Exposition, sect. 188a, pp. 100-38. This view is countered by commentaries that see Israel destined for this New Covenant eschatology (Duhm, *Jeremiah*, 256-57; Kraus, "Der Erste," 65).

30. Duhm, *Jeremiah*, 256-57; Weiser, *Jeremia 25.14-52.34*, 295; Kraus, Der Erste," 65; 2 Macc 12.31-32; 1QS 1.16-2.25 parallel to Deut 27-28; 1Q22; 1Q34bis 3 ii 6; 4Q378 frg. 19 col. ii; 4Q379 frg. 17; though such covenant renewal begins the eschatological era (1QSa 1.5).

31. Augustine, *Contra duas epistulas Pelegianorum*, sect. 3.6; *Enchir.* sect. 46; Calvin, *Institutes*, 2.11.7-8; Moon, *Jeremiah's New Covenant*.

32. Calvin, *Institutes*, 2.11.8; Moon, *Jeremiah's New Covenant*, 88-89.

33. Watson, *Text and Truth*, 215; Moon, *Jeremiah's New Covenant*, 256.

peaceful circumstances that the watchmen can leave the vineyard to worship Yahweh in Zion (Jer 31:5–6). Yahweh will fill the lives of His people with healing joy and abundance (Jer 31:12–14; 33:6). This restoration imagery prompts praise and prayer among Israel and Judah (Jer 31:7). So much peace and good will be theirs from Yahweh that other nations will tremble in amazement and fear (Jer 33:9).

These restoration blessings serve as an intersection of the Mosaic, Davidic, and the New Covenants. The Mosaic covenant applicability can be seen through the lens of chapter thirty in Deuteronomy, but that is developed elsewhere.[34] Here in Jeremiah the realization of the land promise is grounded in returning to Yahweh's giving the nation the land to possess at first under the Mosaic covenant (Jer 30:3). The Mosaic covenant will still be operative because Levitical priests offering and sacrificing[35] continually will be there as certainly as the Davidic King[36] (fulfilling the Davidic covenant) will be there (Jer 23:5–6; 33:18, 21 within 33:14–26).[37]

---

34. See volume one, Kennard, *Biblical Covenantalism in Torah*, ch. 5, "Deuteronomy."

35. Often the everlasting covenant is a fusion of the Abrahamic and Mosaic covenants (Polaski, "Reflection on a Mosaic Covenant," 55–73). Elsewhere the New Covenant is also identified with the practice of the Mosaic Covenant. In the spirit of remembering the Mosaic covenant, Yahweh will establish an everlasting covenant and forgiving relationship with Israel which extends that foundational covenant (Ezek 16:60–63). When this everlasting covenant of peace is established with them, Yahweh will multiply them and establish His sanctuary, as His dwelling place, in their midst forever (Ezek 37:26–28). Ezek discusses at great length the kingdom temple, priests, sacrifices, festivals and Sabbaths (Ezek 40–46). In Ezek 40–46 the functioning Kingdom Temple is described where sacrifices are offered by the priests including the purification offering (Ezek 43:20–26), and the daily burnt offerings, peace offerings, purification offerings and grain offerings, all of which atone (Ezek 45:15, 17). There will even need to be seventh-day sacrifices to atone for all who go astray or are naïve (Ezek 45:20). Many of these features reflect the Mosaic patterns though there are some small changes like a Temple rather than a Tabernacle and the Day of Atonement being moved to the first month rather than in the seventh month. Freedman and Miano, "People of the New Covenant," 7–26.

36. Elsewhere the New Covenant is also identified with the realization of the Davidic Covenant by a Davidic king reigning on earth (Isa 55:3; Ezek 37:24–26). Freedman and Miano, "People of the New Covenant," 7–26.

37. Jer 30:8–12 and 33:14–26 is absent from the LXX but present in the MT. Some conjecture that the difference is reflective of the Zadokite eclipse of the Davidic line (McKane, *Jeremiah*, 2:862) or the rise of the Hasmoneans (Duhm, *Jeremiah*, 276; Holladay, *Jeremiah*, 2:230). However, beyond these textual critical ellipses, the everlasting character of the Davidic Kingly reign is amply supported in LXX Jer 23:5–6 and among the other prophets in the MT and their LXX counterparts (Isa 55:3–5; Ezek

Israel will serve Yahweh their God and David their king (Jer 30:9). This return to serving Yahweh rests on the basis of Yahweh's redemption and Israel's repentance, which is the balance in Deuteronomy thirty (Jer 31:11, 18–20). The dispersion was like another wilderness experience ended by Yahweh's love (אָהַב/'hb and חֶסֶד/ḥsd both strongly covenantal words, Jer 31:2–3). Within this context God makes another covenant with Israel that He will maintain forever (עוֹלָם/'lm, Jer 32:40; also Ezek 37:26–28). This New Covenant also serves as the basis for certain re-gathering of Israel into the land and owning the land (Jer 32:36–44). However, this New Covenant transforms Israel's heart so that they always fear Yahweh and continue in the one way (Jer 32:39–40). This internal transformation was promised in the Mosaic covenant but is at the center of the New Covenant (Deut 30:6; Jer 31:32–34).

The New Covenant is "new" (חֲדָשָׁה/ḥdšh). By this word חֲדָשָׁה, Jer means *fresh, recent* and *novel*.[38] The word "new" (חֲדָשָׁה/ḥdšh) is described as *fresh* like God's faithfulness even though it has been there before (Lam 3:23). Jeremiah also used this word "new" (חֲדָשָׁה/ḥdšh) to mean "recent" as in the new gate of the Temple (Jer 26:10; 36:10). The word "new" (חֲדָשָׁה/ḥdšh) for Jer also means "novel" or unique like a woman encompassing a man[39]. (Jer 31:22). This role reversal, women likely

---

34:23–24; 37:24–25; Hos 3:5) and Qumran (4QJer c 33:16–21). So both source critical explanations are unlikely (Leuchter, *The Polemics*, 72). However, the LXX ellipsis of Jer 33:14–26 also removes the Jeremiah commitment to the everlasting Priestly Covenant and their Mosaic Covenant atoning sacrifices (Jer 33:18, 21). Perhaps the dispersion context of the LXX does not see the need to emphasize the everlasting Priestly Covenant in the Temple and their functioning atoning sacrifices. However, the Hebrew MT and 4QJer c retain this commitment to the everlasting Priestly Covenant, while Ezekiel in MT and LXX and second Temple documents continue to describe eschatological sacrifices in the Temple that atone and forgive (Ezek 44:11–31; Sir 45.25; 47.11; 1QM 2.5; 11QT 25.10–27.10; *Shemoneh Esreh*. benediction 14). So there is support for Davidic and Priestly Covenants in both MT and LXX.

38. "New Covenant" is also discussed in early Judaism in CD 6.19; 8.21; 19.33; 20.12; 1QpHab 2.3; 1QSb 3.26; 5.5, 21; 1Q34bis 3 ii 6.

39. The phrase "a woman will encompass a man" is difficult to interpret, though it clearly indicates a new order which at least in some way indicates a role reversal (Jer 31:22). Calvin suggests a highly plausible view concerning the role of warriors. Since in the midst of the Babylonian captivity male warriors become so terrorized that they become as a woman birthing a child (Jer 30:6), it could be that in Yahweh's new peaceful order even women can perform the defending of their man. That is, the new order will be profoundly peaceful and reverse a well-established covenant curse of warriors becoming like women. There are other views as to what in the established order changes, such as women initiating in the sexual relationship or the virgin Israel

becoming warriors, undoes the covenant curse elsewhere mentioned in which warriors become as women (Jer 50:35–38; 51:30).40. In this sense this New Covenant initiates a "new creation" (Jer 31:22). The new (חֲדָשָׁה/ ḥdšh) covenant reflects a fresh, recent and novel approach to Israel's relationship with Yahweh when contrasted with the Mosaic Covenant (Jer 31:31–32). In this novel relationship the New Covenant is not like the Mosaic in certain ways.

The New Covenant brings about the new order of blessing out of a context of destroyed dispersion (Jer 31:27–28). The freshness of replanting Judah and Israel to increase their numbers of man and beast is inaugurating. The freshness of planting them in the land to rebuild them focuses on the new blessed order that will come about in their lives.

The New Covenant will bring about a new legal order of individual moral responsibility (Jer 31:29–30; Ezek 18:3). Individual moral responsibility was present before in the Mosaic Covenant (Deut 24:16), but the Mosaic Covenant set up a multi-generational judgment which Yahweh executed even to four generations for a previous generation's sin much like the Hittite suzerainty treaties utilize (Exod 20:5–6; 34:6–7; Num 4:18, 33; Deut 5:9–10; Jer 25:11–12 and 29:10 with 2 Chr 36:21; Jer 32:18; Lam 5:7; Ezek 18:2).[41] However, such a multi-generational curse is completely absent from all ancient Near East law codes, so it has a suzerainty treaty quality. Within ancient Near East covenantal standards this Mosaic

---

embracing Yahweh again but there is not as much ancient Near Eastern treaty evidence to understand the phrase in these ways.

40. The reverse of men becoming as women is a treaty curse for weakness and cowardice (Jer 30:6; 31:22; *Ashurnirari treaty* rev. 5.9, 12–13; an old Babylonian prayer *CAD*, Z:110b; Hittite prayer to Ishtar, lines 25–29 in F. Sommer, "Ein hethitisches Gebet," *ZA* 33(1921): 98; Hittite soldiers oath in Pritchard, *Ancient Near Eastern Texts*, 354; Era Epic 4.55–56 in *AfOB* 9, 99; Hillers, *Treaty Curses*, 66–68; Isa 19:16; 2 Sam 3:29).

41. Beckman, *Hittite Diplomatic Texts*, 14, no. 1A "Treaty Between Arnunda 1 of Hatti and the Men of Ismerika" 3 (obv. 12–18); pp. 40–41 no. 5 "Treaty Between Suppiluliuma 1 of Hatti and Aziru of Amurru" 17 (A rev. 12'–16'); p. 48 no.6A "Treaty Between Suppiluliuma 1 of Hatti and Shattiwaza of Mittanni" 15–16 (A rev. 58–75); p. 52–54 no. 6B "Treaty Between Shattiwaza of Mittanni and Suppiluliuma 1 of Hatti" 9–11 (rev. 25–62); p. 58 no. 7 "Treaty Between Suppiliuma 1 of Hatti and Tette of Nuhashshi" 17 (A 4.44'–57); p. 64 no. 8 "Treaty Between Mursili 2 of Hatti and Tuppi-Teshshup of Amurru" 21–22 (A 4.21–32); pp. 65, 69 no. 9 "Treaty Between Mursili 2 of Hatti and Niqmepa of Ugarit" 1 and 20–21; p. 73 no. 10 "Treaty Between Mursili 2 of Hatti and Targasnalli of Hapalla" 15; pp. 92–93 no. 13 "Treaty Between Muwattalli 2 of Hatti and Alaksandu of Wilusa" 21 (A 4.31–46); p. 99 no. 15 "Treaty Between Hattusili 3 of Hatti and Ramses 2 of Egypt" 19 (A obv. 65–70); p.112 no. 18B "Treaty Between Hattusili 3 of Hatti and Ulmi-Teshshup of Tarhuntassa" 9–11 (rev. 5–14).

Covenantal multi-generational judgment is still gracious. However, the New Covenant carries no judgment over to the next generation, so it is even more generous than other ancient Near Eastern covenants. Said in a proverbial manner, only the one who eats the sour grapes will have his teeth set on edge.

The New Covenant will bring about a new internalization of the Mosaic Law for Israel (Jer 31:33). In this sense Tiberius Rata defends that the term "new" (חֲדָשָׁה/ḥdšh) in Jer 31:31 could also mean "Renewed" covenant, which would draw the New Covenant tightly with the Mosaic Covenant,[42] or a New Covenant nomism.[43] The Mosaic Covenant commanded Israel to circumcise their heart (Deut 10:16). The Mosaic Covenant promised that Yahweh would eventually bless Israel by circumcising their heart (Deut 30:6). The New Covenant institutes this blessing within the heart of each Israelite. The Law (תּוֹרָתִי/trt) placed within them is singular in the Hebrew text and thus is best taken as the Mosaic Law which the context develops was given when Yahweh brought them out of Egypt (Jer 31:32-33). The New Covenant internalized Mosaic Law includes specifics like a functioning Temple, Levitical priests, animal sacrifices, Mosaic feasts and Sabbaths (Jer 33:18, 21; Ezek 40-46).[44] For Yahweh to place this Law within Israelites' hearts benefits them significantly so that they will affirm their relationship to Yahweh and obey Him as their God instead of breaking covenant as did their forefathers (Jer 31:32-34; 32:40). There will be no need for Israelites to evangelize, teach, or exhort each other to know Yahweh for all Israel will be in intimate relationship with Him (Jer 31:33-34). They will corporately be God's people for Yahweh will ground their relationship with Him in His complete forgiveness of their sin. From this intimate relationship with Yahweh, God will

---

42. Rata, *The Covenant Motif*, 2; Talmon, "The Community," 12–13; Christiansen, *The Covenant in Judaism*, 56–57; Moon, *Jeremiah's New Covenant*, 160–61; 2 Macc 12.31–32; Josephus, *J. W.*; 1QS 1.16-2.25 parallel to Deut 27–28; 1QSb 3.26; 5.5, 21; 1Q22; 1Q34bis 3 ii 6; 4Q378 frg. 19 col. ii; 4Q379 frg. 17; though such covenant renewal begins the eschatological era (1QSa 1.5).

43. *Ep. Barn.* 2.6; Gräbe, *New Covenant*, 153; Backhaus, *Der neue Bund*, 312.

44. Early Judaism continues the hope of the construction of the Temple as identified with the new creation at the end time (1 Chr 17:12–14; Ezek 40:1–43:5; *Jub.* 1.27–28; 1QS 8.6–7; 4Q 174), which Temple is indwelt by the presence of God (Pss 11:4; 79:1; Isa 6:1; 66:6; Ezek 43:2–5; 11QTa 29.7; 45.12–14; 46.3–4) and populated by functioning priests in a covenant relationship with God where sacrifices atone and forgive (Ezek 44:11–31; Sir 45.25; 47.11; 1QM 2.5; 11QT 25.10–27.10; *Shemoneh Esreh.* benediction 14). This central focus of Temple in eschatological Israel becomes a metaphor for the community of Israel (1QS 8.5–6; 9.6).

internally unify Israel in one heart and way (Jer 32:38–40). Yahweh will also provide the internal motivational fear of Yahweh to prompt obedience, to accompany the internal Law which is to be obeyed.

Ezekiel joins Jer in taking up the re-affirmation of Israel in New Covenant through the echo of Yahweh's covenant formula: "Israel shall be a people for Me, empowered by My Spirit, and Yahweh will be their God and I will transform Israel's heart to be responsive in love and obedience" (a composite of: Ezek 11:14–21; 14:1–11; 36:22–35; 37:23, 28; Isa 59:21). Such New Covenantal transformation does not remove Israel from the synergistic responsibility to make a new heart and spirit for themselves (Ezek 18:31; Deut 30:2, 11–14). Zechariah is the only other O.T. prophet to join Jer and Ezek in utilizing the covenant formula, "Israel will be My people and I will be their God in truth and righteousness" (Zech 8:8).[45]

Similarly, Yahweh promises a future covenant initiating a Kingdom of peace with animals and Israel in which all warfare will cease (Isa 11:6–10; 54:10; Ezek 34:25; 37:26; Hos 2:18).[46] The Kingdom will be begun with Yahweh marrying Israel forever in righteousness and His faithfulness (Isa 62:4–5; Hos 2:19–23). This betrothal language expresses a monogamous election marriage vow that initiates the eschatological expression of Kingdom between Yahweh and Israel.

While the O.T. development of the New Covenant is primarily Israel-focused, Isa includes Gentiles in a second tier role of servants who can see the glory of God in Kingdom as they also are permitted to enter the Temple and experience Sabbath, Temple prayers and sacrifices (Isa 51:4; 56:6–7; 60:10; 61:5; 66:18).[47] Overseeing them, the Jews will be as priests of Yahweh.

As second Temple Judaism translates the Jeremiah text into the LXX, the singular expression in Hebrew for Mosaic Law (תּוֹרָתִי/trt) is translated into Greek in the plural as God's laws (νόμους), which broadens this New Covenant commitment beyond that of the Mosaic Law to signify broad obedience to God (LXX Jer 38:33 which is MT Jer 31:33). Internalized obedience is thus a broad New Covenant commitment. However, the rabbinics and medieval Judaism continue to maintain that the *torah* is everlastingly binding on Israel and that which must be obeyed.[48]

---

45. Rendtorff, *The Covenant Formula*, 37.

46. 1QM 12.3; 18.7–8.

47. 2 Macc 3.1–3, 12, 33–39; 13.23; Tob 1.8; 13.11; Jdt 14.10; Theodotus, frag. 4 *P.E.* 9.22.4–6.

48. Sir 45.7, 24–25; Bar 4.1; *Midr. Ps.* 119:10 cited by Montefiore and Lowe, *A*

Isaiah, Ezek, and Joel shift the internalizing language of the Law to the enlivening language of the Spirit upon the people (Isa 59:21; Ezek 36:27; Joel 2:28-29). God's covenant with Israel signifies the Spirit of the Lord upon the people. With the Spirit upon the people they will continue to speak the words of the Lord. Much like the prophetic ministry and especially the Messianic prophet (Isa 11:2; 61:1) so the people will prophesy and see visions, declaring God's word in this New Covenant era without end (Isa 59:21, Joel 2:28-29). However, in this covenantal language, as in Jeremiah there is still a fusion of the New covenant with the Mosaic Covenant, for in the eschatological covenant and Israel's holding fast to covenant, Sabbath and sacrifices will be an expression of those the Lord gathers to His House of prayer (Isa 56:4-8).

The New Covenant is a certain and everlasting covenant (Jer 31:35-37; 32:40; also Isa 59:21; 61:8). These New Covenant blessings are as certain for Israel as the continuing fixed order of creation since they all depend upon Yahweh. Israel is guaranteed a continued relationship with Yahweh. The covenant guaranteeing this relationship is an everlasting covenant because Yahweh promises never to turn away from Israel, but to continue to do them good.

Summarizing Jeremiah's relationship of covenants shows that the New Covenant realizes the benefits of both the Mosaic and Davidic covenants with slight modifications to the Mosaic covenant. The New Covenant is more explicit than the Mosaic covenant in: 1) internalizing the Law code and motives, 2) individualizing moral responsibility, and 3) guaranteeing the continuing relationship with Yahweh through His forgiveness and blessing.

New Covenant in Second Temple Judaism

Reflecting on Israel's rebellion under the Mosaic Covenant, the mainstream Pharisaic document Bar 2:30-35 shows the influence of Jeremiah's prophecy.

> Israel is a stiff-necked people. But in the land of their exile they will come to themselves and know that I am the Lord their God. I will give them a heart that obeys and ears that hear; they will praise me in the land of their exile, and will remember My name

Rabbinic Anthology, 125; rabbi Joseph in *BT Nidah* 616; Maimonides ninth of thirteen principles of Judaism *Commentary on the Mishnah*, 159-60.

and turn from their stubbornness and their wicked deeds; for they will remember the ways of their ancestors, who sinned before the Lord. I will bring them again into the land that I swore to give to their ancestors, to Abraham, Isaac, and Jacob, and they will rule over it; and I will increase them, and they will not be diminished. I will make an everlasting covenant with them to be their God and they shall be my people; and I will never again remove My people Israel from the land that I have given them.[49]

Such an everlasting covenant with Israel blessed in intimate relationship with the Lord is the New Covenant. As in Jeremiah, this New Covenant expression is seen as a divine internalization that has God resolving the problems from Israel's Mosaic Covenant rebellion and curse.

The concept of New Covenant was used at Qumran to indicate the faithful or "true Israel" who walked in the proper order of the Qumran Covenanters and obeyed the previous covenants.[50] In contrast to the Mosaic Covenant, the New Covenant is for them a new beginning of the faithful keeping of the Mosaic Covenant by those who follow Abraham.[51] As such, the New Covenant is a sectarian route of repentance so that they return to the Mosaic Covenant.[52] Such a New Covenant is not merely the status quo of Mosaic Law compliance for the Pharisaic rabbinics rather, a new era has begun.[53] In this narrow way, Qumran sees that there is divine grace, reflecting a New Covenant transformation empowered by God's Spirit (Ezek 36:24–37:28; Joel 2:28–29).[54] Furthermore, for Qumran and Pharisee alike, the Divine Spirit will expiate the righteous person in covenant in this life from his iniquity into an enlightened Spirit-enabled

---

49. Bar 2:30–35.

50. *Charter of a Jewish Sectarian Association* (1QS, 4Q255–264a and 5Q11) 3.7–12, 26; 4.22–23; 5.5, 21; 9.6; *Damascus Document* (CD 4Q268 frag. 1=4Q266 frag. 2 Col. 1) ver. 6; 6.9, 19; 8.21=19.33–34; 14.1–2; 20.12; B col. 19, ver. 12–13 here the New Covenant is clearly still Law like Jer 31:33 Hebrew; 19.33; 20.12; 1QpHab 2.3; 11.13 "circumcision of heart's foreskin"; *4 Ezra* 9.31; There is also a lacuna in 1QpHab 2.3 where likely בְּרִית stood as referring to new "covenant"; Freedman and Miano, "People of the New Covenant," 7–26; Evans, "Covenant in the Qumran," 55–80.

51. CD 1.3–5; 2.14–3.21; 5.20–6.3.

52. 1QS 4.22; 1QSa; CD 8.16–18; possibly a reference in *Hab. Pesher* 2.3 "those who betr[ayed] the new [covenant]."

53. *Lev. Rab.* 9.7; 13.3; *Eccl. Rab.* 11.8; *S. of S. Rab.* 2.12, 4; Targum on Isa 12.3 and Song 5.10; *Yalkut Isa.* 26.2; Midrash to Ps. 146.7; *b. Sanh.* 51b; *b. Shab.* 151 b.

54. *Charter of a Jewish Sectarian Association* (1QS; 4Q255–264a; 5Q11) 3.15–4.1; 4.5; *The War Scroll* (1QM, 4Q491–496) 1.1–20; 16.11; 1QH 4, 5, 18; 4Q548 frag. 1 col. 2 9–16; 11Q13 22–25.

pure living of the narrow way, utilizing New Covenant terminology such as: "empowered by Spirit", "circumcision of heart" and "internalization of Law" to describe this life transformation (Deut 30:6; Jer 31:33, Joel 2:28-29).[55] For example, Pharisaic *Jub.* describes Israel as in New Covenant and returning to Yahweh.

> After this they will return to Me in all uprightness and with all of their heart and soul. And I will cut off the foreskin of their heart and the foreskin of the heart of their descendants. And I shall create for them a holy spirit, and I shall purify them so that they will not turn away from following me from that day and forever.[56]

---

55. *Jub.* 1.23; 6.17; *Odes Sol.* 11.1-3; *Charter of a Jewish Sectarian Association* (1QS, 4Q255-264a and 5Q11) 3.7-12; 4.18-23; 5.5; *Damascus Document* (CD 4Q268 frag. 1=4Q266 frag. 2 Col. 1) ver. 6; 14.1-2; B col. 19, ver. 12-13 here the New Covenant is clearly still Law like Jer 31:33 Hebrew; 1QpHab 2.3; 11.13 "circumcision of heart's foreskin"; *4 Ezra* 9.31; *Ex. Rab.* 19(81c) and *Targum Cant.* 3.8.

56. *Jub.* 1.23; also *Jub.* 1.17-18 and 24-25; Bar 2.35.

5

Instances of Covenant Nomism in Second Temple[1] Judaisms

THIS CHAPTER PRESENTS A brief look at historical instances of Jewish covenantal nomism which underlie the Jewish perspectives of the third quest for the historical Jesus[2] and the New Paul.[3] E. P. Sanders defined the Jewish pattern of religion to be covenant nomism, namely that in which God elects His people to a covenant which governs their experience of blessing or curse from Him. Sanders defined covenantal nomism as follows:

> Covenant nomism is the view that one's place in God's plan is established on the basis of the covenant and that requires as the proper response of man his obedience to its commands, while providing means of atonement for transgression ... *Obedience maintains one's position in the covenant, but it does not earn God's grace as such* ... Righteousness in Judaism is a term which implies the *maintenance of status* among the group of the elect.[4]

While Jacob Neusner is deeply critical of Sanders methodology, he accepts that Sanders has accurately described Judaism as within such covenant nomism and considers that such a description is "wholly sound

---

1. The second Temple context is Judaism from fifth century B.C. with the construction of Ezra's Temple to the second century A.D. with the destruction of Herod's Temple, through the Jewish war (66–73 A.D.) and Bar Kochbah rebellion (132–135 A.D.).

2. Sanders, *Jesus and Judaism*; Dunn, *Jesus Remembered*. vol. 1; Wright, *Jesus and the Victory of God*; Flusser, *Jesus*; Kennard, *Messiah Jesus*.

3. Sanders, *Paul, the Law, and the Jewish People*; Dunn, *The Theology of Paul the Apostle*; Wright, *What Saint Paul Really Said*.

4. Sanders, *Paul and Palestinian Judaism*, 75, 420, 544; "Common Judaism Explored," 11–23.

and self-evident."[5] While the evidence is not monolithic, Morna Hooker concludes that the second Temple Jewish evidence substantially supports covenant nomism.

> Beginning with Palestinian Judaism, Sanders argues persuasively against the very negative view of Judaism which has dominated much Christian biblical scholarship. His conclusion is that Judaism is not a "legalistic" religion, since salvation is seen as a matter of God's grace, not of works, the "pattern of religion" which emerges from the great majority of Jewish writing of the period 200 BC–AD 200 is that of "covenantal nomism."[6]

Edward Cook identifies that covenant nomism is the widely accepted description of second Temple sources.[7] Within such a covenant nomist view, Israel enters covenant by God's electing grace and continues in the covenant by the gracious means which God has supplied for guidance and recovery.

One of the primary claimed competitors to the covenant nomist paradigm is that of variegated nomism. That is, Judaisms of this period are varied with regard to features of the Law.[8] This varied nature of Judaisms is generally accepted even by lead advocates of the covenant nomist thesis.[9] This chapter is not trying to demonstrate that the only second Temple Jewish model is covenant nomism but rather merely that covenant nomism is a significant paradigm within the mix of early Jewish Law options. My thesis for this chapter is defended as accurate by two thirds of the authors writing in the primary volume advocating variegated nomism.[10] Reviewers of *Justification and Variegated Nomism* have

---

5. Neusner, "The Use of the Later Rabbinic," 2:47–48; "Paul and Palestinian Judaism," 177–91, esp. 180 and 191; *Judaic Law*, 53, 105, 232; *Judaism*; *Sifre to Deuteronomy*, 60, 145; *Performing Israel's Faith*.

6. Hooker, *From Adam to Christ*, 155; "Paul and 'Covenant Nomism,'" 47–56.

7. Cook, "Covenant Nomism," 203.

8. Carson, especially pressed this interpretation of *Justification and Variegated Nomism*, 1:5, 544.

9. Sanders, *Paul and Palestinian Judaism*, 423; Dunn, *The Parting of the Ways*, 18.

10. Falk considers the *Pss. Sol., Pr. Man., Pr. Azar.* 11–13, and *2 Bar.* 14.6 to be covenant nomist texts ("Psalms and Prayers," 1:15, 51); Bauckham concludes that the apocalypses "broadly coincide with Sanders" in covenant nomism ("Apocalypses," 1:148, 172, 179, 180); Kugler concludes that the *Testament of the Twelve Patriarchs* support covenant nomism ("Testaments," 1:190); Salisbury concludes that Josephus views Israel in obedience as in a covenant nomist relationship with the Law ("Josephus," 1:259); Alexander, "Torah and Salvation," 1:273; McNamara agrees that the

concluded that the variegated nomist model neither excises nor performs a requiem for a part of its strategy, that of covenant nomism.[11] So I do not consider variegated nomism to be a competitor but rather an ally to my thesis that covenant nomism is a significant paradigm among second Temple Judaisms.

This chapter is a historical study to demonstrate that all the components for covenant nomism are available in the early Jewish context, though not in as dominant an emphasis as Sanders claimed. This largely historical study of Jewish covenant nomism builds upon the O.T. Suzerainty (or Great King) Treaty work of Mendenhall, Baltzer, McCarthy, and Kline which see Mosaic Covenant documents such as Deuteronomy as within a suzerainty treaty format.[12] Such a covenant includes Israel as elect by God within the Mosaic Covenant which provides blessings if Israel obeys the covenant stipulations, and curses from the Great King if they disobey the Law. Such a framework is essentially covenant nomism. It is this covenantal program that drives covenant nomism in Judaism, but instances of covenant nomism appear in second Temple Judaism, even though they are rarely the emphasis.[13]

Extending such covenant nomism to the second Temple era does not mean I am trying to portray a monolithic pan-Judaism (a criticism that could be levied against Sanders methodology) but I am trying to identify that all the important elements for a viable covenant nomist view are

---

targums have many themes but that one of them is covenant nomism ("Some Targum Themes," 1:355); Bockmuehl agrees with this assessment of the presence of covenant nomism in the Qumran texts mentioned ("1QS and Salvation at Qumran," 1:381–414, especially 412 but considers that there is much more evidence since then); Winninge, *Sinners and the Righteous*, 9–180, especially 125–136; Evans, "Covenant in the Qumran," Abegg, "The Covenant of the Qumran," and Cook, "Covenant Nomism," 55–80, 81–98, and 203–20 respectively; Beale, "The Overstated," 93–94; Avemarie, *Torah und Leben*; "Bund," 176–224; "Erwählung," 108–26; Gathercole, "Early Judaism," 153–62 esp. 161; covenant nomism is also affirmed by Joslin, *Hebrews*, 23–87; Hogerterp, "4QMMT," 359–79.

11. Byron, and Eisenbaum http://www.bookreviews.org/bookdetail.asp?TitleId=1887&CodePage=1887,4658; also Gathercole, "Early Judaism," 153–62; Yinger, "The Continuing Quest," 382–85.

12. Mendenhall, "Covenant Forms," 50–76; Muilenberg, "The Form," 347–65; Baltzer, *Das Bundesformular*; Lohfink, "Der Bundesschluss," 32–56; *Das Hauptgebot*; McCarthy, *Treaty and Covenant*; Kline, *Treaty of the Great King*.

13. This is obvious by reading the manuscripts but one volume that intentionally repeatedly makes this point is: Carson, *Justification and Variegated Nomism*, vol. 1.

amply exampled within second Temple Judaism.[14] Additionally, some of the second Temple documents (such as: Dan, Sir, *Bar., Pss. Sol., The War Scroll* [1QM], *Charter of a Jewish Sectarian Association* [1QS], and the *Damascus Document* [CD]) have all the features needed for a full covenant nomist view within them.[15] Many other second Temple documents in their fragmentary condition have support for some of the essential points. Additionally, other second Temple sources do not raise the subject of covenant nomism or everlasting life because they are narratives focused on a different thrust such as contemplating the pre-Law heritage such as with Adam, Enoch or Abraham, but even here they occasionally attempt to show that these pre-Law patriarchs did in fact keep the Law.[16] Furthermore, the prayers and psalms are worshipping or requesting petitions from God, not really a covenant nomist task but occasionally even there, covenant nomism shows through.[17] Through all these different flavors of second Temple Jewish religious expression there is however no alternative route to everlasting life explained except through covenant nomism.

14. I realize that challenges to this view have been marshaled. Probably one of the most formidable challenges was raised by Elliott in his *The Survivors of Israel*. However, the impact of this work on this question is in my opinion significantly diminished because of the highly selective sectarian documents it surveys and admits it surveys (13-26). At this point I believe Sanders and Dunn to be presenting a broader reflection of Judaism of this era. Additionally, Biblical texts like James, Matthew and Acts indicate that Jews and Jewish Christians were zealous for the Law.

15. These texts even have the eschatological aspects which make them a soteriological strategy beyond merely the foundational covenant nomism of Deut and other covenant renewal documents (Exod 20:1–Lev 26:46; Deut as a whole; Josh 24; and in fragmentary ways in the following: 1 Sam 12; 2 Chr 29:6–31:21; 34:13–35:19 [parallel 2 Kgs 22:9–22]; Ezra 9:2–10:44; Neh 9:5–10:34; and the Asaph covenant renewal liturgies of Pss 50 and 81). This kind of covenant extension is commented upon by second Temple sources (*L.A.B.* 23). Bockmuehl agrees with this assessment of the presence of covenant nomism in the Qumran texts mentioned ("1QS and Salvation," 1: 381–414, especially 412 but considers that there is much more evidence since then); cf. Evans, "Covenant in the Qumran," 55–80; Abegg, "The Covenant of the Qumran," 81–98; Cook, "Covenant Nomism," 203–20.

16. *Jub.* 16.20–31; 22.1–9; McNamara agrees that the targums have many themes but that one of them is covenant nomism ("Some Targum Themes," 1:355). Likewise, Bauckham concludes that the apocalypses "broadly coincide with Sanders" in covenant nomism ("Apocalypses," 1: 148, 172, 179, 180). Furthermore, Kugler concludes that the *Testament of the Twelve Patriarchs* support covenant nomism ("Testaments," 1:190).

17. Falk considers the *Pss. Sol.* and the *Pr. Man.* to be covenant nomist texts ("Psalms and Prayers," 1:15, 51); Winninge, *Sinners and the Righteous*, 9–180, esp. 125–136; Edward Cook, "Covenant Nomism," 203–220; Beale, "The Overstated," 93–94.

Furthermore, while covenant nomism is broadly represented from within second Temple Judaism, such early Judaism is not monolithic, and thus the chapter title "Judaisms." For example, some Sadducees criticize Pharisees for not being faithful enough to *torah*.[18] Additionally, some of the Pharisees do not think that the Sadducees are appropriately zealous for *torah* either.[19] Furthermore, some of the sectarian Jews (such as some at Qumran) do not think that the Sadducees and Pharisees are appropriately zealous for the covenant either.[20] In this framework, the less powerful forms of Judaism especially judge the more powerful as inappropriate and thus destined for covenant curse.[21] Additionally, some of these categories, such as Pharisees, have variety within them as evident in the rabbinic debates[22] and unique positions Josephus airs. Furthermore, the *halakah* from Alexandria (such as Philo) or from Elephantine papyri do not often get into the fray of condemning the alternative forms of Judaism but still maintain covenant nomism for daily life.[23] Furthermore, various Jewish groups and their writings defined the *Torah* and the era of expected covenant nomism differently, as Marv Pate summarizes.

> *Sirach, Baruch* and *Psalms of Solomon* equate the Torah exclusively with the law of Moses, believing that it could be obeyed in the present age. *Fourth Esra* and *2 Apocalypse of Baruch* reinterpret the law apocalyptically, relegating Israel's full compliance with it to the age to come. *First Enoch* and DDS redefine

---

18. *m. Yad.* 4.6; *Nahum Commentary* 3:1–4 (col. 2.1–10); *The Fathers According to Rabbi Nathan* A 5; 37.

19. Josephus, *J. W.* 1.5.2; 2.8.14; 2.162–63; *Ant.* 13.10.6; 13.172; 13.288 and 298 indicate their authority among Hasmonean dynasty and people; 17.2.4; 18.12–15, 17 has Sadducees even submitting to Pharisean teaching [cf. *b. Yom.* 19b; *b. Nidd.* 33b]; *Life* 12; 4QMMT C 5–21a indicates the need to separate from those who will be destroyed in judgment; *Yadayim* 3.7; 4.6–7; *Makkot* 1.6; *Niddah* 4.2; perhaps (*Pss. Sol.* 1.8; 2.3; 7.2; 8.12–13; 17.5–8, 23) either here or on the next note from the sectarians Jews dependent on how one interprets 'devout' (*Pss. Sol.* 3.3–7; 4.1, 8; 9.3; 10.6; 13.6–12; 15.6–7).

20. 1QpHab col. 8–12 on the wicked priest; 4QoNah 1.6–7; 2.2, 4; Josephus, *J. W.* 1.97; *Ant.* 13.380.

21. 1QpHab 9.6–7; *T. Lev.* 15.1; *T. Mos.* 6.8–9; Josephus, *Ant.* 18.85–87; *J. W.* 2.161–3; 6.5.3.

22. Prior to 70 A.D. the rulings of the house of Shammai prevailed with usually a more stringent conclusion (80 percent of time) but after 70 A.D. the house of Hillel gained ascendancy, occasionally even being more stringent (20 percent of time) (Tob 4.15a; *y. Ber.* 1.7; *m. Šabb.* 1.4–11; 31a; *m. Miqw.* 4.1; *b. ʿEd.* 5.3; *m. Yad.* 3.5).

23. Philo, *Decal.*; Josephus, *Ant.* 3.5.4–5, 90–92; *m. Tamid* 5.1; *Nash papyrus.*

the Torah in terms of their respective sectarian readings, while Diaspora Judaism emphasizes the moral summary of the law in the hope that Gentiles would thereby be attracted to the God of Israel.[24]

Notice that, herein I am not trying to justify the New Jesus or the New Paul, which of course would need to be warranted within the near contextual analysis of gospels or Pauline texts. I am only attempting to clarify that everything needed for covenant nomism is sufficiently exampled in second Temple Jewish source material.

I do not claim that the extra-biblical material is divinely authoritative or is always stating truth, but I consider it a helpful study to have an accurate historical record of Jewish self-reflection, to frame the context for the biblical texts. To reflect the non-canonical quality of the second Temple sources I place the addresses in the notes, while I usually place the biblical addresses in the text itself.

To develop a view of covenant nomism in the second Temple writings one needs to recognize that some Jews of this era see and express: 1) themselves as elect of God, 2) God's election brings them into covenant, 3) Israel is not trying to get into covenant but is trying to live within covenant, 4) there is a two ways strategy[25] in which Israel maintains its place in covenant blessing by obeying the Law, and 5) this narrow way of virtue righteousness (or appropriate covenantal living) is both a gracious accomplishment by God and a way of life (for which those who are on the narrow way are responsible). Within this narrow way there is covenantal means of atonement providing gracious means of retaining place within the narrow way. Thus, God graciously elects, forgives, and recovers the righteous in the narrow way of salvation. With such grace, covenant nomism would probably best not be described as earning blessing or salvation.

For covenant nomism to be configured as an eschatological soteriology strategy, an additional fact would also be required, namely: for Israel's eschatological condition to be resurrected to the blessed Kingdom, then their lives need to be broadly characterized as righteous. All five of these covenant nomist features, including this soteriological facet are included in: Dan, *The War Scroll* (1QM), *Charter of a Jewish Sectarian Association* (1QS), and the *Damascus Document* (CD). That is, to get a clear

---

24. Pate, *Communities of the Last Days*, 28.
25. Notice only the narrow way brings blessing, the broad way begets destruction.

statement of eschatological judgment and everlasting life one needs to be in the second Temple era of Pharisaic and sectarian Jewish development or at least in its wake. The only O.T. book which contains this perspective is Daniel, with an early clear view concerning personal resurrection within Judaism (Dan 12:2).[26] Furthermore within this Jewish theological era the documents do not provide an alternative approach to everlasting life than that of covenant nomism.

God Graciously Elects and Recovers Israel in Covenant

God's election of Israel to His covenant meant that if Israel obeyed, then God would bring about blessing, hope, and everlasting life. God elects (בְּחִירַי/*bḥîrî*) and binds Israel into the benefits of the Mosaic Covenant for gathering after the Captivity and into the final Kingdom (1 Chr 16:13; Ps 105:6; Isa 43:20; 45:4; 65:9, 22). God initiated this choice of Abraham and his descendants (Israel) in the Abrahamic promise and covenant (Gen 12:1–7; 15:1–21; 17:1–21). Reflective of this Abrahamic Covenant, God initiated Israel's rescue out from Egypt to make them a great nation (Exod 3:2–19:6). Chris VanLandingham claims that the Abrahamic election as "initiated by God does not appear in second temple texts."[27] However contrary to that, biblically and through some second Temple Jewish texts, Yahweh initiated relationship and covenant with Abram on the basis of His choice and promise of blessings (Gen 12:1–3; Mal 1:2–3).[28] This initiating divine choice continues within a Deuteronomist perspective, God initiated the election, revelation and movement of Israel toward the

---

26. Kennard, *Messiah Jesus*, 333–35.

27. VanLandingham, *Judgment & Justification*, 36.

28. Mal 1:2–3 joins the Gen emphasis in identifying God's election as grounded in God's choice to love Jacob. Several second Temple Jewish sources support that God's election is initiated by Him in His choice and grace (1QH 11.11–15; 15.18–20; *T. Mos.* 3.9; 4.5–6; *Pr. Azar.* 11–13; Philo, *Sacr.* 57; 2 *Apoc. Bar.* 48.18–20; 75.5–7; *m. Sanh.* 10.1). In contrast, a number of second Temple Jewish texts identify God's choice of Abraham is because he is righteous in the narrow way (1 *En.* 89.10–12; CD 3.1–4). The extension of the Abrahamic Covenant is in some second Temple Jewish texts identified by Isaac and Jacob being righteous, while Ishmael and Esau are not (Philo, *Sobr.* 8–9; *Sacr.* 17–18; *Virt.* 208–11; *Rewards* 59; L.A.B. 32.5 quoting Mal 1:2–3), whereas Genesis emphasizes these choices as initiating with God (Gen 17:19; 25:23), and 2 Macc 1.2 combine both sentiments together. Bird, "Salvation in Paul's Judaism?," 16.

Promised Land (Deut 1:6–8).[29] It is the Great King Yahweh Who imposes His covenant upon His vassal Israel.

Such covenant making is another level of God's election of Israel exclusively. Israel elected in Mosaic Covenant is created by God to be a holy nation, thus requiring them to live in a separate manner (Exod 19:6; Lev 11:44; Deut 4:6–8). So second Temple sources exhort Israel to reside with the geography, mindset and practice of Israel in covenant.[30] As such, *Pseudo-Philo* describes the Mosaic Covenant to be "the laws of our race."[31]

Within this perspective, Moses calls Israel to obey the Law and if Israel obeyed they would be wonderfully blessed (Deut 28:1–14), whereas if Israel does not comply with the Law then they will be horribly cursed (Deut 28:15–29:28).[32] If Israel repents and complies with the Law then God will graciously bless Israel within the covenant blessing again (Deut 30:2–10).[33] Friedrich Avemarie and Philip Alexander claim that salvation in the rabbinics is either by Law or grace because both themes are present there to be emphasized at different times.[34] I think that some of the rabbinic texts could be read as more synergistically affirming both Law and grace simultaneously, and some of the grace texts more deterministically. Notice, these themes do not need to be mutually exclusive since the provision of the Mosaic Covenant is both gracious and obligates Israel in Law, as was developed within Deuteronomy above. I think that a synergism of graciously funded rigorism is especially the case among Qumran texts where responsibility within determinism is more an emphasis. In fact, these Jewish sources teach both Law and grace in a synergism of grace and works that affirms both without mutually excluding either. This recognition that God had elected Israel into covenant and that in their disobedience He brought captivity and curse is expressed by Daniel (Dan 9:2–4; 11:28–32). Likewise Daniel recognizes that the prophecy of Jeremiah places limits on this Babylonian captivity curse to seventy years (Jer 25:11–12; 29:10) and he prays to the covenant-keeping God for a gracious recovery.

---

29. Echoed in Bar 2.35 and 4Q504-506 3.4–7.

30. Sir 24.8, 23; Bar 3.36–4.4; *L.A.B.* 12.2, 4.

31. *L.A.B.* 12.2; 9.13, 15; Sir 24.23.

32. A number of second Temple Jewish documents echo this Deuteronomistic perspective especially 1Q22; *T. Mos.* 1–2; *Jub.* 1.5–6.

33. *Esth. Rab.* 11.1.11; 1Q22; *T. Mos.* 1–2; *Jub.* 1.5–6.

34. Avemarie, *Torah und Leben*; "Bund," 176–224; "Erwählung," 108–26; Alexander, "Torah and Salvation," 1: 273.

> Alas, O Lord, the great and awesome God, who keeps His covenant and lovingkindness for those who love Him and keep His commandments, we have sinned, committed iniquity, acted wickedly, and rebelled, even turning aside from Thy commandments and ordinances ... O Lord our God, who hast brought Thy people out of the land of Egypt with a mighty hand and hast made a name for Thyself, as it is this day-we have sinned, we have been wicked. O Lord, in accordance with all Thy righteous acts, let now Thine anger and Thy wrath turn away from Thy city Jerusalem ... O my God, incline Thine ear and hear! Open Thine eyes and see our desolations and the city which is called by Thy name; for we are not presenting our supplications before Thee on account of any merits of our own, but on account of Thy great compassion. O Lord hear! O Lord forgive! O Lord listen and take action! For Thine own sake, O my God, do not delay, because Thy city and Thy people are called by Thy name (Dan 9:4-19).

Such a gracious theme of election into covenant and recovery is broadly supported from both Scripture as well as sectarian Jewish writings. The fact that such a view is not limited to a particular Jewish community underscores the likelihood that Israel in general thought of themselves as graciously in covenant with God. This possibility of gracious blessing fosters hope.[35] For example, *Jubilees* sees *torah* as an everlasting Law obeyed by both angels and patriarchs before Moses receives it.[36] Then Yahweh generously extends His election choice to include Israel through the Mosaic Covenant, binding them into a covenant nomist relationship of obedience and blessing. In contrast, Chris VanLandingham claims that "Post-biblical Jewish literature introduces the idea that God has chosen Israel because of its merit."[37] VanLandingham's view is challenged by the gracious two ways passage of the *Charter of a Jewish Sectarian Association*, namely "God has chosen them for an everlasting covenant; all the glory of Adam shall be theirs alone."[38] Additionally, VanLandingham's view is further challenged by Philo, and *The Damascus Document*, and

---

35. Sanders, *Jesus and Judaism*, 335–36; 2 Bar. 14.12.

36. *Jub.* 15.25–34.

37. Van Landingham, *Judgment & Justification*, 43; he claims these support his point: 1QM 10.9–11; Philo, *Prelim. Studies* 51; L.A.B. 11.1; 2 Bar. 48.20; Pss. Sol. 9.8–10; however these texts might be better understood in later recognizing the chosen rather than being the basis of God's choice, as in 1QpHab 5.5.

38. *Charter of a Jewish Sectarian Association* (1QS; 4Q255–264a; 5Q11) 3–4; 4.22–23.

other documents which see God's choice of Israel based upon Abraham's previous righteousness and God's faithfulness to this previous promise.[39] Additionally, 1QM 10.9–11 does not justify God's election as responding to Israel's righteousness but as grounding their privilege. Even if the covenant is made with the righteous among Israel, God is the One Who makes it a covenant and guarantees it forever (especially for subsequent generations).[40]

Thus for Qumran, God's election of Israel graciously grounds Israel's recovery in the Mosaic Covenant. For example, both a remnant and Israel's recovery are guaranteed in the Mosaic Covenant; "When He [God] remembered the covenant of the forefathers, He left a remnant to Israel and did not allow them to be totally destroyed."[41] The remnant which God graciously rescues is a participant and beneficiary in the Mosaic Covenant (though this probably subsumes the Abrahamic Covenant too); "Because God loved the ancients who bore witness following him, so too He loves those who follow them, for such truly belongs the covenant of the fathers."[42]

In Qumran manuscripts the term "covenant" (בְּחִירָי/bḥîrî) identifies a covenant that may be more penetrating than the Mosaic Covenant but is centered on the Mosaic Covenant with obligations that they need to obey, once they are within the covenant.[43] God rescues Israel from their disobedient condition and the *Charter of a Jewish Sectarian Association* identifies that God will "induct all who volunteer to live by the laws of God into a Covenant of Mercy, so as to be joined to God's society and walk faultless before Him, according to all that He has revealed for the times appointed them."[44] The act of obedience does not include Israel

---

39. CD 3.1–4; Philo, *Spec.* 4.180–81; *T. Reu.* 15.1–4; *T. Ash.* 7.7; L.A.B. 35.3b.

40. CD 3.12–13; 7.5–6, especially Geniza B.

41. CD 1.4; 3.10; 4.9; 6.2; 4Q267 frag. 2, line 7; 4Q268 frag. 1, line 12; 4Q269 frag. 2, line 5; and perhaps 4Q512 1–6 xii 12; Abegg, "The Covenant of the Qumran," 81–98, especially 83.

42. CD 8.16b–18; 19.31; 1QM 13.7; 14.8; 4Q385 16 i 9.

43. 1QS 1.16–17; 5.1–3, 7–8, 20; 10.10; CD 15.5–6.5, especially Geniza A; 1QpHab. 1.11; 1Q22 1–2; *Charter for Israel in the Last Days* (1QSa; 1Q28a, 4Q249a-i) 1.11; 4Q280 frag. 25-6; 4Q398 frags. 11–13 with 4Q397 frags. 14–21 and 4Q397 frag. 22 verses 17–18, 23–25; 4Q525 frag. 2–3 2.4; *Apocryphal Psalms of David* (11Q5–6; 4Q88; 4Q448) psalm 154.12 and psalm 155 col. 24.8; *The Temple Scroll* (11Q19–21; 4Q524; 4Q365a) 59; *Apoc. El.* 1.13.

44. *Charter of a Jewish Sectarian Association* (1QS; 4Q255–264a; 5Q11) 1.7–9; CD 3.9–10 identifies God initiates His covenant with Israel so that He will atone for their sins.

in covenant, but rather a divinely initiated oath of allegiance to God includes them in covenant, but covenant does require obedience for those within covenant.[45] More deeply, *The War Scroll* identifies that covenant is ultimately grounded by God keeping it throughout Israel's generations.[46] As such, God's covenant is everlasting and grounds the Mosaic Covenant priesthood.[47] Yet even beneath this covenant, it is God Who graciously opens the salvation and peace for His people because God is righteous and He accomplishes this covenant restitution for His own honor.[48] Pseudo-Philo also expresses a hope to God for covenant blessing based upon God's gracious character and covenant oath, "The Lord will take pity on you today, not because of you but because of His covenant that He established with your fathers and the oath that He has sworn not to abandon you forever."[49] Such sentiment motivates prayers to God for His gracious and merciful salvation. One example is the *Prayer of Azariah*.

> For your name's sake do not give us up forever.
> And do not annul your covenant.
> Do not withdraw your mercy from us,
> For the sake of your servant Isaac and Israel your holy one,
> To whom you promised to multiply their descendants like the stars of heaven.[50]

Such prayers are answered by thankfulness to God. For example, there is such gratitude in the *War Scroll*.

> Blessed is Your name, O God [of god]s, for You have done wondrous things for Your people, and have kept Your covenant for us from of old. Many times You have opened the gates of salvation for us for the sak[e of] Your covenant. [And You provided f]or our affliction in accord with Your goodness toward us. You, O God of righteousness, have acted for the sake of Your name.[51]

---

45. *Charter of a Jewish Sectarian Association* (1QS; 4Q255-264a; 5Q11) 1.16-17; 5.1-3, 7-8, 20; 10.10; CD 15.5-10.

46. *The War Scroll* col. 14, verse 8-9; 1QM frag. 11 col. 2, ver. 18.

47. *Pss. Sol.* 10.4; *Jub.* 1.4-5; 1 Macc 1.57; *The War Scroll* col. 17, ver. 3; col. 18, ver. 7; *L.A.B.* 11.5.

48. *The War Scroll* col. 18, ver. 8-9; 1QM frag. 11 col. 2, ver. 18; Philo, *Somn.* 2.237.

49. *L.A.B.* 30.7.

50. *Pr. Azar.* 11-13; similar in *2 Bar.* 14.6 and *Prayer of Manassah*, which Falk considers is a covenant nomist text ("Psalms and Prayers," 1:15).

51. *The War Scroll* (1QM, 4Q491-496) 18.6-9.

E. P. Sanders develops that the Rabbinic material and religion was covenantally gracious and grounded in God's election of the people.

> The Rabbinic religion was framed by election at one end and a share in the world to come at the other. All those who remained within the covenant partook of the covenant promises. As we have repeatedly pointed out, the Rabbis never doubted God's fidelity to the covenant. What they dealt with was how man could best be faithful.[52]

G. F. Moore summarizes this gracious salvation emphasis within Judaism.

> "A lot in the World to Come," which is the nearest approximation in rabbinical Judaism to the Pauline and Christian idea of salvation, or eternal life, is ultimately assured to every Israelite on the ground of the original election of the people by the free grace of God, prompted not by its merits, collective or individual, but solely by God's love, a love that began with the Fathers . . . "A lot in the World to Come" is not wages earned by works, but is bestowed by God in pure goodness upon the members of his chosen people.[53]

Moore, again citing Pharisee Antigonus of Socho's famous exhortation not to work for a reward, concludes that "there is a certain irony in the fact that the first recorded word of a Pharisee should be repudiation of the supposed 'Pharisaic' wage-theory of righteousness."[54] Moore's statements are accurate to the second Temple Jewish sources but probably framed with some slant so as to not cross the Pauline material or possibly Paul himself reflects this gracious Pharisaic emphasis against a minority view evident in some second Temple documents. I think that blessing and salvation in second Temple Judaism are more gracious than Moore portrays, with the divine initiative and guarantee with God. For example, Qumran documents indicate this divine gracious initiative: "By Thy goodness alone is man righteous;"[55] "Thou will pardon iniquity and through Thy righteousness You will purify humans of sin."[56] God gra-

---

52. Sanders, *Paul and Palestinian Judaism*, 177.
53. Moore, *Judaism in the First Centuries*, 2:94–95.
54. Moore, *Judaism in the First Centuries*, 2:96.
55. 1QH 13.16–17.
56. *Jub*. 22.14; *Ps. Sol*. 13.10; *4 Ezra* 7.138–40; 1QH 4.37; 7.18–19; 16.11; 1QS 10.11; 11.2–3, 10–15; 4Q417 frag. 2 1.15; 11QS 14–15; Prayer for Deliverance 14[11Q5

ciously forgives and cleanses sin.[57] In spite of the stiff demand for Israel's obedience, God makes room for mercy.[58]

Such divine sourcing of the cleansed life sets up a synergism of Jewish free-will (even among the deterministic Essenes and certainly also among the libertarian Pharisees) with this divine work in the believer such that righteous deeds indicate both gratitude to God within covenant as well as an allegiance to God indicative of one who is Kingdom bound.[59] In second Temple Judaism, righteousness is not a "getting in" earning, nor is it a "staying in" but rather it is *an identification of those who graciously remain in unto Kingdom inclusion*. Or as N. T. Wright concludes, "the real Judaism" was "based on a clear understanding of grace," and that "good works" were meant to express this "gratitude and demonstrate that one is faithful to the covenant."[60] Part of the reason the demonstration of Israel's faithfulness to covenant unto Kingdom does not earn place in second Temple Judaism is that it is a God-initiated framework placing Himself under obligation to save those who comply with His covenant which was initiated by Him, as Moore concludes.

> The reflection may be made that man's good deeds do not of themselves lay God under obligation; God does not *owe* him a recompense for doing his duty. But God has put himself under obligation by his promise of reward, and in this sense man, in doing what God requires of him, deserves the recompense.[61]

Additionally, though the righteous live virtuously in the narrow way, Israelites still need forgiveness up until the Last Judgment, when God will also graciously forgive them.[62] Furthermore, the Divine Spirit will expiate the righteous person in covenant in this life from his iniquity into an enlightened pure living of the narrow way, which utilizes New Covenant terminology to describe life transformation (Deut 30:6; Jer

---

57. Sir 2.11, 30–31; 16.116; 18.12; 23.10; *Pr. Man.* 13; *Pss. Sol.* 9.6–7; *Jub.* 5.17; 22.14; *4 Ezra* 7.139; 4Q504 frag. 4 7; prayers for deliverance 13[11Q5 19.13]; 14[11Q5 19.14].

58. Sir 16.14; 18.11–12; 1QS 11.12.

59. 1QH 1.36 with the previous notes; 1QS 5.7–10; CD 15.8–9, 12 (=4Q266 17 i 3); 16.1–2, 5(=4Q271 2 ii 3–4); 19.33–20.10; Bowley, "Moses," 159–81; Smith, *What Must I do to be Saved?*, 4–72.

60. Wright, "The Paul of History," 61–88, especially 79–80.

61. Moore, *Judaism in the First Centuries*, 2:90; McGrath, *Iustia Dei*, 1:112.

62. CD 20.27–34 ms B; 1QS 4.18–23; 11.9–11; 1QHa 12.29–30.

31:33).⁶³ Here, the Divine acceptance is based on the covenant and the atonement which God graciously provides to cleanse and transform the community and its persons.

In second Temple Judaism the Mosaic Covenant framework is an everlasting economy for Israel. For example, *Baruch* declares *torah* is forever and thus requires continuous compliance by Israel.

> She is the book of the commandments of God
> And the Law which stands forever.
> All who cling to her will live,
> But those who forsake her will die.⁶⁴

Covenant Nomism Entails a Two Ways Strategy

The Mosaic Covenant is perceived in second Temple Judaism to develop a two ways strategy.⁶⁵ In such a view there is only one narrow righteous way for blessing and Kingdom, while the broad way leads to curse and destruction.⁶⁶

While most Jewish second Temple documents that address sin do so from the angle of personal responsibility, a few do so to explain why evil persists. For example, *2 Baruch* and *4 Ezra* bemoan that Adam has fallen into sin in a manner that burdens all humanity "with an evil heart" and

---

63. *Charter of a Jewish Sectarian Association* (1QS, 4Q255-264a and 5Q11) 3.7-12; 4.22-23; 5.5; *Damascus Document* (CD 4Q268 frag. 1=4Q266 frag. 2 Col. 1) ver. 6; 14.1-2; B col. 19, ver. 12-13 here the New Covenant is clearly still Law like Jer 31:33 Hebrew; 1QpHab 2.3; 11.13 "circumcision of heart's foreskin."

64. Bar 4.1; Sir 1.26; 2.15-16; *T. Iss.* 5.1; cf. rabbi Joseph in BT *Nidah* 616; Maimonides ninth of thirteen principles of Judaism *Commentary on the Mishnah, Nissan*, b. Moses, *Ma'aseh Nisim*, 159-60.

65. *Jub.* 20.6-10; 21.21-24; 30.21-22; *1 En.* 94.1-5; 98.6-8; *Charter of a Jewish Sectarian Association* (1QS; 4Q255-264a; 5Q11)1.9-10; 2.11-17; 3-4; 4.20-22; 5.22; 8.22; 4Q228; 4Q473 frag. 2; 4Q176 frags. 12-13 16, frags. 10+11+7+9+20+26 verse 7; 4Q504 3.4-13; 4Q548 frag. 1 2.2-16; Philo, *Post.* 1.67-68 obedience identifies good; *2 Bar.* 85.12-15; *Sib. Or.* 8.399-401; *T. Ash.* 1-7 in *T. 12 Patr.*; *T. Ab.* 11; these are similar to Matt 7:7; 13:43; 25:46.

66. *Jub.* 1.15-16, 20, 22-25; 5.11, 15; Sir 11.26; 16.12, 14; 17.23; *1 En.* 95.5; 100.7; *Pss. Sol.* 2.7, 16, 25, 34-35; 17.8-9; *Jos. Asen.* 28.3; Philo, *Spec.* 4.164; *L.A.B.* 3.10; 44.10; 64.7; *2 Bar.* 54.21; 1QS 2.7-8, 11-14; 10.11, 17-18; 1QH 4.18-19, 31-32; 5.5-6; 14.24; 1QM 6.6; 11.3-4, 13-14; 18.14; CD 3.4-5; 5.15-16; 7.9; 19.6; 20.24; 1QpHab. 12.2-3; 4QpPs37 4.9; 4Q266 18.6 (=4Q270 11 I 19-20) exclude disobedient from people of God; Josephus, *Ant.* 10.138; *J. W.* 1.378; Gathercole, "Torah, Life," 126-139.

with consequences of death.[67] Such an original and universal sin leaves all humans with a tendency to do sins,[68] but the choice to do those sins even in these contexts is still the choice of the human agent, and thus humans are responsible for our own sins.[69]

In this condition, there is acknowledgement that no human is righteous as God is righteous,[70] nevertheless God's people are called to be righteous as God is righteous.[71] That is, God graciously conferred the status of righteousness in atonement onto community members.[72] For example, Anderson Das says, "The righteous were typically sinners who availed themselves of God's mercy and election even while falling short."[73] This means that there is no contradiction with the same hymns declaring humans to be both *unworthy* and *righteous* (as a member of the covenant community).[74] With regard to the *Pss. Sol.*, Franklyn describes the godly as "not free from sin, but are sinfully pious, unrighteously righteous. Their opponents are the sinners."[75] Bruce Longenecker describes it as follows, "The antithetical status of these two groups (viz. the righteous and the sinners) is wholly determined by whether or not one is, and intends to remain, a member of the covenant community, for common to both groups is sin, but restricted to the covenant community is the grace of God which is efficacious for the repentant members of that community who seek his forgiveness."[76] A dedication on the wall of an ancient synagogue identifies the stated purpose of synagogue as about reading the Law, teaching the commandments and hosting those who need the

---

67. 2 Bar. 54.15, 19; 4 Ezra 7.118; 3.21.

68. 2 Bar. 54.15, 19; 4 Ezra 4.35–38; 7.118; 3.20–21.

69. 2 Bar. 54.19; 4 Ezra 3.20; 7.72, 119-26; 1QS 11.9–10.

70. 11Q5 24.7; 1QH 1.25–27;7.28–29; 8.19; 9.14–17; 10.3–12; 12.19, 24–31; 15.28; 17.14–15; 11QPs 155.8; 1QS 11.9–11; *Pss. Sol.* 3.5,9; 9.7; *L.A.B.* 12; 13.9; 26.14; 19.9–10, 44; Philo, *Mos.* 2.147.

71. *Sifre Deut.* 49.

72. Das, *Paul and the Jews*, 147; 1QHa 19[=11].29–32; 1QS 2.25–3.9; 11:12.

73. Das, *Paul and the Jews*, 147.

74. Hymn 1 1.22, 25–27 with 1.36; Hymn 5 3.23–25 with 3.19–23; Hymn 7 4.29–30 with 4.31–33 1nd 4.35–37; Hymn 11 7.16–17 with 7.17–25; Hymn 12 7.28–29 with 7.29–31; Hymn 14 9.14–16 with 9.12–14; Hymn 17 11.3 with 11.9–12; Hymn 18 11.20 with 11.17–18 and 11.29–32; Hymn 19 12.19, 24–31 with 12.20–23, 32; Hymn 20 13.13–16 with 13.16–19; Hymn 25 alternating in 17.26–18.30; Vermes, *The Dead Sea Scrolls*; Longenecker, *Eschatology and the Covenant*, 26.

75. Franklyn, "The Cultic and the Pious," 8; *Ezra* 6.32; 7.60, 92.

76. Longenecker, *Eschatology and the Covenant*, 27.

mikvot and are in need.⁷⁷ So the community expression of Judaism is all about keeping and being recovered in the Law.⁷⁸ E. P. Sanders describes what is meant by the faithful righteous life in covenant.

> Man's faithfulness to the covenant, negatively, is not renouncing it, not treating the decrees of God as of no effect, not scorning the law and not treating his brother in such a way as to show that in fact he has no respect for God who commanded love of the neighbor. Positively, it is doing one's best to obey the commandments and doing what is appropriate in case of failure. "Doing what is appropriate" always involves repentance, for the unrepentant person does not take steps to redress his disobedience. "What is appropriate" may include the bringing of a sacrifice, making restitution and other obvious acts of contrition. After the destruction of the Temple, repentance was substituted for all the sacrifices prescribed in the law, although the Day of Atonement maintained a special place in Jewish life. Ultimately, what is required is that one intends to remain in the covenant, intends to be obedient.⁷⁹

This righteous way is described by the *Sibylline Oracles* and other second Temple texts as those "concerned with righteousness and fine deeds, piety and righteous thoughts."⁸⁰ Occasionally, such righteousness is identified as grounded upon other virtues, namely: fearing God,⁸¹

---

77. Theodotus dedication on synagogue wall found in Jerusalem in 1914; Strange, "Synagogue," 614.
78. LXX addition Dan 3:34; *Pr. Azar.* 1.11.
79. Sanders, *Paul and Palestinian Judaism*, 176.
80. *Sib. Or.* 2.313-14; *1 En.* 1.8.
81. *Pss. Sol.* 2.33-34; 13:11-12.

loving God,[82] faithfulness,[83] maturity/perfection,[84] serving God,[85] and walking honestly.[86] Individuals of such piety are identified with this label of being "righteous."[87] Solomon Schechter defends that the rabbinics were joyfully optimistic that a Jew in such circumstances could obey the Law.[88] Such human obedience to the Law gives life (Deut 30:14, 17; Lev 18:5; Ezek 33:16; Neh 9:29).[89]

This optimism developed a synergism of God graciously enabling the Jew to obey the Law.[90] That is, second Temple Jewish literature strongly develops God's grace as effectively transforming the Israelite to righteous living.[91] The divine initiation and determinism is especially ap-

82. *Pss. Sol.* 10.3; *Sifre Deut.* 10.

83. 4Q521 2.2. 5–6.

84. CD 1.20–21; 2:15; Philo, *Migr.* 127–130; *Abr.* 275–76; *Her.* 6–9; however Das ("Beyond Covenantal Nomism," 237) overplays his case for perfection, since several of his texts actually support that the Lord's way is perfect rather than the believer must be perfect (1QS 1:13). Furthermore, this misrepresents Sanders (Das, 237; Sanders, *Paul and Palestinian Judaism*, 288–90) who argues for a gracious accomplishment, which view Das correctly acknowledges but considers contradictory. Instead the gracious perfection that Sanders claims fits better with the admission of sin that Sanders and Das admit and is itself contradictory to only Das' view, and thus motivating Das' rejection of the straw man view. Thus Das ignores some second Temple texts as impossible. However, I appreciate Das' appeal to maintain tension on these areas (Das, 238) and the recognition that Noah's "perfection" is qualified "relative to his generation" (240; Philo, *Deus* 117, 122, 140; *Abr.* 34, 36–39, 47).

85. CD 20.20–21.

86. 4Q184 1.14–15.

87. 4Q378 3 ii 5, 26 1–3; *Sifre Deut.* 1.

88. Schechter, *Aspects of Rabbinic Theology*, 149–69; Philo uses Deut 30:10–14 to indicate that the Law can be lived (*Post.* 84–85; *Virt.* 183; *Mut.* 236–37; *Somn.* 2.180; *Good Person* 68; *Praem.* 79–80); *L.A.B.* 11.2; *Tob* 3.5; *4 Ezra* 7.19–25.

89. Sprinkle, *Law and Life*; Sir 45.5; 4 Ezra 14.22, 30; Bar 4.1; *Pss. Sol.* 14.2–3; Philo, *De Congr.* 86–87; 4Q 266; CD 3.15–16; 4Q 504 frag. 6 2.17.

90. Philo, *Post.* 84–85; *Virt.* 183; *Mut.* 236–37; *Somn.* 2.180; *Good Person* 68; *Praem.* 79–80; *L.A.B.* 11.2; *Tob* 3.5; *4 Ezra* 7.19–25; Yinger, "The Continuing Quest," 385; Laato (*Paul and Judaism*) over presses this optimistic case; likewise, Thielman over presses Jewish pessimism (*From Plight to Solution*, 28). Morton suggests that Paul's pessimism emerges from a pessimism in Jewish apocalyptic (4 Ezra and 1QM) while granting generally rabbinic optimism ("Review of *Paulus*," 375–77); Sprinkle, *Law and Life*. While not pretending to know the origin of Paul's ideas, I think that multiple genres of second Temple Judaism hold these issues in tension, pessimistically confessing sin in dispersion and optimistically advocating obedience to Torah.

91. *Pss. Sol.* 2.33–35; 10.4; 11QPs 155.20–21; *Pr. Man.* 13–14; *Jos. Asen.* 10–13; *L.A.B.* 11.1, 6; 13.10; 14.2; 18.10; 19.8–11; 21.4, 9; 22.5–7; 23.4–14; 28.4–5.

parent among Qumran. For example, this two ways view is presented by the *Charter of a Jewish Sectarian Association* rooted and enabled by two spirits. In this presentation the way of light is gracious, reflecting a New Covenant transformation empowered by God's Spirit.

> God created humankind to rule over the world, appointing for them two spirits in which to walk until the time ordained for His visitation. These are the spirits of truth and falsehood. Upright character and fate originate with the habitation of Light; perverse, with the fountain of Darkness. The authority of the Prince of Light extends to the governance of all righteous people; therefore, they walk in the paths of light. Correspondingly, the authority of the Angel of Darkness embraces the governance of all wicked people, so they walk in the paths of darkness . . . Yet the God of Israel (and the Angel of His Truth) assist all the Sons of Light. It is actually He who created the spirits of light and darkness, making them the very cornerstone of every deed, their impulses the premise of every action. God's love for one spirit lasts forever. He will be pleased with its actions for always. The counsel of the other, however, He abhors, hating its every impulse for all time.[92]

Thus, for some second Temple texts there is a synergism of divine direction and enablement with human responsibility and free will. Elsewhere second Temple Judaism often presents this two-ways strategy with a strong call on responsibility and a divine judgment according to deeds (1 Kg 8:32; Ps 28:4; Ezek 7:4; Jer 16:18; 17:10; Hos 4:9).[93] For example, several of the pseudonymous psalms develop this two ways strategy clearly.

> To distinguish between the righteous and the sinner,
> To recompense sinners forever according to their deeds.
> To have mercy on the righteous, delivering him from affliction
>   from the sinner,
> And to recompense the sinner for what he has done to the
>   righteous.

---

92. *Charter of a Jewish Sectarian Association* (1QS; 4Q255–264a; 5Q11) 3.15–4.1; *The War Scroll* (1QM, 4Q491–496) 1.1–20; 16.11; 4Q548 frag. 1 col. 2 9–16; 11Q13 22–25; 1QH 1.21–23; 4.31–32; 7. 6–7, 14; 13.16–17; 14.25–26; 15.13.

93. *Jub.* 5.11, 15; *1 En.* 95.5; 100.7; *Pss. Sol.* 2.7, 7, 16, 25, 34–35; 17.8–9; *Jos. Asen.* 28.3; *L.A.B.* 3.10; 44.10; 64.7; *2 Bar.* 54.21; 1QS 2.7–8; 5.10–13, 18–19; 1QX 10.11, 17–18; 1QH 4.18–19; 5.5–6; 14.24; 1QM 1.2; 11.3–4; 18.14; CD 1.16–18; 3.4–5, 10–11; 5.15–16; 7.9; 8.1; 20.24; 1QpHab 12.2–3; 4QpPs 37.4–9; 4Q 463 1 1; 4Q387 3 6–8; *Sifra Beḥukotai, pereq* 6.1; *Mekh. Yito* 10; Yinger. *Paul, Judaism*, 285 summary but argued through the book; Shiffman, *Qumran and Jerusalem*, 237–50.

> For the Lord is good to those who call on him in patience,
> Acting according to his mercy towards his holy ones.[94]

> Know today that if you proceed in the ways of your God, your paths will be made straight. But if you do not heed his voice and you become like your fathers, your affairs will be spoiled and you yourselves will be crushed and your name will perish from the earth.[95]

Rabbi Akiva developed that the consequences for each way might not be so clear in this life but in the world to come they would be definitive, because God deals strictly with all.

> He deals strictly with both [righteous and wicked], even to the great deep. He deals strictly with the righteous, calling them to account for the few wrongs which they commit in this world, in order to lavish bliss upon and give them a goodly reward in the world to come; He grants ease to the wicked and rewards them for the few good deeds which they have performed in this world in order to punish them in the future world.[96]

Unfortunately, Israel did not always keep the narrow way of the Mosaic Covenant. Within this pessimistic recognition, *4 Ezra* calls Israel to optimistic faithfulness in God's gracious sowing of the everlasting Mosaic Law into Israel.

> "Hear me, O Israel, and give heed to my words, O descendants of Jacob. For behold, I sow my Law in you and you shall be glorified through it forever." But though our fathers received the Law, they did not keep it, and did not observe the statutes; yet the fruit of the Law did not perish-for it could not, because it was yours ... For we who received the Law and sinned will perish, as well as our heart which received it; the Law, however, does not perish but remains in its glory.[97]

This optimistic narrow way purifying of Judaism is consistent with the Mosaic Covenant that God made with Israel, especially from the perspective of the Mosaic Covenant as a Suzerainty treaty binding Israel in a covenant relationship that offers blessing or curse dependent upon their

---

94. *Pss. Sol.* 2.34–36; cf. 9.3–4.
95. *L.A.B.* 20.3; similar to *Sib. Or.* 8.399–401; *T. Ash.* 1–7 in *T. 12 Patr.*; *T. Ab.* 11.
96. *Gen Rab.* 33.1; parallel in *Lev. Rab.* 27.1; *Sifre Deut.* 53 has a similar but anonymous saying.
97. *4 Ezra* 9.30–37; *T. Iss.* 5.1.

obedience.[98] In this, Israel is already blessed in a covenant relationship with Yahweh. This relationship is expressed as coming from the exodus and heading toward the Promised Land and the Kingdom. Furthermore, if Israel obeyed all the Law then they would be wonderfully blessed, enabling Kingdom to come (Deut 28:1–14; 30:8–20).[99] However, if Israel disobeyed then they will be horribly cursed (Deut 28:15–30:20). This sets up a narrow way of blessing and a broad way of wrath. The prophets call Israel back from their wandering ways to the narrow way of covenant faithfulness (1 Kgs 19:10; Jer 21:8; Ezek 9:8–10).

However, these two ways are also evident in the wisdom tradition, for wisdom optimistically calls the wise to follow in a narrow way, fitting into the patterns of creation, in contrast to the many broad ways of the fool that lead to destruction. In this approach, wisdom is vindicated in people showing consistency to the narrow way of the wise, in contrast to the broad way of the fool (Prov 28:6; Matt 7:24–27; 11:19: Luke 7:35).

These revelational approaches, covenant and wisdom, have come together through a two ways expression in the wisdom and torah psalms (Pss 1:6; 119:29–32; 139:24). This two ways orientation is embraced even more in sectarian purifying Early Judaism Qumran and the Essenes.[100] In this Deuteronomist approach, Israel continuing to be dominated by Gentile powers spotlights that Israel repeatedly chose the way of disobedience (Deut 9:7; 28:15–30:20; 2 Kgs 17:23; Neh 9:32; Isa 9:1–2; Ezek 21:3; 20:31; Mic 5:3–4).[101]

E. P. Sanders describes that Rabbinic Judaism shows its commitment to God and covenant by desiring to remain in the covenant through covenant nomism. That is, Israel does not earn their place but reflects

---

98. Mendenhall, "Covenant Forms," 50–76; Baltzer, *Das Bundesformular*; Kline, *Treaty of the Great King*.

99. Echoed in second Temple texts such as 1QpHab 5.3.

100. Sir 2.12; 15.11–17; 21:10–14; Wis 5.6–7 2 Esd. 7:6–14; 30.15; 42.10; *Pss. Sol.* 4.8; 9.5; 13.6–12; 14.10; 1 Macc 1.34; 2.44, 48; 3 Macc 5.51; *1 En.* 5.4–7; 82. 4–5; *2 Bar.* 59.10; 85.13; *4 Ezra* 7.3–9, 48, 82, 129, 137; *Sib. Or.* 2.150; 1QH 10[=2].8–12; 1QpHab 5.4–8; *b. Ber.* 28b; *m'Abot* 2.9; Philo, *Sacr. AC* 2; *Agr.* 103–104; *ARN* 14, 18, 25; *T. Ash.* 1:3, 5; 6.3; *T. Jac.* 2.17; *Pesq. R.* 179b; *t. Sota* 7.11; *t. Sanh.* 14.4; *b. Hag.* 3b; *b. 'Erub.* 19a; *Mek.* on Exod 14:28; *Sipre* on Deut 11:26; 1QS 3:13–4.26; *Apoc. Zeph.* 3.9. The early church continued in this two ways teaching: *Did.* 1–6; *Barn.* 18–20; *Herm. m.* 6, *s.* 9.12.5; *Ps.-Clem. Hom.* 3.52.2; 5.7; *T. Ab.* 10–11; *Apos. Const.* 1–5; Kennard, "The Two Ways;" Wright, *Jesus and the Victory of God*, 313–314.

101. 1 Esd 8.73–74; 2 Esd 9.7; Bar 1.13, 18–19; 2.6.

God's *gracious* election, and therefore legalism is an inappropriate critique, as Sanders develops.

> The overall pattern of Rabbinic religion as it applied to Israelites (proselytes and righteous Gentiles . . .) is this: God has chosen Israel and Israel has accepted the election. In his role as King, God gave Israel commandments which they are to obey as best they can. Obedience is rewarded and disobedience punished. In case of failure to obey, however, man has recourse to divinely ordained means of atonement, in all of which repentance is required. As long as he maintains his desire to stay in the covenant, he has a share in God's effort to be obedient constitute the *condition for remaining in the covenant*, but they do not *earn* it . . . Only by overlooking this large pattern can the Rabbis be made to appear as legalists in the narrow and perjorative sense of the word. Their legalism falls within a larger context of gracious election and assured salvation. In discussing disobedience and obedience, punishment and reward, they were not dealing with how man is saved, but with how man should act and how God will act within the framework of the covenant. Within that framework, they were determined to understand and obey God's commands as best they could, but they did not think that they earned their place in the covenant by the number of *mitsvot* fulfilled. Nor did they think that the transgression of more commandments than were fulfilled would damn them. They may have made such statements, as they could also say that transgression of *one* commandment would damn, but homiletical exhortation should not be confused with basic belief. As long as a man intended to remain in covenant, and indicated his intention by true repentance, God did not reckon the precise number of commandments fulfilled or transgressed. If God judged strictly, no man would live. Not even the patriarchs could stand God's reproof if he judged strictly.[102]

So salvation is graciously given by God but conditionally evidenced in the believer's life by obedience, like an Edwardsian religious affection.[103]

---

102. Sanders, *Paul and Palestinian Judaism*, pp. 180–81; Sanders cites these rabbis for support: Rabbi Eliezer in a baraita, *Arakin* 17a top, and *Gen. Rab.* 12.15; 39.6; cf. *Pss. Sol.* 2.33–35; Dunn, "The New Perspective," 95–122; *Jesus, Paul, and the Law*, 183–214; Eskola, "Paul, Predestination," 392–94. I think that the Lutheran response (Caird, "Paul and Palestinian Judaism," 542; Gundry, "Grace, Works," 11, 35) is too critical of Sanders and Dunn at this point in their Lutheran loyalty to traditional *sola fide*, pressing traditionally beyond the historical second Temple Jewish texts.

103. Edwards provides a paradigm pattern in *A Treatise Concerning Religious*

Even those who are critical of the New Perspective virtually acknowledge a new consensus of rabbinic soteriology that banishes legalism and positions itself in a gracious narrow way.[104]

While the last judgment is decided by God (on the basis of deeds),[105] it is not earned because the righteous are already in the covenant on the basis of God's gracious choice. Kent Yinger identifies that these deeds taken into account by God's judgment are thus not merits by which a person gains entry into a particular status with God, but a part of the means of recognizing a person's inner character.[106] Yinger concludes that with Paul and second Temple Judaism, the relation between grace and works is the same, "the righteousness upon which salvation depends is by grace through faith from start to finish, and receives its *necessary confirmation* in the outworking of obedience to the end."[107] Therefore, second Temple Jewish salvation is similar to a semi-Augustinian or Orthodox synergism that is neither monergistic Augustinian, nor optimistically Pelagian. By synergism I mean a divinely initiated cooperation that the human has a role in obedience, which obedience affects their eschatological salvation.[108] On the other hand, Simon Gathercole concludes that final vindication is on the basis of the conjunction of divine election and righteous works, which leaves open an inappropriate form of Jewish boasting in themselves that should have no place.[109] Resolving this, N. T. Wright explains

---

Affections.

104. Sir 27.3-4; *Pss. Sol.* 2.33-35; 14.6; 16.15; *Pr. Azar.* 1.12; Sanders, *Judaism*; Yinger, "The Continuing Quest," 374-75, 378-82; "Defining 'Legalism,'" 91-108; "Reformation Redivivus," 89-106; Jackson, "Legalism," 1; Laato, *Paulus und das Judentum*, 34-37; Silva, "The Law and Christianity: Dunn's Synthesis," 339-53, esp. 340; even though on a more popular level most presentations still reflect the pre-1977 view of legalistic Judaism (Anderson, Miller, and Travis, *Breaking the Bondage of Legalism*, 51, 60, 155); However a search for a natural tendency of humans toward legalism in the fields of anthropology, sociology or psychology yields little (Shklar, *Legalism*; Shapiro, *Autonomy*, 69-73).

105. *Jub.* 30.19-23; Sir 16.12-14; *1 En.* 89.70; 98.8; *2 En.* 52.15; *2 Bar.* 24.1; CD 20.19-20; *Sib. Or.* 2.93-94; *L.A.B.* 3.10; Yinger, *Paul, Judaism*; Gathercole, "After the New Perspective: Works," 97; somewhat revised as: *Where is Boasting?*, 111.

106. Yinger, *Paul, Judaism, and Judgment*, 159; nuanced by "The Continuing Quest," 388.

107. Yinger, *Paul, Judaism, and Judgment*, 228.

108. Yinger, *Paul, Judaism, and Judgment*, 159; nuanced by "The Continuing Quest," 389; Eskola, "Paul, Predestination," 396-97, 404-6; Gathercole, *Where is Boasting?*

109. Gathercole, *Where is Boasting?*, 163.

how present and eschatological justification fit (from his exposition of Romans 2:12–16), and how one's whole life matters for such a future salvation view.

> It is vital to note that the justification and the judgment spoken of in this paragraph are inalienably *future*. This is not *present* justification; Paul will come to that in chapter 3. Nor can the two be played off against one another. They belong together: present justification, as Romans makes clear, is the true anticipation of future justification. And in Romans as elsewhere in Paul, it is present justification, not future, that is closely correlated with faith. Future justification, acquittal at the last great Assize, always takes place on the basis of the totality of the life lived.[110]

If Israel is appropriate in covenant then they are righteous.[111] For example, *Testament of Levi* identifies that "doing righteousness" is obeying the Law and teaching it to others.[112] This form of righteousness shows itself in practical covenant nomist ways such as being there for the vulnerable ones of society, to meet their needs.[113] At Qumran terms like "justification" have an eschatological meaning of *"divinely approved status in covenant"* rather than views more familiar within evangelicalism.[114] For example, N. T. Wright summarizes this eschatological emphasis from Qumran as follows:

---

110. Wright, "The Law in Romans 2," 143–144. Van Landingham claims that many of these second Temple texts signify that Jews are trying to earn their salvation through works (*Judgment & Justification*, 66–171), however, they can instead be read as Wright proposes showing evidence of righteousness to indicate who will be the ones God saves for His reasons rather than that they earn such a salvation. Those who also agree with Wright that this Romans text is Christian New-Covenant Gentiles as a foil for Jewish disobedience, thus indicating a divine gracious life transformation: Zahn, *Der Brief*; Mundle, "Zur Auslegung," 249–56; Flückinger, "Die Werke," 17–42; Barth, *A Shorter Commentary on Romans*, 36–39; Souçek, "Zur Exegese," 99–113; Cranfield, *Romans*, 1:155–63; König, "Gentiles," 53–60; Salas, "Dios premia," 265–86; Bergmeier, *Das Gesetz*, 31–102; Watson, *Paul, Judaism*, 118–22; Wright, "The Law in Romans 2," 131–50; Robert Jewett, *Romans*, 212–14.

111. Kennard, *Messiah Jesus*, 300–302.

112. Tob 3.5; *T. Levi* 13.1–4; 4 Ezra 7.19–25; *L.A.B.* 11.2; Gathercole, *Where is Boasting?*, 76.

113. Job 22:7; Isa 58:7; Ezek 18:7, 16; *T. Jos.* 1.5–7; *T. Jac.* 2.23; 7.24–25; *2 En.* 9.1; 10.5; 42.8; 63.1; *Mek.* on Exod 14.19; *b. Soṭa* 14a; *m. Qidd.* 1.10; *t. Qidd.* 1.13; *Tg. Ps.-Jn.* on Deut 34:6; *Eccl. Rab.* on 11.1; Justin, *1 Apol.* 67. Much of this material is nicely laid out in chart form in Davies and Allison, *Matthew*, 3:426.

114. One example is how 4QMMT develops the term righteousness, especially frag. 14, col. 2, text: 2.3 "justification by works;" cf. 1QS 5.21; 6.18; *2 Bar.* 57.2.

> Justification in this setting, then is not a matter of *how someone enters the community of the true people of God*, but of *how you tell who belongs to that community*, not least in the period of time before the eschatological event itself, when the matter will become public knowledge.[115]

Thus justification in second Temple Judaism has more of an ecclesiological (within the covenant community of Israel) and eschatological meaning than an initial salvation meaning. Israel keeping of God's gracious Law was the covenant obligation to remain within God's gracious divine blessing of being reckoned as righteous.[116] From his work with the *Pss. Sol.*, Mikael Winninge reminds us that Jewish materials present a universality of sinfulness such that the righteous within the two ways could be more accurately called the "sinfully righteous" as opposed to the "stubbornly disobedient 'sinners.'"[117] Qumran's *Charter of a Jewish Sectarian Association* conveys this sentiment of covenant nomism graciously applied by God in His justification of the covenant community, that is, sinners who are being transformed by God to be righteous too.

> As for me, my justification is with God. In God's hand are perfection of my way and the uprightness of my heart. He will wipe away my transgression through his righteousness . . . From the source of his righteousness is my justification, and from his marvelous mysteries is the light in my heart . . . As for me, I belong to wicked humankind, to the company of ungodly flesh . . . For humanity has no way, and humanity is unable to establish their steps since justification is with God and perfection of way is out of his hand . . . As for me, if I stumble, the mercies of God shall be my everlasting salvation. If I stagger because of the sin of flesh, my justification shall be by the righteousness of God which endures forever . . . He will draw me by his grace, and by his mercy he will bring my justification . . . Through his righteousness he will cleanse me of the uncleanness of humankind and of the sins of humankind, that I may confess to God his righteousness, and his majesty to the Most High.[118]

Additionally, second Temple Jewish literature expected the Teacher of Righteousness to teach righteous Jews God's Law and revelation in a

---

115. Wright, *What Saint Paul Really Said*, 119.
116. 4QMMT 30–31; 4 Macc; Sir; Bar.
117. Winninge, *Sinners and the Righteous*, 264, 305.
118. *Charter of a Jewish Sectarian Association* (1QS, 4Q255–264a, 5Q11) 11.

New Covenant form.[119] In this, Qumran added that this righteousness was also brought about by "faith in the Teacher of Righteousness."[120] He will serve as a rival to the man of the lie, a wicked priest who tried to destroy the Teacher of Righteousness. However, the Teacher of Righteousness (as the Messiah of Aaron)[121] will prepare those faithful to the Law for eschatological blessing of everlasting life[122] instead of the judgment God will mete out on the unfaithful.[123] 4QMMT develops divine grace through forgiveness while retaining covenant nomism as the normative human narrow way.[124] Additionally, on the basis of God's justification through covenant nomism and the Teacher of Righteousness, the Qumran community became called the "sons of righteousness" or the "elect of righteousness."[125]

Works of the Law

The concern of how to interpret the phrase "works of the Law" has developed a variety of descriptions. The new perspective on Paul includes: E. P. Sanders' "pattern of religion" and James Dunn's "boundary markers." Whereas, the reformation tradition focuses on "Jews legalistically earning salvation by keeping the Law." However, neither is the emphasis of second Temple Jewish sources where the phrase primarily refers to *community behavior in conformity to the Law*.[126] That is, the emphasis is on

---

119. 1QpHab 1.11–13; 2.1–3; 7.1–5, 10–11; 8.1–3; 9.9–10; 11.4–8, 13; 4Q165 frag. 1–2; 4Q171 3.14–17; 4.3–4, 26–27; 4Q173 frag. 1 4.

120. 1QpHab 8.1–3 on Hab 2:4.

121. 1QpHab 2.2–9; 4Q171 3.15.

122. CD 3.12–16, 20; *Tg. Onq. Lev.* 18.5; *Ps.-Jn.*; *Sipre Lev.* 193 on Lev 18:1–30.

123. 1QpHab 2.2–10; 5.3–8.

124. *Jub.* 4.5–6; 16.9; 19.9; 30.19–29; 31.32; CD 3.12–14; 1QS 3.11; 4.22–23; 5.5; 8.9–10; Hogerterp, "4QMMT," 359–79.

125. 1QS 9, 14; 1QH 2, 13.

126. Several different Hebrew phrases translate as "works of the Law" (ἔργων νόμου) from either "works" (מַעֲשֵׂה) or "faithfulness" (עוֹלָם חַסְדֵי): Neh 13:14; 1QS 5.21, 23–24; 6.18; 1QpHab 7.11; 8.1; 12.4–5; CD 13.11; 4Q171 frgs. 1–2 ii 14; 4Q174 frgs. 1–3 ii 2; 4Q176 frg. 17 line 7; 4Q394 frag. 3–7 col. 1–2.1–3; 4Q398=4QMMT frag. 14 col. 2.3; C.23–28; 4QFlor. 1.1–7; 4Q470 frg. 1 line 4; 4QpPsa 1–2.2.14, 22; 11QT 56.3; 2 *Bar.* 57.2; 4 *Macc.* 7.9; cf. Lohmeyer, *Probleme paulinischer*, 31–74; Christianson, *The Covenant in Judaism*; Watson, *Paul and the Hermeneutics*, 334–35; Evans, "Paul and 'Works of Law,'" 201–26; Hofius, "'Werke des Gesetzes,'" 271–310; Dunn, *The New Perspective on Paul*, especially chapters 1, 8, 10, 14, 17, 19 which were articles from

Jewish compliance to the whole of the Law. Michael Bachmann follows Käsemann's lead and translates the phrase as "regulations of the Law" or "*halakhot* of the Law."[127] Thus the whole of the Law is emphasized, though on occasion it can refer to that which would defile, as in 4Q394. In such contexts where Jews are separated from Gentiles it could especially indicate boundary markers, but the context must decide. However, the second Temple Jewish emphasis of the phrase "works of the Law" is not about these boundary markers or legalistically earning salvation as much as *whole Law compliance*. Michael Bachmann develops that these statements of "works of the Law" have nothing to do with individual achievements to be judged because they are never accompanied by "good" or "bad works of the Law."[128] In Qumran texts "works of the Law" is never about earning salvation. There is no second Temple Jewish text which takes this phrase in a legalistic direction for earning salvation. The issue is whole Law compliance. That is, doing *torah*, namely deeds of righteousness, is identified as the lifestyle for which God reckons someone righteous. For example, making *torah* practically true in one's life is the attitude by which a person in 4QMMT "will be reckoned to you as righteousness, since you will be doing what is righteous and good in His eyes, for your own welfare and for the welfare of Israel."[129] Here "Reckoned as righteousness" identifies an acknowledgement of *the status of those within the Mosaic Covenant who keep the Law*. Just before this text is a call to reflect on past examples of righteousness where the pious kings do exemplary deeds and how they were committed to *torah* as evident in

---

1992–2008 on works of the Law which nicely provides a trajectory for how the view grew; de Roo, "The Concept of 'Works of the Law,'" 116–47; "*Works of the Law*," esp. 1–26; Cranfield, "The Works of the Law," 89–101; these contrast with Dunn, *Romans*, 1:159; Sanders, *Paul and Palestinian Judaism*, 118; for example, of Reformation view: Moo, *Romans 1–8*, 216–17; "'Law', 'Works of the Law,'" 82; Bachmann, "Rechtfertigung," 1–33; "4QMMT," 91–113. In spite of Dunn's identification of the concept with the "palisades and iron walls to prevent mixing with any other peoples" *Letter of Aristeas* 139–42 (*The New Perspective on Paul*, 8–9), even though the phrase "works of the Law" is not in the *Letter of Aristeas*; Hogerterp, "4QMMT," 359–379.

127. Bachmann, *Anti-Judaism in Galatians?*, 24; *Sünder oder Übertreter*, 93–98; "Rechtfertigung," 15–28; "demands" Käsemann, *An die Römer*, 57–60.

128. Bachmann, *Anti-Judaism in Galatians?*, 11; Lohmeyer, "Probleme paulinischer," 31–74, esp. 59, 64, 68, 71.

129. 4QMMT C 26–32; 4Q397 frag. 23; 4Q399 frag. 1; frags 14–17 col. 2; developed by Dunn, *The New Perspective on Paul* especially chapters 1, 8, 10, 14, 17, 19 which were articles from 1992–2008; a similar point is made by 1 Macc 2.52 and developed by Jewett, *Romans*, 312.

their works of the Law and forgiven of their sins within covenant loyalty. Notice that the issue is not boundary marks or ceremonial rituals.

> Remember the kings of Israel and contemplate their deeds whoever among them feared the Torah was delivered from troubles; and these were seekers of the Torah whose transgressions were forgiven. Think of David who was a man of righteous deeds and who was therefore delivered from many troubles and was forgiven.[130]

Perhaps this text can be seen as following the pattern of David's faithfulness (Isa 55:3; 2 Chr 6:42).[131]

Jacqueline deRoo rejects the new perspective on Paul,[132] developing that "works of the Law" are divinely initiated *deeds*[133] *reflecting the status within Mosaic Covenant keeping* often with a quality of offering these works as *spiritual sacrifices to God*, and that *God atones* the individuals and their community through these "works of the Law."[134] Such a positioning of the Jew in compliance to the center and thus the whole of the Law indicates that they are righteous, while denying the new perspective view of "works of the Law" as boundary markers. Such righteousness is divinely initiated. Such deeds are done by the Jew in obedience to the Law. Such obedience is described by the synonym s as "perfect" and "living blamelessly."[135] This obedience indicates a status that they do not earn because God elected them and He initiates such deeds. However, such obedience is occasionally seen as atoning for the individual and the community, without the need to bring a Temple sacrifice.[136]

This section will explore some of these successes and some martyrs in their commitment to *torah*. Part of the result of new Judaism studies of the second Temple Jewish era is to recognize that at least a broad segment of Judaism expressed a deep commitment to the Mosaic Law as the Covenant document from God to be obeyed if Israel was to be blessed. This sentiment continues the commitment indicated in the Torah and

---

130. 4QMMT C 23–25; Tob 4.12; Jdt 8.26; 1 Macc 2.51; 4.9; Sir 2.10.

131. deRoo takes it this way (*"Works of the Law,"* 24).

132. deRoo, *"Works of the Law,"* 219.

133. deRoo, *"Works of the Law,"* 83 note 35 justifies the deed emphasis.

134. deRoo, *"Works of the Law,"* 20, 36, 41; 4Q174 3.7; CD 5.5b–6a; 4QMMT C 31.

135. CD 2.15–16; 1QS 1.8; 2.2; 3.9; 8.18, 21; 9.6, 8, 19; 1QSb 1.2; 4Q525 frg. 4 line 10; deRoo, *"Works of the Law,"* 27.

136. 4Q174 3.7; CD 5.5–6; deRoo, *"Works of the Law,"* 15, 33–35.

Covenant Renewal Psalms. At Qumran there developed an annual covenant renewal ceremony with public repentance and confession.[137] That is, Israel was already in covenant with God, so that they are not trying to obtain initial blessing; they are recovering the blessing that God has covenanted them to maintain. N. T. Wright writes, "The Torah was the boundary-marker of the covenant people: those who kept it would share the life of the coming age."[138] So this covenantal nomism was the way Israel had of maintaining relationship with God, particularly in difficult times.

With the return from the exile there was an attempt to bring Israel into a strict adherence to the Law to prevent another national apostasy and experience of covenant curse (2 Chr 14:3; Ezra 7:10; 9:10-15; Neh. 9:34; 10:30). For example, Daniel and his three friends insisted on keeping kosher and not participating in idolatry even if it would cost their lives (Dan 1:1-21 and 3:1-20). A similar commitment in the dispersion is made by Tobit who expressed awareness that Israel's defeat and exile had come about as a just divine punishment for their violating the Mosaic Covenant.[139] As such, Tobit determined that while they were living among Gentiles, Israel must observe Jewish marriage and keep kosher in order to preserve Israel's uniqueness in covenant.

When Israel was re-gathered into the land, Martin Hengel argues that Israel considered that the whole land of Israel was God's possession, so Israel tried to purge Gentiles from the land through either evicting them or converting them to become Jews.[140] For example, Tobit's son John Hyrcanus 1 forced the Idumeans in the land to submit to circumcision and other requirements of the Law.[141] His successor, Aristobulus 1, required the same compliance with the Law for the Itureans who lived in the land.[142]

The *Testament of Moses* 9.6 expresses this Jewish attitude from Mattathias against Antiochus IV to Bar Kokhba against Hadrian (175 B.C.-135 A.D.), "Let us die rather than transgress the commandments of the Lord of Lords, the God of our fathers."[143] Such a death possibility might

---

137. CD 9.13; 1QS 1.24–2.1 with possible introduction 4Q256 2.2 and possibly 4Q286 1.1.7-8?, 4-5?; Nitzar, "Repentance," 2:758-59.

138. Wright, *Jesus and the Victory of God*, 301.

139. Tob 1.9-12; 4.12-13; 14.5.

140. Hengel, *The Zealots*, 197.

141. Josephus, *Ant.* 13.9.1; 2 Macc 3.11, 24-29.

142. Josephus, *Ant.* 13.11.3.

143. 1 Macc 1.57, 63; 2.20, 50; *T. Mos.* 9.6; similar statement also by Josephus, *Ag.*

be contemplated by the Covenant Renewal Psalms only when Israel is unfaithful to Covenant (Pss 50:3, 15; 81:7, 11–15).

Israel interpreted God as establishing them in covenant nomism, as within the Mosaic Covenant such that they must obey the Law or else lose God's blessing as a people.[144] These Jews saw this passion for the Law as a realization of the New Covenant in which God was giving them a "new heart" and a "new spirit."[145] As a result, Israel insisted on circumcision, keeping kosher, practicing exclusively Jewish marriage, and Sabbath keeping as expressions of this purity.[146] Likewise Tobit, captive in Ninevah, did not eat Gentile food.[147] Furthermore, when Judith ingratiated herself with Nebuchadnezzer's general, Holofernes (so she could kill him) she took all the kosher food to eat through the fourth day when she carried out the deed.[148] In the LXX version of Esther 4:17 she reminds God that she has not eaten food from Haman's table or drunk wine of libations. Another instance is that seven brothers and their mother were tortured and executed on orders of Antiochus IV rather than eat pork.[149] Furthermore, the Egyptian Jews kept separate from Gentile's food and worship which led to hostility between them.[150] Antiochus attempted to force cultural conformity by forbidding aspects of the Law that distinguished Israel from other people, forbidding circumcision and *kosher*, and ordering Jews to worship foreign gods. However, the Jews resisted such moves.[151] While circumcision was practiced by some other groups, its practice was a strong affirmation of Jewish male identity.[152] Many of the Jews abhorred pagan sacrificial meat as evidenced when Antiochus ordered some Jews to eat pork and food sacrificed to idols but Eleazar

---

Ap. 2.218.

144. Jdt 5:17–21; 8:18–23; 10.5; 12.2; Jub 1.22–25; 2.17–33; 15.11–34; *Pr. Azar.* 6–14; CD 10.14–11.18.

145. As in Jer 31:31–34 and Ezek 36:24–37:28 so too in: Jub 1:22–25; 1Q3 4, 5; 1QH 4, 5, 18; 4Q *Shir Shalb*; CD 4Q266 frag. 2 1.6–8; B 19.12–13; 1QpHab 2.3; 11.13; 4Q434 frag. 1 1.4; 4Q437 frag. 1 1.14.

146. Jub 2:17–33; 15:11–34; Jdt 10:5; 12:2; Tob 1.10–12; 4:12–13..

147. Tob 1.10–12; 4:12–13.

148. Jdt 10.5; 12:2, 9–19; 13:8.

149. 2 Macc 7 especially 7.9 and 8.2; cf. 4 Macc 1.8, 10.

150. 3 Macc 3.4–7; 7.11.

151. 1 Macc 1:15, 45–46, 48, 54, 60–64; 2:15–28; 5.27; 6.10; 2 Macc 6.18–31; Jub 22.16; 30.7–17; Hellerman, "Purity," 401–21.

152. Philo, *Migr.* 89–93; Josephus, *Ant.* 1.10.5.

and others refused, so they were tortured and killed.[153] Furthermore, at Qumran no guilt offering was utilized in public covenant renewal ceremonies, for such a sacrifice was replaced by obedience and purity in covenant nomism.[154]

By the third century B.C. there is evidence of regular readings of *torah* in synagogue liturgy.[155] This practice developed into a regular three year cycle for completely reading the *torah*.[156]

Covenant nomism informed national policy in Israel as well. For example, the Hasmonean John Hyreaus (135-104 B.C.) broke off an important siege because of the coming of the Sabbath year.[157] Likewise, Gaius Caesar granted Israel an exemption from paying taxes in October 47 B.C. because Israel was in the process of celebrating sabbatical year.[158] This theme of commitment to *Torah* regarding the Sabbatical year is reflected also in psalms of his era.[159] The continued commitment among rabbinics to sabbatical year indicates Israel's effort to regain Edenic Kingdom conditions.[160]

Furthermore, this covenant nomist commitment is reflected in the *Letter of Aristeas*.

> In his wisdom the legislator (Moses) ... surrounded us with unbroken palisades and iron walls to prevent our mixing with any of the peoples in any matter ... So, to prevent our being perverted by contact with others or by mixing with bad influences he hedged us in on all sides with strict observances connected

---

153. 2 Macc 6:18-31; 4 Macc 5:1-6:30 also *Joseph and Aseneth*. This issue continues into the Christian community, especially among Jewish Christians (Acts 15:20, 29; 21:25; 1 Cor 8:7-13; 10:7-28; Rev 2:14, 20).

154. 1QS 3.6-12; 9.3-6; Bilha Nitzar, "Repentance," 2:758-59.

155. Acts 15:21; *y. Meg.* 3.4-6; 4.1, 75a; *b. Meg.* 29b; *b. B. Qam.* 82a; Josephus, *Ag. Ap.* 2.175 #362; Philo, *Somn.* 127 #498.

156. The earliest reference to a fixed three year cycle is *b. Meg.* 29b.

157. Josephus, *J. W.* 1.157-60; Jews compliance with Sabbath law was well known in the ancient near East (Josephus, *Ant.* 14.10.12; *Ag. Ap.* 2.2, 39; Philo, *Mos.* 2.21; and even more so in sectarian Judaism [CD 10.14-11.18; *Songs of the Sabbath Sacrifice*; *Temple Scroll*=11Q19]). Salisbury concludes that Josephus views Israel in obedience as in a covenant nomist relationship with the Law ("Josephus," 259).

158. Official Letter from Gaius Caesar to Hyrcanus 2, 47 B.C. included in Josephus, *Ant.* 14.202-210 and Zeev, *Jewish Rights*, # 5, 2.4-5, 25-28, pp. 80-101, 374.

159. *Songs of the Sabbath Sacrifice*.

160. *Sifra* 245.1.2.A-D; Neusner, *Handbook of Rabbinic Theology*, 335.

with meat and drink and touch and hearing and sight, after the manner of the Law.[161]

Additionally, in 63 B.C. when Pompey corraled Jews in Jerusalem, he raised the earthworks on Sabbath without firing missiles; the Jews would not fight the Roman troops under their noses because the Jews would only defend themselves on the Sabbath if they were attacked.[162] In fact, the Jews' strict observance of Sabbath kept them from service in imperial armies, for it became a characteristic feature that marked off Jewish communal life.[163]

Rome and regional political powers repeatedly recognized that Jews had an ancient right to follow the Jewish Law, and extended their legal right to obey the Law. For example, Gaius Caesar in October 47 B.C. identified that Jews and their priests had a legal right to obey the Jewish Law.[164] Likewise in that year an official decree in Sardis and in Laodicea gave Jews of their respective cities the right to obey their Jewish laws including the traditional prayers, Sabbaths, and sacrifices.[165] Miletus, Ephesus, and Halicarnassus followed suit with similar permission of Jews to be faithful to the Jewish laws, including the Sabbath.[166] In 12 B.C. Caesar Augustus issued an edict also granting the Jews of Asia and the Near East the right to obey their Patriarchal Law, including Sabbath.[167] In 41 A.D. Claudius issued a similar edict preserving Alexandrian Jewish rights to obey their tradition, and then he extended these rights to all Jews of

---

161. *Letter of Aristeas* 139–42 specific selection quoted in Dunn and Suggate, *The Justice of God*.

162. Josephus, *J. W.* 1.145–47.

163. Horace, *Sat.* 1.9.69–70; Philo, *Somn.* 2.123–24; *Legat.* 158; Josephus, *Ant.* 13.252; 14.10.12; 14.237. 16.2.3; 16.6.2–4.

164. Official Letter from Gaius Caesar to Hyrcanus 2, 47 B.C. included in Josephus, *Ant.* 14.202–210 and Zeev, *Jewish Rights*, # 5, 2.32–34, pp. 80–101, 375.

165. Official Decree of Sardus, 47 B.C. and magistrates letter to Laodicea included in Josephus, *Ant.* 14.259–261, 241–43 and Zeev, *Jewish Rights*, # 20, 2.10–16, pp. 218–225, 375; #17, 2.7–20, pp. 192–98, 376.

166. Official Permission from Miletus between 46 and 44 B.C.; From Ephesus in 43 B.C. and in 42 B.C., and Decree from Halicarnassus included in Josephus respectively *Ant.* 14.244–246, 225–27, 262–64; 16.167; 14.256–58 and Zeev, *Jewish Rights*, respectively: # 18, 2.10–13, pp. 199–205, 375; #9, 2.12–13, pp. 139–49, 375; #21, 2.13–16, pp. 226–35; #24, 2.10–11, pp. 362–72, 375–76; and #19, 2.11–14, pp. 206–16, 376.

167. Edict of Caesar Augustus of March 6, 12 B.C. included in Josephus, *Ant.* 16.162–65 and Zeev, *Jewish*, #22, 2.7–10, 13–15, pp. 235–257.

the world so that Jews everywhere might be obedient to the Law of their fathers without hindrance from any others.[168]

However, at times the Jews risked their lives to be faithful to the Mosaic Covenant. For example, in 5 B.C. Herod had erected a golden eagle over the temple as a votive offering, and two learned teachers (Judas and Matthaias) inspired the young men to pull down the image.[169] Herod responded with having many of them arrested, tried and burned alive. Furthermore, Josephus describes instances such as that in 26 A.D. when Pilate introduced Roman standards and a bust of Caesar into Jerusalem. Here Jews were ready to die rather than transgress the Law.[170] A large group followed Pilate to his residence in Caesarea and sat outside his house for five days. When they were summoned to tribunal and troops surrounded them with drawn swords, the Jews fell to the ground extending their necks and exclaiming that they were ready to die rather than to transgress the Law. Pilate was impressed and withdrew the standards. Likewise, in 41 A.D. Caligula ordered Petronius to set up his statue in the Temple, Josephus claims that the protestors said, "slay us first before you carry out these resolutions … we will sooner die than violate our laws."[171] During the fifties A.D. King Agrippa tried to placate Torah zealous Jews.[172] Their hope was that God would intervene and prevail with blessing from the Mosaic Covenant.[173] These examples reflect merely a sample of Israel's commitment to Yahweh under the framework of corporate covenant nomism. It is in this framework of sectarian Judaism that the hope for a Messiah includes that He would be a definitive teacher of the Law.[174]

Rome largely maintained Israel's privilege in the dispersion to keep the Law and the Jewish customs which exempted them from emperor

---

168. Edicts of Claudius in 41 A.D. included in Josephus, respectively *Ant.* 19.280–85, 303–11 and Zeev, *Jewish Rights*, respectively: #28, 2.24–27, pp. 295–327 and #29, 2.14–16, pp. 328–344, 375.

169. Josephus, *J. W.* 1.651–55; *Ant.* 17.149–67.

170. Josephus, *J. W.* 2.169–74; *Ant.* 18.55–59.

171. Josephus, *Ant.*18.261–64 and 271.

172. Josephus, *Ant.* 19.292–334; *m. Bik.* 3.4; *m. Sot.* 7.8.

173. Josephus, *Ant.*18.267.

174. 4Q174 (4QFlor) 1.11 (different from the "branch of David"); 4QpPs (4Q171) 3:13–16; 1QpHab 1.13; 2:2, 8–9; 5:10; 7:4–5; 11:5; CD 1.11; 6.7; 7:18 (identified with the star); 20.1, 28, 32.

worship and civic cults,[175] and gave them protection of Sabbath observance including nonappearance in court,[176] the right to operate as an independent organization collecting and distributing tax to the Temple,[177] as well as exemption from military service.[178]

As the Temple in Jerusalem was destroyed initially in 70 A.D. and went into occasional use among the ruins, a Jewish Temple near Elephantine, Egypt continued in use until the fourth century A.D. Additionally, the Samaritan Temple on Mount Gerizim reconstructed in the second century B.C., continued to function as well but Jews had little dealings with Samaritans.

Love for God was shown in obedience to *torah*. For example, the Bar Kokhba rebellion was partially caused by a Roman ban against circumcision which was lifted immediately following the defeat of the rebellion.[179] Additionally, Rabbi Akiva helped to inspire the Bar Kochba rebellion but was tortured to death by the Romans in 135 A.D. for the capital crime of teaching *torah*. When Rabbi Akiva was taken out for execution, it was the time to recite the morning *Sh'ma*, and as he did so the Romans flayed his skin with an iron comb.[180] He encouraged his disciples that now he would have the opportunity to love the Lord with all his soul. With the completion of the *Sh'ma*, he died. During the same persecution Rabbi Hanina ben Teradion, while he was being burned to death for teaching *torah*, clarified that individual *torah* scrolls and individual Jews may be destroyed but the *torah's* words are everlasting.[181]

Michael Bachman makes an extended case for covenant nomism continuing among Jews of the land and dispersion.[182] His case is especially built from analysis of fourth to seventh century A.D. synagogue mosaics prominent with Law themes.

---

175. Josephus, *J. W.* 2.10.4; *Ag. Ap.* 2.6 (77); Philo, *Legat.* 23.157.

176. Horace, *Sat.* 1.9.69–70; Philo, *Somn.* 2.123–24; *Legat.* 158; Josephus, *Ant.* 13.252; 14.10.12, 20–25; 14.237. 16.2.3; 16.6.2–4.

177. Neh. 10:32–34; Josephus, *Ant.* 14.7.2; 16.6.2–7; in Tacitus, *Histories* 5.5.1 even gentiles send tribute to the Jewish Temple.

178. Horace, *Sat.* 1.9.69–70; Philo, *Sonm.* 2.123–24; *Legat.* 158; Josephus, *Ant.* 13.252; 14.10.6, 12–13; 14.237. 16.2.3; 16.6.2–4.

179. Ban: Cassio Dio *Rom. Hist.* 69.121–22; *Historia Augusta* 14.2; Removal of ban: Modestinus, *The Rules* bk. 6; *Digesta* 48.8–11.

180. *Berak.* 61b.

181. *Avodah Zara* 18a.

182. Bachmann, *Anti-Judaism in Galatians?*, 32–59.

In contrast to this zeal for God and covenant nomism, Israel repeatedly rebelled and brought themselves into covenant curse and Gentile dominance (Deut 9:7; 28:15–30:20; 2 Kgs 17:23; Neh 9:32; Isa 9:1–2; Ezek 21:3; 20:31; Mic 5:3–4).[183] Israel continued to describe themselves as in exile from the Babylonian era through that of the rabbinic era.[184] Their precarious condition was confessed by *Baruch*, much as the Covenant Renewal Psalms had confessed previously, "We have disobeyed Him, and have not heeded the voice of the Lord our God, to walk in the statutes of the Lord that he set before us. From the time when the Lord brought our ancestors out of the land of Egypt to this day."[185]

This rebellion was due to Israel's unfamiliarity and disregard for the Mosaic covenant. Judaism's hope for the Kingdom was in part a divine work that would make Israel a transformed New Covenant people (Deut 30:1–6; Jer 31:33–34; Ezek 36:24–37:28).[186] Furthermore, when Israel was in *diaspora*,[187] a Divine re-gathering was the hope of the *diaspora* Jews as they anticipated God's covenant blessing.[188] However, this hope did not remove Israel from their obligation to the Law, rather God would enable them to be faithful to the Deuteronomical framework present in the Mosaic covenant (Deut 30:8–18; Jer 31:29–30).[189] Some second Temple sources envision this New Covenant life transformation as already

---

183. 1 Esd 8.73–74; 2 Esd 9.7; Bar 1.13, 18–19; 2.6; CD 1.13–21; 1QS 2.4–5; 1QH 2.8–19; 1QpHab 2.1–4; 5.3–8.

184. Sir 36.8; *T. Mos.* 10.1–10; *1 En.* 85–90; *T. Levi* 16–18; *Apoc. Abr.* 15–29; *T. Jud.* 24.1–3; *Jub.* 1.15–18, 24; *T. Naph.* 4.2–5; *T. Ash.* 7; *T. Benj.* 9; 2 Macc 1.27–29; 1 Esd 8.73–74; 2 Esd 9.7.

185. Bar 1.18–19 within penitential prayer 1.15–3.8; similar to Dan 9:4–19; Ezra 9:6–15; Neh 1:5–11; 9:5–37; 1 Esd 8.74–90; *Pr. Azar.*; *Pss. Sol.* 2; 8; 9; Jdt 9; 1 Macc 3.50–53; 4.30–33; 3 Macc 2.2–20; 6.2–15; *Jub.* 1.15–18, 22–25; 10.3–6; 2 Bar. 48.2–24; 54.1–22; Tob 3.1–6; *Pr. of Man.*; 1QS 1.18–3.12; 4Q393; 4Q481c; 4Q504; 4Q506; Josephus, *Ant.* 2.334–37; 4.40–50; Boda, Falk, and Werline, *Seeking the Favor of God.* vol. 1–3.

186. CD 6.19; 8.21; 20.12; 1QpHab. 2.3; 1QS 4.5; 1QH 4, 5, 18; 4QShirShalb 2; *Jub.* 1.22–25.

187. Meaning: Jews living outside their home land of Israel. *Sib. Or.* 12.110–14.

188. *Pss. Sol.* 8.28; 11.1–4; 17.28; Falk considers that the *Psalms of Solomon* is more congenial to covenant nomism than to those who would critique this ("Psalms and Prayers," 1:51); *T. Mos.* 4.9; Philo, *Praem.* 162–63; 2 Bar. 14.12; 78.7; *Tg. Isa.* 53.8; *Tg. Hos.* 14.8; *Tg. Mic.* 5.1–3.

189. Kennard, "Jeremiah and Hebrews."

occurring, summing up the previous covenants and enabling enlightened pure living of the narrow way (Deut 30:6; Jer 31:33).[190]

Covenant Nomism as Salvation with an Afterlife

In the O.T., the afterlife is described as in *sheol*. The concept of *sheol* emerges from the Pentateuch as a grave or a cavernous pit to swallow Korah in judgment (Gen 37:35; 42:38; 44:29, 31; Num 16:30, 33). In the O.T., *sheol* broadly becomes a synonym for death[191] and grave.[192] By extension, the concept of *sheol* becomes the lowest pit of the earth and a hidden area, though not hidden from God.[193] In the more developed theology of David, Solomon and the later prophets, *sheol* takes on qualities of a cognitive realm of the dead (Prov 7:27; 9:18; Isa 14:9, 11, 15). In this environment, all the dead are lying in their graves in *sheol* though they can be aroused (Isa 14:9; Ezek 23:21–30). As such, the realm of the dead: weakens, shames and silences proud rebels (Ps 31:17; Isa 5:14; 14:10; Ezek 31:15–17; 32:21). This *sheol* may even reach into this life at precarious times and draw its victims down into its dark domain (Lev 26:16; Job 17:14; Pss 9:15; 23:4; 30:3; 31:9; 32:3–4; 42:4; 88:3; 102:3–7; 103:4; Isa 10:18; Jer 19:9).

The concept of resurrection in the O.T. is marginal at best.[194] For example, the Pentateuch occasionally states that the heros of the faith are gathered to their forefathers. However, when there is no family tomb,

---

190. Bar 2.30–35; *Jub.* 1.16–25; *4 Ezra* 6.26b–28; Sectarian second Temple Judaism considered that the New Covenant was being realized among their New Covenant community and thus fulfilling the Law: *Charter of a Jewish Sectarian Association* (1QS, 4Q255–264a and 5Q11) 3.7–12, 26; 4.22–23; 5.5, 21; *Damascus Document* (CD 4Q268 frag. 1=4Q266 frag. 2 Col. 1) ver. 6; 6.19; 8.21; 14.1–2; B col. 19, ver. 12–13 here the New Covenant is clearly still Law like Jer. 31:33 Hebrew; 19.33–34; 20.12, 19; 1QpHab 2.3; 11.13 "circumcision of heart's foreskin"; *4 Ez.* 9.31; Lehne, *The New Covenant*, 43–61; Freedman and Miano, "People of the New Covenant," 7–26; Evans, "Covenant in the Qumran," 55–80; Gräbe, *New Covenant*, 58–67.

191. 2 Sam 22:6; Job 7:9; Pss 9:17; 18:5; 49:14–15; 55:15; 86:13; 88:3; 89:48; 116:3; Prov 5:5; 27:20; 30:16; Isa 28:15, 18; Hos 13:14.

192. 1 Sam 2:6; 1 Kgs 2:6, 9; Job 17:13–14, 16; 21:13; 24:18; Pss 16:10; 88:3; Prov 1:12; 15:24.

193. Deut 32:22; Job 11:8; 14:13; 26:6; Ps 139:8; Prov 15:11; Isa 57:9; Amos 9:2; Jonah 2:2.

194. von Rad, *Old Testament Theology*, 1:470–71, 2:350; Brueggeman, *Theology of the Old Testament*, 483–84; Wright, *The Resurrection*, 85–128; Kennard, *Messiah Jesus*, 333–35.

such a reference is a very ambiguous comfort (Num 20:24, 26). In a vague event, the witch of Endor conjured up Samuel bodily from the grave (1 Sam 28:14-20). Though he vanished when the conjuring was over, he must have been available from *sheol* in order to temporarily bodily resurrect. Additionally, Ezekiel's vision of the valley of dry bones is better seen as a metaphor describing Israel's national resurrection and reunion, rather than a personal resurrection of individuals (Ezek 37).[195] Perhaps the only clear mention of personal resurrection in the O.T. is that of Dan 12:2-3 where the dead will awake from their sleep among the dust to either everlasting life or everlasting contempt.[196]

This sort of resurrection hope is much more common in second Temple Judaism in the wake of developing Pharisaic and Qumran theology.[197] That is, the faithful in the Mosaic Covenant when they die continue

---

195. Zimmerli, *Ezekiel*, 2:256-257.

196. Joyce Baldwin, *Daniel*, 204-206; Wright, *The Resurrection*, 108-110.

197. 2 Macc 7.9-14, 22-23; 14.43-46; *1 En.* 22; 58.3; 62.14-16; 91.10; 92.2; 104; 108.11-14; *Jub.* 5.10; 10.17; 22.22; *L.A.B.*; CD 3.11-16, 20-21; 7.5, 9; 13.11; 20.17-20, 25-27; 1QH 11.19-23 [3.18-22]; 19.10-14 [11.7-11]; 1QS 3.7-12; 4.7; 4Q228 frag. 1 1.9; 4Q266, frag. 11; 4Q385 2; 4Q386 1-2; 4QMMT C; 4Q521 2.2.12; 5.2.5-6; *2 Bar.* [Syriac] 30.1-5; 49-51; 4 Macc 7.19; 16.25; *4 Ezra* 7.26-44; *Sib. Or.* 4.180; *T. Benj.* 10.6-8; *T. Levi* 18; *T. Jud.* 24; *Tg.* Hos. 6:2 interprets this text to be resurrection whereas the text speaks of the reviving of Israel on the third day; *Tg. Jon.* on Isa 27:12f describes salvation as being accomplished on the third day; *b. Sanh.* 90b where Gamaliel claims that God would give the resurrected patriarchs land, not merely their descendants and Johanan Num 18:28 the portion of YHWH given to Aaron is taken that he will be alive again, likewise Num. 15:31 is claimed that the remaining guilt of the offender will be accountable in the world to come; 91b-92a; *B. Ta'an.* 2a; *B. Ket.* 111; *m. Sanh.* 10.1, 3; *T. Mos.* 10.8-10; *Gen. Rab.* 14.5; 28.3; *Lev. Rab.* 14.9; *Messianic Apocalypse* adds resurrection to a modification of Ps 146:5-9 as a Messianic expectation to be done to others; *T. Jud.* 25.4 claims this Messianic resurrection would begin with Abraham, Isaac, and Jacob; *T. Benj.* claims that after these are raised the whole of Israel will be raised; *Pss. Sol.* 3.11-12; 4Q521 frag. 2, col. 2.1-13; frags. 7 and 5, col. 2.1-7; 1QH 14.29-35; 19.10-14; *Targum Songs* 8.5; the benediction in the *Amidah*, the *Shemoneh Esre*. However, Wis 3.1; 8.19-20; 9.15 and Josephus' description of the Pharisees (*Ant.* 17.152-154; 18.1.3-5; 18.14, 16; *J. W.* 1.650, 653; 2.151-153, 163, 165; 2.8.14; *Ag. Ap.* 2.217-18) follow more a Platonic immortality of the soul view, but even here the soul eventually is given a body to match (Wis 9.15; Josephus, *J. W.* 2.163). Also the Biblical authors (Matt 22:23-33; Mark 12:18-27; Acts 23:6-7) and the *Eighteen Benedictions* present the Pharisees as believing the bodily resurrection of the dead. Beth She'arim Israel catacomb 20 inscription 194 says "Good luck on your resurrection" (Longnecker, "Good Luck on Your Resurrection," 249-70). Gillman, *The Death of Death*, 101-142; Wright, *The Resurrection*, 129-206 for the post-Biblical Jewish view. The early church from patristic through medieval eras embraced bodily resurrection instead of Platonic immortality of the soul with regard to personal eschatology (Bynum, *The Resurrection*;

to be blessed in the afterlife with bodily resurrection unto Paradise.[198] In fact, *Pss. Sol.* 14.3 utilizes Lev 18:5 to show that the Law dependent life continues into everlasting life: "the righteous ones of the Lord will live by it [the Law] forever" and again, "Love is keeping her commandments, Observance of her laws is the guarantee of immortality."[199] Furthermore, with reference to tortured and martyred Jews, 2 Macc identifies the Mosaic Covenant as "God's covenant of or toward everlasting life."[200] This identifies that for 2 Macc, unlike *Pss. Sol.*, resurrection begins with everlasting life[201] and is a life not yet attained.[202] *T. Ash.* 5.2 joins 2 Macc in identifying that "everlasting life waits for death."[203] Taking a step back, some second Temple manuscripts also speak of an afterlife as everlasting life,[204] and possibly others even intimate bodily resurrection for the faithful.[205] Some Second Temple texts extend the Deuteronomic blessing/curse of this life to a post-mortem judgment and afterlife, where the righteous are blessed in the after-life with Deuteronomic blessing including

---

Wright, *The Resurrection*, 480–552); Nickelsburg, "Resurrection," 2:765–66; Bauckham, "Life, Death," 245–56 and Longnecker, *The Resurrection*, 80–95.

198. *4 Ezra* 8.33–36; 9.7–13; *Pss. Sol.* 9.4–5; 14.1–10; 15.6–13; *2 Bar.* 44.12–15; 51.1–6; *2 Apoc. Bar.* 38.

199. *Pss. Sol.* 14.3 repeated with argument from 5.15; and 6.18; *T. Jos.* 18.1; *Jub.* 5.10; 10.17; 22.22; *2 Bar.* 48.22b; CD 3.11–16, 20–21; 7.5, 9; 13.11; 20.17–20, 25–27; 1QS 3.7–12; 4.7; 4Q228 frag. 1 1.9; 4Q266, frag. 11; 4QMMT C; additionally CD col 7, 6 refers to the result of obedience to the Law as living for 1000 generations; Gathercole, "Torah, Life and Salvation," 126–45; Gathercole, *Where is Boasting?*, 66–67; Neusner, *Handbook of Rabbinic Theology*, 559–99; contrary to Dunn, *The Theology of the Apostle Paul*, 152–53.

200. Dan 12:3; 2 Macc 7.36; *Pss. Sol.* 3.11–12; *T. Mos.* 10.9–10; *T. Job*; *2 Bar.* 51.7–12; *Jos. Asen.* 8.9; *L.A.B.* 19.12–13; *Sib. Or.* 4; *Num Rab. Shelaḥ* 17.6; *Tanḥ. B. Shelaḥ* 31.37b; *Pes. K.* 102a fin.–b init; Blanton, "Paul's Covenantal Theology," 70.

201. Arenhoevel, *Die Theokratie*, 159, n. 13.

202. Dunn, *The Theology of the Apostle Paul*, 152-3.

203. *T. Ash.* 5.2; translation following Gathercole, *Where is Boasting?*, 76 contrary to Charlesworth, *Old Testament Pseudepigrapha*, 1:818 "wards off death"; 1QS 4.7.

204. 1QS 4.6–8; CD 3.20; 4Q181 3–4; *1 En.* 37.4; 40.4; 58.3; 4 Macc 15.3; *Pss. Sol.* 3.12; *Sib. Or.* 2.149–53; 3.49 frag. 3; *L.A.B.* 23.10; *Num Rab. Shelaḥ* 17.6; *Tanḥ. B Shelaḥ* 31.37b; *Pes. K.* 102a fin.–b init.; Sprinkle examines all the second Temple 'life' promises for everlasting life or present blessed covenant life in *Law and Life*.

205. 1QH 3.10–22; 6.34; 11.12; 1QM 12.1–4.

the salvation of everlasting life.[206] Likewise, love of God as indicated by obedience to the Mosaic Covenant permits access to Kingdom.[207]

With everlasting life as an outcome from covenant nomism, the Law is an everlasting covenant for Israel[208] with the land as an everlasting national covenant blessing identified as Kingdom.[209] While the O.T. had not identified the land as holy, second Temple literature makes this identification that the land is holy, which further underscores its need to be protected from defilement.[210] George Moore's study of rabbinic Judaism concludes for a national salvation, "A 'lot in the World to come' . . . is ultimately assured to every Israelite on the ground of the original election of the people by the free grace of God."[211] Claude Montfiore moderates this Jewish national election to salvation by a Deuteronomic blessing in his affirmation that "for every decent Israelite there is a place in the future world" where he defines "decent" to be "Torah adherence."[212]

While afterlife is an extension of salvation beyond the grave that the Torah and Covenant Renewal Psalms never developed, such a resurrection idea was seen by second Temple Jews as having basis in biblical and extra-biblical psalms.[213] For example, the rabbinic morning prayer *birkat*

---

206. *T. Jos.* 18.1; *Jub.* 5.10; 10.17; 22.22; *2 Bar.* 48.22b; CD 3.11–16, 20–21; 7.5, 9; 13.11; 20.17–20, 25–27; 4Q228 frag. 1 1.9; 4Q266, frag. 11; 4QMMT C; 1QS 3.7–12; *4 Ezra* 7.34–36; 13.39–40; *Hymn Scroll* 19.12–14.

207. Wis 5.15; 6.18; *Pss. Sol.* 9.3–5; 1QS 3–4; *4 Ezra* 6.5; 7.77; 8.33, 36; *2 Bar.* 14.12; 51.7; Bird, "Salvation in Paul's Judaism?," 16.

208. CD 3.12–14; 1QS 3.11; 4.22–23; 5.5; 8.9.

209. 11QTemple 51.15–16; Philo, *Spec.* 4.164.

210. Lev 27:30 indicates the tithe, seed and fruit as holy but not the land; Ps 78:54 refers to a holy boundary (גְּבוּל) rather than land (הָאָרֶץ); Zech 2:12 Eng or 16 Hebrew (אַדְמַת הַקֹּדֶשׁ) which is parallel in the text to Jerusalem or the land around the Temple cf. Milgrom, *Leviticus 17-22*, 1573 and Weinfield, *The Promise of the Land*, 203; 2 Macc. 1:7 and Philo, *Spec.* 4.215; *Temple Scroll* 48.7, 10; 51.8.10; 1QH 4.25; 7.10; 1QM 3.4; 1QS 2.25; 5.13, 20; 8.17–23; 9.8; 1QSa 1.12; 2.9; CD 20.2, 5, 7, 24; *T. Job* 33.4–7; *T. Dan.* 5.11–13; 11QTemple 51.16; 56.12.

211. Moore, *Judaism in the First Centuries*, 2:95 with reference to *m. Sanh.* 10.1.

212. Montefiore, *Judaism and St. Paul*, 44; Sanders, *Paul and Palestinian Judaism*, 147.

213. Ps 16:1, 8–11 is taken by Peter and Luke in Acts 2:25 as fusing this psalm with 2 Sam 7:12 to proclaim the necessity that David's greatest Son, Jesus must have risen (Acts 2:25–32), which argument reflects a similar fusion of Ps 132 and 2 Sam 7:10–16, which 4QFlor takes to be messianic; *Messianic Apocalypse* adds resurrection to a modification of Ps 146:5–9 as a Messianic expectation to be done to others; *Pss. Sol.* 3.12; the *Eighteen Benedictions* present the Pharisees as believing the bodily resurrection of the dead.

ha torah in the second benediction praises God that within the covenant, *torah* teaches God's commands for the narrow way within which God saves Israel.[214]

Angels accompany God to both gather the elect into Kingdom and gather the unrighteous for damnation (Jer 51:53; Matt 13:41, 49; 24:31; Luke 16:22).[215] The sound of a trumpet or *sophar* horn will signal their gathering (Joel 2:1; Zeph 1:16; Zech 9:14; 1 Cor 15:52; 1 Thess 4:16)[216] much like the *sophar* horn has called Jews to gather for Sabbath or other sacred occasions (Num 10:10; Josh 6:5; 1 Kgs 1:34; Ps 81:3; Isa 27:13; Jer 4:5).[217] This gathering is presented in similar language as the Jews being gathered from dispersion (Isa 27:12–13).[218] This visual and audible coming indicates that redemption is near. Thus Jewish parables commonly emphasize wisdom for being alert unto Kingdom.[219] The righteous are

---

214. Second benediction of *birkat ha-torah* lines 115–17; DiSante, *Jewish Prayer*, 67.

215. Angels aid in the gathering of damned and elect (*1 En.* 1.6–9; 54.6; 62.11; 63.1 *Apoc. Elijah* 3.4; *Asc. Isa.* 4.14; *4 Ezra* 4.26–37; 9.17; *2 Bar.* 70.1–2; *b. B. Mes.* 83b; *Midr. Ps.* on 8:1). Additionally, Gabriel blows the *sophar* for gathering into Kingdom (*Quest. Ezra B* 11; Gk. *Apoc. Ezra* 4.36). Normally second Temple Judaism either has a damnation that destroys (2 Macc 12.43–45; 1QS 4.13–14; *Gen. Rab.* 6.6t. *Sanh.* 13.3–4; *Pesiq. Rab. Kah.* 10.4; *Pesiq. Rab.* 11.5) or a view of temporality in hell then released (*Num. Rab.* 18.20; some texts are often taken this way but are unclear: Sir 7.16; *Sipre Num.* 40.1.9; *Sipre Deut.* 311.3.1; 357.6.7; *'Abot R. Nat.* 16 A; 32.69 B; 37.95 B; 12 months in hell is a familiar duration in Jewish second Temple texts [*b. Šabb.* 33b; *Lam. Rab.* 1.11–12]). In the biblical text there is no dwelling on the punishment like the kind of sadism one finds in: *Apocalypse of Peter*; *Acts of Thomas* act 6; *Sib. Or.* 2.252–312; Tertullian, *Spect.* 30; Dante Alighieri, *The Divine Comedy*, section 1 "Hell," cantos 1–34.

216. *Pss. Sol.* 11.1; *Did.* 16.6; *Apoc. Abr.* 31.1; *Shemoneh Esreh* benediction 10; *Quest. Ezra B* 11.9; Gk. *Apoc. Ezra* 4.36; for texts of these cf. Davies and Allison, *Matthew*, 3:363.

217. *t. Sukk.* 4.11–12; 1QM; *Par. Jer.* 4.2; *Roš. Haš.* 26a.

218. Bar 4.36–37; *1 En.* 57.2; *Pss. Sol.* 11.3; this is not just a re-gathering from the Assyrian and Babylonian captivity as Pitre proposes (*Jesus, the Tribulation*, 4, 35–130), but of the continuing dispersion under any Gentile domination, including Greek, Roman and more recent as well.

219. Similar parables to that of Matt 25:1–13 and Luke 12:35–36 include those of Ben Zacchai occurs in *B.T. Šabb.* 153a with wise and foolish invitees. This follows two parables which contrast the wise from the foolish in *B.T. Šabb.* 152a and b. Likewise, in *Ecclesiastes Rabbah* 3.9.1 there is a foolish traveler who did not seek the protection of a military post on his travels, when he could, so that once night fell and he was terrified, he was then refused. Sometimes, as in *Mek.* on Exod 19:17, God is presented as coming with fire to light the escort of a bridegroom.

then gathered into a Messianic banquet as a metaphor for Kingdom (Isa 25:6–9; Luke 14:15; 22:16–18; Rev 19:9).[220]

Kingdom is occasionally described as a "new creation" (Isa 65:22; 66:22; Jer 31:22 [LXX 38:22]).[221] Such a new creation is clearly novel and fresh. This new creation may be expressed as a return to paradisiacal conditions of the original creation.[222] Such a "new creation" in Isaiah and *Jubilees* especially emphasizes the cosmological and human side of the new creation.[223] That is, not only will the cosmic situation be created anew but also the human condition and the vocation of humanity will be empowered into a new level of victory over any lingering curse.

Spirit Empowerment unto New Covenant

Reflecting on Yahweh renewing Israel back into the land, Yahweh promises an everlasting New Covenant, "I will make an everlasting covenant with them to be their God and they shall be my people; and I will never again remove My people Israel from the land that I have given them."[224]

The New Covenant transformation is empowered by God's Spirit resulting in covenant participants adhering thoroughly to the *torah* (Ezek 36:24–37:28; Joel 2:28–29).[225] Furthermore for Qumran and Pharisee alike, the Divine Spirit will expiate the covenantal righteous person from his iniquity and uncleanness. Such a person is enlightened by the Spirit to

220. 1QSa or 1Q28a 2.11–12, 19–21; *'Abot* 3.16–17; 4.16; *b. Ber.* 34b; *Sanh.* 98b; *Gen. Rab.* 62.2; *Ex. Rab.* 45.6; 50.5; *Lev. Rab.* 13.5; *Num. Rab.* 13.2; *Ruth Rab.* 5.6; *Cant. Rab.* 1, 3.3, on Song of Songs 1:3; *Pesiq. Rab.* 41.5; 48.3; *B. Bab. Bath.* 74b–75a; *Yalqut Shim'oni, Songs,* no. 988; *Sefer Eliahu, BBhM* 3.67; *Nistarot R. Shim'on ben Yohai, BhM* 3.80; *Pirqe Mashiah, BhM* 3.76–77; *S'udat Livyatan, BhM* 6.150–51; *Mid. Alpha Beta diR. Akiba, BhM* 3.33–34; *Mid. haN'elam, Zohar* 1.135b, 136a.

221. *1 En.* 45.4–6; 72.1; *Jub.* 1.29; 4.26; *2 Bar.* 44.12.

222. *1 En.* 61.12; *2 En.* 8.1–3; *T. Levi* 18.10–12; *2 Bar.* 4.3.

223. Hubbard, *New Creation,* 52 focuses on the cosmological nature of the new creation but Jackson, *New Creation,* 39 develops the cosmological and anthropological sides in relation. The Pauline new creation metaphor is better as anthropological (2 Cor 5:17; Gal 6:15 καινὴ κτίσις) though Kingdom caries the cosmological and places the Christian within it (1 Cor 6:9–10; 15:50; Col 1:13; 1 Thess 2:12).

224. Bar 2:33–35; 1QS 4.22; 4Q268 frag. 2 col. 1 6–8; CD B col. 19.12; 1QpHab col. 2.3; col. 11 13; 4Q434 frag. 1 col. 1.4; 4Q437 frag. 1 line 4.

225. *Jub.* 6.17; *Charter of a Jewish Sectarian Association* (1QS; 4Q255–264a; 5Q11) 3.15–4.1; 4.5, 18–23; 1QpHab col. 11.13; *The War Scroll* (1QM, 4Q491–496) 1.1–20; 16.11; 1QH 4, 5, 18; 4Q548 frag. 1 col. 2 9–16; 11Q13 22–25; VanderKam, "Covenant," 1:151–55; Blanton, "Spirit and Covenant Renewal," 137–38.

pure living of the narrow way, utilizing New Covenant terminology (such as: "empowered by Spirit", "circumcision of heart" and "internalization of Law") to describe this life transformation (Deut 30:6; Jer 31:33, Joel 2:28–29).[226] For example, Pharisaic *Jubilees* describes Israel in the New Covenant as returning to Yahweh.

> After this they will return to Me in all uprightness and with all of their heart and soul. And I will cut off the foreskin of their heart and the foreskin of the heart of their descendants. And I shall create for them a holy spirit, and I shall purify them so that they will not turn away from following me from that day and forever.[227]

As such, this New Covenant expression is seen as a divine internalization wherein God resolves the problems from Israel's Mosaic Covenant rebellion and Yahweh's curse toward Israel's unresponsiveness.

The concept of New Covenant was used at Qumran to indicate the faithful or "true Israel" who walk in the proper order of the Qumran Covenanters and obey the previous covenants.[228] In contrast to the Mosaic Covenant, the New Covenant is for them a new beginning of the faithful keeping of the Mosaic Covenant by those who follow Abraham.[229] As such, the New Covenant is a sectarian route of repentance so that they return to the Mosaic Covenant.[230] While empowering living in the Mosaic Covenant, such a New Covenant ushers in a new era.[231]

---

226. *Jub.* 1.23–24; *Charter of a Jewish Sectarian Association* (1QS, 4Q255–264a and 5Q11) 3.7–12; 4.22–24; 5.5; *Damascus Document* (CD 4Q268 frag. 1=4Q266 frag. 2 Col. 1) ver. 6; 14.1–2; B col. 19, ver. 12–13 here the New Covenant is clearly still Law such as Jer 31:33 Hebrew; 1QpHab 2.3; 11.13 "circumcision of heart's foreskin"; *Odes Sol.* 11.1–3; *4 Ezra* 4.26; 7.50; 9.31; *Ex. Rab.* 19(81c) and *Targum Cant.* 3.8.

227. *Jub.* 1.23; also *Jub.* 1.17–18 and 24–25; *1 Bar.* 2.35.

228. *Charter of a Jewish Sectarian Association* (1QS, 4Q255–264a and 5Q11) 3.7–12, 26; 4.22–23; 5.5, 21; 9.6; *Damascus Document* (CD 4Q268 frag. 1=4Q266 frag. 2 Col. 1) ver. 6; 6.9, 19; 8.21=19.33–34; 14.1–2; 20.12; B col. 19, ver. 12–13 here the New Covenant is clearly still Law such as Jer 31:33 Hebrew; 19.33; 20.12; 1QpHab 2.3 there is a lacuna where likely בְּרִית stood as referring to new "covenant"; 11.13 "circumcision of heart's foreskin"; *4 Ezra* 9.31; Freedman and Miano, "People of the New Covenant," 7–26; Evans, "Covenant in the Qumran," 55–80.

229. CD 1.3–5; 2.14–3.21; 5.20–6.3.

230. *Jub.* 6.17; *Charter of a Jewish Sectarian Association* (1QS; 4Q255–264a; 5Q11) 3.15–4.1; 4.5, 18–23; 1QpHab col. 11.13; *The War Scroll* (1QM, 4Q491–496) 1.1–20; 16.11; 1QH 4, 5, 18; 1QSa; 4Q548 frag. 1 col. 2 9–16; 11Q13 22–25; CD 8.16–18; possibly a reference in *Hab. Pesher* 2.3 "those who betr[ayed] the new [covenant]."

231. *Lev. Rab.* 9.7; 13.3; *Eccles. Rab.* 11.8; *S. of S. Rab.* 2.12, 4; *Targum on Isa* 12.3

Gentiles

Many in second Temple Judaism considered that Gentiles and even Samaritans were sinners[232] and unclean,[233] and thus excluded from the afterlife.[234] This view was grounded upon Israel being uniquely chosen by God as God's "portion and inheritance,"[235] thus blessed "above all the nations,"[236] and with a national hope of restoration into Kingdom.[237] This fostered a rabbinic discussion about whether Gentile children would be damned with their parents and the prevailing conclusion was that those who had not reached the age of accountability simply would be neither raised nor condemned.[238]

In contrast to this dominant negative perspective on Gentiles some rabbinics viewed Abraham as called to covenant for the nations,[239] which made Abraham the first Gentile proselyte[240] and missionary to Gentiles.[241] As part of the deeper back story, a few rabbinics conjectured that Gentiles were offered *torah* but they rejected it and thereby were rejected by God.[242] Consequently Jewish practices were to be maintained and Gentile practices (which were seen as akin to idolatry) were to be avoided, as *Jubilees* describes.

> Separate yourself from the gentiles, and do not eat with them, and do not perform deeds like theirs. And do not become associates of theirs. Because their deeds are defiled, and all of their ways are contaminated, despicable, and abominable.[243]

---

and Song 5.10; *Yalkut Isa.* 26.2; Midrash to Ps 146.7; *b. Sanh.* 51b; *b. Šabb.* 151 b.

232. Ps 9:17; Tob 13.6; *Jub.* 33.23-24; *Pss. Sol.* 2.1-2.

233. *b. Šabb.* 17b; *b. AZ* 36b; *y. Šabb.* 1.3.

234. *Tosefta Sanhedrin* 13:2 where rabbi Joshua argues the point from Ps 9:17; *b. 'Avodah Zara* 2b-3a; Joel Kaminsky, "Israel's Election," 17-30.

235. *Pss. Sol.* 17.15, 23; *Jub.* 23.24; *L.A.B.* 7.3; 10.2; 12.4; 14.5; Gal 2:15; 2 Bar. 82.5; Sir 50.25-26; 4 Ezra 6.56; Second benediction of *birkat ha-torah* line 117; cf. DiSante, *Jewish Prayer*, 67.

236. *Pss. Sol.* 11.9; 11.8-11; *L.A.B.* 11.1; 19.8; 30.4; 35.2.

237. *1 En.* 90.34-38; *Jub.* 1.15-25; *Pss. Sol.* 17.21-46; m. Sanh. 10.1.

238. *T. Sanh.* 13.1-2 (434); *Bar. Sanh.* 110b; *'Abot R. Nat.* 36; *p. Šeb.* 4, 35c, 29; Str-B. 1:786.

239. *T. Benj.* 10.9-10.

240. Philo, *Cher.* 31; *Mut.* 76; *Somn.* 161; *Spec.* 1.52.

241. *B. Hag.* 3a; Josephus, *Ant.* 1.161-67.

242. *Sif. Deut.* 343.4.1-2; *L.A.B.* 11; *Mekilta* 2.

243. *Jub.* 22.16; *L.A.B.* 9.1, 5; 12.2-10; 18.13-14; 19.7; 21.1; 25.7-13; 27; 30.1;

As such, God's grace and protection upon Israel is contrasted with His condemnation and destruction of the "unlawful" nations.[244] Uriel is characteristic in *4 Ezra* claiming that there will be great joy in the salvation of the few, but no grief in the damnation of the many (Jew as well as Gentile).[245] Uriel justified his response by appealing to Moses in Deuteronomist covenant nomism, "For this is the way of which Moses, while he was alive spoke to the people, 'Choose for yourself life, that you may live!' But they did not believe him, or the prophets after him, or even myself who have spoken to them."[246]

However, some second Temple documents taught that Gentiles could be included by renouncing idolatry, converting to Judaism, and embracing the benefits of Kingdom (Ps 22:27; Isa 2:2–3; 14:1; 56:6–8; Ezek 47:22–23; Dan 11:34; Mic 4:2; Zech 2:11; 14:16; Ezra 6:21; Esth 9:27).[247] Many diaspora Jews sought the conversion of Gentiles to Judaism.[248] Many proselytes came to Judaism from among these Gentiles.[249] The proselyte experience was initiated by the Gentile accepting circumcision[250] and the purifying process of proselyte baptism in repentance.[251]

34.1–5; 41.3; 43.5; 44; 45.3; *Sifra* 193.1.9–11; 194.2.1, 15; *Bavli 'Abodah Zarah* 1.1.1.2/2a–b; Neusner, *Handbook of Rabbinic Theology*, 148–50, 492.

244. *Pss. Sol.* 7.6–10; 8.23–34; 10.5–8; 11.1–9; 12.6; 17.1–46; *L.A.B.* 10.4–6.

245. *4 Ezra* 7.126–31.

246. *4 Ezra* 7.129–30.

247. Tob 13.11; 14.6–7; *Pss. Sol.* 17.34; *T. Benj.* 9.2; *T. Jos.* 4.4–6; *T. Zeb.* 9.8; *Jos. Asen.* 12.3–5; *Mekhilta* 33.1.1; *Sifre* on Deut 20:16–18; *b. Soṭa* 35b; *b. Sanh.* 96b; Kaminsky, "Israel's Election," 17–30; Donaldson, *Judaism and the Gentiles*.

248. Tob 1.8; 13.11; Jdt 14.10; 2 Macc 3.1–3, 12, 33–39; 13.23; Theodotus, frag. 4 *P.E.* 9.22.4–6; Josephus, *Ant.* 20.34–36; *Ag. Ap.* 2.210; *m. 'Abot* 1.12; *b. Šabb.* 31a; *Sanh.* 99b; *Gen. Rab.* 39.14; 47.10; 48.8; 84.8; 98.5; *Num. Rab.* 8.4; *Eccl. Rab.* 7.8, section 1; *Pesiq. Rab Kah. Sup.* 1.6; *Pesiq. Rab.* 14.2; 43.6.

249. Jdt 14.10; Tob 1.8; 2 Bar. 41.4; Josephus, *Ant.* 18.82; 20.34–53; Philo, *Virt.* 102; *Spec.* 1.51–52; 4.178; *4 Ezra* 3.36; *m. Bik.* 1.4; *b. Pesaḥ* 87b; *m. 'Abot* 1.12; *b. Šabb.* 31a; *Sipre Num.* 108; *Mek.* on Exod 20:10; *b. Sanh.* 97b; petition 13 in *Shemoneh 'Esreh*; Mt. 23:15; Acts 2:11; 6:5; 13:43; Justin, *Dial.* 122; Dio Cassius, *Rom. Hist.* 37.17.1; 57.18.5; 67.14.1–3; Juvenal, *Satire* 14; Horace, *Satires* 1.4.142–43; cf. Pau Figueras, "Epigraphic," 194–206; E. L. Sukenik, *Jüdische*," 13; Donaldson, *Paul and the Gentiles*, esp. 51–78.

250. Jdt 14.10; Josephus, *Ant.* 13.257–58, 318–19; Josephus indicates circumcision caused Izates hesitation in proselytizing (*Ant.* 20.39–42); *Sipre* on Num. 15:14 [108]; *m. Ker.* 2.1; *b. Ker.* 9a.

251. *T. Levi* 14.6; *Midrash Sifre Num.* 15:14; *b. Yebam* 46a–48b; Epictetus, *Ditr.* 2.9.19; Josephus, *J. W.* 2.150; *Ant.* 14.285; 18.93–94; *Sib. Or.* 4.165; *m. Tohar* 7.6; *t. Yoma* 4.20; *t. Pesaḥ* 7.13; Acts 10:28; John 18:28; Jews into Qumran: 1QS 3.3–6; Jews to John's Kingdom Judaism: Matt 3:11; Luke 3:7.

2 Baruch identifies that proselytizing Gentiles must accept "the yoke of [God's] Law."²⁵² *Pseudo-Philo* extends Israel's election experience through the Mosaic Covenant to be accomplished by divine grace within Israel, and then expands culpability for the Mosaic Covenant to the whole world.

> In the third month after the sons of Israel had gone forth from the land of Egypt, they came into the wilderness of Sinai, and God remembered his words and said, "I will give a light to the world and illumine their dwelling places and establish my covenant with the sons of men and glorify my people above all nations. For them I will bring out everlasting statutes that are for those in the light but for the ungodly a punishment . . . [to Moses] I will put my words in your mouth, and you will enlighten my people, for I have given an everlasting Law into your hands and by this I will judge the whole world."²⁵³

A number of second Temple texts clarify that a Gentile proselytizing to Judaism joins the exclusive Jewish community including circumcision. For example, *Judith* describes Achior's proselytizing, after seeing "all that the God of Israel had done . . . he believed firmly in God . . . was circumcised, and joined the house of Israel."²⁵⁴ The hope is as Philo describes that a proselyte is one who is "circumcised not in foreskin but in pleasures, desires, and other passions of the soul."²⁵⁵ Tacitus describes this proselytizing process, "Those who are concerned to their ways follow the same practice [i.e., circumcision], and the earliest lesson they receive is to despise the gods, to disown their country, and to regard parents, children and brothers as little account."²⁵⁶ The disowning may work the other way as well as the Gentile family abandons the proselyte, as occurred to Asenath when she renounced her former gods, she was orphaned.²⁵⁷ Entrance into Judaism made the Gentile "righteous" or appropriate status within the Mosaic Covenant.²⁵⁸ Such righteousness consists substantially

---

252. *2 Bar.* 41.3; Josephus, *Ant.* 20.44-45; *t. Demai* 2.5; *m. 'Abot* 1.12; 3.5; *b. Šabb.* 31a.

253. *L.A.B.* 11.1-2; Philo, *Mos.* 2.36.

254. Jdt 14.10; *Sipre* on Num. 15:14 [108]; *m. Ker.* 2.1; *b. Ker.* 9a.

255. Philo, *QE* 2.2.

256. Tacitus, *Hist.* 5.5.2; cf. Jdt 5.5-21; 7.23-28; Philo, *Virt.* 102; 181-82; 212-19; *Spec.* 1.51-52; 4.178.

257. *Jos. Asen.* 11.4-5; 12.5-15; Philo, *Spec.* 4.178.

258. *T. Sanh.* 13.2.

of living a life of choosing deeds according to *torah*.[259] Some texts include Gentiles proselytizing into the eschatological Kingdom (Isa 56:6 in the MT; LXX; *Tg. Isa.*; and 1QIsa. a).[260] While this global commitment to covenant nomism occasionally appears in later texts, the more common focus is on Israel's unique covenantal relationship, so there is some suspicion of the motive and value of Gentiles proselytizing into Judaism.[261]

There are even some second Temple Jewish texts that predict Gentile pilgrimage into the eschatological Kingdom without requiring them to proselytize to Judaism (Isa 11:22; 66:18–20; Zech 8:23).[262]

However, some texts identify that Gentiles are perpetually outside the Covenant, and thus damned.[263]

Conclusion

In conclusion, second Temple Jewish documents have everything to support a doctrine of covenant nomism. This doesn't mean that all second Temple documents teach covenant nomism. Nor does this require covenant nomism to be a major theme throughout second Temple Jewish writings. Neither does this study require the New Testament to react to covenant nomism. However, covenant nomism is live in the historical-cultural context. Therefore, the nearer exegetical context must be the forum within which particular textual decisions are made with regard to the issues of a New or Reformation Paul view. We should not automatically dismiss the New Paul or New Jesus because it does not fit with our traditions, for the view of covenant nomism (which the New Jesus is claimed to embrace and against which the New Paul reacts) is sufficiently instanced within the second Temple Jewish material to fund these

---

259. *Jub.* 7.20.

260. *1 En.* 90.33–38; Sir 44.19–23; *Pss. Sol.* 17.31; *2 Bar.* 41.1–6; 68.1–8; 70.7–8; 72–73; *4 Ezra* 13.33–50; *Jub.* 22.20–22; *Sib. Or.* 3.719, 757–58; *T. Levi* 18.9; *T. Jud.* 24.5–6; 25.3–5; *T. Benj.* 9.2; 10.6–11; *T. Ash.* 7.2–3; *T. Naph.* 8.3–4; Philo, *Mos.* 2.44; *Ex. Rab.* 19.4; *Num. Rab.* 8.2; Evans, "From 'House of Prayer,'" 439 n. 31.

261. *b. Yeb.* 24b; 47a–b; *Mek.* On Ex. 22:20–21; *Lev. Rab.* 27.8.

262. Tob 13.11; 14.5–6; *Sib. Or.* 3.702–31, 772–75; *Pss. Sol.* 17.31; *1 En.* 90.33 and *2 Bar.* 68.5; Donaldson, "Proselytes," 3–27; Fredriksen, "Judaism," 544–48; Bird, "Justification," 125. A supercessionist approach is presented in *5 Ezra* 1.35–40 as a Christian text claiming Ezra abandoned Israel and transferred allegiance to incipient Christianity (Bergren, "Gentile Christians," 593–612).

263. *Jub.* 15.26.

responses. Thus the New Jesus and the New Paul are possible views from the standpoint of the Jewish source material, provided the near contexts of the biblical texts warrant such conclusions.

6

Matthew's Jesus on the Law[1]

THE ESCHATOLOGICAL EXPECTATIONS AMONG the Prophets and Qumran were for a Messianic teacher to be "the interpreter of the Law" (Isa 42:4).[2] John Collins argued that "the interpreter of the Law" was likely at Qumran to be connected with the priestly "Messiah of Aaron."[3] This expectation floated the possibility that the founder of the Qumran community might be this "teacher of righteousness."[4] Perhaps, the notion emerged from the idea of a prophet like Moses or the son of David, Solomon who was a wise teacher as well (1 Kgs 3:12; Prov; Eccl).

Second Temple Jewish literature expected the Teacher of Righteousness to come and teach the righteous Jews God's Law and revelation in a New Covenant form.[5] He would serve as a rival to the man of the lie, a wicked priest who tried to destroy the Teacher of Righteousness. However, the Teacher of Righteousness (as the Messiah of Aaron)[6] would

---

1. This chapter includes revised material from Kennard, *Messiah Jesus*, 107–152 used by permission from Peter Lang publishers.

2. 4Q174 (4QFlor) 1.11–12 (different from the "branch of David" but possibly identified with the priestly Messiah); CD 6.7; 7:18 (identified with the star but different than the Davidic Messiah).

3. Collins *The Star and the Scepter*, 114–115; cf. 4QFlor 1:6–11; 4QTestim 13–17; CD 7:18–19; 4Q541.

4. 4QpPs (4Q171) 3:13–16; 1QpHab 1.13; 2:2, 8–9; 5:10; 7:4–5; 11:5; CD 1.11; 20.1, 28, 32. In these texts the *torah* was taught, not replaced by the "teacher of righteousness."

5. 1QpHab 1.11–13; 2.1–3; 7.1–5, 10–11; 8.1–3; 9.9–10; 11.4–8, 13; 4Q165 frag. 1–2; 4Q171 3.14–17; 4.3–4, 26–27; 4Q173 frag. 1 4; a rather enigmatic comment is made by Jesus at the last supper identifying that the wine symbolizes the New Covenant in His blood and that his death is on behalf of many for forgiveness of sins (Matt 26:28; Mark 14:24; Luke 22:20). This comment identifies Jesus thinks in New Covenant thought forms.

6. 1QpHab 2.2–9; 4Q171 3.15.

prepare those faithful in the Law for eschatological blessing of everlasting life[7] instead of the judgment God will mete out on the unfaithful.[8] In such a setting vicarious atonement death is not expected though mimetic atonement may be common.

In such a Jewish sectarian context, Matt is written for a Jewish audience following Jesus. With a Jewish audience in view, copies of the gospel were produced in Hebrew, though Ireneaus and a number of fathers claim that the original was in Hebrew.[9]

Matthew's gospel portrays the early Messianic Jewish engagement of the Mosaic and New Covenants as fused together in an intense internalism advocated by Jesus. This salvation and ethic is directly applicable for Jewish followers of Jesus. However, because the view Jesus presents is conveyed through the lens of the New Covenant, much of His teaching is directly applicable for all who wish to follow Jesus (including Gentiles), though the especially Law laden teaching (for Jewish Christians) might need to be modified for them, since the Gentile was never under the Mosaic Covenant unless he sojourned in the land of Israel. This applicability of Jesus' teaching is seen beyond the Jewish Christian by the other synoptic gospels as presenting similar teaching to Matthew's presentation with less presence of the Law (as in Luke's Sermon on the Plain). When this happens in parallel synoptic texts to these which Matt includes within his Law emphasis, the other synoptic gospels will be included in the discussion here showing continued relevance of Jesus' teaching for all Christians. So for example, Jesus discussions about Jewish sacrifices or the Law as for salvation would not be applicable for the Gentile Christian as seen through the lens of the Luke-Acts material which discusses the Jerusalem council decision.[10] Here in Matt, that nuance of the later decision at the Jerusalem Council is not yet apparent since the audience for this gospel is primarily

---

7. CD 3.12–16, 20; *Tg. Onq. Lev.* 18.5; *Tg. Ps-Jonathan*; *Sipre Lev.* 193 on Lev 18:1–30.

8. 1QpHab 2.2–10; 5.3–8.

9. Irenaeus, *Haer.* 3.1.1–2; Eusebius, *Hist. eccl.* 3.24.6; 6.25.4; Epiphanius, *Pan.* 30.3.7; Jerome, *Ep.* 20.5; Augustine, *The Harmony of the Gospels* 1.2–3, 3–6; 1.6.78–79; Hebrew Matt preserved in fourteenth century text *Even Bohan*; Howard Hebrew Matthew text based on Add no. 26964 (British Library) for Matt 1:1–23:22 and Ms. 2426 (Jewish Theological Seminary of America) for Matt 23:23–28:20.

10. See chapter eight "Luke and John: Spirit Extended Salvation to the Gentiles Without the Law" also Kennard, *Messiah Jesus*, 157–176.

the Jewish Christian. Jesus also taught other things than these related to biblical covenants, but those are discussed in my book *Messiah Jesus*.[11]

Jesus as Teacher of the Law

Jesus enters upon the scene characterized as "a teacher of the people," by both the Gospels and early Judaism.[12] Such a designation as teacher is the most common way in which Jesus is referred, especially in Matt and Luke.

A supreme example of Jesus' teaching of the Law is in Matthew's Sermon on the Mount. The audience for Jesus' Sermon on the Mount is that disciple band that He has called from among the Jews to follow Him (Matt 5:2 "them" takes nearest referent in 5:1 "disciples"). The sermon is in a very similar style to that of the rabbis of Jesus' day, much evident in the oral *torah* and the later *Talmud*.[13] Much like these Jewish teachers, Jesus' *midrash* teaching goes beyond Law conformity to press application home in the life of His listeners.[14] However, within the sermon there is a focused section to teach the Law. Jesus' Kingdom teaching to Jews incorporates the Law as the ethic to be lived toward the Kingdom. The Law is the framework for Jesus' context and the context of Matthew's Jewish-Christian readership.[15] The other Synoptic Gospels merely treat the binding nature of the Law as a non-emphasized historical feature of Jesus' ministry[16] while Matt emphasizes Jesus' binding the Law upon His

---

11. Kennard, *Messiah Jesus*.

12. Matt 4:23; 5:2, 19; 7:29; 9:35; 11:1; 13:54; 15:9; 21:23; 22:16; 26:55; 28:15, 20; Mark 1:21–22; 2:13; 4:1–2; 6:2, 6, 30, 34; 7:7; 8:31; 9:31; 10:1; 11:17; 12:14, 35; 14:49; Luke 4:15, 31; 5:3, 17; 6:6; 11:1; 12:12; 13:10, 22, 26; 19:47; 20:1, 21; 21:37; 23:5; John 3:2; 6:59; 7:14, 28, 35; 8:2, 20, 28; 9:34; 14:26; 18:20; Acts 1:1; Josephus, *Ant.* 18.63; *b. ʿAbod. Zar.* 17a/t; *Ḥul.* 2.24; *Qoh. Rab.* 1.8(3). The Babylonian Talmud considered Jesus to be a Jewish disciple who turned out badly (*b. Sanh.* 103a; *b. Ber.* 17b).

13. Bokzer, *Judaism*, 194.

14. Baba Mezia 88a; Mekitta on Exod 18:20; cf. Loader, *Jesus' Attitude*.

15. Saldarini, *Matthew's Christian-Jewish Community*, However, I would date the composition of Matthew as before the destruction of the Temple, since Matthew's comments of Jesus on this topic appear to reflect prophecy awaiting fulfillment rather than having been fulfilled, but likely after the Gentile ministry had begun; cf Overman, *Matthew's Gospel*; Levine, *The Social*.

16. See chapters seven and eight: "The Gospel of Mark and the Controversy of Jewish Traditions" and "Luke and John: Spirit Extended Salvation to the Gentiles Without the Law."

disciples and his readership. In all the gospels, but especially in Matt, Jesus radically teaches and lives the Law in three ways. (1) Jesus maintains a more pervasive internalizing of the Law than the Law itself requires, which should be seen as a New Covenant internalization of the Law (Jer 31:33).[17] (2) Jesus emphasizes the priority of the Law's design over against its permissions. (3) Jesus emphasizes the priorities that the Law sets up within itself. For example, Jesus emphasizes generosity and compassionate love beyond the Law's restrictions. Each of these radical extensions is consistent with both the Law as well as New Covenantizing of the Law, so that, for Jesus in Matthew, the way of salvation is via the Messiah and a New Covenant embracing of Law. This is not surprising in its context, since Jewish contextual communities would have thought the same thing.[18] In fact, the charge that sectarian Jewish communities would have against a pan-Judaism is that of not being faithful enough to the Mosaic Law.[19] In this way, Jesus could be seen as cultivating and raising up a new sect of peace-making Messianic Judaism (that becomes Jewish-Christianity), with the same charge against Judaism that they were not faithful enough to the Law (Matt 5:20; 23:23). In fact, the Sermon on the Mount can also serve as a polemic to Moses receiving the Law on Mount Sinai,[20] for Jesus provides a New Covenant intensification of the Law. We will develop Jesus' agenda for the Law first in this chapter, largely out of the Sermon on the Mount.

This tension for legitimacy of Jesus' Law teaching among Judaism is responded to by the Jews in two ways: (1) the Jews question Jesus' Law commitment based on: (a) His healing on the Sabbath, and (b) His permitting Himself to be touched by the unclean and, (2) then the Jewish

17. Rabbinics saw that there was a continuity of Law into the Messiah's New Covenant ministry and the Kingdom to come (*Gen. Rab.* 98.9; *Eccl. Rab.* 11.1; *Mid. Tanh., Ki Tavo*, par. 4; Midrash fragment, *BhM* 6.151–52; *Halakbot G'dolot*, ed. Hildesheimer, 223 top; Azulai, *Hesed l'Avraham* 13c–14a; Vital, *Sefer haHezyonot*, p. 160; *Mid. Talpiyot* 58a; *Yemenite Midrash*, 349–50; Yitzhaq of Berdichev, *Imre Tzaddiqim*, ed. Tz'vi Hasid, 10 [5b]. There is no evidence that the Sermon on the Mount is constructed in Hittite treaty form (contr Law, "The Law," 27–29), for example: Matt 5:1-2 is simply a narrative context with no throne names given as occurs in Hittite treaties and Matt 5:3–16 is essential virtues not a historical prologue of the Great King's rescue of the vassal like occurs in a Hittite treaty.

18. Sanders. *Jesus and Judaism; Paul, the Law, and the Jewish People.*

19. Elliott, *The Survivors of Israel.*

20. The mountain is treated as location with no development of polemic to Moses' Mount Sinai (Exod 19:3; 24:13, 18), though Jesus does comment on the Law in a New Covenant manner.

leadership tests Jesus' authority as a scribe to authoritatively teach the Law. These agendas of others are important challenges and must be dealt with to demonstrate Jesus' consistency as the Teacher of righteousness and the Law. These issues will constitute the second half of this chapter.

While this chapter is an attempt to develop the historical Jewish Jesus, it is also Matthew's Jewish emphasis for his Jewish-Christian readership. Matthew concurs that Jewish-Christians should live a New Covenant expression of the Law unto Kingdom. However, this presentation should be balanced by the voices of Mark, John and especially Luke on the Law since Gentile believers are included in salvation. Only after we see Luke's resolution can we appreciate Matthew's, Mark's, and John's important but incomplete contributions, and thus maintain them all in tension.

Sermon on the Mount and Plain (Matt 5–7; Luke 6:20–49)

To demonstrate Jesus' continuity with both second Temple Judaism and John's kingdom ministry, it is helpful to examine the core of Jesus' teaching. Here, two introductions to Jesus' characteristic sermons will be examined (the Sermon on the Mount and the Sermon on the Plain)[21] showing Jewish-Jesus continuity within the narrow way unto Kingdom. Jesus has new things to say in these sermons but there is a great degree of continuity with second Temple Judaism as well. Both the new and the continuity will be highlighted throughout this section.

Both the Sermon on the Mount and the Sermon on the Plain are addressed to Jesus' disciples (Matt 5:12; Luke 6:20). Of course, the multitude overheard his teaching (Matt 5:1; 7:28) but the thrust was for those already identified with Jesus as His disciples.

Jesus' sermons position themselves within a two way approach unto Kingdom, much like second Temple Judaism and John the Baptist had before Him.[22] Both the Sermon on the Mount and the Sermon on the Plain

---

21. These two sermons are given historically at different times, since the miracle of healing the leper immediately follows the Sermon on the Mount, as Jesus is coming down from the mountain (Matt 8:1–2) and precedes the Sermon on the Plain (Luke 5:12–15; 6:20–49) and Luke identifies that he writes his gospel in consecutive order (Luke 1:3). Additionally, the geography of mount and plain identify different locations (Matt 5:1; Luke 6:17). Cf. Loehr, "Jesus and the Ten Words" in *Handbook* 4:3135–54.

22. Second Temple Judaism develops a two ways view unto Kingdom especially from a wisdom and prophetic perspective (Sir 35.11; 48.10; *Bar.* 4.37; 5.5; 2 Macc

follow this Jewish orientation as is apparent especially in the beginning and end of the sermons (Matt 5:3–16; 7:13–27; Luke 6:20–26). However, the clearest development of the two ways approach is in the conclusion of the Sermon on the Mount in which five illustrations portray the two ways: 1) gates and ways, 2) sheep versus wolf in sheep's clothing, 3) trees, 4) claims demonstrated, 5) and builders (Matt 7:13–27). Each way has a goal toward which it leads, either that of life and the Kingdom (Matt 7:14, 21) or destruction (Matt 7:13, 19, 27; 16:18). Jesus begins His exhortation to enter by the narrow gate[23] and the way that leads to life. Only one of the two-ways saves, the other damns. The narrowness of the strictured way (στενης and τεθλιμμένη) has implications that there are few who find it (Matt 7:13–14; Luke 13:23–25). While the breadth of the way that leads to destruction indicates that many will follow this way (Matt 7:13, 22). The broad way includes those who take advantage of others as: wolves in sheep's clothing or false prophets. The basic way on which a person travels is evidenced by the consistent obedience in following Jesus' and the Father's teaching (Matt 7:21, 24, 26). However, this is not a way of earning one's place in Kingdom, rather it is showing in a natural fruiting manner that has an intimate internalized discipleship relationship with the Son (Matt 7:15, 17–19, 23). The Kingdom way is not shown in works such as prophecy, exorcisms, or miracles (Matt 7:15, 22). Rather, *the Kingdom way is shown in New Covenant obedience rather than Lawlessness* (Matt 7:21–24, 26). The good man or tree produces the good fruit and generous speech from within his heart (Matt 7:16–20 with vs. 12; Luke 6:43–45).[24] Works show what kind of person someone is. Such a good person builds on the firm rock foundation of obedience to Jesus and the Father (Matt 7:24–27; Luke 6:46–49).[25] *Such strictured but wise living does not remove the troubles of life but instead enables one to survive them, because he has built upon the foundation of Jesus' teachings.* Eschatological justification unto Kingdom assesses the disciple's aligning with Jesus from the evi-

---

1.27; 2.18; *Jub.* 1.15; *Pss. Sol.* 8.34; 11.2; 14.9–10; 15.10; 17.11–12, 28–31, 50; 18.6–9; 1QM 2.2, 7; 3.13; 5.1; 11QT 8.14–16; 57.5; 1QS 3.18–4.26; 4Q228; 4Q473 frag. 2 2–4; *Charter of a Jewish Sectarian Association* 9.21; *Asher* 1.3–5; 6.4–6; Philo, *Rewards* 164; 4 Ezra 7.6–8). W. D. Davies and Dale Allison, *Matthew*, 1:439, 442–480 present these beatitudes as entrance requirements into the Kingdom.

23. Luke 13:24 has narrow door instead of gate.

24. A similar good tree/bad tree comparison is made in the Jewish parables in *M. Aboth* 3.18; *ARNa* 22.2; *ARNb* 34; *Tg. Ps.-J.* on Gen 4:8 and Deut 20:20.

25. *ARNa* 24.1–4, 22 makes similar building materials and on rock or sand comparisons in a two ways Jewish salvation.

dence from virtues of righteousness, forgiveness and doing good to indicate who is granted everlasting life (Matt 13:39–43, 49–50; 18:35; 25:12, 34–46; Luke 13:23–30).

Elsewhere, in the two ways soteriology, there is a way of light and a way of darkness (Matt 7:22–23; Luke 11:34–36).[26] In Judaism, God is seen to dwell in light (Ps 104:2; Dan 3:3–4; Hab 3:3–4)[27] and thus He gives light to His people (Job 29:2–3; Pss 4:6; 18:28; 48:3).[28] The eschatological hope is light (Isa 60:20), but those who are God's are now illuminated by revelation light of life and wisdom (Pss 27:1; 56:13; Hos 10:12 LXX; John 1:4, 9).[29] This illumination impacts the righteous so that they are described as the people of the light who "walk in the light of the Lord" (Isa 2:5; 42:6; 49:6; Matt 5:14; 6:22; 1 John 1:5–10).[30] The way of the light shows the issues and allegiances clearly, demonstrating its sincere allegiance to God (Matt 6:22; Luke 11:34).[31] The way of the darkness cannot see clearly. Darkness is duplicitous and deceived, being unaware of its blindness and separation from God (Job 18:5–6; 38:15; Matt 6:23; Luke 11:34–35; 1 John 1:6, 8, 10).[32] For example, such a condition of Jewish "evil eye" is that of a selfish miser, signifying intent and remaining in darkness (Deut 15:9; Prov 23:6; 28:22).[33] In spite of fire, hell is described as a dark place with the outcome being darkened lives (Matt 8:12; 22:13; 25:30).[34]

Beatitudes-Similitudes

Both the Sermon on the Mount and the Sermon on the Plain begin with beatitudes. In Luke the two ways are more explicit as it includes a section of curses following the beatitudes (Matt 5:3–10; Luke 6:20–26). Each of the beatitudes begins with the word "blessed," serving as a repetitive[35]

---

26. Davies and Allison, *Matthew*, 1:635–36 develop that the eye in ancient Judaism was viewed as a light source and that they embraced an extra-mission theory of vision, unlike modern empiricism which embraces an intromission theory of vision.

27. *1 En.* 38.4; *Jos. Asen.* 6.3.

28. 1QS 11.3; *2 Bar.* 38.1.

29. Sir 8.1; Wis 7.10, 26.

30. *1 En.* 104.2; *T. Levi* 14.3; *LAB* 51.6; *T. Job* 31.5; 53.3.

31. Job 1:1 Aq.; *Barn.* 19.2; *T. Levi* 13.1; *Ps. Phoc.* 50; CR col. 3 and 4.

32. *T. Job* 43.5–6; *T. Sol.* 26.7.

33. Tob 4.7; Sir 14.8; 26.11; *m. 'Abot* 2.9, 11; 5.19; 1QS 4.9–11.

34. 1QS 2.8; *1 En.* 103.7.

35. While the O.T. beatitudes do not group more than two together (e.g., Ps

echo concerning the beneficial condition that a disciple can possess provided he meets the criterion of each verse. This means that the beatitudes are first and foremost blessings that show God's grace, rather than requirements.[36] Conditions evidence which disciples of Jesus will be so blessed, as Albert Schweitzer said it, the beatitudes "define the moral disposition which justifies admission into the Kingdom."[37]

The blessed conditions are to be understood as realized within the Kingdom. Matthew's beatitudes begin and end with identifying blessing with "the Kingdom" (Matt 5:3-10).[38] The *inclusio*[39] (or literary envelope; Matt 5:3, 10) of mentioning the Kingdom serves to identify the other blessings as Kingdom benefits as well. Additionally, some of the benefits are only believably received in the eschatological Kingdom, such as the idea of meek and gentle inheriting the earth (Matt 5:5). Luke's account begins with the Kingdom but does not quite complete an *inclusio* in its close of promising great reward to come from heaven to earth (Luke 6:23).

These Kingdom benefits have both present and future in view. Matthew's *inclusio* and Luke's starting point of "theirs *is* the kingdom" evidences by its present tense verb that present Kingdom benefits are already in play for those who meet the criteria (Matt 5:3, 10; Luke 6:20). The other beatitudes evidence by their future tense verb a future reward that is not yet received but will especially be realized in the future eschatological

---

84:4-5), the listing of nine beatitudes should not overwhelm the reader, since by second Temple Judaism an occasional list of beatitudes is as long (Matt 5:3-11; five in 4Q525 including purity of heart and faithfulness to the Law; four in Luke 6:20-22). 2 *En.* 52.1-14 has seven beatitudes and seven curses. Later, the *Gos. Thom.* has ten beatitudes, some in series (7, 18-19, 49, 54-58, 68-69, 103). Additionally, the Matt beatitudes may have parallels with Isa 61, quoted in Luke 4:18-19; cf. Sir 14.1-2, 20-27; Davies and Allison, *Matthew,* 1:436-439.

36. Beatitudes are found in Jewish wisdom (Sir. 14.20-27) and prophetic texts (2 *En.* 52.1-14). As a genre, it is not really Law or covenant, even though these genres possess statements of blessing and curse, but not in beatitude form (Deut 28-30).

37. Schweitzer, *The Mystery of the Kingdom of God,* 53-54; *The Kingdom of God and Primitive Christianity,* 93-101. Thus the liberal ethical approach (e.g., von Harnack, *Das Wesen des Christentums*; *What is Christianity*; Scott, *The Ethical Teaching of Jesus*; Marshall, *The Challenge of New Testament Ethics*; Cox, *The Secular City* has ignored the Jewish eschatological Kingdom context for Jesus teaching.

38. The Kingdom focus of these beatitudes is like the beatitudes of: *Pss. Sol.* 17.44 or 1 *En.* 58.2-3 "Blessed are you righteous and elect ones, for glorious is your portion. The righteous ones shall be in the light."

39. Latin for enclosing in a literary envelope.

Kingdom (especially clear in: Matt 5:5, 12; Luke 6:23), thus the beatitudes must be taken together. No one benefit can be removed from the rest of the Kingdom framework or a disciple relationship to the King, likewise no one quality can be lifted to promise Kingdom benefits. For example, merely because a person grieves or is gentle does not guarantee her involvement in the Kingdom. However, when someone who *has* a discipleship relationship with Jesus, grieves or is gentle there is in fact an appropriate reassurance that Kingdom blessings are hers.

"Blessed are the poor in spirit, for theirs is the Kingdom" (Matt 5:3). Recognition of poverty in a disciple's spiritual condition identifies the disciple's trust and dependence upon her master (Jas 2:5).[40] It is not a spiritual benefit for the able and wealthy, but rather for those who recognize their need. This reverses the popular secular sentiment: "blessed are the rich." Luke 6:20 simplifies the poverty to be material poverty which is more emphasized in Luke than any other synoptic gospel (Luke 1:53; 4:18; 6:20; 7:22; 14:13, 21; 16:20, 22; 18:22; 19:8; 21:3).[41] This Lukan portrait is similar to Qumran's self-designation of the sect, as the poor.[42] Whether material poverty shows one to be in need of depending upon God or recognition of one's spiritual nature of inadequacy, the results are the same. Both point to humility and dependence on God, as one admits to her own spiritual bankruptcy. Within Jewish tradition, such a reference to the poor refers to the meek, humiliated and oppressed people of God (Isa 10:2; 26:6).[43] This sentiment affirms one sense of the Jewish tradition indicated in the *Sibylline Oracles* 8.208: "Blessed are the poor, for they shall be rich," especially in eschatological reversal. This is rather telling for American Christianity. In the twenty first century, the world's

---

40. Such fiscal poverty was a positive religious designation in Judaism (1QM 11.9, 13; 13.14; 14.7; 1QpHab 12.3, 6, 10; 4QpPs 37 fr. 1, 2.10).

41. This call to the poor is consistent with 4Q88 9.13–14 and the *Passover Haggadah* which calls all the poor (using similar phrases to that of Jesus in Luke) to the Passover feast. *Gos. Thom.* 54 follows Luke on *fiscal poverty* but Matthew on *third person plural* (*their*) with "Blessed are the poor, for theirs is the kingdom of heaven." That is, Luke personalizes it further by the second person "*yours* is the Kingdom." Additionally, the *Gos. Thom.* 69.2 encourages that these hungry and thirsty will be satisfied.

42. 1QpHab 12.2–10; 1QM 11.9, 13; 13.14; 1QH 2.32; 3.25; 5.16, 18, 22, ; 4QpPs 37 1.9; 2.10; 4Q88 9.13–14; with only the *Damascus Document* using the term in the more common sense of poor people; Dunn, *The Christ & the Spirit*, 1:110.

43. *Pss. Sol.* 5.2, 11; 10.6; 15.1–3; 18:2; 5 *Apoc Syr. Ps.* 2:18; 1QpHab. 12.3; 1QM 14.7 where such poverty might mean fainthearted; 1QH 5.13–14; 4QpPs 2.9–10.

richest 15 percent of people are defined as those who own a house that keeps the weather out and also own a car. Whereas, if you own two cars and some recreational equipment as well, then you are among the top 5 percent of the world's wealthy.[44] Luke warns that those who receive comfort now, their riches may indicate that they are not depending upon God and thus they have no more benefits to come (Luke 6:24). Jewish tradition indicates that in the Kingdom age to come there will be no poverty.[45] Luke later goes on to illustrate this point with Jesus' teaching on wealth, in the parable of the rich man and Lazarus (Luke 16:19–31). Abraham in paradise summarized the point for the rich man as "during your life you received your good things and likewise Lazarus bad things; but now he is being comforted here, and you are in agony" (Luke 16:25). The recognition that of one's own spiritual poverty and being other oriented to benefit those in need, such as homeless Lazarus, is affirmed with serving God (Luke 16:13). Jesus warns the scoffers who thought that they could serve God and money that such a selfish broad way was damnable (Luke 16:21, 23). However, for those whose dependence is on God, the present reality of living and benefiting in Kingdom is their very real possession.

"Blessed are those who mourn, for they shall be comforted" (Matt 5:4; Luke 6:21). Perhaps, picking up the Jewish traditional sentiment from Isaiah 61:1–2, quoted by Jesus as He begins His ministry in the Nazareth synagogue, Jesus provides real comfort in kingdom for the downtrodden and oppressed (Luke 4:18–21).[46] Jewish tradition continued to emphasize that the Kingdom should be thought of as broadly comforting to us in our life of mourning (Isa 60:20; 66:10; Jer 31:13; Ps 126:2–6).[47] The mourning (Matthew's emphasis) and weeping (Luke's emphasis) that occur in this life are in contrast to the comfort and laughing which will come upon all who are beneficiaries of the Kingdom in the future. The mourning refers to a sorrow with the world as it is. Perhaps such mourning produces reflective thought and action to provide comfort to those about who are in need.

---

44. My attempt to conceptualize *U.N. Human Development Report 2003* as summarized by www.trentu.ca/said/povertystats.html which for example lists the salary average of the richest fifth of the world population to be on average $31,000 per capita per year in 1993 dollars, while the poorest fifth of the world population lives on less than $1 per capita per day.

45. *Sib. Or.* 3.378; *T. Jud.* 25.4; *b. Pesh.* 50 in contrast to *b. Šabb.* 151b and *Sipre* on Deut 15:11.

46. Sir 48.24.

47. *Thanksgiving Scroll* 13.14–15; *Bar.* 4.23; 1QH 18.14–15; 11QMelch 2.20; perhaps also Ps 126:2–6.

Matt uses "mourning" in one other place to indicate the inappropriateness of mourning when the disciples have Jesus with them, but Jesus reminds them that He will be taken away (Matt 9:15).[48] When Jesus is removed, mourning their loss is quite appropriate. However, this concept of mourning could be much broader, like sorrow for sin in one's life or context (Matt 25:75; Luke 7:38–48; 22:62).[49] This weeping could occur within areas of lack such as hunger or the lack of love (Luke 6:21–22). Mourning can include loss of loved ones and the futility of wasted life (Matt 2:18; Luke 5:38). Jesus grieves over Jerusalem that is rejecting Him, and urges them to grieve as well (Luke 19:41; 22:28). For those who grieve in any of these ways, real comfort will be theirs in future Kingdom benefits. Jesus' present Kingdom healing even removes the cause for grief for some now, in the promise of raising loved ones from the dead (Mark 5:34; Luke 7:13; 8:52). Luke warns that those who laugh now and do not take to heart the present context of grief shall mourn and weep in their destruction as they miss future Kingdom benefits being poured out (Luke 6:25).

"Blessed are the gentle, for they shall inherit the earth" (Matt 5:5). The quality of πραεις is meekness, absence of pretension. As a virtue, gentleness is other oriented with a kindness that includes these others in Kingdom benefits in a particularly soft and sensitive manner. As such, this meek gentleness is a synonym for poverty of material and in spirit (Matt 5:3; Luke 6:20). In this statement, Jesus echoes the Jewish tradition evident in the Law[50] and articulated by 2 *Enoch* 50.2: "In patience and meekness spend the number of your days so that you may inherit everlasting life." This meekness is a quality Jesus displayed in His humble offering of rest for the disciples (Matt 11:29). It is also a quality predicted of Him by Zech 9:9, which indicates Jesus' peaceful intention in coming to Jerusalem on a colt of a donkey, to offer them the Kingdom if they would have Him as King (Matt 21:5). Jesus did not come to conquer but to offer inclusion into the benefits of Kingdom. Those, like Jesus, who display this quality in relationship as He does, shall inherit the whole

---

48. While not in inspired Scripture as the earliest, nor the best manuscript, Mark 16:10 shows one example of how mourning and comfort surround the death and resurrection of Christ.

49. Tob 13.14; *Pesiq. R.* 28.3.

50. The praise of meekness and gentleness is also evident in Jewish tradition through (Deut 4:1; Ps 37:11; Philo, *Mos.* 2.279; Josephus, *Ant.* 19.330; *m. Soṭa* 9.15; ARN 7; *b. Soṭa* 40a, 49b; *b. Šabb.* 30b; *b. Ned.* 38a; 4QPs 2.9–11) and in classical works as well (Plato, *Crat.* 120E; *Resp.* 375C; Lucian, *Somn.* 10; *Ep. Arist.* 257, 263).

earth, and not merely a part of the land (γῆς in Matt 5:5, 13). This hope of land inheritance also reflects the Jewish hope for the Kingdom (Isa 60:21-22; 61:7; Rom 4:13).[51] Eschatological reversal is a common Jewish hope (Luke 1:50-53).[52]

"Blessed are those who hunger and thirst for righteousness, for they shall be satisfied" (Matt 5:6).[53] Those with a desire for appropriate living to be developed in their lives and contexts will have their need amply met. This quality of righteousness is developed in the next section, but here Jesus' sentiment also reflects Jewish traditional expectations (Pss 42:2; 63:1; 143:6; Amos 8:11).[54] Two prongs of this hunger for righteousness include passion and longing for social justice and personal consistent piety. Such personal piety and relational fairness are the food of life here in community. When these are not present or are abused a famine of righteousness ensues and should provoke a person to hunger and thirst for righteousness. This longing is the same sentiment as seeking above all else God's Kingdom and His righteousness, where there is real encouragement that Jesus' disciples needs will be met (Matt 6:33). Luke describes one who hungers for food, thus identifying the hungry with the poor, who may be oppressed (Luke 6:21 and connecting it by synonymy to Matt 5:3-5, 10-12). Especially, the Lukan version resonates with the Jewish tradition of eschatological reversal (Pss 37:19; 107:5-9; 132:15; Isa 25:6-8; 32:1, 16-17; 49:10-13; 55:1-2; 65:13).[55]

"Blessed are the merciful for they shall receive mercy" (Matt 5:7). Jesus' teaching reflects the sentiment of rabbis elsewhere.[56] The merciful

---

51. *Jub.* 32.18-19; *2 En.* 5.7; 11QTemple 59.11-13; 4QpPs 2.9-12; 4QPs 37; *2 Bar.* 51.3; *m. Qidd.* 1.10.

52. *Sir* 35; *Wis* 5.1-20.

53. *Gos. Thom.* 69.2 takes this beatitude with reference to poverty, hungering and thirsting in need will be satisfied.

54. *Wis* 5.15; Philo, *Post.* 172; *Fug.* 139; *b. Sanh.* 100a; *m 'Abot* 2.2; *Sifra A.M.* par. 8.193.1.11; *Sifra Behuq.* pg. 2.262.19; *b. Qidd* 396; *Pesiq. Rab. Kah. Sup.* 2.1; *Deut. Rab.* 7.9.

55. *1 En.* 58.4; 62.14; *2 Bar.* 29.6; *Par. Jer.* 9.20; 1QSa; 4Q525; *T. Levi* 13.5. This theme is continued in 2 Pet 3.13 and *Gos. Thom.* 5.6; 69b.

56. This is parallel in *b. Šabb.* 151b, "He who has mercy on people obtains mercy from heaven;" also *t. B. Qam.* 9.30, "As long as you are merciful, the Merciful One is merciful to you;" *T. Sim.* 4.4; Josephus, *Ant.* 10.41. Additionally, the rabbis identified that God judged the world by two measures: justice and mercy (*Lev. R.* 29.3), so that following a verse about righteousness it is appropriate to develop the theme of mercy. This sentiment continues in early Christiandom, *1 Clem.* 13.2; Polycarp, *Ep.* 2.3.

are the benefactors who attempt to meet other's needs.[57] The dominant expression of mercy in the synoptics is the healing done by the Son of David (Matt 9:27; 15:22; 17:15; 20:30–31; Mark 5:19; 10:47–48; Luke 1:58; 17:13; 18:38–39). Whereas, in Jewish tradition the primary merciful One is God (1 Sam 23:21; Ps 72:13; Prov 14:21; Mic 6:8).[58] Mercy is one of the weightier matters of the Law and unfortunately was neglected by the scribes and Pharisees (Matt 23:23). One form of the Jewish neglect of mercy was their restrictiveness to their own Jewish group.[59] Jesus' disciples must have mercy in ministering to sinners and forgiving others without judging them (Matt 6:12–15; 7:1–5; 9:13; 12:7; 18:21–35; Mark 11:25). The good Samaritan exemplifies mercy in meeting his neighbor's and even an enemy's needs (Matt 5:44–47; Luke 10:37). This sentiment of showing mercy universally was also a factor in some forms of Jewish tradition.[60] The merciful shall receive mercy (Matt 5:7). The future mercy to be received could be in this life or the Kingdom beyond.[61] In response, praise is given to God for His mercy unfolding in His salvation plan (Luke 1:50, 54, 72, 78). Through Luke 16:24, Jesus warns us that those who do not give mercy (such as the rich man's abuse of Lazarus) will not receive mercy in the afterlife.

"Blessed are the pure in heart, for they shall see God" (Matt 5:8). The pure are the clean who recognize that God alone is their hope (Ps 24:3–4; Matt 23:26; 27:59).[62] The kind of purity described is one of whole moral purity and integrity. Such a person is sincere and not divided against himself. Examples of internal anger and adultery are developed as contrast to this purity in this context (Matt 5:22, 28). Purity of heart also has a community role of transparency and authenticity, rather than living as the hypocrites who present an image to others for their own gain. Such a commitment to purity of heart reflects Jewish tradition (Gen

---

57. *T. Jud.* 18.3–4; Epict. *Disc.* 1.18.4.

58. *T. Zeb.* 5.1, 3; 7.1–8.6; Philo, *Spec.* 4.72, 76–77.

59. For example, Qumran, the Essenes and other Jews maintained a mercy within the community and a hate to outsiders (1QS 1.4, 10–11; 2.4–9; 9:21–23; 1QM 4.1–2; 15.6; 1QH 5.4; *b. Ber.* 33a; *b. Sanh.* 92a; Josephus, *J. W.* 2.139).

60. A commitment to universal mercy is present in rabbinic Judaism (*Sipra* on Lev 19:18 and *Mek.* on Exod 21:35) and outside the Jewish tradition (Polybius 18.37.7; Hesiod, *Op.* 342–43, Solon, frag. 1.3–5; Plato, *Tim.* 17d–18a; *Resp.* 375c; *Meno* 71e; Tacitus, *Hist.* 5.5–6).

61. 2 Tim 1:18; Jude 21; *1 Clem.* 28.1.

62. *2 Bar.* 9.1; *2 En.* 45.3.1; *T. Jos.* 4.6; *Benj.* 8.2; 4QBeat.

20:5-6; Ps 24:3-4; Isa 61:1 "broken hearted" as in responsive from one's heart to God).[63] The privilege of the pure in heart in Jewish tradition is to see or know God in the Kingdom (Job 19:26; Pss 11:7; 17:15; Isa 52:6; 60:16; Jer 24:7; 31:31-34).[64] Jewish tradition developed that such a view of God at the present tended to be beyond normal expectation,[65] so that it remained an eschatological hope (as in Matt 5:8).

"Blessed are the peacemakers, for they shall be called sons of God" (Matt 5:9). The peacemaker is one who reconciles humans into peaceful relationships as is evident in Matthew 5:23-26 and Mark 9:50. Such peacemaking is affirmed by Jewish tradition (Ps 34:14; Prov 10:10).[66] A peacemaker will not force God's Kingdom but will humbly wait for it (Isa 25:6-9; 26:8; 30:15, 18; 40:30-31; 49:23; 50:10-11; 57:13; 64:4; Lam 3:22-26; Mic 7:7; Jas 5:7-9). A peacemaker is one who demonstrates that he is a son of the Father by generously loving and praying for his enemies that persecute him (Matt 5:39-45). Such peacemaking may be at significant cost or loss. Such peacemaking may require letting an abuse go, in forgiving one's abuser. However, this peacemaking is not to be at the expense of denying Jesus as the Son, that is, the King. Associating oneself to Jesus' teachings may in fact separate one from others and work against peace (Matt 10:34). In maintaining a relationship with Jesus as the Messiah, we should work for peace and thereby identify ourselves as sons of God (Matt 5:9, 45; Luke 6:35; 20:36). Here, "sons of God" would imply that God has something of the same quality of loving and working toward peace, that peacemakers as sons would have. A model for sons of God is Jesus, *the* Son of God, who by His mandate in the Davidic Covenant, works for peace (1 Chr 22:9-10; Matt 3:17; 4:3; 17:5; 27:9, 40, 43, 54). Being a son of God would identify one as a son of the Kingdom (Matt 13:38) in contrast to the damned sons of hell (Matt 23:15). This hope of becoming "sons of God" is one which Jewish tradition held out for the Kingdom.[67]

---

63. *T. Naph.* 3.1; *T. Jos.* 4.6; 1 Tim 1:5; 2 Tim 2:22; Heb 10:22.

64. *4 Ezra* 7.98; *b. B. Bat.* 10a; SB 1; *b. Sanh.* 98b; Philo, *Contempl.* 11-12; *Abr.* 57-59; *Mut. nom.* 81-82; Matt 16:27; 24:30; 26:64; Mark 13:26; 14:62; 1 Cor 13.12; Heb 12:14; 1 John 3:2; Rev 1:7; 22:4.

65. Exod 3.6; 19:21; 33:20, 23; John 1:18; 1 Tim 6:15-16; *Sipre* on Num 12:8.

66. *2 En.* 52.11-15; *m.'Abot* 1.12; *m. Pe'a* 1.1; *Mek.* on Exod 20:25.

67. *Pss. Sol.* 17.27; *Sib. Or.* 3.702. Everlasting reward is promised for peacemaking (*m. 'Abot* 2.8; *Pe'a* 1.1; ARN 40A).

"Blessed are those who have been persecuted for righteousness sake, for theirs is the Kingdom" (Matt 5:10-12; Luke 6:22).[68] "Those who have been persecuted" is a perfect participle which emphasizes that we are dealing with qualities over which in this case we have little control. This kind of persecution includes: hatred, ostracism, insults, spurning through defamation, excommunicating[69] and saying all kinds of evil against one falsely on account of Jesus (Matt 5:11; Luke 6:22). Such persecution is essentially directed at those who have identified with Jesus and maintain obedient, righteous character. This is consistent with the Jewish traditional expectation that the righteous will suffer persecution.[70] Such persecution has the potential of devastating a person so that they fall away (Matt 13:21; Mark 4:17). Persecution identifies Jesus' disciples with the prophets who were persecuted by the religious leaders in their context. This virtually guarantees the certainty of the religious leaders persecuting the disciples (Matt 10:23, 38-39; 16:21, 24-26; 23:34-35; Mark 8:31, 34-38; 10:30; Luke 9:21-24; 21:12). Second Temple Jewish tradition identified that the fate of God's prophets was that of martyrdom.[71] In this context it is indeed a bad sign if all speak well of you for this is the way the religious leaders' fathers treated the false prophets (Luke 6:26). To be identified with God's prophets and with the Son in persecution is a cause for rejoicing because it indicates that one will be blessed with life and reward in the Kingdom (Matt 5:11-12; 16:24-27; Mark 8:35-38; Luke 9:24-26). Joy in suffering resonates with a Jewish traditional approach,[72] but more clearly provides the Kingdom rationale for such gladness. It is in this way of identifying with God's prophets that Jesus' teaching resonates with the Jewish revelation heritage. Other than this instance, persecution in the O.T. is not developed as a condition of blessing. The encouragement to joy is rather unusual for Matthew's more somber character in his persecution environment, in contrast to Luke

---

68. 1 Peter 3:14 and *Gos. Thom.* 68 retain the same sentiment. Polycarp, *Ep.* 2.3; Clement of Alexandria, *Strom.* 4.6.

69. Perhaps implied by a wooden reading of the text in Matthew 5:11 and Luke 6:22, namely, "cast out your name as evil on account of the Son of Man," which probably has beneath it a Semitic expression "to cause an ill name to go out." Davies and Allison, *Matthew*, 1:462.

70. Wis 1.16–5.23.

71. *Jub.* 1.12; 4QpHos 2.3–6; Josephus, *Ant.* 10.38; *Ascen. Isa.* 2.16; 5.1–14; *Par. Jer.* 9.21–32; *Tg.* on Isa 28:1.

72. Jdt 8.25; 2 Macc 6.28–30; *2 Bar.* 48.48–50; 52.5–7; *b. Sanh.* 101a; Acts 5:41; Rom 5:3–5; Phil 4:10–13; Jas 1:2, 12; 1 Pet 1:6; 4:13–14.

who writes at great length about rejoicing, which Luke normally identifies with Kingdom realizations occurring and the lost being saved (Luke 1:14, 47; 2:10, 13, 20; 10:20; 15:5, 7, 10, 24, 32; 24:41, 52). Perhaps it is in this Lukan joy (when present Kingdom benefits are realized), that Matthew identifies that blessing is also expressed by a *present* benefit of having the Kingdom now (Matt 5:10). However, Matthew's joy goes further in that it realizes that suffering now for Christ identifies one as a beneficiary of greater Kingdom benefit from heaven in the future as well (Matt 5:12).

"You are the salt of the earth" (Matt 5:13). Salt, gathered from evaporation pools or from the edge of the Dead Sea (Ezek 47:9–11; Zeph 2:9),[73] was a primary implement in keeping food from putrefying (Exod 30:35).[74] It was also used as a condiment to season food (Job 6:6; Isa 30:24) and was a mandatory accompaniment in some sacrifices (Lev 2:13; Ezra 6:9; Ezek 43:24).[75] As such, salt was considered one of the valuable staples of life along with oil and wine.[76] For example, Antiochus IV gave salt, oil and wine to all the Jews who aided him against Ptolemy Philopater (c.a. 170 B.C.). It is important to note that none of the synoptics describes an ethical meaning to this salt description, as though we had a salty task to perform. In fact, since the statement is a descriptive comment of being, "You *are* salt," there is no charge at all to do some salty purpose such as preserving the world. Rather, as a descriptive comment, it recognizes these disciples to be valuable as they are identifying with these beatitude traits. The contextual emphasis of Jesus and all the synoptics is to take this condition of saltiness as something that unfortunately can be lost (Matt 5:13; Mark 9:50; Luke 14:34). That is, salt is more soluble than the impurities contained within it, so the salt could be leached out leaving a non-productive soil worthy only to be trod upon by feet.[77] This loss of salt (μωρανθῇ) is elsewhere taken as an ethical condition of becoming fools (μωρανθῇ; Matt 5:13; Luke 14:34; Rom 1:22; 1 Cor 1:20).[78] Here is where the ethical charge lay: in the same way that salt can leach out and become unrecoverable unproductive soil, so too could the disciples depart from their beatitude traits and be rejected from the Kingdom program already

---

73. Josephus, *Ant.* 13.128.

74. Ignatius, *Magn.* 10; Diogenes Laertius, *Vit.* 8.1.35.

75. *Jub.* 21.11; 11QTemple 20; *m. Mid.* 5.3.

76. Sir 39.26; Pliny the Elder, *Nat.* 31.102; *m. Sota* 9.15.

77. Pliny the Elder, *Nat.* 31.82.

78. This allusion also works in Aramaic and Hebrew, further underscoring that loss of salt and foolishness are related.

begun with them. The exhortation is for one to stay true to the beatitudes as qualities of one's being, for this indicates the blessing of the Kingdom.

"You are the light of the world" (Matt 5:14). Again, this is a declaration of a quality of being. Jewish tradition developed that people could be light (Isa 42:6; 49:6; Dan 12:3).[79] The disciples in their beatitude traits were like light. Here the emphasis is not on the losing of the quality of being (such as with salt) but on doing what light does. A lit-up city is visible on a hill at night, so also oil lamps that are lit are used to shine light to their whole environment, not to be hidden under a basket (Matt 5:14–15; Mark 4:21; Luke 8:16; 11:33).[80] The disciple is to let this light quality of his life be visible to others *by doing good works reflective of the beatitude virtues* (Matt 5:16). The purpose (ὅπως) of being light is so that others may see our good works and praise the Father as a result.

This look at the beatitudes and similitudes has provided a brief overview of the way to obtain the Kingdom. It is a virtue salvation in discipleship relationship with Jesus, possessing beatitude qualities of behavior or character, while aligned with Jesus. For example, evangelicals tend to emphasize salvation by faith. Jesus in the gospel of John would recognize faith as the critical salvation virtue. However, this current discussion is trying to unpack the Sermons on the Mount and Plain, which neither deny nor develop faith in that manner. Actually synoptic gospels identify faith with obtaining healing.[81] This virtue salvation is dependent upon a relationship with Jesus, which obtains, retains, and exhibits these Beatitude qualities evidenced through good works. Loss of these qualities spells a rejection from the Kingdom. Continuation in these qualities as a disciple of Jesus indicates great blessing in the Kingdom.

Excursus on Righteousness in the Synoptics

Righteousness is central to Jesus' Kingdom program in Matt. The author Matthew ties with Paul for the most instances of δικαιος in any N.T. authors (17 times). Luke also reflects the emphasis of righteousness but not to Matthew's extent (11 times). For Mark the quality is peripheral (2

---

79. *1 En.* 104.2; *2 Bar.* 77.13–16; *T. Levi* 14.3–4; *T. Job* 31.5; *Par. Jer.* 9.14; *Apoc. Adam* 83.3–4; *b. Sanh.* 14a; *b. B. Bat.* 4a; *ARN* 25; 1QS 3.3, 19–22; 1QM 13.5–6, 14–15; *T. Job* 43.6/4; *Sib. Or.* fr. 1.26–27.

80. A similar point is made in *Gos. Thom.* 33b about preaching instead of good deeds.

81. Kennard, *Messiah Jesus*, 33–36.

times). The word δικαιος means one who does right. The related word δικαιοσύνη expresses the quality of righteousness. Matthew (6 times) dominates Luke (1 time in gospel, though 4 times in Acts) in using this word but Paul controls the N.T. emphasis with 60 times. The related word δικαιοω means justify or vindicate. Luke (5 times in gospel and 2 times in Acts) dominates Matthew in using the word but Paul controls the N.T. emphasis with 26 times. The following instances are δικαιος unless otherwise indicated.

Righteousness is grounded in the Law. The Old Testament, Second Temple Judaism, and Rabbinic Judaism identified righteousness as conformity to the Law.[82] Therefore, there is great continuity between second Temple Judaism and the synoptic presentation of Judaism. For example, Luke identifies that the blameless walk includes keeping God's commandments as righteousness (Luke 1:6). In fact, the Law is so identified with righteousness as to let the cognate δικαιομα mean commandments (Luke 1:6). Matthew retains Jesus' identification that loving one's neighbor is an instance of righteousness in keeping the Law (Matt 5:43, 45). The righteous conform themselves with the Law in opposition to sin (Matt 9:13; Mark 2:17; Luke 1:17; 5:32; 15:7). These sinners need to repent to become identified with righteousness.

Righteousness extends beyond the Law to include any appropriate action when viewed from the perspective of integrity, thus continuity with what was considered appropriate in second Temple Judaism is also the issue in righteousness. Joseph is described as a characteristically righteous man even though in mercy he does not insist on the Law by not exposing Mary for adultery which he thought she must have done in order to be pregnant with Jesus (Matt 1:19). This reference expands righteousness to appropriate integrity. So that if a person trusts a man of integrity for an appropriate wage, it will be a righteous wage (Matt 20:4). Furthermore, the ones who generously meet needs are righteous, for they are ones who do what is appropriate (Matt 25:37). In this way righteousness becomes synonymous with "holy," "devout," and "good" (Mark 6:20; Luke 1:75 δικαιοσύνη; 2:25; 23:50).[83]

---

82. Kennard, *Biblical Covenantalism in Torah: Judaism, Covenant Nomism, and Atonement,* chapter six on "Hebrew Metaphysic" under the section of "Righteousness."

83. Kennard, *Biblical Covenantalism in Torah: Judaism, Covenant Nomism, and Atonement,* chapter six on "Hebrew Metaphysic" overlap comparing sections "Holy" and "Righteousness."

Luke emphasizes that righteousness includes a correct assessment or vindication. Making a correct judgment is righteousness (Luke 12:57). God is acknowledged to be righteous (δικαιοω) by those who acknowledge John's baptism (Luke 7:29). Wisdom is vindicated (δικαιοω) by the lives of its children (Matt 11:19; Luke 7:35). The following are declared to be righteous: Jesus, John the Baptist, Joseph, Abel, Zechariah son of Berechiah, Zacharias, Elizabeth, and Simeon (Matt 1:19; 10:41; 13:17; 21:32; 23:29, 35; 27:19 and maybe 27:24; Mark 6:20; Luke 1:6; 2:25).

Pursuit of the Kingdom is a pursuit of righteousness. This appropriate way to live is identified with God's Kingdom to the extent that to pursue God's Kingdom is to pursue God's righteousness (Matt 7:33; δικαιοσύνη). Such pursuit is a desire, investigation, striving after, a living for and praying for appropriate living (Matt 6:32–33; 7:7–8). When one is living appropriately he is living in the way of righteousness (Matt 21:32; δικαιοσύνη). Even sinners can recognize the way of righteousness when it is fleshed out and taught by someone like John the Baptist. At the beginning of Jesus' ministry, He desired to do everything appropriately, "fulfilling all righteousness" (Matt 3:2; 21:32). Jesus then called His disciples into the way of righteousness. Those who hunger and thirst for righteousness in their own lives and the society about them will be satisfied (Matt 5:6). For example, a sinner who admits sin to God is vindicated by God, for God has mercy on him (Luke 18:14). This Lukan reference is perhaps the only synoptic reference that approximates a Pauline legal justification and it actually is still very oriented to relational vindication from humility to exaltation. On the other hand, in Matt both the view of Paul's legal justification and Luke's one instance of relational vindication are foreign. A hungering and thirsting for righteousness would constitute a commitment to appropriate living as defined by the rest of the beatitudes (Matt 5:10, 20). Hungering and thirsting are not different levels of desiring righteousness, for each of the beatitudes calls the disciples to one commitment of a virtue and provides one benefit to meet the virtue's need. The only split beatitude, Matt 5:10–12 "persecuted for the sake of righteousness," is also actually unified as well. Matt 5:10 states it simply, and Matt 5:11–12 respectively explore kinds of persecution and the reward of obtaining the Kingdom benefits, with its present joy. Persecution for righteousness' sake is any form of persecution that includes insults and false accusations; it need not be merely religious persecution or doing some right deed, though these could be included. The hungering and thirsting are then descriptive terms which nicely resolve together in mealtime imagery of being filled to satisfaction. These who are righteous will be eventually separated from the sinners, so that they will shine in the Kingdom with everlasting life (Matt 13:43, 49; 25:46; Luke 14:14).

The righteous who can expect to enter into the Kingdom are required to have righteousness surpassing the scribes and Pharisees (Matt 5:20). The religious leaders attempted to vindicate (δικαιοω) themselves before men but God knows their hearts (Luke 10:29; 16:15). For all their legal and religious fastidiousness, the scribes and Pharisees are excoriated by Jesus for their hypocrisy and Lawless living (Matt 23:28). Their righteousness consists of self-trust and pretense (Luke 18:9; 20:20). Jesus' disciples must rise above this brand of righteousness to that of sincere appropriate living if they are to be Kingdom bound.

The rest of the Sermon on the Mount and the Sermon on the Plain explain the core of Jesus' teaching, His teaching on the Law and the sincerity of internal Kingdom virtues. Jesus' emphasis reflects a New Covenantal approach to the Kingdom. All of this New Covenant oriented material strongly identifies Jesus with second Temple Judaism.[84]

Matthew 5:17-20; The Law and the Kingdom Salvation Paradigm[85]

Jesus Himself lives the Mosaic Law zealously in a New Covenantal manner. Furthermore, in Matt, Jesus mandates zealous teaching and living of the Law as part of His way for His Jewish followers to head toward the Kingdom.

In Matt 5:17, "Do not think that" is a rhetorical device designed to set aside potential misunderstandings. It does not require there to be a popular opinion in need of polemic, for the phrase is used in Matthew 10:34 with no evidence of a pacifist group in Jesus' disciples. Furthermore, the phrase does not require an absolute antithesis, for certainly Jesus urged peace as a Kingdom virtue (Matt 5:9) in spite of His insistence that conflicts would come (Matt 10:34). So when Jesus points out that His purpose for coming is not to abolish but to fulfill, His insistence on His disciples doing the Law and Prophets can permit teaching consistent

---

84. As in Jer 31:31-34 and Ezek 36:24-37:28 so too in: *Jub.* 1:22-25; 1Q3 4, 5; 1QH 4, 5, 18; 4Q Shir Shalb; CD 4Q266 frag. 2 1.6-8; B 19.12-13; 1QpHab 2.3; 11.13; 4Q434 frag. 1 1.4; 4Q437 frag. 1 1.14.

85. This discussion appreciates the Jewish *kĕlāl* teaching pattern of a general principle stated first and then developed through examples. The details are consistent with that of: Davies and Allison, *Matthew*, 1:481-503; McIver, "The Sabbath," 231-32, 241-42.

with the Law and Prophets but with qualifications not immediately apparent in His brief statement.

The "Law or the Prophets" here mean the O.T. or the Scriptures of Jesus' day (Matt 7:12; 11:13; 12:5; 22:40; Luke 16:29, 31).[86] The disjunctive "or" makes it clear that neither is abolished. The prophets answer the Law, so that the referent does not change when only the Law is mentioned in verse 18.

Jesus calls His disciples to see that their lifestyles need to be about fulfilling the Law and the Prophets.[87] "Abolish" means a destruction or removal from experience (Matt 24:2; 26:61; 27:40). Jesus denies that He will destroy or remove the Law from the experience of His disciples.[88] "Fulfill" (πληρῶσαι) means to fill or complete. There is no evidence that πληρῶσαι translates the Aramaic קוּם (*qum*) meaning "establish, validate, or confirm" the Law. The LXX never uses πληρῶσαι to render קוּם (*qum*) or cognates. Instead, the verb πληρῶσαι renders the Hebrew מָלֵא (*ml'*), which means "fulfill." Matthew's use of the verb πληρῶσαι is to fill up a pattern, not that of a one to one correspondence.[89] In Matt 5:17 the issue is not Jesus' keeping of the Law and the Prophets so that He might be a perfect human able to die in our place. Rather the issue is that the ethical lifestyle of Jesus' disciples (reflective of His teaching) is to fit within the Law and the Prophets, and contribute toward identifying them with the Kingdom.[90]

In Matt 5:18, "For truly I say to you" emphasizes that the connection with the preceding is very important. It shows why Jesus' disciples need to fit within the Law pattern in identifying themselves with the Kingdom.[91]

The Law is still in effect such that even the smallest letters and stroke remain binding (Matt 5:18; Luke 16:17). The smallest Hebrew letter is *yod*

---

86. 4 Macc 1:34; 2:5–6, 9; 9:2; Josephus *Ant.* 17.151.

87. *Dial. Of Adamantius* 2.5 claims that Jesus was here to destroy the Law but this statement is too extreme for the Jewish Law affirming context to permit so a straight forward reading of Matthew takes Jesus role as preserving and extending the Law. Parallel Jewish statements to Matthew confirm this sense (*Ep. Isidore* 1.371; *b. Shab.* 116b).

88. Rabbi Gamaliel in *Šabb.*116 a–b says, "I came not to destroy the Law of Moses nor to add to the Law of Moses."

89. Kennard, *Messiah Jesus*, 14–19.

90. Davies and Allison, *Matthew*, 1:485–487.

91. Davies and Allison, *Matthew*, 1:487–491; Meier, "The Historical Jesus," 52–79; *A Marginal Jew. Vol. 4*.

or י.⁹² The *yod* is the center of much rabbinic discussion as the smallest letter. For example, rabbi Honnah said that rabbi Acha described a tradition from rabbi Hoshaia.

> The letter yod which God took out of the name of Sarai our mother was given half to Sara and half to Abraham. A tradition of rabbi Hoshaia: The letter yod came and prostrated itself before God, and said, 'O eternal Lord, thou has rooted me out of the name of the holy woman.' The blessed God answered, 'Hitherto thou hast been in the name of a woman, and that in the end [viz. in Sarai]; but henceforth thou shalt be in the name of a man, and that in the beginning.' Hence is that which is written, 'And Moses called the name of Hoshea, Yehoshua.⁹³

This Jewish teaching is concluded "So you see not even the smallest letter can pass from the Bible."⁹⁴ The name *Yehoshua* is that of Joshua or Jesus, so *yod* matters if you say "Jesus." This is speaking in terms of the sages, as John Fisher quotes, "If the whole world were gathered to destroy the *yod* which is the smallest letter in the Torah, they would not succeed (*Song Rab.* 5.11; cf. *Lev. Rab.* 19). Not a letter shall be abolished from the Torah forever (*Exod. Rab.* 6.1)."⁹⁵ When sages declared that Solomon threatened to uproot a *yod* from the Law, God responded that He would instead uproot a thousand Solomons.⁹⁶

Likewise, every stroke is retained in the Law. A stroke is a very small extention on several Hebrew letters which distinguish these letters from similar ones (ה and ח, or ו and נ or ן, or ר and ד, or כ and ב). Even Luke joins Matt in identifying that "it is easier for heaven and earth to pass away than for one stroke of a letter of the Law to fail" (Luke 16:17; Matt 5:18). The rabbis also speak directly to the absolute importance of every stroke in the text.

> It is written (Lev 22:32) לֹא תְחַלְּלוּ אֶת־שֵׁם קָדְשִׁי *Ye shall not profane my holy name*: whosoever shall change ח into ה, destroys

---

92. I realize that the typeset *yod* is smaller than most instances of manuscript written *yod*, but the argument still holds up as is evident by the following manuscript quotes and second Temple discussion about *yod*.

93. *b. Sanh.* 20.3; *Gen. Rab.* 47.1.

94. *b. Sanh.* 107ab; *p. Sanh.* 2.6.2; *Gen. Rab.* 47.1; *Lev. Rab.* 19.2; *Num. Rab.* 18.21; *Song Rab.* 5.11.3–4.

95. Fisher, "Jesus Through Jewish Eyes: A Rabbi examples the Life and Teachings of Jesus," a paper presented at the Evangelical Theological Society, Nov. 2003.

96. *p. Sanh.* 2.6.2; *Ex. Rab.* 6.1.

the world (for then לֹא תְחַלְלוּ written with ה, makes this sense, *Ye shall not 'praise' my holy name*). It is written (Ps 150:6) כֹּל הַנְּשָׁמָה תְּהַלֵּל יָהּ *Let every spirit praise the Lord:* whosoever changeth ה into ח destroys the world. (It would read *"Let every spirit profane the Lord"*). It is written (Jer 5:12), כִּחֲשׁוּ בַּיהוָה *They lied against the Lord:* whosoever changeth ב into כ destroys the world. (It would read *"Like the Lord they lied"*). It is written (Deut 6:4) יְהוָה אֱלֹהֵינוּ יְהוָה ׀ אֶחָד *The Lord our God is one Lord:* he that changeth ד into ר destroys the world. (It would then read *"The Lord our God is another [god]"*).[97]

Much like the rabbis claiming that the world would be destroyed if strokes were changed, so Jesus claims that the strokes of the Law will be preserved until heaven and earth pass away (Matt 5:18). In a parallel construction, the descriptive event that heaven and earth *will pass away* (παρέλθῃ) is mentioned as contrast for not even the slightest letter or portion of a letter from the Law *will pass away* (παρέλθῃ). Jesus affirms that what the Law says about all its minutiae being preserved is still applicable for His disciples. Using the same verb "*pass away*" (παρέλθῃ) Jesus makes the same kind of parallel statement in Matt 25:35 "Heaven and earth *will pass away*, but My words *will not pass away*." In both these statements, the ethical binding condition is in view and not merely a remembrance or preservation of words. The two "until" (ἕως) clauses in Matthew 5:18 designate the duration of the binding authority of the Law. The first "until heaven and earth pass away" means "until the end of the age" or "never, as long as the present world order persists." The second "until" (ἕως) clause "until all is accomplished" is parallel to the first. The word πάντα ("all" or "everything") probably refers to the prophecies in the Law or the whole O.T. that carry on through the whole eschatological Kingdom program. An example of the Law's prophecies that have not happened yet would be that Israel will be re-gathered into the land in a responsive believing condition (Deut 30:3–10). So until the present order of the world realizes the complete description of this O.T. program, the Law and the rest of the O.T. are still binding upon Israel and Jesus' Jewish followers (Deut 30:3–10; Matt 5:18).[98]

---

97. *Tanchum* 1.1 (*Tachum* is a compilation of midrashic comments which feature the *derashot* of Rabbi Tanhuma Bar Abba, a Palestinian *amora*. His principal teacher in *halakhah* and *aggadah* was Rabbi Huna; cf. Lightfoot, *A Commentary*, 2:102.

98. Betz, *The Sermon on the Mount*, 184.

This doctrine of the everlasting immutability of the Torah is consistent with the Jewish teaching that understood the *Torah* would in the future be understood better than it had to that point (Jer 31:33).⁹⁹ Therefore, Jesus' revisions and intensifications are consistent with the practice of the Jewish rabbis affirming the *Torah*.¹⁰⁰

In Matt 5:19, "these commandments" refer to the ethically binding material in the O.T., especially the Law.¹⁰¹ In Matt, ὅς ("this" or "these") never points forward, so Jesus does not include His commands of Matt 5:20–7:27 within "these commands." It is possible that "these commands" could include Matt 5:3–16. Matthew elsewhere uses the verb cognate to "commandments" (ἐντολῶν) of Jesus' teaching in Matt 28:20 (ἐνετειλάμην) but the noun as used in Matt 5:19 is never used of Jesus' teaching. Much more likely than referring to the preceding discussion of Matt 5:3–16, is the immediate context concerning the continued ethical relevance of the Law. Here it cannot be restricted to the Ten Commandments since the entire O.T. program is still in effect within this age, even those funded by the minutiae of the Law. Furthermore, the kind of commands that Jesus has in mind with regard to the Law, and these commands come from all over the Law, even several minor laws beyond the focus of the Ten Commands.

All these commandments are still binding so that they inform the disciple's life and teaching. The one who by lifestyle or teaching *annuls* or *loosens* (λύσῃ) one of the *least* (ἐλαχίστων) commandments has consequences in his life of being *least* (ἐλάχιστος) in the Kingdom. Likewise, the one who keeps and teaches the commandments has the consequences of greatness in the Kingdom. "Least and greatness" refer to gradation with the Kingdom ranks as is evident elsewhere in Matthew (11:11; 18:1–4). "Least and greatness" probably do not refer to exclusion and inclusion, for Jesus is not placing the disciples under a standard of absolute perfection to be included; there is still a place for poverty of spirit and forgiveness. John Fisher concludes:

---

99. 1 Macc 4:46; CDC 2.16; 3.4, 13; 1QS 3.12; 4.23; 5.6; 1QM 17.3; *b. Sabb.* 151b; *Lev. Rab.* on 7:11–12 and 11:2; *Yal.* on Prov 9:2; and *Midr. Ps.* 146.7; Bar 4.1; rabbi Joseph in BT *Nidah* 616; Maimonides ninth of thirteen principles of Judaism *Commentary on the Mishnah, Nissan, b. Moses, Ma'aseh Nisim*, 159–60; Davies and Allison, *Matthew*, 1:492; Banks, *Jesus and the Law in the Synoptic Tradition*, 33.

100. 11QTemple or Hillel introduction of the prozbul (*m. Seb.* 10.3–4).

101. Davies and Allison, *Matthew*, 1:496.

No one can break or set aside even the least of the commands, without jeopardizing his future status (v. 19). As if this were not enough, he concluded this section (v. 20) by emphasizing that his followers needed to be even more observant and devout than the Pharisees, going beyond even their exemplary practice of the traditions![102]

Jules Isaac summarizes this as, not only did Jesus "not overthrow the Law . . . or empty it of its content, but on the contrary I increase that content, so as to fill the Law to the brim."[103] So part of Jesus correct teaching of the Law includes the full implications and complete meaning of the spirit of the commandments. In effect, this New Covenant spirit of the commandments is building a "fence around the Law," which would be indicative of the Aramaic for "fulfill" (קוּם/*qum*) and consistent with what earlier sages had done.[104]

Jesus points out that entrance into the Kingdom requires a practice of righteousness surpassing the scribes and Pharisees (Matt 5:20). Practiced righteousness, not imputed righteousness is in view in this text.[105] Jesus' criticism here is not that the scribes and Pharisees were not ethically good, but rather that they were not good *enough*. As the scribes and the Pharisees taught the Law from "Moses seat," they could encourage their society to be good, but their pattern of life did not match their teaching (Matt 23:2–3). They placed a burden upon the people that was too heavy for even them to comply, with such peripheral matters as tithing, clothes, baths, and monuments for the dead (Matt 23:4–36). Later Jesus confronts the negative qualities in the scribes and Pharisees that needed to be transcended. Their fundamental failure was a disregard for the weightier matters of the Law, such as Kingdom, the Messiah, justice, mercy, and faithfulness. In some Jewish leaders' radical externalizing of the Law they show themselves to be hypocrites, appearing to be righteous, while they themselves were full of robbery, self-indulgence and lawlessness. Jesus was instead calling for a proper valuing of the Law from the weightier matters down to the minutiae.

The righteousness that is required in the passage is not a past positional righteousness; for the passage is on *doing and teaching the Law*

---

102. Davies and Allison, *Matthew*, 1:496.

103. Jules Isaac, *Jesus and Israel*, 66.

104. Pirke Avot 1.2; cf. Lachs, Montefiore, Finkel, Friedlander, *The Jewish Sources*; Lapide *The Sermon on the Mount*.

105. Betz, *The Sermon on the Mount*, 190; Przybylski, *Righteousness*, 80–87, 121–23.

within a disciple relationship to Jesus, and *looking ahead* to that which will in the future provide entrance into the Kingdom.[106] So to these Jewish disciples, Jesus identifies that those who will enter the Kingdom identify themselves by a radical practice of righteousness that surpasses the scribes and Pharisees' practice and teaching of the Law, all within a disciple relationship that views Jesus as the authority in their lives. Jesus has already shown Himself to be a practitioner of such righteousness (Deut 6:13–14; 8:3; Matt 4:4, 7, 10). Of course such a radical practice of righteousness is evident in the preceding beatitudes (Matt 5:6, 10) but also in Jesus subsequent teaching. Probably also the woe side to the Sermon on the Plain indicates what needs to be transcended: the rich, well fed, laughing life, of which all speak well (Luke 6:24–26).

It is in this light that Jesus' comments to the rich young ruler support in a practical manner what has been taught so far in the Sermon on the Mount (Matt 19:16–26; Mark 10:17–30; Luke 18:18–30).[107] Jesus is asked "What good thing shall I do that I may obtain everlasting life?" Here obtaining everlasting life is analogous to entering the Kingdom and being saved (Matt 19:16, 23–25; Mark 10:17; Luke 18:18, 24–25).[108] Jesus' answer for this Jewish ruler is to keep the commandments of the Law. Jesus does not say to try to do the Law until you find out you can't and then throw yourself on the mercy of God; Jesus tells His Jewish disciples to *keep* the Law. This should not surprise us because it is what Jews repeatedly expected and Christian Jews for several centuries tried to live.[109]

---

106. Westholm, "The Righteousness," 253–62; Blanton argues that Matthew especially sees salvation accomplished by obeying *Torah* ("Saved by Obedience," 412).

107. Also corroborated by *Gos. Naz.* 1, as recounted by Origen, *Matt.* 15.14.

108. Second Temple sources support this point as well (1QS 4.6–8; CD 3.20; 4Q181 1.3–4; *1 En.* 37.4; 40.9; 58.3; 4 Macc 15.3; *Pss. Sol.* 3.12).

109. Jer 31:31–34 and Ezek 36:24–37:28; Jdt 5:17–21; 8:18–23; 10:5; 12:2, 9–19; 13:8 *Pr. Azar.* 6–14; *Jub.* 1:22–25; 2:17–33; 15:11–34; 1Q3 4, 5; 1QH 4, 5, 18; 4Q Shir Shalb; Tob 1.10–12; 4:12–13; 1 Macc 1:48; 2:15–28; 2 Macc 6:18–31; 7; 3 Macc 3.4–7; 4 Macc 5:1–6:30; *T. Jud.* 26; *Jos. Asen.*; Josephus, *J. W.* 1.145–147, 157–60, 651–655; 2.169–74; *Ant.* 13.252; 14.237; 17.149–67; 18.55–59, 261–64, 267, and 271; cf. Wright, *Jesus and the Victory of God*, 301; Sanders, *Paul and Palestinian Judaism*; *Paul, the Law, and the Jewish People*; *Jewish Law from Jesus to the Mishnah*; and *Judaism*; and Dunn, *Jesus, Paul and the Law*; *Jews and Christians*; and *Paul and the Mosaic Law*, especially interesting is Wright's chapter "The Law in Romans 2," 131–150. Furthermore, Biblical texts like Jas, Matt and Acts indicate that Jews and Jewish Christians were zealous for the Law. However, especially at focus is Matt 5:17–48 and 19:16–22; cf. Saldarini *Matthew's Christian-Jewish Community* and Kennard, "The Way to Kingdom Salvation;" "The Law in James;" "Paul and the Law;" Klijn, "The Study of Jewish Christianity,"

This is a New Covenant form of covenant nomism that obtains everlasting life because it acknowledges if a person follows Jesus in loving his neighbor like he loves himself, then he shows forth transformed Kingdom character. Since God alone is good, Jesus' answer points to God's commands. Even Mark and Luke (who do not emphasize the keeping of the Law as does Matthew) declare on Jesus' lips that keeping the Law is the way to everlasting life (Mark 10:17–19; Luke 10:25, 28; 18:18–20).[110] Additionally, Matt and Luke present that such a Law oriented pious life is able to be lived and in fact was lived by Zacharias, Elizabeth, Joseph, and Simeon who "walked blamelessly in all the commandments and requirements of the Lord" (Matt 1:19; 5:17–20, 48; Luke 1:6; 2:25). Or as N. T. Wright describes it, the Kingdom is obtained by following "Jesus in finding a new and radicalized version of Torah-observance."[111] Jesus further clarifies that the commandments He has in mind are those like the fifth, sixth, seventh, eighth, and ninth of the Ten Commandments, and Lev 19:18, all of which have financial overtones.[112] Jesus recognizes that the Law has as its primary focus the loyalty relationship to the Lord (Matt 22:37–38) however, Jesus focuses on the human side of the Law here emphasizing the love relationship to others which shows whether one truly loves the Lord (Matt 22:39). Jesus has in mind here particularly those commandments that others can see and benefit from or at least not suffer under their violation. The last one, which is of course beyond the Ten Commandments, sums up all the minutiae of relationships one to another in the Law (Matt 19:19; 22:39–40). The young man affirmed that

---

419-31; Taylor, "The Phenomenon," 313-34 and Velasco and Sabourin, "Jewish Christianity," 5-26; Klijn and Reinink, *Patristic Evidence*; Strecker, "Appendix 1: On the Problem of Jewish Christianity," 257; Strecker, "The Kerygmata Petrou," 2:102-27, esp. 210-22 and 270-71; Strecker, *Das Judenchristentum,*; Schoeps, *Theologie*; *Jewish Christianity*; van Voorst, *The Ascents of James*; Skarsaune and Hvalvik, *Jewish Believers in Jesus*.

110. Origen affirms that Jesus teaches everlasting life is available for those who align with Jesus and live the Law in this deeply internalized manner (*Matt.* 15.14 on Matt 19:16–22; Skarsaune and Hvalvik, *Jewish Believers in Jesus*, 249).

111. Wright, *Jesus and the Victory of God*, 307.

112. These commandments are from the broadly Protestant numbering of the Decalogue. All the synoptic gospels list the fifth command last after the others, however, Luke 18:20 reverses the first two (giving the order as: seventh, sixth, eighth, ninth and fifth, and Mark inserts "do not defraud after the ninth and before the fifth command. Neither Mark nor Luke has Lev 19:18 as does Matt, so their statement is more Decalogue focused while Matt presents a fuller Law as binding for his Jewish Christian readership.

under a legally tight reading of the Law, he had kept all these commands. However, he sensed that in some way, he is still failing through a lack in his life. Whereas, in the Mark and Luke accounts, Jesus is the One who declares that the rich young ruler still lacks (Mark 10:21; Luke 18:22). Jesus offers him completion (which He has commanded in Matt 5:48) and obtaining his goal of the Kingdom by means of a radical extrapolation of Lev 19:18: to really love your neighbor as yourself[113] means sharing the proceeds of the sale of your possessions with those in need, the poor. Jesus does not develop the attitude of being willing to give to the poor; His emphasis is on doing: keeping the commandments, selling and giving (Matt 19:16, 17, 21). Giving up these possessions would enable the young man to follow Jesus in His itinerant ministry as Peter and the disciples had done (Matt 19:21, 27). Perhaps Matt includes Jesus' statements of giving to the poor for purposes of the itinerant ministry, to address issues in his readers' lives such as: the poor from famine, or the itinerant dispersion of the Jewish Christians outside their homeland due to persecutions. If the young man had complied, he would have had Kingdom treasure as the disciples were to receive (Matt 19:21, 29). Unfortunately, the young man was unwilling to pay the price of Jesus' radical Law demands, and so His departure provided an opportunity to instruct the disciples in the near impossibility of a rich person pursuing the Kingdom (Matt 19:24–26).[114] The primary focus of the Law is evident as serving God, rather than money (Matt 6:24). The fact that the young man went away with his riches shows that ultimately he was unwilling to serve God. In this case the Kingdom is missed for failure to keep the Law and align with Jesus.

At this point Peter chimes in and says "Behold, we have left everything and followed you; what gain will there be for us?" (Matt 19:27). Jesus reassures the disciples that they have complied with this radical paying the cost of the Law, and that they will have a unique role of judging Israel (Matt 19:28). In fact, everyone who has left house and family

---

113. Such a love of one's neighbor as oneself is supported throughout early Judaism (*Jub.* 7.20; 20.2; 36.4, 8; Tob 4.15; Sir 19.13–17; 1QS 5.24–6.1; CD 6.21–7.3; 9.2–8; *T. Reu.* 6.8; *T. Sim.* 5.7; *T. Zeb.* 8.5; *Let. Aris.* 207; Livneh, "Love Your Fellow as Yourself," 173–99).

114. The camel (the largest beast of burden for Israel) is impossible to go through a sewing needle (Matt 19:24–26) in the same manner as in Babylon (where the largest beast of burden is the elephant) it was said that it is impossible for an elephant to go through the eye of a needle (*b. Ber* 55b; *B. Meṣ.* 38b). The disciples get the point and Jesus reiterates it as well.

members for Christ's sake shall receive many times as much and will inherit everlasting life (Matt 19:29).[115]

Matthew 5:21–48; Jesus Teaching of the Law

Interpretation of the Law is a political act of control in society. Small changes in behavior signify major changes in outlook, and mark off one group from another. The early Jewish Christian community saw Jesus' Kingdom teaching in a new flexible enough arrangement that appreciated their Jewish heritage (like new wine skins; Matt 9:16–17).[116] The agenda of this section is set primarily by what Jesus identifies to be significant for Kingdom and secondarily by how Jesus responds to questions and issues asked of Him. These questions asked expose rigidity of those around Jesus' context who will try to tear the garment or burst in rejection.

Jesus' emphasis is on the practice of keeping the Law, for the way to the Kingdom is matched by His teaching of the Law as well. Jesus is the supreme example of the fact that the one who keeps and teaches the Law shall be called great in the Kingdom (Matt 5:19). Given ample opportunities, none of His opponents accused Him of violating the Law (Matt 26:59–60; Mark 14:55–56; John 8:46; 18:23). The Orthodox Jewish scholar Pinchas Lapide described Jesus as a traditional observant Jew.

> Jesus never and no where broke the law of Moses, nor did he in any way provoke its infringement-it is entirely false to say that he did . . . In this respect you must believe me, for I know my Talmud . . . This Jesus was as faithful to the law as I would hope to be. But I suspect that Jesus was more faithful to the law than I am-and I am an Orthodox Jew.[117]

The second main portion of the Sermon on the Mount, the six "antithesis," contains the major section where Jesus teaches the Law. However, the pattern of "*and* (δὲ) I say unto you" is quite consistent with the structure of oral torah and the rabbinic form of teaching the Law.[118] John

---

115. Actually, the text sandwiches family members between houses and lands.

116. This text should not be seen as a cause to reject the Mosaic Law emphasis of Jesus teaching; Davies and Allison, *Matthew*, 2:112–117.

117. Lapide, in Kung, "Jesus in Conflict," 74–75.

118. Bokzer, *Judaism*, 194; Fisher, "Jesus Through Jewish Eyes;" Betz, *The Sermon on the Mount*, 210; possibly 11QT as Wacholder (*Dawn of Qumran*, 4) proposes unusually uses first person singular.

Fisher summarizes the rabbinical pattern as evident from rabbi Ishmael (one of the foremost scholars cited in the Talmud and alive in Jesus day), "One might hear so and so . . . but there is a teaching to say that the words should be taken in *this* sense."[119] Then John Fisher concludes, "the point being made by the formula is that to some people Scripture appears to have a certain meaning, but that apparent meaning is an incomplete, or inaccurate understanding."[120] Thus, these statements are Jesus' rabbinical corrections as New Covenant extensions of the Law. Normally, what followed was some form of the verb "to say" such as "there is a teaching to say," which leaves the authority in the logic of the argument. However, Jesus' authoritative, "I say," with the "I" emphatic in all the "I say" statements, utilizes the rabbinical pattern to present Jesus as the final or supreme authority. Often in rabbinic circles one might expect an appeal to an influential rabbi at this point or occasionally God is the one who undertakes these corrections.[121] So part of the issue in Jesus' Law teachings is to recognize and submit to Jesus as the definitive authority (normally associated with God) to extend the Law in an internal active practice of New Covenant life. This approach goes beyond the above rabbinical pattern and the prophet pattern "Thus says the Lord," to highlight that Jesus is the authority. Therefore, the authority of Jesus in this teaching role is being emphasized throughout this section. This section is thus more than the Law, it is about Jesus' authority to extend the Law throughout the disciple's life. It is quite clear that Jesus' teaching does not annul or loosen (λύσῃ) any teaching of the Law (Matt 5:19). As in Jesus' dealings with the rich young man, mandating that the young man radically keep the Law, so Jesus' authoritative teaching should be considered to be consistent enough with the Law to be teaching the Law (Matt 5:19). Since Jesus' teaching is calling the disciple to internalize the Law, it is helpful to remind oneself that the Law always has had a central concern for the Law being internalized and not merely complied with externally (Deut 6:5–6; 10:16).

---

119. *Mekita* 3a, 6a; Fisher, "Jesus Through Jewish Eyes"; cf. Schechter, "Rabbinic Parallels," 1:16.

120 Fisher, "Jesus Through Jewish Eyes;" an early example of this practice is in: *Mekhilta* on Exod 19:20.

121. Rabbis shied away from first person reference in teaching Hans Betz, *The Sermon on the Mount*, 210; Daube, *NT and Rabbinnic Judaism*, 59, 62; Midrash Tanhuma, Jer 4:2 on goodness; Daube, *The NT and Rabbinic Judaism*, 55–62.

Love.

One of the last points of this section but the priority and summary of the Law is love (on the basis of the question in Matt 22:36–40). Jesus identifies the greatest commandment in the Law as "You shall love the Lord your God with all your heart, and with all your soul, and with all your mind" (Matt 22:37; Mark 12:30; Luke 10:27).[122] Such a love for God should captivate one's whole being. Such a focus on love resonates with the Jewish traditional understanding that the Love of God is the greatest commandment (Deut 6:4–5; Luke 10:26–27).[123] The second command is like it in loving your neighbor as yourself (Matt 22:39; Luke 10:27).[124] This love emphasis is so critical that the whole Law and the prophets depend upon (or are suspended from) this backbone of love (Matt 22:40). This whole section of Jesus as Law teacher should then be seen as explaining aspects of this love relationship. The affirmation of love as the core does not deny any of the specifics of the Law for Jesus is recognized as teaching the Law correctly and thus not annulling any part of the Law (Mark 12:32–34). In fact, it is the very same answer a lawyer had earlier given to him when Jesus asked him to summarize the Law (Luke 10:26–27).

The golden rule is another summary statement of the Law which motivates the choice to benefit others in love (Matt 7:12).[125] "Therefore, whatever you want others to do for you, do so for them" (Matt 7:12; Luke 6:31).

Jesus calls His disciples to a New Covenant internalism of this love commitment significantly beyond the teaching of other Jewish views in His call to "love your enemies" (Matt 5:43–47 and Luke 6:27–38 compared to Lev 19:18).[126] During the conquest, Jews were to doom their enemies by holy war slaughter (Deut 7:1–5, 24–26; 26:17–19; Josh 6:16–17, 21; 8:24–25; 1 Sam 15:1–35). David and second Temple confessions

---

122. Mark 12:30 and Luke 10:27 add strength (ἰσχύος) either before or after "mind" to reflect MT: מְאֹדֶךָ and LXX: δυνάμεως.

123. T. Iss. 5.2; 7.6; T. Dan. 5.3; Jub. 36.3–8; Josephus, Ag. Ap. 2.206; Philo, Spec. 2.63; Decal. 20.154; 108–10; Abr. 208; m. Sanh. 10.1; Rabbi Akiva in Sifra Lev. 19:18; Sifre on Deut. 6:4; b. Šabb. 31a; b. Ber. 63a.

124. Rabbi Akiva considered love of neighbor in Leviticus 19:18 to be the great commandment (T. Iss. 5.2; 7.6; T. Dan. 5.3; Sifra Qed. 4.200.3.7; Sifra on Lev 19:18; Gen. Rab. 24.7; Šabb. 31a).

125. Sir 31/34.15; ARN 25, par. 53B; 26A; 29, par. 60B; Targ. Ps-J. on Lev 19:18; Gos. Thom. 6.3; Sent. Sext. 179–80; b. Šabb. 31a by Hillel.

126. Meier, A Marginal Jew. Volume 4: Law and Love, 528–51.

affirm the value of loathing God's enemies, those who bring significant detriment to Israel (Ps 139:21-22).[127] These statements are sufficient to fund the disciples' awareness of statements of hatred concerning enemies (Matt 5:43). Jesus however calls His disciples to a higher standard of generosity: "love your enemies, do good to those who hate you, bless those who curse you, pray for those who mistreat you" (Luke 6:27-28). This commitment to love and peace goes far beyond non-retaliation, becoming a significant identification of those who are children of God (Matt 5:45; Luke 6:35). The point is, when you behave as sons, you are and will *be* sons.[128] Such generosity identifies us with the character of our Father who shows His generosity by bringing rain to the unrighteous as well as the righteous (Matt 5:45; Luke 6:35). Practicing such love consistently identifies one within the family of God.

Affirming this love commitment identifies one as not far from the Kingdom (Mark 12:34). Practicing this radical love commitment obtains the inheritance of everlasting life as sons of the divine Father (Matt 5:45; Luke 10:25, 28). It is a common occurrence to love those who love you back, for even tax-gatherers and Gentiles do this. As such, the woman whom Jesus forgave much loved Him much and demonstrated it by washing His feet with perfume, tears, and her hair (Luke 7:36-50). Such a mutually beneficial love has a way of funding the tradition of love within the community (Matt 5:44).[129]

The Law was clearly more radical in its command to love sojourners (Lev 19:19, 33-34; Matt 22:39).[130] Jesus radically extends the concept of

---

127. Sir 50.25-26 states openly loathing Edom and Philistia. Several texts advocate hating the sons of darkness (Josephus, *J. W.* 2.139; 1QS 1.3-4, 9-10; 2.7-9; 9.16, 21-22) but call for renunciation of retaliation because that is God's role (1QS 10.11-18; *Jos. Asen.* 23.9; 284, 14; 29.3; 2 *En.* 50.3-4). Some documents also call for continuing the conflict against Seleucids and Romans (1QM, 4QM; 4 Macc 12.18) and having no associations or meals with Gentiles (*Jub.* 22.16).

128. Compare *b. Quid.* 36a says this in the present tense while Matt 5:45 says it in the aorist middle and Luke 6:35 identifies it in a future middle.

129. For example, Qumran, the Essenes and other Jews maintained a love within the community and a hate to outsiders (1QS 1.4, 10-11; 2.4-9; 9:21-23; 1QM 4.1-2; 15.6; 1QH 5.4; *b. Ber.* 33a; *b. Sanh.* 92a; Josephus, *J. W.* 2.139). The commitment is present in rabbinic Judaism (*Sipra* on Lev 19:18 and *Mek.* on Exod 21:35) and outside Jewish tradition (Polybius 18.37.7; Hesiod, *Op.* 342-43; Solon, frag. 1.3-5; Plato, *Tim.* 17d-18a; *Resp.* 375c; *Meno* 71e; Tacitus, *Hist.* 5.5-6; Davies and Allison, *Matthew*, 1:549-552.

130. Other O.T. and Second Temple texts which anticipate Jesus expansive love include also: Exod 23:4-5; 1 Sam 24:17-19; 2 Sam 19:6 LXX; 1 Kgs 3:11; Job 31:29

neighbor in the parable of the Good Samaritan to any who show mercy (Luke 10:29–37). Even a despised individual such as a Samaritan[131] who inadvertently happens upon someone in his travels is a neighbor. The issue of *compassion* took precedence over issues of *ritual cleanliness*.[132] The compassion shown costs time, effort, and money, but it was right to recover the man from his plight. Jesus commands the resistant lawyer to follow the same pattern and to show mercy to others who can never repay his service. However, among Jesus' disciples He commands an even more radical extension of love to include personal enemies who persecute you (Matt 5:44).[133] This love of one's enemies should include doing good deeds to them and praying for them (Matt 5:44; Luke 6:27–28). Jesus shows a prime example of loving and praying for the welfare of His persecutors during His crucifixion (Luke 23:34). To evidence such broad love to one's enemies is to evidence a quality of sonship to the Father, for the Father provides sun and rain for both righteous and unrighteous alike (Matt 5:45).[134] The disciple is not to settle on common mutuality but is to seek perfect righteousness in evidencing love as the Father is perfect (Matt 5:48). Such perfection fits the Jewish pattern of obedience to God's Law,[135] thus realizing maturity, following Jesus and full obedience to the Father's will (Matt 5:48 in its context; 19:21). The specific issues that make up the rest of this sermon flow out from this commitment to love.

(Eusebius, *Dem. ev.* 1.6); Ps 7:3–5; Prov 24:17–18 (cf. *m.' Abot* 4.19); 24:29; 25:21–22; Jer 29:7; Jonah 4:10–11; *T. Iss.* 7.6; *Jub.* 7.20; 20.2; 36.4; Philo, *Decal.* 108–10.

131. There is antipathy between Jew and Samaritans in this second Temple Judaism (John 8:48; *Sir* 50:25–26; Josephus, *Ant.* 18.2.2; *B.T. San.* 57a, where a Samaritan is not worthy of receiving aid from a Jew).

132. There is no evidence in Jesus' parable that the Jew is dead (as is developed in *Mish Berak.* 7.7), but these religious leaders do not even want to check his condition, but rather avoid the injured.

133. Jewish parallels include: *Ep. Arist.* 207, 227, 232; Philo, *Virt.* 116–18; *T. Gad.* 6.1–7; *T. Zeb.* 7.2–4; *T. Iss.* 7.6; *T. Benj.* 4.2–3; *2 Bar.* 52.6; *2 En.* 50.4; *b. Ketub.* 68a; *m.'Abot* 1.12; 2.11; 4.3; 5.16. Early Christian literature echoes this love of enemies: Acts 7:60; Rom 12:14, 17–20; 1 Cor 4:12–13; 1 Thess 5:15; 1 Pet 3:9; Polycarp, *Ep.* 12.3; Irenaeus, *Adv. haer.* 3.18.5; *Ps.-Clem. Hom.* 3.19; *Ep. Apost.* 18; *2 Clem.* 13.4; Justin, *1 Apol.* 14.3; Athenagoras, *Supp.* 12.3.

134. Several rabbinic texts affirm that God is good to the just and the unjust (*b. Ta'an.* 7a; *Mek.* on Exod 18:12; *Pesiq. R.* 48.4; *b. Sanh.* 111a; *2 Bar.* 12.1–4).

135. Gen 6:9; Deut 8:13; 1QS 1.13; 5.24; 8.1–2, 20–21; 1QSb 1.2; Philo, *Det.* 132, 160; *Decal.* 175; *Deus* 4; *Sacr.* 120.

Murder.

Jesus begins His legal teaching with the sixth law of the Ten Commandments, "You shall not commit murder" (Exod 20:13; Deut 5:17), the consequences of murder being judgment before the court (Matt 5:21).[136] In the Law the word תִּרְצָח (*trṣḥ*) means murder or unlawful violent death. The Law expands this to include primarily willful murder as is done out of a context of hatred, rather than manslaughter (Num 35:16–31). The word is also used of "capital punishment," which should be done to a murderer, and the word also is used of the one who commits "manslaughter," which of course is accidental (Num 35:27; Deut 4:42). The organization of the stipulations in Deut include issues of chapters 19:1–22:4 within the umbrella of this command.[137] These issues include manslaughter, rules for capital punishment, capital punishment of a rebellious child, rules for warfare in taking life and taking a wife, forgiveness in untraceable homicide and appropriate care in issues which cause disputes (such as boundaries, legal witness, inheritance, and possessions belonging to others).

Internalization of the Law would certainly exclude angry plots and attempts to defraud another. Jesus' authoritative teaching extends the Law by going to the source and rooting out all anger, consistent with Jewish tradition[138] and commanding a zeal for reconciliation (Matt 5:22–26). Jesus forbids anger (ὀργιζόμενος) and any verbal expression which begins to show itself like calling a brother a fool.[139] In this context a brother could be a family member or a fellow traveler heading toward the Kingdom (Matt 4:18, 21; 5:9). The Aramaic word רבע transliterated as *raca* means "fool, imbecile, or blockhead." The Greek word μωρέ (*mōre*) would also mean "fool," but for the Hebrew speaker it might also have overtones of "apostasy, rebellion and wickedness," through the Hebrew word מרה (*mrh*).[140] Since both words mean "fool" and sound similar, the judgment should be seen as the same: eschatological condemnation, which excludes one from the Kingdom.

---

136. Sir 34.25–27.

137. Kaufman, "The Structure of the Deuteronomy Law," 105–158.

138. T. Gad. 4.1–7; Tg. Ps.-J. and Tg. Onq. on Gen. 9.6; Tg. Ps.-J. on Deut 5.21; Der. Er. Rab. 11.13; m.'Abot 4.21; b. Qidd. 39b; b. Ned. 22b; b. Pesah. 66a-b; 1QS 6.26; 7.2–4; Sifre Deut. to Deut 19:10–11 and 22:13; T. Soṭah 5.11; b. Kidd 41a; Tosefta Derech Eretz vol. 2 quoted from Flusser, *Judaism*, 117; Geza Vermes, *The Religion of Jesus*, 31.

139. Similar to Sir 28.3–4.

140. Carson, "Matthew," 8:149.

Within this framework where one's legal religious duty included offering sacrifices at the altar (for recovering from sin as well as for gratitude), the more important duty is to live peacefully with all.

Such peacemaking as to be reconciled with a brother takes precedence over one's sacrificial duty (Matt 5:24-25).[141] When reconciliation is accomplished then the Kingdom bound Jew should bring his sacrifice to the altar for Covenantal purposes like atonement, forgiveness, and peace (Lev 1-7). Jewish Christians continued to offer Jewish sacrifices in such settings and in recovery from uncleanness (Matt 5:24; 8:4; Mark 1: 44; Luke 2:22-24; 5:14; Acts 18:18; 21:23-26).[142] This practice of reconciliation as *more important* than sacrifice complies with Judaism's valued piety and ethical behavior as more significant than issues of formal observance of religion.[143] Elsewhere, Jesus underscores the need to reconcile to maintain a community heading toward the Kingdom (Matt 6:14-15; 18:21-35). To emphasize the urgency of reconciliation, Jesus uses a standardized story (elsewhere used in Luke 12:58 to warn Israel of its eschatological judgment) to emphasize that judgment will be meted out to the fullest extent. There may be a parallel with verse 22 which would mean that fullest judgment might entail eschatological condemnation, which excludes one from the Kingdom.

Jesus has taken the Law (which forbids angry plots and attempts to defraud another) and radically extends it under His own authority (consistent with Jewish tradition) to forbid anger and to mandate a zeal for reconciling with others. Jesus' teaching is a consistent Jewish extension of the Law.

---

141. The Jewish practice would have sacrifice complete the reconciliation process (Lev 1-7; *Ep. Aristeas* 170-71; Sir 34.18-19; 35.12; Philo, *Spec.* 1.236f.). Continuing this practice, Matt 5:23-24 and Acts 18:18; 21:23-27 supports Jewish Christian participation in Jewish sacrifices. In contrast, *Gos. Eb.* 7 as recorded by Epiphanius, *Pan.* 30.16.4-5 has Jesus condemn such practice of Jewish sacrifices. Of course, the Law prescribes the Levitical sacrifices for Israel (Lev 1-7, 16:1-17:9). Additionally, the O.T. describes the Kingdom era under the Messiah as continuing to practice these sacrifices that atone (Jer 33:18; Ezek 43:18-46:24), though the Hebrews 10:1-8 ceases the sacrifices for now for any new Covenant people who would be disturbed by their reminder, and *Lev. Rab.* 9.7, written four centuries after the destruction of the Temple (i.e. 5th cent. A.D.), ceases the ritual sacrifices in the Messianic Kingdom.

142. Jewish sacrifices among Jewish Christians continued to be offered for the issue to be addressed in Heb 10:1-4 and *Gos. Eb.* frag. 5 30.16.5; Betz, *The Sermon on the Mount*, 175.

143. 1 Sam 15:22; Hos 6:6; *T. Isaac* 4.18-22, 39; *m. B. Qam.* 9.12; *b. Yoma* 87a.

Adultery.

The second point of the Law that Jesus takes up is the seventh law of the Ten Commandments, "You shall not commit adultery" (Matt 5:27; Exod 20:14; Deut 5:18). In the Law, the Hebrew word נאף (n'p) and the Greek word μοιχεύσεις means "an illicit sexual relationship." Such an act of adultery would occur if any man or woman would have a sexual relationship with another human than one's spouse. Such adultery was condemned by the participants' receiving capital punishment (Lev 20:10–21). The Law prohibits bestiality as well (Lev 20:15). The organization of the stipulations in Deut includes issues of chapters 22:5–23:18 within the umbrella of illicit mixtures and epitomized by this command.[144] The core of this section is the resolution of claims and practices of illicit sexual relationships (Deut 22:13–30; Exod 22:16–17). While capital punishment was executed upon proven claims, the claims against one who is vindicated bring a monetary fine upon the faulty claimant. Furthermore, the sexual act of a man with a virgin betrothed to him requires them to get married (with no divorce) and pay the girl's father a dowery for her. Other issues in this section of the Law, include rules concerning: appropriate clothing, obtaining food, access to the assembly, ceremonial cleanliness in the army, preservation of escaped slaves and exclusion of prostitution. Internalization of the Law would exclude any mental plots involving illicit sexual relationships. Such an exclusion of an adulterous eye and heart is common in the Jewish traditions.[145]

Jesus' authoritative teaching extends the Law's idea of adultery in one's heart (consistent with Jewish tradition) to even *look* upon a woman to *desire* her. The word βλέπων constitutes a simple *look*. The word ἐπιθυμῆσαι means to *desire* even in a positive manner (Matt 13:17) but here it means *lust*. The simple act of looking upon to lust seems to carry simplicity of internalization that extends beyond the Law but is consistent with it. Such a view censors internalization of lust, such as occurs even when there may not be an actual woman present such as internet porn or sensual imagination.

---

144. Kennard, chapter five of *Biblical Covenantalism in Torah*.

145. 1QpHab 5.7; 1QS 1.6; CD 2.16; 11QTS 59.14; Josephus, *C. Ap.* 2.183, 217; *Yoma* 29a; *T. Iss.* 7.2; *Reub.* 4.8; *b. Nid.* 13b, bar.; *Shab.* 64ab; *Lev. Rab.* 23.12; *Mek.* of R. Simeon 111; *Jub.* 20.4; *T. Isaac* 4.53; *Sifre* on Num. 15:39; Sextus, *Sent.* 233; *Pesiq. R.* 24.2; cf. Davies and Allison, *Matthew*, 1:522; Montefiore *Rabbinic Literature*, 41 for quote of these texts; Vermes, *The Religion of Jesus*, 32–33; "A Summary of the Law," 303.

Jesus then makes his New Covenant extension of the Law: if a body part such as an eye or a hand causes you to stumble, excise it[146] so that you do not end up perishing in hell. The concept of hell (γέενναν) is the eschatological place of judgment modeled after the valley of Hinnem, once associated with pagan rites of Molech, but in Jesus' day was used as a rubbish pit with smoldering fires. Stumbling (σκανδαλίζει) is the sin of falling away in Lawlessness and unbelief (Matt 13:21, 41–42, 57–58; 18:6–9). Those who stumble over Jesus are condemned in judgment. Persecution, affliction, or perhaps restricting access to Jesus can set up the possibility of stumbling. Jesus' disciples committed a temporary betrayal (σκανδαλισθήσεσθε) when Jesus was taken and they all fled (Matt 26:31, 33). Usually such stumbling was not temporary, for those who fell were damned the same as Satan, Pharisees, Nazareth occupants, and eschatological traitors (Matt 13:57–58; 15:12; 16:23; 24:10). The strong language here presents an extreme insistence upon abstaining from *any* form of mental adultery. The repetition of "stumbling" and "hell" shows that compliance with Jesus' radical extension of the Law is imperative. If one permits unbelief or lawlessness in his life (e.g., desiring lust concerning a woman), then that person is in serious threat of damnation.

---

146. The removal of body parts for convicted criminals was sometimes done (Deut 25:11–12; Judg 16:21; Josephus, *Vita* 171–173, 177; *J. W.* 2.642–644; *b. Pes.* 57b) but it is probably not encouraging maiming but rather the seriousness to make sure that you miss hell (cf. *Ps.-Clem. Rec.* 7.37; Origen, *Comm. Matt.* 15:1). Rabbinic literature discusses the removal of a hand to: 1) to excise habitual sin of masturbation (*m. Nid.* 2.1; *b. Nid.* 13a–b; *b. Šabb* 108b metaphorically) because hand is used euphemistically for penis (Isa 57:8; 11QT 46.13), and 2) habitual striking others (*b. Nid.* 13b sect. b and d). In the resurrection, amputated body parts were thought to be restored to the righteous (2 Macc 7.11). The point here is that Jesus' appeal which identifies adultery with heading for damnation underscores the graver seriousness of adultery over the Law's capital punishment practice. Some may appeal to Jesus activity in John 8 or 4 to soften the judgment on an adulteress. However, John 7:53—8:11 is not in the earliest or best manuscripts and if one includes it here its presence distracts from the continuing argument of John. The same could be said for the other placement in the text (after 7:36 or 7:44 or 21:24 or Luke 21:38), so I do not consider that this pericope is Scripture. There is also something awkward and perhaps a frame-up for only one participant to be accused. In the other situation with the woman at the well, though Jesus knows her through prophecy to be a serial divorcee and an adulteress (John 4:18), Jesus uses the opportunity to bring this non-Jew and her village into the Kingdom way. To bring her to trial would require witnesses catching her in the act; instead Jesus has her convert to the Kingdom.

Divorce.

The next point of Law that Jesus considers is the permission and process of divorce (Deut 24:1-4; Matt 5:31). Deuteronomy permits the husband to divorce his wife if he has found some *indecency* (עֶרְוַת/'rwt) in his wife. This indecency (עֶרְוַת) is best taken as *indecent exposure* or *public nakedness* (Gen 9:22-23; 42:9, 12; Exod 20:26; 28:42). Even in the near context, the word is used of *indecent public exposure* (that is, excrement needs to be buried and not left exposed, Deut 23:13-14; עֶרְוַת). In the Deut instance, עֶרְוַת/'rwt cannot mean "sexual immorality," for the punishment for sexual immorality is not being sent away in divorce but rather capital punishment (Lev 18:6-19; 20:11-21). In this Deut instance, legal dissolution of marriage is permitted for indecency.

This legal framework was taken in divergent views in Jesus' day, though there is strong agreement that the process required a bill of divorce and a return of the dowry.[147] By the fifth century B.C., in the Jewish military colony on the island of Elephantine, Egypt permitted either spouse the authority to divorce their mate as is evident from three marriage contracts of the time.[148] The Herodian royals divorced at will including the women initiating such as did Herodias and Salome (Mark 6:17-18).[149] Roman Law permitted either partner to initiate divorce. For example, we either have a divorce certificate from a Jewish lady dated 135 A.D., or a quit claim document from her releasing her former husband of financial obligations.[150] However, such egalitarianism was advanced when compared to commoners in Palestinian Judaism where the husband kept the marriage settlement and thus was the empowered one who could initiate a divorce.[151] Qumran judged that divorce and remarriage was illicit in all circumstances because God *made* the "male and female"

---

147. CD Df 3.10-15; 11Q19-21 57.15-19 (also 4Q524 and 4Q365a); Josephus, *Ant.* 15.7.10; *Nahal Hever Babatha Ketubba,* Obverse 1-17; *Mur* 19 Bill of Divorce; *Nahal Tse'elim* 13 Waiver of Claims; Yardin, *Textbook of Aramaic,* 2:56 & 58.

148. *The Context of Scripture,* 3:153-57 especially 3:155-56 "Document of Wifehood 3.63" vs. 23-29 (dated 14 Oct. 449 B.C.), 171-73 "Document of Wifehood 3.71" vs 9-10 (dated 9 Aug. 449 B.C.), 182-86 esp. 184-85 "Document of Wifehood 3.76" vs. 25-27 or lines 33-34; Brody, "Evidence for Divorce," 230-34, esp. 231; Instone-Brewer, "Jewish Women Divorcing," 249-57; Lipiński, "The Wife's Right," 9-27.

149. Josephus, *Ant.* 15.7.10; 18.5.1.

150. Papyrus Ṣe'elim 13; Tal Ilan, "Notes and Observations," 195-202; Rabello, "Divorce of Jews," 79-102.

151. *Tosefta Ketubet* 12.1.

and "they *became* one flesh."¹⁵² In mainstream Judaism, opinion was divided between the school of Shammai, which permitted divorce with the possibility of remarriage to another for gross indecency,¹⁵³ and Hillel, who permitted divorce for real or imagined offenses, including an improperly cooked meal. For example, the Hillelite rabbi Aiba permitted divorce and remarriage to another for a case of a roving eye for pretty women, the sin Jesus had just condemned in Matt 5:28–29.¹⁵⁴ Josephus even permitted divorce "for any causes whatsoever."¹⁵⁵ Others tried to diminish divorce as a practice because they saw its abuse to be so devastating.¹⁵⁶

The discussion of divorce was conducted concerning a male perspective in all the biblical texts except perhaps Mark 10:12 where there is some concession to non-Palestinian circumstances where a woman could more easily divorce her husband.¹⁵⁷ Divorce was envisioned as a possibility for Jewish women living in the colony of Elephantine in Egypt in the fifth century B.C. A number of Aramaic marriage contracts mention a wife divorcing her husband explicitly and one rabbinic text mentions it,¹⁵⁸ but the evidence for such a practice in Israel itself is almost nonexistent.¹⁵⁹

---

152. CD 4:21 justifies no divorce on the basis of original design, the pattern in the ark during the flood, and the command for the king not to multiply wives in Deut 17:17 which is interpreted as no second marriage while wife is still alive; because the ensuing defilement of another in intimate sexual union would separate the previous marriage partner (1QApGen. 20.15 Abraham's prayer against loosing Sarah to Pharaoh), thus an argument against serial polygamy in 11QTemple 57:17–19; Angelo Tosato, "The Law of Leviticus 18:18: A Reexamination," *CBQ* 46(1984): 199-214; 11Q19 57.15–19 permits a second marriage only after spouse is dead; 4Q271 frag. 3 lines 10–15 identify that neither a divorcée nor a woman with previous sexual experience is an acceptable wife; thus, remarriage after divorce is fornication (CD 4.21); Elledge, "'From the Beginning," 380–86.

153. These followed this interpretation: Philo, *Spec.* 3.30; Josephus, *Ant.* 4.253; Sipre on Deut 24:1; *m. Giṭ.* 9.10.

154. *M. Giṭ.* 9:10 or 90b.

155. Josephus, *Ant.* 8.23; also Rabbi Eliezer in *m. Gittim* 9.1–3..

156. *b. Giṭ.* 90b; *m. Giṭ.* 9.10; *Sifre Deut.* 269.

157. *Elephantine* papyri in Bammel, "Markus 10:11f und das jüdische Eherecht" *ZNW* 61(1970): 95–101; and Philo, *Spec. Laws* 3.30 in Treggiari, *Roman Marriage*, 441–46; *Se'elim get* 13; Instone-Brewer, *Divorce*, 89–90.

158. *M. Yebam.* 13.1; Cowley, *Aramaic Papyri*, 45; Fitzmyer, "The Matthean Divorce Texts," 205; "A Re-Study of an Elephantine," 137–68; cf. Kraeling, *The Brooklyn Museum Aramaic Papyri*, 142–43 (*BMAP* 2:9), 206–207 (*BMAP* 7:25); compare *AP* 9:8.

159. There is only one instance, Josephus, *Ant.* 15.7.10.

Jesus stands out starkly in contrast to most of these views as He through a New Covenant manner extends the Law. Matthew 5:31 begins with δέ, implying that the preceding argument continues: divorce is the moral equivalent to adultery. For Jesus, God's design sets the priority: do not divorce or try any other form of separation because God has joined the two together (Gen 2:24; Matt 19:3-6; Mark 10:5-9; 1 Cor 7:10).[160] Jesus admits that the Mosaic process of divorce was permitted for those who have hardness of heart. Jesus was not annulling the Law as some of the divergent views in the first century context evidence annulment of the Law. That is, Jesus permits those who are willfully rebellious from God's design to have a legal loophole which permits divorce, but such an option is precarious at best. However, Jesus transcends the issue of the legal and permissible, to a higher order of what is right by God's design. The remainder of Jesus' teaching on divorce reflects a moral problem which is comparable to adultery.

The statements in Matt 19 and Mark 10 are roughly equivalent in emphasizing design priority over legal permission. The statements in Matt 5:32 and Luke 16:18 come in contexts that emphasize the binding nature of the Law. The Matthew context identifies divorce as part of the Pharisaic concerns which fall short of Kingdom (Matt 5:20, 31-32; 19:3). The Luke 16:1-13 and 19-23 context identify that such divorce is akin to apostatizing from God to a selfish loyalty to money which damns. Likewise, the Mark 9:42-48 and 10:13-16 context identify that divorce is akin to selfish distraction to damnation. Three of the divorce passages make it clear that the husband commits adultery (μοιχεύσεις) if he remarries after divorce (Matt 19:9; Mark 10:11).[161] Mark 10:12 clarifies that the wife also commits adultery (μοιχεύσεις) if she remarries after divorce. Furthermore, if anyone would happen to marry a divorced woman, then even this previously unmarried individual would commit adultery (μοιχεύσεις) in marrying a divorcee (Matt 5:32; Luke 16:18). Unlike the Mark and Luke passages which have no exception clauses, the two Matt passages do have exception clauses to the effect of "except for the cause of

---

160. Some claim that Jesus' absolute prohibition echoes the view of Tob 6:18 "she was destined for you [to be with in marriage] from eternity," however, Jesus' rationale merely goes back to the design of creation (Gen 1:27; 2:24); Fitzmyer, "The Matthean Divorce Texts," 203.

161. Qumran agrees that remarriage is adultery (11Q19 57.15-19 permits a second marriage only after spouse is dead; 4Q271 frag. 3 lines 10-15 identify that neither a divorcée nor a woman with previous sexual experience is an acceptable wife; thus, remarriage after divorce is fornication [CD 4.21]).

unchastity" (πορνείας). For example, Matt 5:32 says that a husband who divorces his wife except for the cause of unchastity (πορνείας) makes her commit adultery (μοιχεύσεις).

The word πορνείας includes every kind of unlawful sexual intercourse including the complete semantic field of μοιχεύσεις.[162] For anyone who is married, the two words are synonymous; a married person who does πορνείας does μοιχεύσεις and a person who does μοιχεύσεις does πορνείας. The illicit sexual act speaks of a deed, not a characteristic of life (such as being a perpetual adulterer or prostitute). However, acts described by these words constitute sexual immorality in which the Law required the participants to be executed under capital punishment (Lev 18:6-19; 20:11-21). That is, the sin in the Law's exception clause (indecency or public nakedness) is not as grave a sin as sexual immorality (πορνείας), since divorce is permitted in that case instead of death sentence.

The exception clauses in Matt in no way imply that divorce is acceptable. Remember that the whole discussion of divorce and remarriage has been rendered equal to adultery (by the δέ; Matt. 5:31), and rebellious by the disregard for God's design and involvement in making the couple one flesh (Matt 19:3-6; Mark 10:5-9). There is no substantial reason for Matthew's exception clause to be read into Mark or Luke, since they are themselves inspired Scripture. Mark and Luke have not included an exception clause, and their texts are understandable without any exception clause. Therefore, any remarriage of a divorced person is an act of adultery for both persons being married (Mark 10:10-12; Luke 16:18). Thus, the exception clause in Matt 5:32 and 19:9 does not prevent adultery in a remarriage situation if the divorce was motivated by immorality. Remember Jesus' ethic on this point of the Law is more restrictive than the Law in its appeal.[163] Therefore, Jesus' exception clause cannot be softening and expanding the Law's exception clause. If Jesus is saying that it is acceptable to divorce a wife for her sexual immorality, then He is denying several commands of the Law that required capital punishment (Lev 18:6-19; 20:11-21) and rendering Himself under His own declaration to be least in the Kingdom and therefore self-contradictory (Matt 5:18-19; Mark 10:11-12; Luke 16:18). Not only does the prior context call for a higher ethic but the subsequent context shows that the disciples

---

162. In Matt 15:19 and Mark 7:21 these words are synonyms; *BDB*, 528 and 699.

163. Jesus appeals to: God's design, God's involvement in making the couple one flesh, and Moses' permission to accommodate moral hardness of heart (Matt 19:4-8).

got the point that a higher ethical order was demanded, as evidenced by their statement, "if the relationship of the man with his wife is like this, it is better not to marry" (Matt 19:10). Furthermore, Jesus affirms the disciples in their conclusion that some for various reasons will prefer celibacy. Those who prefer celibacy have it as a gift (Matt 19:11) even though it might have been a condition from birth or a condition of employment or a condition for Kingdom service (Matt 19:12). Jesus concludes His discussion of celibacy by urging those able to accept the preference of a celibate life to accept such a life. This higher ethic does not encourage divorce, but rather warns that persons do an adultery deed if they divorce and remarry (Matt 5:32; 19:9). That is, one who remarries after divorce does the deed of sexual immorality (πορνείας). Therefore, the exception clause describes that a divorcée commits sexual immorality (μοιχεύσεις) in the act of remarriage, except in the case that she has done so previously, in which case an additional act of sexual immorality does not render her immoral for she is already in an immoral condition. This interpretation permits the inspired passages without the exception clause to declare that remarriage is sexual immorality (μοιχεύσεις; Mark 10:11–12; Luke 16:18), and the whole travesty of divorce and remarriage is a violation of sexual immorality (μοιχεύσεις), unless the persons have already violated sexual immorality (πορνείας; Matt 5:32; 19:9). In English the phrase is: "Anyone who divorces his wife makes her commit adultery (μοιχεύσεις) provided she has not already committed adultery (πορνείας)." The verbal construction of the consequences of the divorce force the divorced wife into the act of adultery (μοιχεύσεις). This does *not* mean that a divorced wife becomes a prostitute and starts taking in clients. The grammatical description of the consequences constitute an act of adultery and not necessarily a characteristic lifestyle of being an adulteress. In this first century context, for the average divorced woman to make her way virtually requires her to remarry in order to deal with her vulnerability and come within the oversight of a man in a male dominated society, unless she has significant wealth (Ruth 1:20–21; Isa 1:23; 10:2; 54:4; Jas 1:27). The act of remarriage would be an act of adultery (Mark 10:12). On the other hand, perhaps this making her commit adultery (μοιχεύσεις) builds off the preceding verses which discuss the committing of adultery (μοιχεύσεις) through the process of internalized lust (Matt 5:28). That is, in the same way that a man may lust after a woman, prompted by the visual stimulation, so a divorced woman may lust after a man, prompted by the experience of the sexual intimacy which marriage brought and divorce removed. The exception clause fits, in that if she has already done the deed of adultery (πορνείας) in mind or body then she is not somehow in her divorce being forced to do adultery (μοιχεύσεις) by the divorce; she already did adultery (πορνείας) by her own choice.

Oaths.

The next issue which Jesus takes up is that of vows, insisting that Jesus' followers should be outstandingly honest, and thus need no oaths. Jesus summarizes the ancient teaching on vows to be "you shall not make false vows, but shall fulfill your vows to the Lord" (Lev 19:12; Num 30:2; Deut 23:21; Matt 5:33). Likewise, oaths taken in the name of the Lord were binding and perjury was strongly condemned in the Law (Exod 20:7; Lev 19:12; Deut 19:16–19). Every oath contained an affirmation or promise and an expressed or implied appeal to God as the guarantor, which made the oath binding. Once Yahweh's name was invoked, the vow was a debt that had to be paid. To protect from taking the Lord's name in vain, oaths began to refer to other things than God Himself. By Jesus' time, a sophisticated casuistry of technical expression had developed in order to assess which oaths were binding and which were not. This casuistry appears to have been the result of rabbis' fighting abuses of vows among the masses.[164] Their way of fighting abuses was to develop ways of differentiating between the binding and non-binding oaths. In this way, non-binding oaths included swearing by heaven, by earth, by Jerusalem, by the temple, by the altar, or by one's own head (Matt 5:34–35; 23:16–22).[165] On the other hand, binding oaths included swearing by Yahweh, toward Jerusalem, by the gold of the temple, and the offering on the altar. Such techniques encouraged evasive oaths, and therefore deception. If oaths, designed to encourage truthfulness and greater certainty (as when God swears by an oath; Gen 15), became occasions for clever lies and causistical deceit, then Jesus' abolishment of oaths is consistent with second Temple integrity (Matt 5:34–37).[166] When Jesus is charged to speak under oath, He refuses and simply replies "You have said so" (Matt 26:63–64).

164. Lieberman, *Greek in Jewish Palestine*, 115–143.

165. 1 Chr 12:19; CD Geniza A 15.1–5; 11Q19 53.11–54.7; *m. Šebu.* 4.13; *m. Ned.* 1.3; *m. Sanh.* 3.2; Philo, *Spec.* 2.3–5.

166. Jas 5:12. This stand is similar to the rabbinic teaching in: *Sir* 5.4; 23.9; and *Baba Metzia* 49a. It is also similar to that of the Essenes, except for only their entrance oath; cf. Josephus, *Ant.* 15.370–71; *J. W.* 2.135, 139; Philo, *Prob.* 84; Stobaeus, *Eclogae*

Jesus recognizes that oaths are used and neither condemns them nor contradict his higher ethic (Matt 23:20-22). The use of oaths indicates that all oaths are related to God and are therefore binding. Swearing by heaven is swearing by both the throne of God and Him who sits upon it (Matt 5:34; 23:22). Swearing by earth is swearing by the footstool of God's feet and thus by God (Matt 5:35). Swearing by or toward Jerusalem is swearing by God since it is the city of the Great King (Matt 5:35). Swearing by the Temple is swearing by the God who dwells within the Temple (Matt 23:21). Furthermore, God and the Temple are more important than the gold of the Temple, which the Pharisees and scribes saw as binding, because God and the Temple sanctify the Temple gold (Matt 23:16-17). The altar is more important than the offering on the altar, because God and the altar sanctify the offering (Matt 23:18-19). In this way the supposedly non-binding oath of swearing by the altar actually includes the binding oath of swearing by the offering within it (Matt 23:20). All these casuistic oaths are actually binding and obligate the one who swears them because they are actually swearing by Yahweh.

The issue in Matt 5:34-37 involves forbidding oaths where there is abuse: He is not annulling the Law. God binds Himself by an oath when He established covenant grants (Gen 9:9-11; 15:17-18). The Law even requires Israel to vow to obey Yahweh in suzerainty treaty (Deut 27). Jesus is not absolutely excluding all oaths; He even testifies under oath (Matt 26:63-64).[167] What the Law permits as a way to evidence the truth, Jesus forbids, calling His disciples to a higher standard than the Law (Matt 5:34, 37). So, like the previous issue on divorce, the divine priority of simple honesty transcends oaths in the disciples' lives.

Jesus calls his disciples to say that which is within their own control. Therefore, one should not make an oath by one's head for you cannot

---

1.41.44. However, the Dead Sea scrolls are ambiguous on the issue (11QTemple 53-54; CD 7.8; 9.9-12; 15-16; 1QS 5.8; 6.27). Certain Jewish texts identify doubling, as it appears here in Matthew 5:37 "yes, yes" and "no, no" as a legitimate oath (*b. Šebu.* 36a; 2 *En.* 49.1-2), but that clearly is opposed to the sense of Jesus' command here. Deliberate abstaining from oaths (like Jesus advocates) is part of integrity within Judaism, wherever possible (Philo, *Prob.* 84; *Spec.* 2.2; *Decal.* 84; Josephus, *J. W.* 2.135). There is also some aversion to oaths in the Non-Jewish world (Sophocles, *Oed. col.* 650; Cicero, *Balb.* 5, Plutarch, *Quaest. rom.* 2.127d; *Mor.* 46A; Epictetus, *Ench.* 33.5; Marcus Aurelius, *Antonius* 3.5; Diogenes Laertius 8.22; Iamblichus, *Vit. Pyth.* 47). The early church followed this no oath policy but said it as: "let your yes be yes and your no no" (Justin, *1 Apol.* 16.5; Clement of Alexandria, *Strom.* 5.99.1; 7.67.5; *Const. Apost.* 5.12.6; *Ps.-Clem. Hom.* 3.55; 19.2; Eusebius, *Dem. ev.* 3.3; Epiphanius, *Haer.* 19.6.2; 2 *Jehu* 43).

167. Paul also testifies under oath (Acts 26:63-64).

even change the color of your hair (Matt 5:36). Rather a simple statement of yes or no is the best way to reflect honesty (Matt 5:37). Any further complexity that might confuse a simple honest answer is from the evil one,[168] and is thus identified with the way to hell rather than Kingdom.

Insisting on Legal Rights.

The next point of the Law which Jesus takes up is the issue of insisting on legal rights, which He replaces with generosity, even if it dishonors the giver. He quotes the *lex talionis* passage of "an eye for an eye, and a tooth for a tooth." (Matt 5:38). The *lex talionis* context provides the legal framework to guide the judges for any crime to an appropriate punishment, excluding excessive abuse or leniency (Exod 21:22–24; Lev 24:20; Deut 19:21).[169] Jesus calls his disciples to transcend the Law by *not* insisting on their legal rights by not resisting the evil person who might abuse him (Matt 5:39a). Out from this general teaching Jesus applies illustrations that explain his commitment to peace even at one's own expense.[170] For example, if you as an individual are slapped[171] by someone who is evil, you are to turn the other cheek, thus permitting a continuation of the violation of your rights (Matt 5:39). In the second Temple culture, such abuse or being taken advantage of would mean dishonor. However, Jesus' disciples were to allow themselves to be dishonored if it provided an opportunity to be generous instead. Jeremias identified that such a blow to the right cheek might likely be given to Jesus' disciples as they follow Him and are considered heretics by the Jewish leadership.[172] Furthermore, if anyone attempts to press a legal claim against you (as in a suit for your shirt or the Roman impressments commanding civilians to carry luggage of military personnel a Roman mile), then be doubly generous and give *more* than is asked (Matt 5:40–41). The disciple is to give up his outer cloak as well instead of fighting for legal action, even though this

---

168. The article (τοῦ) before evil (πονηροῦ) indicates a person (Matt 4:1; 5:39; 6:13; 13:38).

169. 11QTemple 61.10–12; *Jub.* 4:31–32.

170. Davies and Allison, *Matthew*, 1:538–540 analyze the similarity of Matt and *Did.* 1:4–5, in contrast to Luke 6:27–36.

171. Slapping on the right cheek probably means to strike the cheek with the back of the hand as in an insult (Job 16:10; Ps 3:7; Lam 3:30; *1 Esdr.* 4:30; Arisophanes, *Ra.* 149–150; *m. B. Qam.* 8.6).

172. Jeremias, *The Sermon on the Mount*, 29.

cloak is a possession (Exod 22:26; Deut 24:13).[173] Likewise, Jesus' disciple should carry the Roman soldier's baggage twice the legal distance.[174] In such a Roman setting, a person who owns possessions can insist on his legal rights in keeping them to himself. However, Jesus' disciple is commanded to be generous like the Jewish traditional emphasis on mercy (Matt 5:42).[175] If someone asks for a possession the disciple is to give it to a person. If someone wishes to borrow something, the disciple is to loan it to the person.[176] With this trajectory, Jesus is not annulling the Law but calling His disciples to a higher ethic of generosity in not insisting on their legal rights. Additionally, part of this generosity is to forgive those who make these demands upon you.[177] Such generosity reflects the love that summarizes the whole Law.

Conclusion

Jesus' Kingdom way incorporates the Law as part of the ethic to be lived in order for His Jewish disciples to obtain Kingdom everlasting life. Jesus radically extends the Law in three broad patterns. (1) The first radical extension of the Law is through a more pervasive internalization of the Law consistent with the New Covenant appropriation of the Law. This approach is evident in Jesus' treatment of anger, adultery, and seeking God's Kingdom and righteousness. It is clear indication that Jesus is calling His disciples to a New Covenant approach to the Law. (2) The second radical extension of the Law emphasizes the priority of design over permission. This approach is evident in Jesus' treatment of commitment in marriage, honesty and Sabbath strictness. (3) The third radical extension of the Law emphasizes the priority of generosity. This approach is evident in Jesus' treatment of legal rights, practical love, judging and Sabbath healing. It is quite clear that Jesus, especially as Matthew portrays Him, requires His

---

173. *b. B. Mes.* 78b; 113b.

174. This would normally mean carrying the pack for two miles, though the Western text says two more miles, for a total of three.

175. *b. Bava; Metzia* 24b, 30b; *b. Avodah Zera* 4b.

176. Matt 5:42; Luke 6:30; cf. Exod 22:25; Lev 25:36–37; Deut 15:7–11; Prov 28:27; Sir 4.1-10; 29.1-2; Tob 4.7; *Jub.* 9.1–12.4; *T. Zeb.* 7.2; Heb 10:34. There are also rabbinic texts in which the sages are encouraged to give even to deceivers (*b. Ketub.* 68a).

177. The rabbis likewise urge a person not to seek redress or retaliation but pray for and forgive the offending party even if he does not ask for forgiveness, cf. *T. Jos.* 18:2; *Tosefta Baba Kamma* 9:29-30; *Yoma* 23a.

Jewish disciples to keep the Law in order to obtain the Kingdom, and its everlasting life. Jesus' New Covenant oriented Mosaic Covenant material strongly identifies Jesus with a sectarian second Temple Judaism.[178]

Jewish Legal Controversies with Jesus

A number of biblical and a few extra-biblical texts accuse Jesus of violating the Law, so a defense of Jesus' consistency with the Law supports Jesus as a Mosaic teacher of the Law. The biblical accusations concern issues of Sabbath violation, and that of touching the unclean. Additionally, the first account of the *Egerton Papyrus* 2 accuses Jesus of breaking the Law and threatens Him with stoning but fragment 1 is sketchy and does not cohere with other accounts of Jesus and the Law.

Sabbath

Sabbath had become an identity marker for Judaism in the first century.[179] The Jewish commitment to Sabbath meant that some Jews waited until Sabbath was over to carry the sick to Jesus (Mark 1:29–32; Luke 4:38–40). However, Jesus healed on the Sabbath without disputes arising, sometimes because He was among friends (Mark 1:29–31; Luke 4:38–39). At other times Sabbath synagogue healings would take place without dispute because those present were simply amazed at the healing (Mark 1:21–28). Sabbath compliance was deep within Jesus' own followers, for example, the believing Jewish women waited until Sabbath was past in order to attend to Jesus' body after His death (Matt 28:1; Mark 16:1; Luke 23:56–24:1).

In the gospels, the most repeated issue on which the religious leadership question Jesus is the violation of Sabbath. This issue rises especially during Jesus' healing ministry. The issue is important to the Law, since: (1) the Sabbath Law is in the Decalogue, (2) the severity of the command to "rest from your work" places the violator under sentence of capital punishment, and (3) keeping Sabbath is the everlasting sign of the everlasting Mosaic Covenant (Exod 20:8–11; 31:12–17; 34:21; 35:2;

---

178. As in Jer 31:31–34 and Ezek 36:24–37:28 so too in: *Jub.* 1:22–25; 1Q3 4, 5; 1QH 4, 5, 18; *4Q Shir Shalb*; CD 4Q266 frag. 2 1.6–8; B 19.12–13; 1QpHab 2.3; 11.13; 4Q434 frag. 1 1.4; 4Q437 frag. 1 1.14.

179. Josephus, *Ag. Ap.* 2.8.20–21; 2.40.282; Philo, *Mos.* 2.21; Doering, *Schabbat*.

Num 15:32–36; Deut 5:12–15).[180] Those who failed to see beyond the pursuit of their business found the Sabbath an irritation (Amos 8:5; Jer 17:19–27; Neh 13:15–22). However, faithful Jews saw its observance as a delight (Isa 58:13–14). Furthermore, Sabbath keeping was well known as a characteristic which marked off Jewish communal life.[181] As we evaluate this issue, it is important that we do not read Jesus' activity as severely unraveling the Law. We have just seen that Jesus in fact supports the Law. There are thirty nine second Temple Jewish prohibitions on the Sabbath.[182] However, there is no written ban on healing on the Sabbath among second Temple Jewish documents. So on the whole, healing on the Sabbath was not seen as a significant issue in second Temple documents that the rabbinics felt needed to continue to be addressed. Instead, there is generally permission and some discussion among second Temple Judaism concerning sensitive Sabbath caretaking for the sick and needy.[183]

Deuteronomy's development of the Sabbath idea emphasizes generosity within this rest (Deut 5:12–15; Exod 23:12). For example, the sabbatical moratorium extends the seventh day to include a seventh year release of debt and obligation of servitude (Deut 14:28–16:17). Between the seventh year release (both temporally and structurally within the section) is the charge to be generous in lending to a brother Israelite and the needy (Deut 15:7–11). Even Jewish Christianity later conceived of the Kingdom as through the lens of continuing future Sabbath rest for the people of God (Heb 4:9). This blessing in Sabbath indicates that at the heart of the sabbatical release is *generosity* meeting needs in a manner that does not make oppressive obligations on the debtor. This Deuteronomic ideal predisposes Jesus to view the Sabbath as a time of release and freeing the oppressed. This is most apparent in His healing ministry. For example, when a woman bent over for eighteen years was healed, the Synagogue official became indignant at Jesus healing on the Sabbath.

---

180. *Jub.* 2.29–30; 50.6–13; CD 10.14–11.18; *m. Šabb.* 7.2; *Sipre* on Num. 15:33; McIver, "The Sabbath," 231–32, 241–42.

181. Horace, *Sat.* 1.9.69–70; Philo, *Somn.* 2.123–24; *Legat.* 158; *Mos.* 2.21; Josephus, *Ant.* 13.252; 14.10.12; 14.237. 16.2.3; 16.6.2–4; *Ag. Ap.* 2.39; 2.8.20–21; 2.40.282; *Tosefta Erubin* 3.5.

182. *m. Šabb.* 7.2; healing is only banned on Sabbath if it involves special actions beyond one's ordinary actions regularly accomplished (*m. Šabb.* 14.3–4). Basser, *Studies in Exegesis*, 15–34.

183. 1 Macc 2.29–41; CD 11.13–14; *Šabb.* 18.3; *m. Šabb.* 6.3; *T. Šabb.* 15.14; *B. Šabb.* 12 a–b; *Šabb. M. Eduyoth* 2.5; *Yoma* 8.6; 84b; *b. Yoma* 85b; *m. Yoma* 8.6; *T. Yoma* 84.15; *Mek.* on Exod 22:2, 23:13, and 31:13.

Jesus responded, "You hypocrites, does not each of you on the Sabbath untie his ox or his donkey from the stall, and lead him away to water? And this woman, a daughter of Abraham as she is whom Satan has bound for eighteen years, should she not have been released from this bond on the Sabbath day?" (Luke 13:14–16). In the wake of this healing and explanation, the people joined the woman in praising God (Luke 13:13, 17).

In response to some Jewish strictures Jesus identified that "the Sabbath was made for man and not man for the Sabbath" (Mark 2:27). Jesus' approach is instanced also in second Temple Judaism.[184] This approach sees Sabbath as an aid to humans in providing rest, God's generosity, and a time to focus on God, and not a time to be restrictive about the benefits God would have available for those who are His.

In second Temple Judaism, there was considerable debate over what sort of concessions were permitted within the generosity of the Sabbath. A number of texts show considerable restrictiveness concerning healing on the Sabbath.[185] Other texts show concessions of leniency that were broadly recognized including: saving of a life, rescuing from a pit but without tools, alleviating acute pain, curing snake bite and cooking for the sick.[186] Quoting Isa 58:13, the rabbis also allowed acts of service to others as in deciding on grants of charity, watering animals, or making arrangements on a child's education (Luke 13:15).[187] As Jesus summarized, "it is Lawful to do good on the Sabbath" (Matt 12:12; Mark 3:4). So Jesus healed on the Sabbath (Matt 12:13; Mark 3:5; Luke 13:10–13; John 5:8; 7:23), which healing, the rabbis say, is a permitted good to occur on the Sabbath, in contrast to Jesus' opponents.[188] Also, the rabbis frequently used the quotation from Hosea 6:6, as Jesus did in Matthew 12:7, to argue that helping others was of greater importance than observing the

---

184. Mek. Abbeta on Exod 31:13.

185. CD 10.14–11.18; 4Q265 frag. 6; 4Q218 frag. 1; 4Q251 frag. 1–2; m. Šabb. 22.6; 14.3–4; 19.2; m. ʿEduy 2.5; Misc. Rules 6.8.1–7; t. Šabb. 16.22.

186. 1 Macc 2.29–41; 4Q265 frg. 6 lines 6–8; Šabb. 18.3; T. Šabb. 14.3; 15.14; Šabb. M. Eduyoth 2.5; m. Šabb. 6.3; Mek. Rabbi Ishmael, Šabb. 1; Yoma 8.6–7; 84b; b. Yoma 85b; M. Yoma 8.6; T. Yoma 84.15; Mek. on Exod 22:2 and 23:13.

187. Fisher, "Jesus Through Jewish Eyes;" countering this the more rigid sectarian Jewish community at Qumran prohibited helping an animal give birth or out of a pit on Sabbath (e.g., CD 11.13–14; 4Q270; 4Q271; T. Šabb. 14.3).

188. M. Šabb. 22.6; m. Yoma 8.6; Mek. on Exod 22:2 and 23:13; B. Šabb. 12a-b; whereas other Pharisees oppose treating minor medical cases on the Sabbath (m. Yoma 8.6; t. Šabb. 12.12–13; 17.14; p. ʿErub. 10.11; Maʿaś. Š. 2.1.4).

rituals and customs.¹⁸⁹ Since good deeds were God's business, they were allowed.¹⁹⁰ The basic rabbinic principle was as Jesus said, "The Sabbath was made for man, and not man for the Sabbath" (Mark 2:27).¹⁹¹

The most obvious example of potentially violating the command to not work on the Sabbath is the instance in which Jesus said to the paralytic "Pick up your mat and walk" (John 5:8). On this point, Rabbi John Fisher says, "Upon examining early Jewish sources, we find that what constitutes work was yet to be fully defined. So for example, carrying things within a walled city (Jerusalem) was not always considered work."¹⁹² However, burdens were not to be carried (Jer 17:21-22).¹⁹³ When Jesus caught up with the healed paralytic, Jesus told him to not sin anymore (John 5:14). Perhaps if a paralytic carried his mat it was a demonstration of praise, but if he kept it up, harm would come to him because he was being viewed as sinning and so the Jews were seeking Jesus' life (John 5:10-14). In this second Temple context, Josephus describes that many of the traditional Sabbath regulations were not in force in Jesus' time.¹⁹⁴ The Pharisees in the gospel accounts insist upon the strictures of Sabbath-keeping so tightly as to annul other features of the Law. As we have seen on questions that are not fully settled, Jesus took clear positions and usually opposed the extreme views of Shammai, sometimes in favor of those of Hillel, as on Sabbath.¹⁹⁵ As Safri concludes "Jesus' Sabbath healings which angered the head of the synagogue were permitted by tannaitic [early rabbinic] law."¹⁹⁶ In fact, as Samuel Cohon develops, "What is puzzling to Jewish students is that the attitude about the Sabbath as reflected in rabbinic Judaism is near to that ascribed to Jesus and remote from that ascribed to his opponents."¹⁹⁷ While this is true, there are traditional texts to which the Pharisees of the gospels could appeal, but Jesus an-

---

189. *Suk.* 49b; *Rab.* on Deut 16:18.

190. *Šabb.* 150a.

191. *Mek. Sabta* 1; *Mek.* on Exod 31:14, 104a; *Yoma* 85b.

192. Fisher, "Jesus Through Jewish Eyes;" additionally, *Eccles Rab.* 9.7 and *m. Šabb.* 7.2 permitted carrying the sick on Sabbath.

193. *Jub.* 2.30; 50.8; CD 11.8-9; 4Q251 frag. 1-2.

194. Fisher, "Jesus Through Jewish Eyes."

195. *T. Šabb.* 16.21-22; *b. Šabb.* 5b, bar., 18b; *Gen. Rab.* 7.2; Josephus, *J.W.* 2.147; CD 10.9; 11.4-5; Strabo 16.2.40; Mart. *Epig.* 4.43; Suet. *Aug* 76; Lee, *The Galilean Jewishness*.

196. Safri, "Religion in Everyday Life," 2:805.

197. Cohon, "The Place of Jesus in the Religious Life of His Day," *JBL* 48(1929): 97.

swered their argument with a wisdom appeal.[198] The Pharisees counseled together to destroy Jesus when He violated their view (Matt 12:13–14; Mark 3:5–6; Luke 6:10–11). However, John Fisher shows an example of this resonance of Jesus and the rabbis in the event of eating heads of grain on the Sabbath, in light of sowing and reaping being forbidden (Exod 16:25–30; 34:21; Lev 19:9–10; 23:22; Deut 23:24–25; Matt 12:1–5; Mark 2:23–28).[199]

> In the first century, it was also apparently the general opinion, at least in Galilee, that it was acceptable not only to pick up fallen ears of grain but also to rub them in one's hand to get to the grain. Some Pharisees objected to this practice, but according to others it was perfectly permissible. The Talmud itself says: "Bundles which can be taken up with one hand may be handled on the Sabbath ... and he may break it with his hand and eat thereof" (*Shabbat* 128a). This certainly allows for what the disciples did; their actions fall well within the bounds of acceptable practice.[200]

When questioned on the Sabbath healings, Jesus gave a standard Jewish response as John Fisher explains.

> He made these replies in typical rabbinic fashion and form as well, frequently using a specific kind of homily called *yelammedenu*. This involves a question addressed to the teacher, followed by his answer based on a *midrash* (interpretation) or *halakah* (authorized opinion). The Sabbath passages (Matt 12:1–13; Mark 2:23–28; 3:1–6; Luke 13:10–17; 14:1–6; John 5:1–16; 7:22–23) record Yeshua's response in this form, in which he cited an interpretation of Scripture or an accepted rabbinic opinion, e.g., "Is it lawful to save life or let it die on the Sabbath?"

---

198. CD 10.15–11.18 and especially 11.13–14 argue that one should not lift an animal out of a pit on the Sabbath; cf. 4Q265; *Miscellaneous Roles* fragment 7, 1.6–9; m. *Besa* 3.4. However, Jesus obviously takes issue with this view when He asks the question, "What man shall there be among you, who shall have one sheep, and it falls into a pit on the Sabbath, will not take hold of it, and lift it out? Of how much more value then is a man than a sheep! So then it is lawful to do good on the Sabbath." (Matt 12:11–12; Luke 14:5).

199. 4Q159; Josephus, *Ant.* 4.231–39; m. *peʾa passim*; b. B. Mes. 92a.

200. Fisher, "Jesus Through Jewish Eyes." Gleaning from another's field was permitted (Deut 23:25; Ruth 2:2) but the Essenes would not even permit scooping up water on Sabbath (CD 11.1–2) and the extremists excluded gleaning on Sabbath (p. *Maʿaś* 2.6; CD 10.14–11.18; *Jub.* 50; m. *Šabb.* 7.2). Cf. b. *Šabb.* 127a; Pines, "The Jewish Christians," 66.

(*Yoma* 35b). In fact, his argument closely parallel that of the somewhat later Rabbi Ishmael (*Yoma* 85a), particularly in Mark 3. In typical rabbinic fashion he also frequently cited both the principle and an example which helped clarify it. In making his case in situations such as this, he used a variety of familiar Jewish concepts, *halakic* conclusions and rabbinic methods.[201]

Part of the regular rabbinic argument about the needs of life overriding the Sabbath restrictions include David's taking the tabernacle bread (1 Sam 21:6; like Jesus mentioned in Matt 12:3-4; Mark 2:25-26),[202] the Temple offerings and circumcisions made on the Sabbath (as Lev 24:5-8 and Num 28:9-10 require these sacrifices, they were offered on Sabbath [1 Chr 23:31], Jesus pointed to this fact in Matt 12:5; Luke 7:22-23).[203] So the Pharisees are hypocrites in fault-finding when Jesus, the disciples and the priests transcend the Sabbath by the Law.

It is important to notice that Jesus entered into discussions with others concerning the prohibitions about Sabbath, He did not just suspend Sabbath and its traditions. The *Gospel of Thomas* 27.2 presents Jesus affirming Sabbath keeping as including the blessing of seeing the Father in Kingdom. In Matthew, Jesus implied the continuance of Sabbath Laws when He urged the disciples to "pray that your flight is not in winter or on the Sabbath" (Matt 24:20). A legitimate Sabbath day's journey was limited in distance (Exod 16:29; Isa 58:13).[204] Furthermore, if He had broken Sabbath, then evidence of this would have been used against Him at His trial, but there is no trace of that.

Matthew goes beyond these common Jewish appeals in having Jesus claim that something[205] is present, namely the Kingdom of love, that is greater than the Temple (Matt 12:6). In this context, where something transcends legal features like the Temple, the Son of Man transcends the Sabbath in any way He wills (Matt 12:8; Mark 2:28; Luke 6:5). However, the way in which He transcends Sabbath is consistent with the Law and

---

201. Fisher, "Jesus Through Jewish Eyes;" Cohon, "The Place of Jesus," 98; Finkel, *The Pharisees*, 163-172; Flusser, *Jesus in Selbstzeugnissen*, 43-63; Sanders, *Jesus and Judaism* 245-69; Back, *Jesus of Nazareth*.

202. The availability of the bread implies that the bread had just been changed, which occurs on the Sabbath.

203. 11QTemple 13.17; *Y'lomm'denu, Yalkut* 2, par. 130; *T. Šabb.* 15b.

204. For example, Qumran prohibited walking more than 1000 cubits on the Sabbath (CD 10.21).

205. "Something" is neuter, therefore not just a person but a quality like Kingdom of love.

Prophets. Jesus does not annul the Sabbath, rather He limits its legal strictures by transcending it by means of *higher* legal restrictions, namely those of: design, Kingdom, and especially compassion.

Touched by the Unclean

That which is clean is a measure of what is cultic appropriate for Israel in light of their relationship with Yahweh.[206] Uncleanness is then a measure of what is inappropriate within this relationship with Yahweh with regard to the cult. Cleanness and uncleanness are metaphysical concepts and not merely ethical ones. Therefore, a leper, or a person who has a hemorrhage, or the dead are all unclean (Lev 12–14; 15:4–27; Num 19:11–12). Such uncleanness is transferred by touch like a communicable disease (Lev 5:2–3; 7:19–21; 11:4–47; 12:2; 15:2–33; 17:15; 18:19; 20:25; 22:4–8; Num 19:11–22; Deut 23:10; Ezek 22:10; Hag 2:12–13).[207] This derived uncleanness is usually not as potently unclean as the source, in that the remedy for derived uncleanness is usually washing and a day's time, and sometimes a sacrifice (Lev 15:4–27). This recovery process or atonement is costly with time and sometimes money because of the cost of a sacrifice. However, there are forms of uncleanness that are more virulent and lasting. For these, priestly inspections and more elaborate sacrifices may need to be provided for atonement to recover one to a clean condition. Ultimately the atonement process included the Israelite's compliance with the Mosaic Covenant. The famous first century rabbi, Yohanan ben Zakkai stated, "In life it is not the dead who make you unclean; nor is it the water, but the ordinances of the king of kings that purifies."[208] That is, faithfulness to the Mosaic Covenant relationship identifies one for cleansing and unfaithfulness identifies the unclean. Yohanan ben Zakkai was once asked if a corpse becomes purified by the water from red heifer, to which he responded publicly, that to take it as such was no different than paganism. However, privately to His disciples he responded "Neither was uncleanness caused by the corpse nor cleanness by the 'water of separation,' but the statute of the red heifer was one of those which had

---

206. For a more complete discussion of this issue cf. Kennard, "Hebrew Metaphysic: Life, Clean, Holy, Righteousness, and Sacrifice" in *Biblical Covenantalism in Torah*, ch 6.

207. *m. 'Ohal.* 18.7 even considers Gentiles and their dwellings unclean.

208. Fisher, "Jesus Through Jewish Eyes."

to be accepted as the will of God though no rational basis for it could be discerned."[209] Such features are clearly seen as direct obedience to Yahweh through the Mosaic Covenant, rather than natural law.

From within this framework it is amazing that Jesus actively touched the unclean in healing and allows Himself to be touched by them for healing to occur.[210] It is as though the presence of the King did not become unclean by their communicable uncleanness. Rather, the King possessed a dynamic purity rendering the unclean to be clean in the Jubilee healing process that is occurring in the surrounding Kingdom expression of Jesus' healings.[211] Jesus took on Himself the infirmities in such an atonement manner as to render the infirmed clean and healed (Isa 53:4; Matt 8:17). For example, a leper was touched by Jesus and the leper was healed (Matt 8:3; Mark 1:41; Luke 5:13). Jesus told the healed leper that he needed to present himself to the priest and make the appropriate offering that Moses' Law demanded (Matt 8:4; Mark 1:44; Luke 5:14). Likewise, a woman with a hemorrhage was both cleansed and healed by her touch of one of Jesus' Jewish corner tassels (κράσπεδα used here commonly translates the Hebrew commanded tassels צִיצָת; Matt 9:20–22; Mark 5:27–31; Luke 8:44–47; cf. LXX: Num 15:38–41 and Deut 22:12). Likewise, Jesus took a dead girl by the hand to bring her back to life (Matt 9:25; Mark 5:41; Luke 8:54).

The Pharisees criticize Jesus because He allows the unclean to touch Him (Luke 7:39). The particular criticism took place in the house of a Pharisee, when a sinful woman broke an alabaster vial and began to anoint Jesus' feet with the perfume and wipe them with her hair (Luke 7:37–38). The Pharisee who had invited Jesus said to himself, "If this man were a prophet He would know what sort of person this woman is who is touching Him, that she is a sinner." The Pharisees were overly concerned with not being touched by sinners so that they would not defile themselves. For example, *As. Mos.* 7.9–10 describes these Jews as "their hands and hearts are all corrupt, and their mouths are full of boasting—and yet they complain: Do not touch me lest you make me unclean." Jesus responded to this Pharisee with a parable about a certain moneylender

---

209. Daube, *The New Testament and Rabbinic Judaism*, 141–142.

210. Jesus actively touches the unclean in healing (Matt 8:3, 15; 9:25, 29; 20:34; Mark 1:41; 5:41; 7:33; 8:22; Luke 5:13; 7:14; 8:54; 22:51). Jesus also allows Himself to be touched by the unclean for healing (Matt 9:20–21; 14:36; Mark 3:10; 5:27–31; 6:56: Luke 6:19; 8:44–47).

211. Kazen, *Jesus and Purity Halakhah*, 24.

who forgave a debtor who owed five hundred denarii, and another who owed fifty denarii (Luke 7:41–42). Simon the Pharisee recognized that the one forgiven more would love more (Luke 7:43). Jesus applied the parable by reminding the Pharisee of his lack of providing hospitality (no foot washing, no kiss, no anointing) which are all made up for by the woman who had washed Jesus' feet with her tears and hair, providing the rest as well. "For this reason I say to you, her sins, which are many have been forgiven, for she loved much; but he who is forgiven little, loves little" (Luke 7:47).[212]

What these critics did not realize is that instead of Jesus becoming unclean by the touch of unclean people, He banishes uncleanness from His context. That is, the Kingdom is an era of banishing uncleanness through healing (Isa 61:1–3). Jesus is the King and He brings a present expression of His Kingdom into whatever setting He locates Himself. So instead of uncleanness communicably making Jesus unclean, His level of holiness banishes uncleanness by healing within the present context of Kingdom that surrounds Him as King.

Jesus' banishment of uncleanness is not to be construed as a disregard for the issue because He grew up in a home committed to Law practice and recovery from uncleanness. For example, circumcision was the first Jewish ceremony that a Jewish male experienced. A discharge of blood during the birth rendered both Mary and Jesus unclean, requiring purification (Lev 12:2–8). On the eighth day, circumcision must be performed, accompanying the purifying of the child. Mary would remain unclean for thirty three days (Gen 17:12; Lev 12:3–4). Perhaps, Luke or the Jews at that time had conflated the eight days for Jesus' purification and circumcision with the thirty three for Mary into "*their*" purification on the eighth day (Luke 2:22). Being a poor woman, Mary sacrificed two turtle doves instead of a one year old lamb. This law indicates that the two sacrifices are for purification[213] offering and a burnt offering, each contributing to the separation of this Israelite from her uncleanness. Since Jesus was also their first born, he would need to be redeemed according to the law of the redemption of the first born (Exod 13:12–16). This redemption process reminds the Jews of the generosity of God, Who rescued the Israelites when the death angel passed over them, thus begin-

---

212. For comments on Luke 7:48–50 see discussions of forgiveness and faith in Kennard, *Messiah Jesus*, 33–36.

213. The Hebrew texts develop this as purification, though the LXX and N.T. call it "sin offering;"

ning the exodus. Joseph and Mary were in the Temple with Jesus in order to carry out for Him the custom of the Jewish Law (Luke 2:27).

When Jesus' purification took place, two Jews came up to baby Jesus, and express Jewish aspirations for Him that reflect Kingdom cleansing consistent with His Kingdom healings (Luke 2:25–38). The first, Simeon, was righteous and devout. He was looking for the consolation of Israel that is the Kingdom.[214] The Holy Spirit was upon him, and had revealed to him that he would not die until he had seen the Lord's Christ. He took Jesus into his arms and blessed the sovereign God for letting him see the salvation personified by Jesus, Who will bring Kingdom glory to Israel and extend such light of revelation even to Gentiles (Luke 2:29–32). He then blessed the family and pointed out that Jesus will reveal the hearts of men, so as to split Israel so that some fall, while others rise (Luke 2:34–35). The other, Anna the Jewish prophetess, also gave thanks to God and spoke of the redemption of Jerusalem to be accomplished in Jesus' Kingship (Luke 2:36–38).

Jesus as the Superior Jewish Scribe (Matthew 21–23)[215]

In this section we shift from Jesus' message content to Jesus' *authority* to teach this content. Here we explore the authority of Jesus as Messiah who teaches this Law and judges the leadership of Israel and their Temple (the symbol of their authority). As Jesus challenges their authority through His teaching on the Law, the religious leaders respond back with a challenge of their own: namely, trying to discount Jesus' authority to make

---

214. The Abrahamic Covenant promised an abundant land as Israel's possession (Gen 15:13–21) which was embraced within the Mosaic Covenant promise for peace and blessing of renewal in the land (Deut 28:1–14; 30:1–30). The Davidic Covenant added the element of Kingship into this hope (developed in the chapter on "Messianic King"). The prophets develop this Kingdom era with the wonderful transforming benefits that will accrue especially to Israel (Jer 31:27–33:26). For example, in a context of Gentile domination, Isa 9 speaks of the birth of a king that will enlighten a new Kingdom era for Israel, bringing peace to the world. Second Temple Judaism hungers and longs for this hope.

215. Most Matthew specialists see chapter 21 beginning a new section (Davies and Allison, *Matthew*, 3:111–112) leaving the Galilean ministry for the rejection of Jewish temple and leadership, which sets the tone for: 1) Jesus' rejection and death, 2) the destruction of the temple and Israel, and 3) eschatological Kingdom. The unit also begins with a phrase that returns at the end as an *inclusio*, namely, "Blessed is He Who comes in the name of the Lord" (Matt 21:9; 23:39). Much of the unit explores Jesus as Messianic judge.

these challenges. This operates on two levels. One level of challenge is, Jesus' level of scribal authority. The professional scribes would usually grant unusually able scribes a level of authority on the basis of tests and demonstrated competency. This level of challenge we will investigate here. The other level of challenge goes further into the content of Jesus' challenge to that of His Messianic authority to judge them. This material has been examined already under Jesus teaching of the Law but is also supportive of Jesus as the Davidic King, Who will judge peoples who resist His Kingdom (see chapter on Davidic Covenant). However, if Jesus is stumped, shamed and ridiculed as an inferior scribe it would indicate that He could not therefore be a suitable candidate for Messiah. So the issue of scribal authority is quite significant to this topic. The authority of Jesus as a superior scribe fits in this chapter since it is another expression of Jesus teaching of the Law.

Jesus bests the best that the establishment has to offer. Utilizing Jewish rhetorical criticism the kind of questions indicate that the level of scribe is being assessed. For example, the Talmud describes standard forensic interrogation of a rabbi's acumen by means of rhetorical questions in four distinct styles: (1) *halachic* or scientific questions about the application of Torah to specific situations, (2) nonsense question designed to rattle and ridicule a scholar and his interpretations of Scripture, (3) conduct questions larger than any one text, and (4) *haggadic* or contrary question.[216] The Jewish leadership broadly wished to use these rabbinical techniques to trap Jesus and show His deficiency and overreaching claims (Matt 22:15–46; Mark 12:13–37; Luke 20:19–44). Instead, the approach backfired on them, showing Jesus' superior ability as a scribe and the religious leadership's further deficiency. This issue of superior scribe is explored here.

The Jewish authority structure during second Temple Judaism meant that the Herodians held the highest posts of authority, surrounded by the Sadducees and the Pharisees. The Herodians were those religious leaders or chief priests and their scribes that accepted Roman dominance and tried to please Herod so that they could maintain themselves in their political power as religious leaders (compare Luke 20:19 with Matt 22:16 and Mark 12:13). The Sadducees were the conservative Jews closely associated with power block of religious leaders in the Temple, who only

---

216. Daube, *The New Testament and Rabbinic Judaism*, 158-69 and "Rabbinic Methods," 239–264; Molina and Neyrey, *Calling Jesus Names*, 73–74; Owen-Ball, "Rabbinic Rhetoric," 2–4, 7, 9–10, 12.

tended to treat the Pentateuch as Scripture and thus did not embrace a clear encouraging afterlife and resurrection view. The Pharisees were progressive Jews, tending to accept the prophets and writings, and thus embraced a hopeful resurrection view for the afterlife. The Pharisees' power block existed especially in the village synagogues but they had considerable adherents at the Temple as well. In general these Pharisees were hoping for a Messiah who would free them from the Romans and to bring in the Kingdom.

The first challenge comes from the Herodians (especially the chief priests and their scribes) and Pharisees in the form of a *halachic* or scientific question, identified by "Is it lawful to . . . ?" (Matt 22:15-22; Mark 12:13-17; Luke 20:19-26). Notice that the Herodians (who had accepted Roman dominance) and the Pharisees (who usually opposed Roman domination), cooperated to try to trap Jesus between their concerns. Flattery begins the trap, "Teacher, we know that You are truthful and teach the way of God in truth." Then the critical issue of Jesus' authority is raised, since He defers to no one and is not partial. Now the *halachic* question tried to tighten the noose around Jesus neck: "is it lawful to give poll-tax to Caesar, or not?" The poll-tax was the most obvious sign in Jewish life of submission to Rome. For example, in A.D. 6 Judas of Galilee led a revolt against the procurator because he took a census for the purpose of collecting the poll-tax.[217] If Jesus said that the poll-tax was unlawful, or as against the Jewish Law, then the Herodians would have Him trapped in advocating seditious activity, a capital offense under Rome. If Jesus said that the tax was lawful, then the Pharisees and Herodians would have Jesus buckling to the Roman dominance in a manner that would alienate the Jewish populous and deflate their hopes for a removal of the Roman oppressors. Many Jews resented the poll-tax, repeatedly finding that the poll-tax was an oppressive burden and had petitioned for its reduction but to little avail.[218]

Jesus perceived their malice in this dilemma and called them down for their hypocrisy. His response was to consider a denarius, the coin used to pay the poll-tax each year.[219] Jesus lays His trap by asking His

217. Josephus, *Ant.* 17. 204; 18.3.i.1; *J. W.* 2.118.
218. Tacitus, *Ann.* 2.42 referring especially to A.D. 17.
219. Palmyra inscription in Dittenberger, *OGIS* 629.153-56= IGR 3.1056 is of 137 AD but it quotes a letter of 18-19 AD showing the relevance of this discussion in Jesus' time including that taxes were calculated in denarii but often paid in local coinage (Matthews, "The Tax Law," 157-80; Kennard, *Render to God*, viii, 51-55; Collins,

accusers whose face and inscription is on the coin. The coin identified Tiberius Caesar by head and inscription.[220] So, they responded that it was Caesar's. Jesus sliced through the issue with his succinct statement, "render to Caesar the things that are Caesar's and to God the things that are God's." The religious leaders and the people[221] were amazed at His answer. Jesus had removed Himself from the trap and reaffirmed the obligation they had to their authorities, while neither aligning Himself with Caesar nor being seditious. The people as well as the religious leaders were amazed at the skill with which He had answered them.

The second challenge comes from the Sadducees in the form of a nonsense question (Matt 22:23–33; Mark 12:18–27; Luke 20:27–40). They begin with flattery by calling Him teacher, even though they do not seek to be instructed. The Sadducees instead built a theological riddle on the law for Levirate marriage, which identified that in order to provide for keeping an inheritance within the family, if a husband died without a child, his brother was to sire a child in his brother's name so that his brother would have an heir (Deut 25:5).[222] The Sadducees (who do not believe in a resurrection)[223] weave a nonsensical question about marriage continuing in the afterlife, and wonder if a wife had seven husbands whose wife would she be in the resurrection.[224] The absurdity is made particularly acute by: (1) their conjectures of marriage in resurrection, which is foreign to the Law[225] and (2) polyandry, which is foreign to Judaism.

Mark, 553–54). Additionally, denarii have been found in Jerusalem before Jesus' time in 46 and 32/1 BC (Ariel, "Survey of Coin Finds in Jerusalem [until the End of the Byzantine Period]," *LASBF* 32[1982]: 273–326, esp. 284 #22 in table 3 on p. 312 and # 31 on p. 313). Jesus in the synoptic gospels makes a superior presentation than the account transpiring in *Gos. Thom.* 100 and Justin Martyr, *1 Apol.* 17.2, because it used audiovisuals that were accurate to the context (a denarius was a silver coin, not a gold one like Thomas claims) and verbally sliced through the issue instead of a blunt response. Additionally Matthew has increased the parallelism over Mark and Luke.

220. Davies and Allison, *Matthew*, 3:216, 218.
221. Luke 20:26; *Gos. Thom.* 100.
222. Josephus, *Ant.* 4.8.23; *m. Yebamot.*
223. Josephus, *Ant.* 18.1.4; *J. W.* 2.8.14.
224. "The resurrection" is a Jewish way of referring to the afterlife, especially from a Pharisaic point of view (Wis 2.1–5; *1 En.* 102.6–11; *m. Sanh.* 10.1; *b. Sanh.* 90b).
225. There is no clear development of resurrection in the Pentateuch. Furthermore, there is only a brief mention of procreation and fertility within marriage in the Kingdom (Isa 54:1–2; *1 En.* 10.17–19; *B. Šabb.* 30b; *Pirqe Mashiah, BhM* 3.77–78.), but it does not raise the issue of how this works out in the resurrection. However, fertility of the barren in these contexts fits within the broader theme of the fruitfulness of the

Jesus' response first deals with the Sadducees' ignorance about the resurrection, which He takes is evident from the Scriptures more broadly as in a Pharisaic orientation, and that the power of God is very able to accomplish these promises. So Jesus' charge back to them is that they are playing with only a half deck of Scriptures and too small a God concept. Jesus then returns to the resurrection and instructs them. The resurrection is an arena that the initiating of marriages to have kids does not apply, because those in the resurrection are like angels in heaven, living forever so there is no need to procreate to raise up an inheritor.[226] Perhaps, also the whole framework of Levirate marriage does not apply to the resurrection because there will be no need to raise up a descendent to inherit in the resurrection because the living will continue to live. So these Sadducees through their misapplication further show that they are out of touch with the purposes of the Law. Jesus then passes from the *manner* of the resurrection to its *fact* of continuing existence, accompanied by at least some of the patriarchs of the faith, like Abraham, Isaac, and Jacob.[227] To demonstrate this, Jesus cites Exod 3:6, wherein God said to Moses, "I am the God of Abraham, and the God of Isaac, and the God of Jacob," and

---

Kingdom (Isa 54:1-3; 55:1-13; 56:9-12; *1 En.* 10.17-19; *2 Bar.* 29; *M. Mid.* 2.6; *T. Suk.* 3.3, 10; *B. Yoma* 77b-78a; *Y. Šeqal.* 50a mid.; *B. Šabb.* 30b; *B. Ket.* 111b; *Pirqe Mashiah, BhM* 3.74, 77-78).

226. Jesus does not develop the similarity to angels for those in resurrection beyond the lack of marrying, so to extend this text to similarities like being spirit beings without bodies (*T. Abr. A* 4.9; Philo, *QG* 1.92; maybe LXX of Ps 103:4) or undergoing angelification, would be conjecture, though Jewish tradition does comment upon such a process (Wis 5.5; 4QSb 4.25; 4Q511 fr. 35; 4QM; *1 En.* 70-71; 104.1-6; *2 En.* 22.4-112 *Bar.* 51.5, 10; *T. Isaac* 4.43-48; Philo, *Sacr.* 1.5; Acts 12:15 may also apply). Jewish afterlife developed to include an astral immortality (Dan 12:2-3; *1 En.* 15.6-7; 104.2-7; 4 Macc 17.5; *2 Bar.* 51.10; *L.A.B.* 33.5; *As. Mos.* 10.9; *CU* 2.43-44, no. 788). For example, Jesus does not develop the Jewish view that as Adam became heavenly he became genderless (Philo, *Opif.* 151-52; *Mek.* on Ex. 12:40; *b. Ber.* 61a; *b. Meg.* 9a; *b. 'Erub.* 18a; *Gen. Rab.* on Gen 1:26). Remember that the Jewish tradition understood Gen 6:2 to mean that at least some angels engaged in sexual intercourse with human women (*1 En.* 6-7; 19.1; 86.1-6; 106.13-17; *Jub.* 4.15, 22; 5.1-11; 1QapGen. 2.1, 16; *2 Bar.* 56.12; *T. Reub.* 5.6; *T. Naph.* 3.4-5; 2 Pet 2:4; Jude 6-7; Justin, *2 Apol.* 5; Tertullian, *Virg.* 7; *Tg. Ps.-Jn.* on Gen 6:1-4. Unfortunately, Christiandom accelerated toward asceticism because of this text, as Christians tried to become like angels in Neo-Platonic ways.

227. Vermes argues that Pharisaic rabbis of the third century supplied similar arguments (*The Religion of Jesus the Jew*, 69). For example, Rabbi Simai argues for historical past resurrection of Abraham, Isaac and Jacob for God to be in covenant relationship with them, likewise, Rabbi Yohanan argues for the continued life of Aaron for tithes to be paid to him (*b. Sanh* 90b).

then Jesus affirmed that God is not the God of the dead but of the living. Jesus claims that the resurrection is already occurring for the dead (cf. Luke 16:19–31) and that in this resurrection, Abraham, Isaac and Jacob are already alive and not merely historical figures of the past.[228] Mark's account has Jesus returning to emphasize that the Sadducees are greatly mistaken (Mark 12:27). Luke's account has some of the scribes affirming that Jesus as a teacher had spoken very well (Luke 20:39). Matthew indicated that the multitude was astonished at His teaching and the Sadducees were silenced (Matt 22:33–34).

The third challenge comes from a Pharisee legal expert in the form of a conduct question (Matt 22:34–40). The lawyer asked Jesus about prioritizing the Law into the greatest commandment. In response, Jesus provides the correct answer of the *shema* as the greatest commandment, "You shall love the Lord your God with all your heart, and with all your soul, and with all your mind." He quickly followed this with a second command of "You shall love your neighbor as yourself." These two commands are alike in that the whole Law and prophets depend or hang upon these two for their unifying framework. This is not a novel perspective, for it is the very answer given to Jesus by a lawyer earlier in his ministry and elsewhere in Jewish tradition (Luke 10:25–28).[229] At that earlier time Jesus had said that such a Law-oriented way of living was salvific. However, in this inquisition, none were seeking such a salvation; they were simply frustrated at not being able to trap Jesus.

Each of these three questions demonstrated a superiority of Jesus' scribal ability. So Jesus turned the tables on the Pharisees gathered there and asked a *haggadic*[230] or contrary question (Matt 22:41–46; Mark 12:35–37; Luke 20:41–44). He did not wait for them to approve Him as in an ordination exam; He had demonstrated His authority and used their own tools to further question their authority and show His scribal pro-

---

228. Jesus view (Luke 16:19–31) is consistent with Jewish tradition (*Abr.* 50–55; 4 Macc 7:18–19; 13.17; 16:25; Philo, *Sacr.* 1.5; *T. Abr.* 20.8–14; *Qoh. Rab.* 9.5.1; *b. Sanh* 90b; *Ex. Rab.* 1.8; *Deut. Rab.* 3.15; *LAB* 4.11; *T. Isaac* 2.1–5; *T. Benj.* 10.6; *Apoc. Sed.* 14.3; *3 En.* 44.7). The sages could also read "living God" as "God of the living" (*Pesiq. R.* 1.2).

229. Akiva, *Sipre* on Lev 19:18; *T. Iss.* 5.2; 7.6; *T. Dan.* 5.3; Aristeas, *Ep.* 229; Philo, *Virt.* 51; 95; *Spec.* 2.63; *Abr.* 208; *T. Naph.* 8.9–10; *Jub.* 7.20; 20.2; 36.7–8; Josephus, *J. W.* 2.139. The early church was quite committed to following the same perspective (1 John 4:21; *Did.* 1.2; Polycarp, *Ep.* 3.3; Justin, *Dial.* 93; Sextus, *Sent.* 106a–b; Tertullian, *Marc.* 5.8).

230. Owen-Ball, "Rabbinic Rhetoric," 4; Keener, *Matthew*, 532.

ficiency by asking them the final kind of rabbinic question. His question raised the real issue, the authority of the Messiah. "Whose son is the Christ?" The religious leaders answered "The son of David."[231] While not denying their answer, Jesus then asked the contrary question, "Then how does David in the Spirit call him 'Lord,' saying, 'The Lord said to my Lord, Sit at My right hand, until I put Your enemies beneath Your feet?' If David calls Him 'Lord,' how is He his son?" This contrary question pressed the authority of Christ consistent with rabbinical reasoning[232] beyond the Davidic king idea to a One, Who was more. No one was able to answer Him. Furthermore, Jesus had demonstrated His superior scribal ability, so from that day on no one asked any more entrapment questions.

Excursus on Jesus' Death in the Synoptics: Service and Martyrdom

When evangelicals consider the message about everlasting life and Kingdom they normally think about the vicarious atonement death of Jesus Christ for the believer's salvation. This understanding is foreign to the synoptics.[233] For example, when an interpreter uses Jesus' words like "the Son of Man came to seek and save the lost" (Luke 19:10) as referring to the effectiveness of Jesus' atonement, the interpreter ignores the contextual meaning of this text. These words do not come in a context of Jesus' death, but rather Jesus' present earthly ministry to forgive sin.[234] That is, they show that Jesus is committed to include among His disciples unto Kingdom even the unattractive people such as a short tax collector named Zaccheus.

The synoptic treatment of Jesus' death is almost entirely just a straightforward historical narrative. This means that the story of Jesus' death is valued on its own merits without rendering it into a forum of apologetics or a fountain of theological significance. The synoptic death narrative is not repeatedly punctuated by statements of fulfilling Scripture (as occurs in John), or miracle, or Spirit-fostered prophecy or

---

231. *Pss. Sol.* 17.21–25; 4QFlor. 1.11–13; Justin Martyr, *First Apology* 45.

232. None of the following sources is pre-Christian but they show Jesus to probably be unoriginal about the application of Psalm 110 to Messiah (Akiva, *b. Sanh.* 38b; *Gen. Rab.* 85.9; *Num. Rab.* 18.23; *Tg.* on Ps 110; echoed in *Barn.* 12.10–11; Davies and Allison, *Matthew,* 3:253–54).

233. Pate and Kennard, *Deliverance Now and Not Yet,* 316–325, 413–421, 461–467.

234. Bock, *Luke,* 2:1523.

explanation of a deeper meaning (as in the birth narratives). The other comments about Jesus' death and resurrection are rare in the synoptics but tend to fit into two basic categories: (1) prediction that Jesus would suffer, die and resurrect, and (2) statements about a cup. This section examines these three developments of Jesus predicted death and cup statements to show that the synoptics do not contribute to covenantal atonement on the basis of Jesus' death but to mimetic atonement following Jesus in the narrow way to Kingdom.

Jesus' Death in Prediction

Jesus predicts His death and resurrection as historical events. For example, Jesus predicts that He must suffer many things from the elders, chief priests and scribes, and be condemned to death (Matt 16:21; 17:12, 22–23; 20:18; Mark 8:31; 9:12, 31; Luke 9:22, 44; 17:25; 18:31; 22:22). In the synoptics, Jesus does not explain why this must happen; He just says it must take place. Wicked religious leaders were simply following in the foolish way to kill the righteous man who showed up their evil ways.[235] Jesus predicts that His death will be by crucifixion but that He would resurrect on the third day (Matt 16:21; 17:9, 23; 20:19; Mark 9:31; Luke 9:22). At times the disciples did not understand what Jesus was saying (Luke 9:44).

Jesus steels Himself to suffer (Isa 50:6–7) because He realized that the Kingdom is only obtainable by going through the Messianic woes (Dan 9:24–27). It is these Messianic woes that begin His martyrdom and the potential martyrdom of His disciples. Albert Schweitzer developed this briefly as follows:

> In order to understand Jesus' resolve to suffer, we must first recognize that the mystery of this suffering is involved in the mystery of the kingdom of god, since the kingdom cannot come until the [tribulation] *peirasmos* has taken place ... The novelty lies in the form in which [the sufferings] are conceived. The tribulation, so far as Jesus is concerned, is now connected with an historical event: He will go to Jerusalem, there to suffer death at the hands of the authorities ... In the secret of His passion which Jesus reveals to the disciples at Caesarea Philippi the pre-Messianic tribulation is ... concentrated upon Himself alone, and that in the form that they are fulfilled in His own passion

---

235. This fits the Jewish pattern spoken by Wis 2.12–20.

and death at Jerusalem. That was the new conviction that had dawned upon Him. He must suffer for others ... that the Kingdom might come.[236]

These predictions of Jesus' crucifixion provide a call to the cost of discipleship and reassurance that the death and resurrection were God's plan. The main contextual implication for Jesus death in these predictive comments is an undergirding of the cost of discipleship; since Jesus is heading for crucifixion, the true disciple must follow him by taking up his cross in impending martyrdom as well (Matt 10:38-39; 16:24-26; Mark 8:34-37; Luke 9:23-26; 14:27).[237] That is, the disciples must be ready for the live possibility that those who will kill Christ, may kill them as well (e.g., Acts 7:54-60; 12:1-6).[238] This mimetic atonement view was common in Jewish,[239] Greek and Roman literature.[240]

Likewise, the one contextual implication for Jesus' resurrection predictions is to point out that Jesus' resurrection would be a sign like that of Jonah so that when it happens others would know who Jesus is as One greater than Jonah (Matt 12:38-41).[241] Likewise, John also reflects an enigmatic prediction from Jesus of His resurrection as a sign which was misunderstood as His opposition to the Temple (John 2:18-22; Matt 26:61; 27:40; Mark 14:58; 15:29).[242] Instead, Jesus referred to the raising of the temple of His body.

---

236. Schweitzer, *The Quest for the Historical Jesus*, 384-90; for an expansion of this perspective see Pate and Kennard, *Deliverance Now and Not Yet*.

237. This emphasis is in line with that of scholarly commentators on these verses. Davies and Allison, *Matthew*, 2:222-223, 670-671; Senior, *The Passion*, 40-45; Gundry, *Mark*, 452-454; Bock, *Luke*, 1:850-857, and 2:1286-87; Beck, "*Imiatio Chisti*," 28-47.

238. Nero's persecution of Christians, Tacitus, *Ann.* 15.44; 1 Clement 6; *Did.* 16.3-5.

239. 1 Macc 2.27-28; 2 Macc 6.12-7.42; 4 Macc 1.8-11; 6.27-30; 7.8-9; 9.23-24; 10.10; 11.12-27; 12.16-18; 16.16, 24-25; 17.2, 11-22; 18.1-5; Wis 2.12-20; 3.5-6; 4.18-5.14; 7.14; 11.19; 12.22; *T. of Moses* 9-10.10; cf. Pate and Kennard, *Deliverance Now and Not Yet*, 29-71; Seeley, *The Noble Death*; Joel Green, *The Death of Jesus*, 168.

240. Seneca, *Lucil.* 24.4-7; 98.12-14; Silius Italicus, *Punica* 6.531-38; Tacitus, *Ann.* 15.62 and 16.35; *Epictetus* 4.1.168-172; Pate and Kennard, *Deliverance Now and Not Yet*, 19-28; Seeley, *The Noble Death*; Charles Talbert, *Learning Through Suffering*, 17-29.

241. Gundry, *Matthew*, 242-45.

242. The Messiah is predicted to be the builder of the Temple (2 Sam 7:13; 1 Chr 17:12; Zech 4:7-10; *Sib. Or.* 5.420-33). 4QFlor. 1.1-13 identifies that in the end times (utilizing 2 Sam 7:13) the Jerusalem Temple will be built but by someone other than the Messiah. Elsewhere, God is portrayed to be the builder of the Temple: *1 En* 90.28-29;

Most of these predictive statements about Jesus' death and resurrection are removed some distance away from the narrative of Jesus' death and resurrection, whereas the primary predictions that are close to the crucifixion narrative are predictions about Judas' betrayal, Peter's denials, and the disciples' scattering. For example, Jesus identifies that one of His disciples would betray Him, the one who dips his hand in a bowl with Jesus and to whom Jesus gives a piece of bread (Matt 26:23–25; Mark 14:18–21; Luke 22:21–22; possibly hinted at earlier by John 6:70–71). Judas as the betrayer fulfills O.T. prophecy, namely: (1) betraying for thirty pieces of silver, which bought a potter's field, and that (2) Judas forfeits his portion and position through this betrayal (Pss 69:25; 109:8; Zech 11:12–13; Matt 26:54–56; 27:9–10; Mark 14:49; Acts 1:20). Jesus does not develop His own death here but rather the horrible consequences of dishonor and damnation that await Judas, since he is described as: "a devil," "lost," and "the son of perdition" (John 6:70–71; 17:12).[243] The potential damnation is also hinted at: (1) by Jesus through His statement that "it would have been better for him to have never been born," (Matt 26:24; Mark 14:21),[244] (2) by Luke's description that Satan enters Judas (Luke 22:3), and (3) that Peter mentions that Judas goes "to his own place" (Acts 1:25).[245] The disciples are clearly upset about such a revelation and repeatedly claim that they will be loyal.

In contrast, Jesus predicts that the disciples will all scatter (Zech 13:7; Matt 26:31–32; Mark 14:27). The disciples are not as loyal as they think when brought face to face with their impending martyrdom. Peter's denials (which Jesus predicts) are a special example calling down this overconfidence (Matt 26:33–35; Mark 14:29–31; Luke 22:31–34). Jesus disorients Peter with the claim that Satan will sift him, which results in Peter's denying Jesus three times. Jesus reassures Peter that he will strengthen the disciples after his denials. The passion narrative alludes to this prediction very softly by recounting that after Peter denied Jesus and the cock crowed, Peter remembered Jesus' statement that he would deny Him.

Jub. 1.17; 2 *Bar.* 4.3; 32.4; 11QTemple 29.8–10; 4QFlor. 1.3, 6; *Midr. Ps.* 90.17; *Mekilta of R. Ishmael* 3.

243. Brown, *John (xiii–xxi)*, 760; This is the more damning evidence against Judas, but the other two notes to follow, speak in this direction.

244. Compare: Matt 18:6–9; 2 Pet 2:20; 1 *En.* 38.2; 1 *Clem.* 46.8; Hermas, *Vis.* 4.2; *m. Hag.* 2.1.

245. Lightfoot, *A Commentary*, 4:19.

Only Luke 22:37 mentions as they are leaving the upper room that Jesus is to be classed among criminals. This mention of Isa 53:12 is the section of the Servant Song that emphasizes how to recognize this servant, much like Luke cites from the same section in Acts 8:32–33 (Isa 53:8–9), Luke does not develop any atonement issue surrounding these Isa quotes. They only serve as issues of recognizing the servant.[246] Without Luke's developing the atonement theme, it would be a reader's assumption to claim that it was there. In fact, Luke diminishes this quote by preceding and following the quote with what they have to carry. None of these predictions develops the significance of Jesus' death but all of them explain the disciples' own lives as the drama unfolds around them.

Cup Descriptions of Jesus' Death

There are three cup descriptions of Jesus' death: (1) the cup that the Zebedee brother's will also take, (2) the cup in the Gethsemane prayer, and (3) the last supper cup.

The first two cup accounts are often assumed by interpreters to allude to Jesus' death through the O.T. metaphor of the cup of God's wrath as penal atonement (Pss 11:6; 75:8; Isa 51:17, 22; Jer 25:15, 17, 27; 49:12; 51:7; Rev 16:1–18:6), as evident by the juxtaposing of Jesus' suffering and cross closely to these cup references (Matt 20:18–19, 22–23; 26:36–44; Mark 14:33–41; Luke 22:42 with ch. 23). These cup references apply God's judging wrath in Babylonian conquest over Israel and ultimately in God's conquest of Babylon the Great. To assume this metaphor of Jesus and those who share such tribulation with Him, this cup becomes the Messianic woes.

In the first account, Mother Zebedee asked for her sons to sit at Jesus' right and left in the kingdom (Matt 20:18–24; Mark 10:35–41). Jesus responds to the Zebedee boys and mother, that they do not know what they are asking. "Are you able to drink the cup that I am about to drink?"[247] The Zebedee boys do not realize what Jesus is asking but they

---

246. Notice Biblical theology's goal is not to expound what is in the mind of the Biblical author, but to expound what the Biblical author actually said. Luke never said Jesus atones as in Isa 53:5–6, 10, Luke merely claims Jesus death is recognizable by his silence (quoting Isa 53:7–8 in Acts 8:32–33). Likewise, Matt only connects this Servant song to be an expression of Jesus' healing (Matt 8:17).

247. This mimetic atonement suffering is additionally supported by Jesus' metaphor of baptism within an O.T. concept of suffering by submersion (2 Sam 22:4–7,

respond, "we are able," to which Jesus responds, "My cup you shall drink," fulfilling their disciple role of being like their master in martyrdom. James dies under the zeal of Herod to persecute the church (Acts 12:2), and John dies exiled to Patmos after being boiled in oil under Domitian persecution and surviving till Nerva's reign.[248] Bear in mind that if the disciples partake of the cup of God's wrath in mimetic atonement, then Jesus' experience as developed in this context is not a unique vicarious atonement, the disciple would also contribute. It is better to see neither the disciples' nor Jesus' cup taking *developed in this context* as depicting a vicarious atonement rather than to fund a conjectured vicarious atonement off the martyrdom of the disciples and Christ, because mimetic atonement coheres strongly within the second Temple Jewish pattern.

In the context, repeated issues of selfishness are shown by 1) the rich ruler who did not love others enough to meet their needs (thereby not internalizing the Law in a New Covenant manner, Matt 19:21–22; Mark 10:22), 2) disciples who wished reassurance (Matt 19:27, 30; Mark 10:28, 31), seeking greatness (Matt 20:20–21; Mark 10:35–37), and 3) grumbling workers of the vineyard (Matt 20:11–16).

In this context, Jesus says, "The Son of Man did not come to be served, but to serve, and to give His life as a ransom for many" (Matt 20:28; Mark 10:45).[249] In these statements, Jesus life is given "in place of" or "in exchange for" (ἀντί) the many, however this preposition does not require a vicarious atonement in Jesus death. By contextual emphasis, Jesus' life given emphasizes His life spent in service as the example of true Kingdom greatness which His disciples are to follow (Matt 20:25–28; Mark 10:42–45). That is, mimetic atonement has Jesus' servanthood life as the price of ransom (λύτρον) rescuing the many from an ambiguous bondage into His Kingdom way. If λύτρον is defined by the other synop-

---

17–18; Pss 18:4–6, 16–17; 32:6; 42:7; 69:1–2, 13–17; 124:1–5 [repeated liturgically as a song of ascent]; 144:7–11; Job 22:11).

248. Ireneaus, *Haer.* 3.1.1; Eusebius, *Hist. eccl.* 3.34.13; Lightfoot, *Apostolic Fathers*, 513–31.

249. A defense of the authenticity of this statement, cf. Feuillet, "La coupe et le baptême de la passion (Mc, x, 35-40; Mt. xx, 20–23; Lc., xxii, 50)" *RB* 74(1967): 356–91; Howard, "Did Jesus Speak," 515–27; Casey, *Aramaic Sources*, 206; Sanders, *Jesus and Judaism*, 147; McKnight, *Jesus and His Death*, 356–58 conjectures that Mark reflects Isa 53. However, in Pate and Kennard, *Deliverance Now and Not Yet*, 316–18, 328–332, we explore the possibility of Isa 53 lying beneath these verses, examining the alternatives and concluding that the near context emphasis should not be overruled by the pendulum swing of plausible academic conjecture.

tic references, such ransoming has to do with God's raising up a Davidic King to deliver Israel from their enemies (Luke 1:68–69; 2:38; 24:21), not a vicarious atonement for sin. This follows the Jewish pattern where a martyr's death ransoms the Covenant people Israel from the sins of the nation.[250] For example, in 4 Macc 6.29 a prayer is uttered by one on the battlefield, "Make my blood their purification, and take my life in exchange for theirs." The speaker goes on to exhort others to "imitate me" in remaining faithful on the battlefield even if martyrdom is their lot.[251] 4 Macc 17.20–22 praises the martyrs for becoming "a ransom for the sin of our nation. And through the blood of those devout ones and their death as an atoning sacrifice, divine Providence preserved Israel." In second Temple Jewish Greek manuscripts of mimetic atonement, this atonement is conveyed by words like through (διὰ), example (ὑπόδειγμα), and the contextual pattern imitative of death.[252] George Nickelsburg explains this second Temple Jewish mimetic atonement option from passages in 2 Macc 6:18–7:44, 1 Macc 2 and the *T. Mos.* 9.

> Each instance recounts the event which the respective author interprets as the catalyst that turns God's wrath from Israel and brings release from the persecution. Each is a story about parent and sons who are ready to die rather than transgress the Torah. The *Testament of Moses,* written in the heat of persecution, anticipates an apocalyptic denouement in which God will avenge the innocent blood of his servants, notably Taxo and his sons. The Deuteronomic scheme of the *Testament of Moses* turns on this author's interpretation of Deuteronomy 32:43 (9:7; 10:2). For the pro-Hasmonean author of 1 Maccabees, Mattathias' zealous deed stays God's wrath (cf. Num 25:8, 11). The Maccabean victories are an answer to the dying patriarch's appeal to execute judgment on the Syrians (2:66–68; cf. Deut. 32:43). The version of the story in 2 Maccabees 7 takes cognizance of the fact that it was Judas Maccabeus who turned back the Syrian armies and brought deliverance to Israel. However, although Taxo's prediction has not been fulfilled as stated, our author nevertheless espouses in part the ideology of the *Testament of Moses.* The innocent deaths of the martyrs and their appeal for vengeance before and after death (7:37; 8:3) contribute to turn

---

250. 1QpHab. 8.1–3; 2 Macc 6.30; 7.9, 11, 14, 16–17, 22–23, 29, 30–38, 36–38; 4 Macc 6.27–29; 9.23–24; 17.21–22.

251. 4 Macc 9.23–24.

252. 2 Macc 6:31; 4 Macc 17:20–22.

God's wrath to mercy (8:5) and facilitate the Maccabean victories that are recounted through the rest of the book.[253]

Gaining Kingdom is the goal in both the Maccabean and Jesus' humble service. However, in this synoptic context, battlefield service is not in view but rather serving through humility as Jesus provides the example. Jesus had repeatedly called His disciples to take up their cross and follow Him in this mimetic atonement (Matt 10:38; 16:24–27; Mark 8:34–38; Luke 9:22–26; 14:26–27; John 12:24–25).

In the synoptic passages, "the many" is the New Covenant people, whom Jesus is gathering around Himself. Such a Kingdom meaning fits delightfully in this passage that acknowledges Jesus as the King in His Kingdom but not like other kings (Matt 20:21, 25; Mark 10:42). This ransom is "for" (ἀντί) the many in this gospel context. That word ἀντί has the sense of "on behalf of" or "in place of." In this case both could apply. Jesus shows His greatness as King in taking the place of servants and serving on their behalf throughout His kingly life on earth. The point of the passage is not vicarious atonement but by contextual emphasis this passage shows that disciples are also to be servants after Jesus' pattern. As such, this passage follows the Jewish mimetic atonement pattern.[254]

The Gethsemane prayer might also be assumed by an interpreter to develop the cup of God's wrath. Jesus identifies this judgment imagery with his impending death (Matt 26:37–38; Mark 14:33–34). Jesus is deeply grieved, sweating what looked like drops of blood (Luke 22:44). Jesus prayed, "If it is possible let this cup pass from Me" (Matt 26:39, 42, 44; Mark 14:36, 39, 41; Luke 22:42). Jesus is not trying to get out of His death in a moment of weakness; He knows full well and is committed to taking the cup God provides in His death (John 18:11). Rather Jesus knows His death is imminent. It is a death which in the Jewish tradition could be either vicarious[255] or mimetic atonement.[256] Both options are available in

---

253. Nickelsburg, *Jewish Literature*, 119–120.

254. 1 Macc 2.27–28; 2 Macc 6.12–7.42; 4 Macc 1.8–11; 6.27–30; 7.8–9; 9.23–24; 10.10; 11.12–27; 12.16–18; 16.16, 24–25; 17.2, 11–22; 18.1–5; Wis 2.12–20; 3.5–6; 4.18–5.14; 7.14; 11.19; 12.22; 1Q5 5.6; 1QS 9.4–5; 1Q34 bis 3 1, 5; 4Q508 1,1; 4Q513 frag. 2 2.4; 11Q10 (*Tg. Job*) 38.2; *Sipre Deut.* Pisqa 333.5; *T. of Moses* 9–10.10; Pate and Kennard, *Deliverance Now and Not Yet*, 29–71; Gundry, *Mark*, 869; Ignatius, *Rom* 6.

255. Isa 53; *1 En.*; Pate and Kennard, *Deliverance Now and Not Yet*, 73–115.

256. 1 Macc 2.27–28; 2 Macc 6.12–7.42; 4 Macc 1.8–11; 6.27–30; 7.8–9; 9.23–24; 10.10; 11.12–27; 12.16–18; 16.16, 24–25; 17.2, 11–22; 18.1–5; Wis 2.12–20; 3.5–6; 4.18–5.14; 7.14; 11.19; 12.22; *T. of Mos.* 9–10.10; cf. Pate and Kennard, *Deliverance*

Jewish literature, though mimetic atonement has more emphasis in the Jewish literature and is the only option clearly developed in the synoptics. However, in this context, neither Jesus nor the biblical authors explain which option is to be understood. Jesus has been prophesying throughout His ministry and just a few moments before at the Passover that He was about to die. So since Jesus is not asking "Do not let Me die" then His request must be: "Father let the severity of death pass on from Me after I die." That is, Jesus is praying for His own resurrection on the other side of the judgment.[257] Matt 26:42 implies that the cup cannot pass away unless He drinks it. This would mean that Jesus' "will" is for release from death to obtain resurrection, though He is open to the Father's will if it should be otherwise. As understood, Jesus in fact did receive from the Father the passing on of the cup in resurrection after His death, as Jesus had asked for in His prayer. This interpretation also best fits with the description of the Gethsemane prayer in Heb 5:7 as being answered in the affirmative since the word "heard" means a positive answer (1 John 5:14-15 and in the Ps). So while the cup briefly alludes to the impending cost of Jesus' death, the Gethsemane passages actually emphasize the effectiveness of Jesus' prayer life to obtain resurrection on the other side of death.

In the account of Passover or Lord's Supper, brief allusions to Jesus' impending death are made. Jesus desired to eat the Passover with His apostles *before* He suffered (Luke 22:14-15).[258] These synoptic accounts contrast with John, who instead places the Passover celebrated by those in Jerusalem on the night *after* Jesus dies (John 18:28). Presumably, those who were visiting in Jerusalem had to fit their celebration of Passover around the availability of rooms, which were of course already booked for the regular time by those who lived in Jerusalem.

A Passover celebration evidenced a liturgical pattern. The meal would begin with the head of the family blessing the feast day and then passing the first cup of wine, which was followed by passing preliminary dishes of bitter herbs and fruit purée. The Passover liturgy would follow with some instruction on the meaning of the commemoration and likely singing of Psalms 113-14. The liturgy concluded with a second cup

---

Now and Not Yet, 29-71.

257. Blaising, "Gethsemane," 333-43; this view is not sufficiently countered by the disjunction (contrary to Gundry, *Mark*, 870) because Jesus is willing to be damned (as the alternative to resurrection) if the Father wills, but Jesus asks for resurrection.

258. Because the Last Supper is with Jesus and the apostles (Luke 22:14-15), Mary Magdalene would not be present, since she is nowhere described as an apostle.

of wine. The meal would follow with roasted lamb, the breaking of the unleavened bread, and bitter herbs with fruit purée (Exod 12:8). This portion of the meal has concluded with the third cup of wine, which was blessed as the cup of blessing. A further time of praise (normally singing Psalms 115–18) was followed by the praise or Kingdom cup.

In Jesus' celebration of the Passover, Matthew and Mark describe the bread broken as "This is My body" symbolizing Jesus' impending death. Jesus in Luke says, "This is My body given for you" (Luke 22:19, ὑπέρ). Here Jesus' body is given in death for the disciples benefit. However, the cup of wrath meaning will not work well for this Lord's Supper cup even though it is symbolizing Jesus death because this cup is already laden with meaning. From Passover the cup hints at a rescue to a new beginning and perhaps by the third or fourth cup it hints at Kingdom (Matt 26:29; Mark 14:25; Luke 22:20; 1 Cor 11:25–26). Additionally, Jesus specifically identified this cup with His blood in His death and the initiation of the New Covenant (Matt 26:28–29; Mark 14:24–25; Luke 22:20; 1 Cor 11:25). Luke and Paul are clearer in identifying this covenant with the New Covenant but all identify the cup and death with Kingdom benefits, so the New Covenant is best seen as what is initiated in this cup. Kingdom benefits like forgiveness emerge from Jesus' death and are celebrated in this cup.

Jesus' death in the Jewish tradition could be either vicarious[259] or mimetic atonement.[260] However, no specific benefit is developed in the bread/body phrases. Only Luke 22:16 develops that Jesus will not eat bread again until the Kingdom comes. The cup[261] statement is a little more fruitful since it is developed as Jesus' blood poured out *for* many (Matt 26:27–28, περί; Mark 14:24 and Luke 22:20, ὑπέρ). The covenant alluded to in Matthew and Mark is rendered explicit in Luke as the New Covenant. However, the New Covenant in the O.T. passages develop Kingdom imagery rather than death imagery (Jer 31:31 and perhaps a

---

259. Isa 53; *1 En.*; cf. Pate and Kennard, *Deliverance Now and Not Yet*, 73–115.

260. 1 Macc 2.27–28; 2 Macc 6.12–7.42; 4 Macc 1.8–11; 6.27–30; 7.8–9; 9.23–24; 10.10; 11.12–27; 12.16–18; 16.16, 24–25; 17.2, 11–22; 18.1–5; Wis 2.12–20; 3.5–6; 4.18–5.14; 7.14; 11.19; 12.22; 1Q5 5.6; 1QS 9.4–5; 1Q34 bis 3 1, 5; 4Q508 1,1; 4Q513 frag. 2 2.4; 11Q10 (*Tg. Job*) 38.2; *Sipre Deut.* Pisqa 333.5; *T. of Moses* 9–10.10; cf. Pate and Kennard, *Deliverance Now and Not Yet*, 318–319, 332–333.

261. There is no evidence that the cup (holy grail) has been preserved though many medieval quests pursued the possibilities. Likewise, there is no evidence from Da Vinci's Renaissance rendering of the "Last Supper" that Mary Magdalene is a holy grail as Brown's fanciful *Da Vinci Code*, 230–239 claims.

future predicted everlasting covenant of Kingdom peace in Isa 55:3; Jer 32:40; Ezek 16:60-63; 37:26). This could be a sacrificial statement either as was required: (1) to begin the Mosaic Covenant (Exod 24:5-8), or (2) in mimetic atonement as the Maccabean revolt, as soldiers on the field of battle gave their lives as sacrifice.[262] If the synoptic gospels had developed Levitical sacrifice imagery or imagery of sprinkling the people, as Heb 9:11-10:18 and 1 Pet 1:2 develop, then the synoptics would be clearly developing a *vicarious* atonement, but there is no development of vicarious atonement in these synoptic passages. Likewise, if this passage developed the need for disciples to take up their cross and follow Him in servant martyrdom as elsewhere in the synoptics (Matt 10:38; 16:24-28; 20:26-28; Mark 8:34-38; 10:42-45; Luke 9:23-26; 14:26-27; John 12:24-25), then this passage would be explaining a *mimetic* atonement. However, no synoptic gospel explains this Last Supper atonement in this passage. So perhaps this reference should be seen as making the point of identifying many, especially the disciples, with Kingdom. In Matt 26:28 the manner of benefit of Jesus' death is explained as for (εἰς) or to the outcome of forgiveness of sins. Elsewhere such forgiveness is granted by fiat from the Divine and His King as part of the Jubilee ministry in Jesus' life (Matt 6:13-14; 9:2-6; 18:27-35; Mark 2:5-10; 11:25-26; Luke 5:20-24; 7:47-49).[263] The time of forgiveness is not explained in the Last Supper but by connecting Matthew with Luke, this forgiveness can be seen as the forgiveness in the New Covenant, which Jeremiah identifies as in the days when Israel will be responsive to the Law and the Lord, such that there will be no need for evangelism (Jer 31:33-34). This had not happened yet. Eschatological forgiveness is not required by Matthew here but it would be consistent with his development elsewhere (Matt 18:22-35). Thus, the manner in which Jesus' death brings about forgiveness is not developed in the synoptics, and since it is merely one obscure clause in the synoptics it is certainly not an emphasis.

Following their Passover and Gethsemane prayer, the three synoptic passion accounts each treat the death and resurrection of Jesus in a straightforward historical manner, without embellishments of fulfilling prophecy

---

262. 1 Macc 2.27-28; 2 Macc 6.12-7.42; 4 Macc 1.8-11; 6.27-30; 7.8-9; 9.23-24; 10.10; 11.12-27; 12.16-18; 16.16, 24-25; 17.2, 11-22; 18.1-5; Wis 2.12-20; 3.5-6; 4.18-5.14; 7.14; 11.19; 12.22; *T. of Moses* 9-10.10; cf. Pate and Kennard, *Deliverance Now and Not Yet*, 29-71.

263. Kennard, *Messiah Jesus*, 23-68.

or explaining their theological significance. If there is an emphasis beyond the historical witness, it is that Jesus is the King of the Jews.

Jewish-Christian Lineage

Jesus' adherence to the Mosaic Law places Him in the context of second Temple Judaism. Part of the rise of the new perspective on Jesus, Paul and Judaism is a greater awareness of the corporate allegiance that Israel had to the Mosaic covenant during the second century B.C. on to the second century A.D.[264] However, the Jewish side of N.T. interpreters even before the new perspective valued Jewish Christian compliance to the Law, while Gentiles did not.[265] This Jewish commitment to covenantal nomism was sampled in the chapter entitled: "Instances of Covenant Nomism in Second Temple Judaism," however many of those Jews who followed Jesus continue with covenant nomism.

This commitment to the Law as a corporate commitment continued among many Jewish sects which embraced Jesus as Messiah. The Messianic Jewish group, especially known as the Nazarenes was the audience of Matthew's gospel, and thus the direct inheritors of this teaching. Jerome repeats that they had a Hebrew version of Matt that they utilized as part of their Scripture.[266] The Nazarenes maintained a high view of Messiah Jesus and yet maintained a consistent lifestyle commitment to the Law as did other Jews.[267] This perspective is evident in the biblical text in how

---

264. This New Paul and Israel studies has followed the wake of Sanders including *Paul and Palestinian Judaism*; *Paul, the Law, and the Jewish People*; *Jewish Law from Jesus to the Mishnah*; and *Judaism*; and Dunn *Jesus, Paul and the Law*; *Jews and Christians*; and *Paul and the Mosaic Law*; Lieu, "The Parting of the Ways," 101–19; *Image and Reality*; Becker and Reed, *The Ways that Never Parted*; Häkkinen, "Ebionites," 247–78; and Luomanen, "Nazarenes," 279–315; Skarsaune and Hvalvik, *Jewish Believers*.

265. Commentators sensitized on the Jewish side even before New Perspective recognize Jewish Christians will be keeping the Law while Gentile Christians are not (Schweitzer, *The Mysticism of Paul the Apostle*, 180, 187; Davies, *Paul and Rabbinic Judaism*, 71, 81–84, 136–45, 221–23; Stendahl, *Paul Among Jews*, 1–7, 80–81, 93; Tomson, *Paul and the Jewish Law*.

266. Jerome, *Vir. Ill.* 3; Klijn and Reinink, *Patristic Evidence*, 210–11; Skarsaune and Hvalvik, *Jewish Believers*, 542–43.

267. Epiphanius, *Pan.* 29.7.5; Skarsaune and Hvalvik, *Jewish Believers*, 478.

Matt,[268] Jas[269] and some in the book of Acts practice their Jewish-Christianity.[270] The Jews attacked and cursed in prayer the Nazarenes for being Jews who align themselves with Jesus as Messiah.[271] Rabbinic literature prohibits contact with Jewish Christians as heretics even more strongly than with non-Jews.[272]

This passion for the Mosaic Covenant among Jewish sects which embrace Jesus as their Messiah continued for centuries.[273] Ireneaus, Epiphanius, and other heresiologists and historians named several groups of Jewish-Christians, but their reports are biased against the group's commitment to the Law.[274] For example, the Ebionites were primarily named as the "poor ones," who had a poor understanding of the place of the Law (they continue to practice it) and primarily use the gospel of Matt.[275] Ebionites are also criticized by the Patristics for their vegetarianism, commitment to purity, daily use of *mikvot* ritual baptisms, and for celebrating Passover when the Jews do so.[276] Justin Martyr identified that these Ebionites require all believers to keep the Law and support an

---

268. Especially at focus is Matt 5:17-48 and 19:16-22; Saldarini, *Matthew's Christian-Jewish Community*; Kennard, "The Way to Kingdom Salvation."

269. Especially at focus is Jas 1:25 and 2:8-26; Kennard, "The Law in James" which has been reworked into chapter 12; Notice the similarities between Matt and Jas in Mayor, *The Epistle of St. James*, lxxxiv-lxxxvi.

270. Especially at focus is Acts 10:14-16, 28; 11:2-3; 15:1-29; 18:18 and 21:20-26; Kennard, "Paul and the Law" and "The Law in James."

271. Epiphanius, *Pan.* 29.9.2; Jerome, *Epist.* 112.13; 12th benediction of *Birkat Haminim*; Skarsaune and Hvalvik, *Jewish Believers*, 482-3.

272. *t. Ḥul.* 2.20-24; *Šabb.* 13.5.

273. Klijn, "The Study of Jewish Christianity," 419-31; Taylor, "The Phenomenon," 313-34 and Velasco and Sabourin, "Jewish Christianity," 5-26.

274. Epiphanius, *Pan.* 30.7.1-7; 30.9.4; Irenaeus, *Haer.* 1.26.2; Hyppelytus, *Refut.*; Clement of Alex., *Strom.* 2.9.45.5; Tertullian, *Marc.* 4.8; Origen, *Princ.* 4.3.8; *Pseudo-Clementines Recognitions* 1.28.1-2; 1.32.4; 1.35.2; 1.37.1-4; Klijn and Reinink, *Patristic Evidence*.

275. Celsus statement in Origen, *Cels.* 2.1 and *Hom. Gen.* 3.5; Eusebius, *Hist. eccl.* 3.27.1-6; Skarsaune and Hvalvik, *Jewish Believers*, 442-46.

276. Epiphanius, *Pan.* 2.3-5; 9.3.6; 15.3; 18.7-19.4; 21.1-6; 22.1-11; Hippolytus, *Haer.* 8.18.1-2; *Pseudo-Clementine Homilies* 7.8; *Didascalia Apostolorum* 21; Rouwhorst, "Jewish Liturgical Traditions," 82; These polemics against the Jewish-Christians are essentially the same polemics made against the Jews (Aphrahat of Persia, Syriac *Demonstrations* 12-16); Skarsaune and Hvalvik, *Jewish Believers*, 446, 456, 459, 520-22, 628-31.

adoptionist Christology.[277] Additionally, Epiphanius identified the Elchesaites as followers of Elchasai and his *Book of Elchasai* (a Mesopotamian Jewish apocalypse). Both the Ebionites and the Elchesaites were Jewish Messianic movements which had a deficient view of Jesus deity, which Heb 1:4–13 could be addressing. Furthermore, the Christian community addressed by *Didascalia* in the third century sought to establish and protect its orthodoxy among a majority of the Jewish-Christian community that practiced the Law.[278]

In the second century, Justin Martyr, in *Dialogue with Trypho the Jew*, addressed the possibility of authentic salvation of Jews, who practice their Judaism and believe in Christ and obey Christ's teaching.[279] Justin concedes that Christians who have faith in Christ may keep the Law if they wish but it is not for salvation.[280] Consistent with this, the communities behind the *Kerygmata Petrou* (c.a. 200 A.D.) and the *Ascents of James* were Jewish-Christians with a high Christology.[281] Justin Martyr suggests that *diaspora* Jewish synagogues rooted out Christians from their midst by denouncing them and their faith in Christ as incompatible with synagogue participation.[282]

Chrysostom reiterated that the Law and circumcision were not required for salvation.[283] Chrysostom also attacked Christian participation in Jewish festivals[284] as joining with apostate Jews, who he identifies as "Christ killers."[285]

---

277. The view that Jesus is a human (not God) adopted to a unique empowered role at his baptism by God, Justin Martyr, *Dial.* 47–48.

278. Epiphanius, *Pan.* 30.7.1–7; Irenaeus, *Haer.* 1.26.2; Ps.-Clementines *Recognitions* 1.37.1–4; Georg Strecker, "Appendix 1: On the Problem of Jewish Christianity," 257.

279. Justin Martyr, *Dial.* 46.1; also 1 *Apol.* 11.

280. Justin Martyr, *Dial.* 47.

281. Strecker, "The Kerygmata Petrou," 2:102–27, esp. 210–22 and 270–71; Strecker, *Das Judenchristentum*, no. 2; Schoeps, *Theologie*; *Jewish Christianity*; van Voorst, *The Ascents of James*.

282. Justin Martyr, *Dial.* 16, 95–96, 110.

283. Chrysostom, *Hom. Act.* 32; *The Acts of the Apostles* 1.11.

284. Chrysostom, *Hom. Act.* 1.1 and 8.1, 48.844 and 927; Meeks and Wilken, *Jews and Christians*, 32, 86, 105.

285. Chrysostom, *Patrologia graeca* 48.849; Murray, *Symbols of Church and Kingdom*, 41; Meeks and Wilken, *Jews and Christians*, 31.

These sects with a high regard for the Law were often villainized as Judaisers, a different kind of Christianity.[286] This situation was normal throughout the East. For example, the writings of Aphrahat show that Christians in Adiabene during the fourth century engaged in vigorous debate concerning the Law with the Jewish community.[287] According to these texts, the Nazarenes survived at least until the fourth century as an independent Jewish-Christian sect that believed in the virgin birth, a high Christology, acceptance of Paul's writings, and continued practice of the Jewish Law.[288] For example, Jerome writes to Augustine about 404 A.D. that the Nazarenes "believe in Christ, the Son of God, born of Mary the Virgin, and say about Him that He suffered under Pontius Pilate and rose again."[289] Additionally, before A.D. 428, Epiphanius describes these Nazarenes in *Panarion* 29[290] especially chapters 6 and 7, as a band of Jewish-Christians primarily in Syria, who believe in God as Creator, Christ as Lord, the resurrection of the dead, and use the N.T. as do other Christians. However, the Nazarenes, according to Epiphanius, also use the Hebrew O.T. like Jews and practice circumcision, Sabbath,[291] and the Law as do Jews. In fact, as late as the eighth century in Syria the works of Sergius the Stylite suggest that ordinary Syrian Christians could not distinguish between Judaism and Christianity in their practice and so the leadership of the Gentile expression of the church attempted to create an image of the Jews which would discourage lay people from having any contact with them.[292] This expression of Jewish-Christianity disintegrated in the region, being caught between the pincers of rising Islam and Christian anti-semitism. Today, less than a tenth of all the Jewish-Christian

---

286. Ignatius, *Magn.* 8–11; *Phld.* 6–9; Jerome, *Comm. Isa.* 3.30 on Isa 9:1; Augustine, *Faust.* 19.7; Wilken, *John Chrysostom and the Jews*, 94.

287. Murray, *Symbols of Church and Kingdom*, 8; Neusner, *Aphrahat and Judaism*.

288. Epiphanius, *Pan.* 29.3.5–6; 30.7.1–7; Tertullian, *Marc.* 4.8; Pritz, *Nazarene Jewish Christianity*, 108–9; Bagatti, *The Church from the Circumcision*. For example, *Pseudo-Clementine Homilies* 42, 355–56 describes the Nazarenes as bishops of the circumcision, who resisted the change of worship day from Sabbath to Sunday at the council of Caesarea (196 C.E.).

289. Jerome, *Ep.* 112.13 contained in Pritz, *Nazarene Jewish Christianity*, 53–54.

290. Epiphanius, *Pan.* 29 is contained in its entirety in Pritz, *Nazarene Jewish Christianity*, 30–35, but the more helpful parts are in chapters 1, 6 and especially 7 on 33–34.

291. Eusebius, *Hist. eccl.* 3.27.5; Skarsaune and Hvalvik, *Jewish Believers*, 446.

292. Hayman, "The Image of the Jew," 440.

synagogues continue in this Nazarene spirituality, which celebrates a high Christology and continue to practice the Mosaic Law as Jews.

The broader Christian approach attacked Judaism as inadequate.[293] The *Epistle of Barnabus* presented Christians as the true heirs of the covenant, for Israel had forfeited it by idolatry, disobedience, and ignorance.[294] These approaches attack Jewish sacrifices and Jewish fasts as inappropriate, for they all point to Christ through typology.[295] Tertullian saw that these sacrifices were also replaced by praise and spiritual sacrifice.[296] Tertullian also argued that Sabbath, circumcision and in fact the whole Law were temporary and abolished in Christ.[297] From a similar perspective, Chrysostom argued that the New Covenant in Christ replaced the Sabbath and circumcision.[298] Origen maintained a supercessionism in which God divorces Israel for their blindness to the Law (thus unbelief in Christ), in order to marry all followers of Christ.[299] Cyprian identified that Israel was judged and dispersed by God for their blindness to Law and Christ.[300] The *Canons of the Council in Trullo* attack Sabbath fasting as a damning practice for which any of the church are to be "cut off" from the church and salvation.[301] The *Laodicean Canons* attack Christians who fraternize with Jews or join in the practice of Jewish festival celebrations such as Passover.[302]

Other Christian traditions such as Orthodox, Roman Catholic, Anglican, Episcopalian, and Wesleyan retain the possibility of gaining Kingdom by following Christ through such a faithful love relationship with God as is expressed in the Decalogue. From a Gentile perspective they diminish the Mosaic Law to be essentially the Decalogue. These are the same traditions that embrace a two ways soteriology, and consider that

---

293. Ignatius, *Letter to Magn.* 10; *Phld.* 6; *Barn.* 2–4.

294. Christians as true heirs (*Barn.* 4.8; 6.19; 13.6; 14.45–46) with Israel forfeiting the covenant by: idolatry (*Barn.* 4.8; 16.1–2), disobedience (*Barn.* 8.7; 9.4; 14.1–4), and ignorance (*Barn.* 10.2, 9).

295. *Barn.* 2–3, 8; Justin, *Dial.* 18–19, 43.

296. Tertullian, *Adv. Jud.* 5.

297. Tertullian, *Adv. Jud.* 4, 6; also Cyprian, *Treatises* 12.1.16–17.

298. Chrysostom, *Hom. Phil.* 1.13.

299. Origin, *Comm. Matt.* 11.13–15; 14.19–20.

300. Cyprian, *Test.* 12.1.6.

301. *The Canons of the Council in Trullo*, canon 55.

302. *Laodicean Canons* 37 and 38, also 35 raises the issue around angelology; von Hefele et. al. *Histoire des conciles d'après les documents originaux*, 1.2, 989–1028.

in this two ways salvation the Law matters. For example, N. T. Wright addresses this perspective from the account of the rich young ruler, "The Torah was the boundary marker of the covenant people: those who kept it would share the life of the coming age."[303] Wright explains how the Law matters for a future salvation view within a two ways soteriology from Rom 2:12–16:

> It is vital to note that the justification and the judgment spoken of in this paragraph are inalienably *future*. This is not *present* justification; Paul will come to that in chapter 3. Nor can the two be played off against one another. They belong together: present justification, as Romans makes clear, is the true anticipation of future justification. And in Romans as elsewhere in Paul, it is present justification, not future, that is closely correlated with faith. Future justification, acquittal at the last great Assize, always takes place on the basis of the totality of the life lived.[304]

After establishing this two ways soteriology, Wright continues to place the Law as mattering within it.

> First, we may consider the peculiar situation of those described here. [Rom] 2.13 and 2.14, taken together, indicate quite clearly that those described in the latter as 'doing the law' will, according to the former, be justified (remember, again that we are here dealing with *future*, not present, justification).[305]

Before long people other than Jews followed Jesus. On this issue of Law and Jewish tradition, the gospels that go to the Gentiles also have a contribution for their Gentile readership. The chapter, "The Gospel of Mark and the Controversy of Jewish Traditions" brings some balancing tension for the Gentile follower of Jesus. The chapter after that, "Luke and John: Spirit Extended Salvation to the Gentiles" resolves this tension with a unified body of Christ that includes Jewish Law compliance and Gentile eschewing of the Law, while both head toward Kingdom.

---

303. Wright, *Jesus and the Victory of God*, 301.

304. Wright, "The Law in Romans 2," 143–144. Those who also agree that this text is Christian New-Covenant Gentiles as a foil for Jewish disobedience: Zahn, *Der Brief*; Mundle, "Zur Auslegung," 249–56; Flückinger, "Die Werke," 17–42; Barth, *A Shorter Commentary on Romans*, 36–39; Souček, "Zur Exegese," 99–113; Cranfield, *Romans*, 1:155–63; König, "Gentiles," 53–60; Salas, "Dios premia," 265–86; Bergmeier, *Das Gesetz*, 31–102; Watson, *Paul, Judaism*, 118–22; Wright, "The Law in Romans 2," 131–50; Jewett, *Romans*, 212–14.

305. Wright, "The Law in Romans 2," 146.

7

As a Gentile Gospel, Mark Eschews Mosaic Law and Jewish Tradition[1]

ONE OF THE RARE texts that is longer in Mark than either Matt or Luke is the account of the Pharisees and scribes taking issue with Jesus concerning His disciples lack of compliance with Jewish tradition of ritually washing hands before eating (Matt 15:1-20; Mark 7:1-23; Luke 11:37-41).

Such Pharisaic tradition had a controversial status before A.D. 70, but it was a significant emphasis with 67 percent of the discussion between Hillel and Shammai consisting of such ritual purity concerns.[2] The pre-Pharisaic "washing of hands" was necessary before handling holy objects,[3] but it was being extended to the handling of food. Shammai insisted on washing hands before filling the cup.[4] However, the view of Hillel won out, "Washing hands before a meal is a matter of choice, ablution after a meal is obligatory."[5] The politically connected Sadducees repudiated all this

---

1. Revised from Kennard, *Messiah Jesus*, pp. 153-156 used by permission from Peter Lang publishers.

2. This tradition was widespread during 2nd-4th century A.D. (*m. Hag.* 2.5-6; *b. Šabb.* 13b-14a; 62b; *y. Šabb.* 1.3d; *b. Yoma* 87b; *TB Berakot* 8.2; 60b; *TB Sotah* 4b). Especially *m. 'Ed.* 5.6 places hand washing in the category of heresy. R. P. Booth argues that the practice was not widespread before 70 A.D. (*Jdt.* 12.7; *Ep. Arist.* 305-306; *Sib. Orac.* 3.591-593; Booth, *Jesus and the Laws of Purity*, 159-160; Brandt, *Die jüdischen*; Räisänen, "Jesus and the Food Laws," 79-100; Schiffman, *Sectarian Law*, 136-41; "The Temple Scroll," 249-55; Dunn, "Jesus and Ritual Purity," 37-60; "Pharisees, Sinners," 61-88; Davies and Allison, *Matthew*, 2:521-522; Sanders, *Judaism: Practice and Belief*, 431-440; Deines, *Jüdische*; Gundry, *Mark*, 358-371; Klawans, *Impurity and Sin*, 146-150; Basser, *Studies in Exegesis*, 34-49; Regev, "Pure Individualism," 176-202; "Moral Impurity," 383-411; Chancey, *The Myth*, 63-119; Kazen, *Jesus and Purity*, 60-88; Poirier, "Purity beyond the Temple," 247-65).

3. *Ep. Aris.* 305; *Šabb.* 14b.

4. *m. Ned.* 9.1; Philo, *Hypoth.* 7.5; Finkel, *The Pharisees*, 140-141, 152-156.

5. *T. Berak.* 5.13; *Tosefta trac. Berak.* 4.8; *Bavli trac. Hullin* 105a.

washing before meals and saw that these purity laws applied only to those who were entering Temple.[6] Likewise, the sectarian Qumran community repudiated them, but with regard to washing before meals, they required total immersion before meals.[7] With the destruction of the Jewish Temple and the success of the Pharisaic synagogue movement, these Pharisaic traditions became codified in the Mishnah.

Within the preceding context in mind, Matt presents this text as a matter of fact to an informed Jewish reader, whereas, Mark adds explanation for a Gentile reader, possibly in Italy, who is not so well-informed.[8] This is an important distinction because it shows that Mark is presenting Jesus for a Gentile audience and thus shows the applicability of Jesus' teachings for that audience. This is especially apparent by comparing the additions that Mark includes over Matthew's parallel account. Furthermore, the Gentile agenda of Mark is also enabled by the immediately following account of the healing faith of the Canaanite woman, specifically designated by Mark as a Gentile (Mark 7:26). On this issue of the Pharisaic washing tradition, Luke does not have a parallel but he raises the issue in another setting.

The Pharisees and scribes raised the issue with Jesus, "why do your disciples eat with unwashed hands?"[9] Mark points out an explanation (from this Jewish traditional perspective) that meant the disciples were rendering themselves impure by eating with impure hands (Mark 7:2). That is, the washing concerning ceremonial defilement and ritual impurity (Exod 30:17–21; Lev 15:11). Mark also points out a parenthetic comment about the Jewish tradition.

> For the Pharisees and all the Jews do not eat unless they carefully wash their hands, observing the traditions of the elders; and when they come from the market, they do not eat unless they cleanse themselves; and there are many other things which

---

6. Josephus, *Ant.* 13.297; 17.41.

7. 1QH 4.14–15 identifies their rejection of the traditions. Immersion before meals is supported by: Josephus, *J. W.* 2.129, 138; 1QS 3.8–9; 5:13; CD 10.10–13; Newton, *The Concept of Purity*, 26–40.

8. Irenaeus, *Haer.* 3.1.1–2; Eusebius, *Marc. Prologue*; *Hist. eccl.* 2.15.1–2; 6.14.5–7.

9. Luke records a parallel account in which the Pharisees take issue with Jesus for not washing before He ate a meal (Luke 11:37–41). Jesus responded to this critic by calling him a fool for emphasizing external cleansing while they neglected internal robbery and wickedness. Jesus' solution was to call him to internal "charity, and then all things are clean for you" (Luke 11:41).

they have received in order to observe, such as the washing of cups and pitchers and copper pots *after their use* (Mark 7:3–4).

This Markan explanation helps his intended Gentile readership to enter into this Jewish traditional issue. I even add a little more explanation to help the contemporary reader understand that while the washing at issue was that of hands before eating, part of the tradition included the washing of pots after use. The tradition permits a pot to be externally unclean without defiling the inside of the pot, but if it is defiled on the inside then the whole pot is ritually unclean.[10] When the question is asked a second time in Mark, Jesus responds that Isaiah rightly prophesied that these Jewish hypocrites will be condemned to captivity and dispersion, which Israel continues to suffer, "This people honors Me with their lips, but their heart is far away from Me. But in vain do they worship Me, teaching as doctrines the precepts of men" (Isa 29:13 quoted in Mark 7:6–7; Matt 15:8–9).[11] In Mark, Jesus summarizes the Jews' problem twice as "neglecting the commandment of God, you hold to the tradition of men" (Mark 7:8–9).[12] After summary, Mark quotes from the Decalogue concerning honor due parents (Exod 20:12; Deut 5:16; Mark 7:10; Matt 15:4). In Matt when the question is asked, Jesus responds with this summary in question form and then addresses the Mosaic Law concern first, and then only after that addresses the Isaiah quote (Matt 15:3–10). So for Mark the issue is that the Jews prefer their tradition over the Mosaic Law, in contrast to the Matt development, which by order could be summarized that the Jews are violators of the Mosaic Law for tradition. Perhaps Matt is showing the Law's binding nature more than Mark presents it. Furthermore, Matt prefaces this quote of the honor due parents by "for God said" still giving some credence for its applicability to his Jewish-Christian readership, while Mark phrases the applicability to the Jewish leaders as "for Moses said," thus potentially distancing his Gentile readership from implications of the Mosaic Law. However, both agree that the main issue being worked here is an unrighteous illustration of how Jewish leadership permit Jews to not honor their parents by rendering their material goods inaccessible for meeting family needs (Matt 15:6; Mark

---

10. *m. Kelim* 25.6; however, utensils used as holy things in the temple have no division between inside or outside, for if one is unclean then the whole vessel is unclean (*Tosefta Kelim Baba Batra* 3.12; *Sifra* 114.1.6; Matt 23:25–26).

11. This is similar to the description of the Jews in the *As. Mos.* 7.9–10, "their hands and hearts are all corrupt, and their mouths are full of boasting."

12. Also an accusation echoed by: *T. Levi* 16.2.

7:9, 12–13). Mark names the process as "*corban*" and then explains for his Gentile readers that this means "given to God" (Mark 7:11).[13]

Jesus then taught the multitude that what defiles a person, is not something that goes into him but rather that which comes out of the person's heart (Matt 15:11–20; Mark 7:15-23).[14] That is, things from outside do not defile a person because it passes through them and then out as waste.[15] Whereas, what proceeds out from a person's heart is what defiles: "evil thoughts and fornication, thefts, murders, adulteries, deeds of coveting, wickedness, deceit, sensuality, envy, slander, pride, foolishness. All these evil things proceed from within and defile the man" (Mark 7:21–23). Matt reduces the vice list to those that concentrate on the Noahic commandments (Matt 15:19).[16] Both of these lists reflect Jesus' New Covenant internalizing obedience and an internalized uncleanness.

Mark adds a comment which Matt does not include, that Jesus "declared all foods clean" (Mark 7:19). This comment is at least identifying that kosher law is not applicable to Mark's Gentile readership, though this may go further and identify that the whole Law concerning clean and unclean may not be applicable to Mark's Gentile readership. It is important to remember that the food Law was binding upon only the Jews of the covenant and the Gentiles within the land (Lev 11; Deut 14:3–20; Dan 1:5, 8–16).[17] Those[18] who are inclined to disband the Mosaic Law altogether on the basis of this comment must remember, that in the previous chapter, "Matthew's Jesus on the Law," Mark recorded that Jesus said to the Jewish ruler that everlasting life and Kingdom is obtained by complying with the Mosaic Law with a generosity that both meets the needs of the poor, and follows Christ (Mark 10:17–24).

---

13. Throughout the LXX, is rendered by קָרְבָּנוּ, δῶρον or "given." cf. Josephus, *Ant*. 4.4.4; *Ag. Ap.* 1.167; and in *m. Ned*. 1.2; 3.11; 4.7–8; 5.6; 9.1 it means sacrifice and vow. The particular issue of depriving relatives by a vow is acknowledged and countered in *Instr*. 2.3.15–18; *m. Ned*. 5.6 and Philo, *Spec*. 2.16–17.

14. CD 16.6–20; *Gos. Thom*. 14. A similar point is made of defilement from within by Jesus' judgments in Matt. 23:25–28 and Luke 11:39–44. Additionally, Mark 7:16 is not the earliest and best manuscripts, so I do not consider it Scripture.

15. This elimination picks up the idea of the latrine drain that carries away the portion of food that does not provide nourishment.

16. Davies and Allison, *Matthew*, 2:536.

17. Esth 14.17; Tob 1.10–12; Jdt 10.5; 11.12; 12. 1–2; 1 Macc 1.62–63; 2 Macc 6.5–7, 18–28; 7:1–2, 42).

18. Some Lutherans and dispensationalists.

Mark also records Jesus as teaching Jewish disciples to be saved through a Law prompted love for others combined with following Christ (Matt 19:16–26; Mark 10:17–30; Luke 18:18–30).[19] Jesus is asked by the rich ruler, "What good thing shall I do that I may obtain everlasting life?" Here obtaining everlasting life is analogous to entering the Kingdom and being saved (Matt 19:16, 23-25; Mark 10:17; Luke 18:18, 24-25).[20] Jesus' answer for this Jewish ruler is to keep the commandments of the Law. Jesus does not say to try to do the Law until you find out you can't and then throw yourself on the mercy of God; Jesus says keep the Law. This should not surprise us because that is what Jews repeatedly expected and Christian Jews for several centuries tried to live.[21] Since God alone is good, Jesus' answer points to God's commands. Even Mark and Luke (who do not emphasize the keeping of the Law as does Matt) declare on Jesus' lips that keeping the Law is the way to everlasting life (Mark 10:17-19; Luke 10:25, 28; 18:18-20) or as N. T. Wright describes it, the Kingdom is obtained by following "Jesus in finding a new and radicalized version of Torah-observance."[22] Jesus further clarifies that the commandments He has in mind are those like the fifth, sixth, seventh, eighth, and ninth of the Ten Commandments, all of which have financial overtones.[23]

---

19. Also corroborated by *The Gospel of the Nazareans* 1, as recounted by Origen, *Matt.* 15.14.

20. Second Temple sources support this point as well (1QS 4.6-8; CD 3.20; 4Q181 1.3-4; *1 En.* 37.4; 40.9; 58.3; 4 Macc 15.3; *Pss. Sol.* 3.12).

21. Jer 31:31-34 and Ezek 36:24-37:28; Jdt 5:17-21; 8:18-23; 10:5; 12:2, 9-19; 13:8 *Pr. Azar.* 6-14; *Jub.* 1:22-25; 2:17-33; 15:11-34; 1Q3 4, 5; 1QH 4, 5, 18; 4Q Shir Shalb; Tob 1.10-12; 4:12-13; 1 Macc 1:48; 2:15-28; 2 Macc 6:18-31; 7; 3 Macc 3.4-7; 4 Macc 5:1-6:30; *T. Jud.* 26; *Joseph and Aseneth*; Josephus, *J. W.* 1.145-147, 157-60, 651-655; 2.169-74; *Ant.* 13.252; 14.237; 17.149-67; 18.55-59, 261-64, 267, and 271; Wright, *Jesus and the Victory of God*, 301; Sanders, *Paul and Palestinian Judaism*; *Paul, the Law, and the Jewish People*; *Jewish Law from Jesus to the Mishnah*; and *Judaism*; and Dunn, *Jesus, Paul and the Law*; *Jews and Christians*; and *Paul and the Mosaic Law*, especially interesting is Wright's chapter "The Law in Romans 2," 131-150. Furthermore, Biblical texts like Jas, Matt and Acts indicate that Jews and Jewish Christians were zealous for the Law. However, especially at focus is Matt 5:17-48 and 19:16-22; cf. Saldarini *Matthew's Christian-Jewish Community* and Kennard, "The Way to Kingdom Salvation;" "The Law in James;" "Paul and the Law;" Klijn, "The Study of Jewish Christianity," 419-31; Taylor, "The Phenomenon," 313-34 and Velasco and Sabourin, "Jewish Christianity," 5-26; Klijn and Reinink, *Patristic Evidence*; Strecker, "Appendix 1: On the Problem of Jewish Christianity," 257; Strecker, "The Kerygmata Petrou," 2:102-27, esp. 210-22 and 270-71; Strecker, *Das Judenchristentum*; van Voorst, *The Ascents of James*.

22. Wright, *Jesus and the Victory of God*, 307.

23. These commandments are from the broadly Protestant numbering of the

Jesus recognizes that the Law has as its primary focus the loyalty relationship to the Lord (Mark 12:29–30), however, Jesus focuses on the human side of the Law here emphasizing the love relationship to others which shows whether one truly loves the Lord (Mark 10:19; 12:31). In contrast to the Matt and Luke parallels, Mark does not include Jesus also adding Lev 19:18. Jesus has in mind here particularly those commandments that others can see and benefit from or at least not suffer under their violation. The young man affirmed that under a legally tight reading of the Law, he had kept all these commands. However, in the Mark and Luke account, Jesus declared that the rich young ruler still lacks (Mark 10:21; Luke 18:22). Jesus offers him completion and obtaining his goal of the Kingdom by means of a radical expression of love for one's neighbor, sharing the proceeds of the sale of your possessions with those in need. Jesus does not develop the attitude of being willing to give to the poor; His emphasis is on doing: keeping the commandments, selling and giving (Mark 10:21). This is a New Covenant form of covenant nomism that obtains everlasting life because it acknowledges if a person follows Jesus in loving his neighbor as he loves himself, then he shows forth a transformed Kingdom character. Giving up possessions would enable the young man to follow Jesus in His itinerant ministry as Peter and the disciples had done (Mark 10:28–30). Perhaps Mark includes Jesus' statements of giving to the poor for purposes of this itinerant ministry, to address issues in his readers' lives such as poverty due to famine, or the itinerant dispersion of the Jewish Christians outside their homeland due to persecutions. If the young man had complied, he would have had Kingdom treasure such as the disciples were to receive (Mark 10:28–30). Unfortunately, the young man was unwilling to pay the price of Jesus' radical Law demands. His departure provided an opportunity to instruct the disciples in the near impossibility of a rich person's pursuing of the Kingdom. The primary focus of the Law is evident as serving God, rather than money (Mark 10:23–27; 12:17). The fact that the young man went away with his riches shows that ultimately he was unwilling to serve God. In this case the Kingdom is missed for failure to keep the Law and align with Jesus.

In Jesus' demonstration of His scribal ability in Mark, the lawyer's response is added over the other synoptic gospels (Mark 12:32–34).

Decalogue. The synoptic gospels list the fifth command last after the others, however, Luke 18:20 reverses the first two (giving the order as: seventh, sixth, eighth, ninth and fifth, and Mark 10:19 inserts "do not defraud after the ninth and before the fifth command. Neither Mark 10:19 nor Luke 18:20 has Lev 19:18 as does Matt.

After Jesus has identified that complete love of God is the first command and the second is like it, that of loving one's neighbor as himself (Mark 12:29–31; Deut 6:4–5; Lev 19:18), the lawyer responds with an affirmation much like an earlier account in Luke 10:28. The lawyer's complete repetition of these commands underscores their binding nature as covering for the rest of the Law. However, the lawyer then identifies the priority that this expression of the Law of love is "much more than all burnt offerings and sacrifices" (Mark 12:33). So this comment diminishes the ritual aspects of the Law, like Mark's earlier comment about "all things clean" (Mark 7:19).

So, while Mark sees a freedom from ritual aspects of the Law for his Gentile readership, he also appreciates that the historical Jesus was more committed to the Law for His Jewish audience. Mark's emphasis on loving God and humans retains this central concern of the Law as applicable for his Gentile audience. The story continues in the next chapter titled, "Luke and John: Spirit Extended Salvation to the Gentiles Without the Law."

8

Luke and John: Spirit Extended Salvation to the Gentiles Without the Law[1]

THE MESSIAH WHO BRINGS eschatological salvation was expected to be endowed with the Spirit (Isa 11:1–2; 42:1; 61:1–2).[2] Likewise the Kingdom was to be initiated by the Spirit being poured out upon all humanity (Joel 2:28–32 [in MT 3:1–5]; Zech 6:1–8), which of course includes Israel (Isa 44:3; Ezek 36:27; 37:14; 39:29)[3] and the disciples (Luke 3:16; Acts 1:5; John 14:26; 15:26; 16:13). The Holy Spirit purifies people so that they will be set apart for God (Ezek 36:25–27; John 3:5–6; 1 John 4:2).[4]

The conversion of the Gentiles is not usually developed in the Biblical expectations for Kingdom, but rather as a *leit motif*. For example, Zech 14:16 anticipates "the remnant of all nations."[5] Second Temple Judaism expected that Gentiles would be converted, destroyed or subjugated (Isa 60:10–14; Dan 2:44–45; 7:14).[6] Craig Keener identifies that "Genuine proselyetes did embrace the covenant (*Sipra VDDen.* par. 2.3.3.1; *Qed. pg.*

---

1. This chapter is revised from Kennard, *Messiah Jesus*, 157–176 used by permission from Peter Lang publishers.

2. *Pss. of Sol.* 17.37; 18.7; *Test. Levi* 18; Eth. *1 En.* 49.3; 62.2.

3. *Jub.* 6.17; *Charter of a Jewish Sectarian Association* (1QS; 4Q255–264a; 5Q11) 3.15–4.1; 4.5, 18–23; 1QpHab col. 11.13; *The War Scroll* (1QM, 4Q491–496) 1.1–20; 16.11; 1QH 4, 5, 18; 1QS 3.7; 4Q548 frag. 1 col. 2 9–16; 11Q13 22–25; VanderKam, "Covenant," 1:151–55; Blanton, "Spirit and Covenant," 137.

4. *Jub.* 1.20–23; 1QHa 8.20; 1QS 3.4, 8–9; 4.21; 4Q255 2 1; 4Q257 3.10; Keener, *John*, 1:546–55; *Acts*, 1:533–34.

5. Joining this text are: Isa 19:23–25; 56:2–8; 66:15–21; Amos 9:12; Zech 2:11 (LXX: 2:15); Ps 47:9; *1 En.* 90.19–33; *Sib. Or.* 3.357–731; 1QM 12.7–14; *Pss. Sol.* 17.21–31.

6. Sir 36.1–9; *Jub.* 24.29; *1 En.* 90.19; *Ps. Sol.* 17.24, 31; *T. Mos.* 10.7; 1QM; CD 14.6; *Sib. Or.* 3; Philo, *Rewards* 93–97, 164.

8.205.1.5) and did share Israel's eschatological hopes (2 *Bar.* 41:4; 42:5–7; *Lev. Rab.* 2:9; 3:2; *Pesiq. Rab.* 35:3)."[7] Among these, the righteous Gentiles were to rise and join Abraham, Isaac and Jacob at the eschatological banquet.[8] Isaiah and Jesus predicted that the Temple would include a benefit for Gentiles in prayer (Isa 56:7; quoted in Mark 11:17).[9] This pattern of Gentiles joining into the Jewish benefit is realized momentarily in John's gospel where certain Greeks worshipping at the Temple during Passover ask Phillip if they can see Jesus (John 12:20–23). This request of Gentile inclusion identifies for Jesus that His hour of death and ascension is at hand; "The hour has come for the Son of Man to be glorified" (John 12:23). This sets up Jesus for a reflective moment in which He knows that He is now to be glorified, but that this glorification in John's gospel includes His death (John 12:20–27) in contrast to the synoptic pattern emphasizing glory with ascension and second coming (Matt 19:28; 24:30–31; Mark 13:26; Luke 21:27; Acts 3:15). In John's gospel, Jesus prays, "Father glorify Thy name" (John 12:28). A voice from heaven (the *bath qol*)[10] responded, "I have glorified it and will glorify it again," though some observed this voice to be merely thunder (John 12:28–30). Jesus pointed out that the divine voice was for the sake of those around Him, thus marking off that it is the time for judgment, because the ruler of this world is cast out and that Jesus would be lifted up in glory to draw all men to Himself (John 12:31–34).

Isaiah predicted that the Messianic King would emerge from and be a great light within the Gentile-dominated Galilee region (Isa 9:1). Furthermore, the Isaianic Servant Songs identify that the outgrowth of the Servant's proclamation is that God will make His Servant "a light to the nations so that salvation may reach to the end of the earth" (Isa 42:6;

---

7. Keener, *Acts*, 3:2258.

8. 4 Macc 7.19; 13.17; 16.25; *T. Benj.* 10.6, 11; *T. Jud.* 25.3–5; *T. Ash.* 7.2–3.

9. Jesus quotes of the Temple being a house of prayer in Matt 21:13 and Luke 19:46 leave out mentioning the Gentile purpose of the Temple.

10. On the concept and instance of *bath qol*: Dan 4:31; Jos. *Ant.* 13.282–83; *Song Rab.* 8.9.3; *b. 'Abot* 6.2; *B. Bat.* 73b; 85b; *Mak.* 23b; *'Erub.* 54b; *Šabb.* 33b; 88a; *Soṭa* 33a; *p. Soṭa* 7.5.5; *Pesiq. Rab. Kah.* 11.16; 15.5; *Lev. Rab.* 19.5–6; *Deut. Rab.* 11.10; *Lam. Rab. Proem* 2, 23; *Lam. Rab.* 1.16.50; *Ruth Rab.* 6.4; *Qoh. Rab.* 7.12.1; *Sib. Or.* 1.127, 267, 275; Artapanus in Eusebius *P.E.* 9.27.36; Dion. *Hal.* 1.56.3; 5.16.2–3; 8.56.2–3; Arrian *Alex.* 3.3.5; Lucian *C.W.* 1.569–70; Plutarch *Is. Os.* 12; *Mor.* 355E; *Mart. Pol.* 9. The *bath qol* was present in Israel before the spirit of prophecy departed (*b. Pesaḥ.* 94a; *Ḥag.* 13a; *Sanh.* 39b) and a few sources give it future ramifications as well (*Lev. Rab.* 27.2; *Pesiq. Rab. Kah.* 17.5).

49:6 cited in Acts 13:47). This means that as Jesus calls His disciples to be His witnesses to the "end of the earth," He is calling them to a ministry that includes Gentiles (Acts 1:8).[11]

Gentile Recipients of Luke and John

Traditionally, Luke and John are written primarily to Gentiles. Author Luke, of Antiochian parentage,[12] wrote both the Gospel of Luke and the Acts to Theophilus, a Greek by name (Luke 1:3; Acts 1:1). The explanation of cultural practice and affirmation of Gentiles in both books renders it likely that Theophilus is likewise a Gentile who as a patron wanted to have an accurate account of the message of the Kingdom from Jesus through Paul. Irenaeus reports that Luke wrote of the gospel preached by Paul, likely implying that Theophilus might have had previous contact or heard of the reputation of Paul on his missionary travels.[13] Irenaeus also wrote concerning John's Gospel as sent to the Christians in Asia, especially around Ephesus.[14] Both of these gospels primarily have a Gentile readership in view and translate the Kingdom message to them.

The Spirit in the Synoptics and Acts

The concept of spirit (πνεῦμά) in the gospels especially emphasizes the conflict Christ has with demons. For example, Mark includes 56 percent of the instances of πνεῦμά as demons (Mark 1:23–27; 3:11, 30; 5:2, 8, 13; 6:7; 7:25; 9:17–25). Luke has the dominant share of πνεῦμά references, retaining 28 percent as demons. The conflict between the Holy Spirit and demons expands these figures a bit more, raising instances within Matt up to 50 percent of his use (Matt 10:1, 20; 12:18, 28–32, 43–45; Mark 3:11, 29–30; Luke 11:13, 24–26; 12:10; Acts 5:3, 9; 7:51; 10:38). This part of this theme supports Christ healing ministry exorcising demons to bring in the Kingdom.

The synoptic gospels as a whole utilize the rest of the Holy Spirit references as identified with three particular limited enablements for ministry, specifically: revelation, baptizing and leading. The Holy Spirit

11. Keener, *Acts*, 1:703–6.
12. Eusebius, *Hist. eccl.* 3.4.7.
13. Irenaeus, *Haer.* 3.14.1.
14. Irenaeus, *Haer.* 3.1.1–2.

sources revelation of the biblical text (Matt 22:43; Mark 12:36; 13:11; Acts 1:16; 10:19; 15:28; 28:25). This divinely fostered foundation provides biblical guidance to which Jesus and believer appeal.

The Holy Spirit coming upon Jesus in His baptism anointed Him for ministry (Matt 3:11, 16; Mark 1:8, 10; Luke 3:16–22; John 1:32–33). John the Baptist hinted that this ministry would not be limited to Jews only, since John admitted that God could raise up children for Abraham even from stones (Matt 3:8–10; Luke 3:7–9). This baptism identified Jesus as the One who would baptize others with fire and the Spirit (Matt 3:11; Mark 1:8; Luke 3:16).

In the same way that Jesus' baptism is a reception of the Spirit, so it is for the believer as well. This baptism by Jesus identifies His own within the benefits of the Spirit (Matt 3:11; Mark 1:8; Luke 3:9). However, this same baptism diminishes unbelievers in the judgment of destroying fire (Matt 3:10–12 πυρί is used in the context for judgment; Mark 1:8; Luke 3:9 πῦρ is used in the context for judgment, 16–17; Acts 1:5; 11:16). The Holy Spirit led Jesus out into the wilderness to be tempted by the devil (Matt 4:1; Mark 1:12; Luke 4:1). Especially in Matthew's version, Satan's offer of the kingdoms of the world serves as a climax to the temptations (Matt 4:8–9). Jesus resists this temptation as a counterfeit way that excluded God and thus did not lead to Kingdom. The leading of Jesus by the Spirit is not developed in the synoptics as extended to believers, rather Jesus instructs His disciples to pray *to the Father* to "not lead us into temptation" (Matt 6:13; Luke 11:4).

Luke-Acts has a unique emphasis on developing the Holy Spirit as empowerment for ministry. Of the instances of πνεῦμά in the gospel of Luke, thirty one percent identify enabling of ministry and in Acts these instances expand to fifty one percent. A major block of this enablement is in the Spirit fostered proclamation (Luke 1:15, 17, 35, 41, 67; 2:25–27; 12:12; John 3:34; Acts 1:8; 2:4, 17–18, 33, 38; 4:8, 31; 7:55; 8:29, 39; 9:17, 31; 10:19; 11:12, 28; 13:9; 20:23; 21:4, 11) which is especially empowering believers (instead of Christ), so that it concentrates in the gospel of Luke toward the beginning where the anticipated baby Jesus has no speaking part. When Jesus instructs the disciples on how to respond to Jewish persecution, the Holy Spirit becomes the critical enabler, "When they bring you before the synagogues and the rulers and the authorities, do not become anxious about how or what you should speak in your defense, or what you should say; for the Holy Spirit will teach you in that very hour what you ought to say" (Luke 12:11–12).

Much of the ministry of the Spirit's enablement to proclaim Christ throughout Acts can be seen as realizing this very help promised by Christ. The mention of "rulers" in this text hints that there will be trials before Gentile rulers as Jesus' Olivet discourse indicates, with Jesus' promise to provide what His disciples were to say (Luke 21:12–14). The rest of these Acts enablements are to proclaim the gospel of the Kingdom as Jesus' witnesses, "you shall receive power when the Holy Spirit has come upon you; and you shall be My witnesses both in Jerusalem, and in all Judea and Samaria, and even to the remotest part of the earth" (Acts 1:8).[15] Each of the promises to enable proclamation indicates that the message will be heard by an audience that includes Gentiles.

The gift of the Holy Spirit is also a foretaste of realized eschatology of the last days when Jesus will return to establish Kingdom (Acts 2:4, 16–21).[16]

In Acts the Holy Spirit also fosters character development which serves to equip some for particular ministries (Acts 6:3, 5, 10; 11:24; 13:52). The conjoining of a virtue with the Spirit to describe the fullness of a person's character indicates that this virtue (whether it is wisdom or faith or whatever) is fostered by the Holy Spirit. The Spirit's fostering of these virtues begins in a Jewish setting but extends with the believers as they travel into Gentile areas. Acts develops that the reception of the Holy Spirit conveys authentic Kingdom salvation onto Gentiles as well.

Synoptic Gospels: Israel Emphasis With Occasional Gentile Events

Jesus primarily restricted His ministry (Matt 15:24; Mark 7:27) and the ministry of His twelve disciples to Israel (Matt 10:6), though He occasionally ministered beyond the bounds of Israel, near Tyre, and in the Decapolis region. He even had a great multitude follow Him from beyond the Jordan, in the Decapolis region (Matt 4:25). Additionally, when Jesus was heading away from Jerusalem He had significant impact on the conversion of Sychar in Samaria (John 4:1–42). The Samaritans acclaimed Jesus as "the Christ, the Savior of the world" (John 4:42). Speaking to

---

15. Bestowal of Spirit also indicates succession of ministry, so the disciples with the Spirit continue where Jesus has left off (2 Kgs 2:9; Acts 1:8; *Mek. Pisha* 1.150–53; *'Abot R. Nat.* 1 A; 1.2B; *Pesiq Rab.* 51.2; Sir 46.1; 48.12; *T. Mos.* 1.7; 10.15; sometimes with diminution of authority [*Pesiq. Rab. Kah.* 24.18]).

16. Von Schlatter, *Die Geschichte*, 16; Lohse, "Die Bedeutung," 436.

Jewish lawyers, Jesus even used a Samaritan to be the hero of a parable (Luke 10:30–37). However, when Jesus was heading toward Jerusalem, Samaria spurned Him (Luke 9:52).

Matthew, Luke and John begin their gospels with a reminder that salvation is for the world. Salvation is a deliverance metaphor indicating rescue from enemies, sin and calamities.[17] John indicates that the Word coming into the world is the One Who enlightens every man (John 1:9). In Luke, when Jesus' purification is taking place, devout Simeon comes to baby Jesus, and expresses Jewish aspirations for Him (Luke 2:25–38). The Holy Spirit was upon Simeon as he looked for the consolation of Israel that is the Kingdom.[18] The Holy Spirit had revealed to him that he would not die until he had seen the Lord's Christ. Simeon took Jesus into his arms and blessed the sovereign God for letting him see the salvation personified by Jesus Who will bring Kingdom glory to Israel and extend such light of revelation even to Gentiles (Luke 2:29–32). Matthew presents the beginning of this salvation light to Gentile wise men[19] arriving from the East having followed a sign star that came to rest over the place where Jesus was born (Matt 2:11). These Gentile wise men offer gifts appropriate in adoring Jesus as the King of the Jews. Additionally, "salvation" includes healing in the synoptic gospels.[20] Ultimately, "salvation" is referencing eschatological Kingdom (Luke 1:69–71).[21]

---

17. LXX: Exod 14:13; 15:2; Judg 15:18; 1 Sam 2:1; 14:45; 2 Sam 19:3[2]; 2 Kgs 13:17; 1 Chron 11:14; 16:35; Pss 6:4–5{5–6}; 32 [33]:17; 68:14[69:13]; 70[71]:15; Isa 25:8–9; 45:17, 21 Tob 8.4–5; 1 Macc 4.25; 2 Macc 14.3; 4 Macc 15.8.

18. The Abrahamic Covenant promised an abundant land as Israel's possession (Gen 15:13–21) which was embraced within the Mosaic Covenant promise for peace and blessing of renewal in the land (Deut 28:1–14; 30:1–30). The Davidic Covenant added the element of Kingship into this hope with the Messianic King. The prophets develop this Kingdom era with the wonderful transforming benefits that will accrue especially to Israel (Jer 31:27–33:26). For example, in a context of Gentile domination, Isa 9 speaks of the birth of a king that will enlighten a new Kingdom era for Israel, bringing peace to the world. Second Temple Judaism hungers and longs for this hope.

19. The wise men are largely undescribed in Matt, though the *Gos. Naz.* Frag. 28 describes their dress in great detail evidencing wealth and dark complexion. Many consider that they are of the best wisdom from Gentiles (Ps 72:10–11; Balaam, Num 22–24; cf. the Persian king arrived in Rome to honor Nero as prompted by Mithras and astrology: Dio Cassius, *Hist.* 63.1–7; Pliny the Elder, *Nat.* 30.16–17; Suetonius, *Nero* 13), or parallel to Egyptian sorceress in the Mosaic account, but there are some of this category elsewhere who are Jews (Acts 8:9–24, Simon; 13:6–11, Elymas; Josephus, *Ant.* 20.142, Atomus).

20. Kennard, *Messiah Jesus*, 25–67.

21. LXX: Ps 98:7–9; Isa 43:1–3; 60:16; 63:9; Jdt 8.17; Wis 16.6; 18.7; Sir 16.1; 1

Jesus begins His ministry of teaching in the synagogues by identifying that the Spirit has empowered Him to proclaim and effect Jubilee freedom as evident in healing (Luke 4:14–30). Jesus is aware that He is God's anointed Savior at the center of eschatological events to bring an expression of God's Kingdom to earth. To present this point, Jesus quotes Isa 61:1–2 and inserts Isa 58:6d from the LXX as a way of continuing His Kingdom theme in the quote.[22]

> The Spirit of the Lord is upon Me,
> Because He anointed Me to preach the gospel to the poor.
> He has sent Me to proclaim release to the captives,
> And recovery of sight to the blind,
> To set free those who are downtrodden,
> To proclaim the favorable year of the Lord. (Luke 4:18–19)

According to the verses, Jesus' ministry is to bring major benefits from a Jubilee Kingdom into the present, namely to: 1) Proclaim good news to the poor, and 2) Proclaim release of captives. This description of Jubilee is not limited to the Jews. In fact, announcing this ministry in Nazareth provides Him with the opportunity to identify that a prophet is not welcome in his home town (Luke 4:24). Jesus then illustrated this Jewish rejection by mentioning how Gentiles have been more responsive to prophets in the past, namely the Sidon widow Zarephath cared for Elijah, and Naaman the Syrian who came for healing when many Jewish lepers did not. Jesus' reputation for healing spread throughout Gentile regions of Decapolis and Syria (Matt 4:24–25). It is in this vein that elsewhere in the synoptics Gentiles mostly appear as recipients of Jesus' miracles.

Jesus resists healing Gentiles, though they show the greatest faith of any throughout the gospels. For example, the Syro-Phonecian woman finds resistance from Jesus (Matt 15:21–28; Mark 7:24–30). This Gentile woman persistently called after Jesus saying, "Have mercy on me, O Lord, Son of David; my daughter is cruelly demonized" (δαιμονίζεται).

Macc 15.62.

22. The substitution of Isa 58:6d for a line in Isa 61:2 may not be apparent in the English text but it is readily recognizable by comparing the LXX with the Greek text of Luke 4:18, which follows the LXX of Isa 61:1–2 until this line. Luke could have paraphrased the Hebrew text on this line but it is likely that he followed the LXX on this line like he did in the rest of the quote. Furthermore, the parts of the pericope of Isa 61:1–3 which Jesus does not quote includes divine vengeance upon Israel's enemies, and an enabled replanting of Israel in the land of Zion. Such a strong Jewish emphasis of Jesus' Kingdom task works against Luke's purposes of Gentile inclusion into salvation in Luke-Acts.

Jesus did not answer her and the disciples wished to send her away. Jesus replied[23] that He was sent only to the lost sheep of the house of Israel (Matt 15:24). The woman fell at His feet and kept asking Him to send the unclean spirit away from her daughter. Jesus responded, "Let the children be satisfied first, for it is not good to take the children's bread and throw it to the small pet dogs" (κυναρίοις).[24] She accepted her secondary status and replied, "Yes, Lord, but even the small house dogs (κυνάρια) feed on the children's crumbs which fall from the master's table." Jesus answered her, "Your faith is great; be it done for you as you wish." Her daughter was healed at once and the demon departed. Returning home she found her daughter healed on her bed. Such long distance miracles were especially counted as miraculous.[25]

In similar vein, it is possible that Matthew's presentation of the healing of the Centurion's servant (Matt 8:5–13; Luke 7:1–10), is also met with similar resistance in Jesus' statement, "Should I coming heal him?" (Matt 8:7). Luke shows no such resistance, perhaps because earlier than in Matthew, the Centurion indicates his unworthiness, and the Jews who make the appeal to Jesus on his behalf show him to be worthy to be granted this miracle (Luke 7:2–10), or because Luke has a more intentional extension of ministry to Gentiles than does Matt. Of course, all descriptions of the Centurion's faith are also among the highest praise Jesus gives to anyone in the gospels: (1) the Centurion's confidence that Jesus can heal his servant, (2) that it can be done with such effectiveness as that of merely delegating the task accomplishes it, and (3) that the healing could be accomplished at such a distance. Jesus responds that "I have not found such great faith with anyone in all of Israel" (Matt 8:10; Luke 7:9). Jesus concludes this healing with teaching on Gentile inclusion in Kingdom and Jewish exclusion in rebellion, "I tell you, that many shall come from east and west, and recline with Abraham, and Isaac, and Jacob, in the Kingdom of heaven; but the sons of the Kingdom shall be cast out into the outer darkness; in that place there shall be weeping and gnashing of teeth" (Matt 8:11–12). Jesus repeats the same statement to Jews in a

---

23. Jesus did not consider it beneath Him to talk with a woman, unlike the Jewish tradition (*m. 'Aboth* 1.5).

24. Both Jesus and the woman refer to κυνάρια, which is the diminutive pet dog of the root word for dog (*kuvwn*). Jesus opens the door with a more familiar image (pet dog).

25. Bultmann, *The History*, 225; *b. Ber.* 34b; Lucian, *Philops.* 16; Diogenes Laertius, *Vit.* 8.67.

synagogue as the Lukan close concerning parables of the Kingdom (Luke 13:28–30). These few Gentiles included dramatically show the Jewish rejection of Jesus to be unreasonable, and certain to be condemned.

In the same pattern Jesus shows in recognizing Gentile healing faith, He also appreciates the gratitude of Gentiles He heals, when compared to Jews who do not turn back and express their faith. For example, at the border between Samaria and Galilee ten leprous men are healed and the only one who turns back with gratitude is the Samaritan (Luke 17:11–19). The others merely headed off to show themselves to the priests as Jews should and Jesus commanded. Jesus was surprised that the others did not join the Samaritan in expressing gratitude, "were none found who turned back to give glory to God, except this foreigner?" (Luke 17:18). Jesus also acknowledged that it is his faith that has made him well (Luke 17:19).

Arriving at the East side of the Sea of Galilee in the Gadarenes[26] region, two demonized (δαιμονιζόμενοι) men came out of the tombs to confront Jesus as the Son of the Most High God, and He cast the demons out of them (Matt 8:28–34; Mark 5:1–20; Luke 8:26–39).[27] These extremely strong violent men did not challenge Jesus directly rather they asked if they were to be tormented before their time. At the same time, Jesus was commanding the demons to come out of them. The legion of demons begged not to be sent to the abyss[28] but to be sent into a herd of swine,[29] perhaps to defeat Jesus' ministry in the region. With Jesus' permission the swine were driven into the sea and drowned. The herdsmen told others and many came out to find the previously demonized men sitting, clothed, and in their right mind, healed or saved (ἐσώθη, Luke 8:36) and listening to Jesus. The city folk implored Jesus to leave their region, perhaps because it had already cost them dearly. Instead, the healed were sent to testify to their friends, so they announced their healing throughout the whole Decapolis region.[30]

---

26. Mark 5:1 "Gerasenes" is a larger and more powerful city about 30 miles from the lake than Matt 8:28 "Gadarenes," which is only six miles from the lake but smaller, so it is accurate to describe the miracle in both regions. This region is a mixed Gentile and Hellenistic Jewish region.

27. Multiple atestation supports the authenticity of this miracle.

28. Judaism saw the deep as the judgment depository of demons (*Jub.* 5.6–7; *1 En.* 10.4–6; 18.11–16; 2 Pet 2:4; Jude 6).

29. For Jews, pig keeping is prohibited (*m. Qam.* 7.7) and eating pork violates kosher (Lev 11:7; Deut 14:8).

30. The population of the region was mixed Jew and Gentiles (Josephus, *J. W.* 3.51–58).

The Gospel of John also primarily connects Jesus within a Jewish setting with a few brief mentions of Gentiles. John 3:16 identifies that God's love for the world was a motivation to send Jesus to save some from the world to everlasting life. After Jesus' triumphal entry into the Temple, certain Greeks worshipping in the Temple wished to see Jesus (John 12:20–22). Philip and Andrew brought them to Him.

Gospel of Luke's View of Law for Jews

Luke's view of the Law is indicated through four terms: "law" (νόμος), "commands" (ἐντολή, Luke 1:6), "custom" (ἔθος, Luke 2:27) and "Moses."[31] Luke uses the term "Law" (νόμος) nine times (one more than Matthew) but five of them explain the Jewish events that surround Jesus' purification as an infant (Luke 2:22–24, 27, 39). Two instances of the term "command" indicate similar compliance with the Mosaic Covenant as in preparing the Passover meal correctly (Luke 1:6; 23:56). Two instances of "law" (νόμος) are shared with Matthew's use showing Jesus audience to be more Jewish and Law-practicing than Luke's audience; John the Baptist's Kingdom message is a continuation of Law and that not even a part of a letter will fail from the Law until all is accomplished in Kingdom (Luke 16:16–17; Matt 5:18; 11:13). Luke records a unique post-resurrection teaching of Jesus to His disciples in which He informs them about how He must fulfill the Law of Moses, Prophets and the Psalms (Luke 24:44). Luke describes a unique event of a lawyer earlier in Jesus ministry asking Jesus to summarize the Law (much like second Temple rabbis had done[32] and Matt 22:34–40 developed occurred for Jesus later). Jesus summary is that there are priorities from the Law of first loving God then loving neighbor, which summarize the whole of the Law.

In Luke 10:25–28 a lawyer asks Jesus what does it take to inherit everlasting life. Jesus responds with a question asking the lawyer to summarize the essence of the Law (νόμος). The lawyer summarized the Law as loving God completely and loving neighbor as oneself (Luke 10:27; Deut 6:5; Lev 19:18). Jesus affirmed him in the accuracy of his answer and replied that if he lived the Law as an expression of loving God and

---

31. Wilson, *Luke and the Law*, 1–3.

32. B. *Šabb.* 31a; b. *Ber.* 63a; Josephus, *C. Ap.* 2.206; Rabbi Akiva considered love of neighbor in Lev 19:18 to be the great commandment (*Sifra Qed.* 4.200.3.7; *Gen. Rab.* 24.7).

others then he would have everlasting life (Luke 10:28; perhaps citing Lev 18:5). It is surprising that unlike other synoptic promises of everlasting life, this one does not place Jesus at the center of the content, so here Jesus is especially consistent with second Temple Judaism's covenant nomism to gain everlasting life.[33] Additionally, Luke presents that such a Law oriented pious life is able to be lived and in fact was lived by Zacharias, Elizabeth, and Simeon who "walked blamelessly in all the commandments and requirements of the Lord" (Luke 1:6; 2:25). Therefore, Jesus was not merely pressing the Law upon the lawyer to show him he could not live it, for Jesus in the parable of the good Samaritan commands the lawyer to go and do the same (Luke 10:29-37). So the emphasis in the context is on doing Law through loving others, not that we cannot do it.

Utilizing the term "commands" (ἐντολή, Luke 18:20), Jesus identifies that everlasting life is obtained by Jewish disciples' compliance with the Mosaic Law and aligning with Jesus (Luke 18:18-30). It is in this light that Jesus' comments to the rich young ruler support in a practical manner what had been taught in the Sermon on the Mount (Matt 5:17-48; 19:16-26; Mark 10:17-30; Luke 18:18-30).[34] Jesus is asked "What good thing shall I do that I may obtain everlasting life?" In this instance obtaining everlasting life is analogous to entering the Kingdom and being saved (Matt 19:16, 23-25; Mark 10:17; Luke 18:18, 24-25).[35] Jesus' answer for this Jewish ruler is to keep the commandments of the Law. Jesus does not say to try to do the Law until you find out you cannot and then throw yourself on the mercy of God; Jesus says *keep* the Law. This should not surprise us because this is what Jews repeatedly expected and Christian Jews for several centuries tried to live.[36] Since God alone is good, Jesus' answer

33. Jesus' teaching on keeping the Law to inherit everlasting life is consistent with second Temple Judaism (2 Macc 7.36; *T. Jos.* 18.1; *Jub.* 5.10; 10.17; 22.22; *2 Bar.* 48.22b;; 1QS 3.7-12; 4.6-8; CD 3.11-16, 20-21; 7.5, 9; 13.11; 20.17-20, 25-27; 4Q181 3-4; 4Q228 frag. 1 1.9; 4Q266, frag. 11; 4QMMT C; *1 En.* 37.4; 40.4; 58.3; 4 Macc 15.3; *Pss. Sol.* 3.11-12; *Sib. Or.* 2.149-53; 3.49 frag. 3).

34. Also corroborated by *Gos. Naz.* 1, as recounted by Origen, *Matt.* 15.14.

35. Second Temple sources support this point as well (1QS 4.6-8; CD 3.20; 4Q181 1.3-4; *1 En.* 37.4; 40.9; 58.3; 4 Macc 15.3; *Pss. Sol.* 3.12).

36. Jer 31:31-34 and Ezek 36:24-37:28; Jdt 5:17-21; 8:18-23; 10:5; 12:2, 9-19; 13:8 Pr. Azar. 6-14; *Jub.* 1:22-25; 2:17-33; 15:11-34; 1Q3 4, 5; 1QH 4, 5, 18; 4Q Shir Shalb; Tob 1.10-12; 4:12-13; 1 Macc 1:48; 2:15-28; 2 Macc 6:18-31; 7; 3 Macc 3.4-7; 4 Macc 5:1-6:30; *T. Jud.* 26; *Joseph and Aseneth*; Josephus, *J. W.* 1.145-147, 157-60, 651-655; 2.169-74; *Ant.* 13.252; 14.237; 17.149-67; 18.55-59, 261-64, 267, and 271; Wright, *Jesus and the Victory of God*, 301; Sanders, *Paul and Palestinian Judaism*; *Paul, the Law, and the Jewish People*; *Jewish Law from Jesus to the Mishnah*; and *Judaism*; and Dunn,

points to God's commands. Even Mark and Luke (who do not emphasize the keeping of the Law for their Gentile audience, as does Matthew for his Jewish-Christian readership) declare on Jesus' lips that keeping the Law is the way to everlasting life (Mark 10:17–19; Luke 10:25, 28; 18:18–20), as N. T. Wright describes it, the Kingdom is obtained by following "Jesus in finding a new and radicalized version of Torah-observance."[37] Jesus further clarifies that the commandments He has in mind are those like the fifth, sixth, seventh, eighth, and ninth Commandments, all of which have financial overtones.[38] Jesus recognizes that the Law's primary focus is on the loyalty relationship to the Lord (Luke 10:25–28). However, Jesus focuses on the human side of the Law here emphasizing the love relationship to others which shows whether one truly loves the Lord (Luke 10:27). Jesus particularly has in mind that those commandments that others can see and benefit from or at least not suffer under their violation. Beyond the Ten Commandments, loving ones neighbor sums up all the minutiae of relationships one to another in the Law (Luke 10:27–28). The young man affirmed that under a legally tight reading of the Law, he had kept all these commands. However, in the Lukan and Markan account, Jesus declares that the rich young ruler still lacks (Mark 10:21; Luke 18:22). Jesus offers him completion and obtaining of his goal of the Kingdom by means of a radical extrapolation of love for others by means of *sharing* the proceeds of the sale of his possessions *with those who are in need*. Jesus does not develop the attitude of being *willing* to give to the poor; His em-

---

Jesus, Paul and the Law; *Jews and Christians*; and *Paul and the Mosaic Law*, especially interesting is Wright's chapter "The Law in Romans 2," 131–150. Furthermore, Biblical texts like James, Matthew and Acts indicate that Jews and Jewish Christians were zealous for the Law. However, especially at focus is Matt 5:17–48 and 19:16–22; cf. Saldarini *Matthew's Christian-Jewish Community* and Kennard, "The Way to Kingdom Salvation;" "The Law in James;" "Paul and the Law;" Klijn, "The Study," 419–31; Taylor, "The Phenomenon," 313–34 and Velasco and Sabourin, "Jewish Christianity of the First Centuries," *BTB* 6 (1976): 5–26; Klijn and Reinink, *Patristic Evidence*; Strecker, "Appendix 1: On the Problem of Jewish Christianity," 257; Strecker, "The Kerygmata Petrou," 2:102–27, esp. 210–22 and 270–71; Strecker, *Das Judenchristentum*; Schoeps, *Theologie*; van Voorst, *The Ascents*.

37. Wright, *Jesus and the Victory of God*, 307.

38. These commandments are from the broadly Protestant numbering of the Decalogue. All the synoptic gospels list the fifth command last after the others, however, Luke 18:20 reverses the first two (giving the order as: seventh, sixth, eighth, ninth and fifth, and Mark inserts "do not defraud after the ninth and before the fifth command. Neither Mark nor Luke has Lev 19:18 as does Matt, so their statement is more Decalogue focused while Matt presents a fuller Law as binding for his Jewish Christian readership.

phasis is on *doing*: keeping the commandments, selling, and giving (Luke 18:20-22). Giving up these possessions would enable the young man to follow Jesus in His itinerant ministry as Peter and the disciples had done (Luke 18:22, 28). Perhaps Luke includes Jesus' statements of giving to the poor for purposes of the itinerant ministry, to address issues in his readers' lives such as: the poor from famine, or the itinerant dispersion of the Jewish Christians outside their homeland due to persecutions. If the young man had complied, he would have had Kingdom treasure as the disciples were to receive (Luke 18:22, 29-30). Unfortunately, the young man was unwilling to pay the price of Jesus' radical Law demands. His departure provided an opportunity to instruct the disciples in the near impossibility of a rich person pursuing the Kingdom. The primary focus of the Law is evident as serving God rather than money (Luke 16:13). The fact that the young man went away with his riches shows that ultimately he was unwilling to serve God. In this Jewish instance, the Kingdom is missed for failure to keep the Law and align with Jesus.

John's Promise of the Spirit

On His last night with His disciples, Jesus tells them He is about to go away and in so doing he will send the Holy Spirit to them to carry on His ministry (John 14:25-28; 15:26; 16:5-8, 12-17). The Messiah was anticipated to be a Comforter to restore the Kingdom of Israel (Isa 40:1; 51:3; 61:2; 66:13; Luke 2:25; John 1:49; Acts 3:19-21).[39] The Holy Spirit would be such a Helper (παράκλητος), after the pattern of Jesus' help to His disciples (John 14:26; 15:26; 16:7, 13-14; 1 John 2:1). Though extrabiblically the term παράκλητος often has a forensic sense as "a legal defender" in classical and rabbinic thought,[40] the majority of the Johannine contexts don't seem to fit that sense very well. In John 14-16 the Holy Spirit extends Jesus ministry. For the specific context of John 16:8-11, the Spirit is the accuser, or the reverse to the forensic sense of παράκλητος. Furthermore, when the term describes Jesus it is as in more of a priestly role accomplishing propitiation rather than a legal role (1 John 2:1). So,

---

39. *Num. Rab.* 13.5; *Lam. Rab.* 1.16.51.

40. A nice discussion and evidence for the view is provided by Keener, *John*, 2:956-57. The classical work by Betz draws the convicting and rebuking work closer to the Qumran teacher of righteousness, but the Spirit works behind the scene continuing Jesus ministry (*Der Paraklet*).

it is better to see the Johainnine παράκλητος in a broadly Messianic like role of Comforter to prepare for Kingdom.

Jesus has many more things to tell His disciples, but they could not bear any more that night and He was going away (John 16:12). Both the Father and Son send the Holy Spirit to the disciples so that in His role as Spirit of truth, the Holy Spirit will bear witness of Jesus (John 15:26).[41] Specifically, the Spirit will teach the disciples all the things which Jesus has been instructing the disciples, and thus He will especially call to their remembrance all that Jesus taught His disciples (John 14:26). Thus, in the same manner as Jesus had pointed out His audience's sin (John 3:17–18; 7:24; 8:15–26, 34, 46; 9:34–41), now the Spirit will continue, calling the world to His righteousness and from judgment (John 16:8–12). Likewise, the Spirit will judge some of the world in sin because they do not believe in Jesus. The Spirit will especially have to demonstrate righteousness, because Jesus who fleshed out righteousness, will no longer be available to physically demonstrate righteousness before them. The Spirit will convict some of the world of judgment because the foe (the ruler of the world) is vanquished and judged. This already realization of judgment unto Kingdom connects the disciples presently with the future grander realization of Kingdom. Furthermore, the Holy Spirit will continue to teach the disciples about the things that the Father and the Son have for them, especially prophecy of what is to come (John 16:13–15).[42] This ministry will therefore glorify Christ among the disciples. Thus, this continuation of the Spirit's presence where Jesus had been, should be profoundly reassuring to the disciples, providing them with peace, so that they might not be destroyed under the hatred of the world (John 14:27–29; 15:18–16:4). This Spirit witness, utilizing what the disciples have seen of Jesus' ministry will equip the disciples to bear witness for Jesus as well (John 15:27; Acts 1:8).[43]

---

41. Wisdom and Spirit are found together (Isa 11:2; Wis 1.6–7; 9.17). The phrase "spirit of truth" is broader than prophecy, including the source for revelation and moral instruction (John 14:13; 15:26; 16:13; 1 John 4:6; *Jub.* 25.14; 1QS 2.1; 3.18–19; 4.3; 4Q381 frag. 69; 4Q444 frag. 1 1.1; 4Q509 5.15–16).

42. John 14:26 and 16:12–14 do not teach that Christians are illuminated (Kennard, "Evangelical," 797–806).

43. Bestowal of Spirit also indicates succession of ministry, so the disciples with the Spirit continue where their master left off (2 Kgs 2:9; Acts 1:8; *Mek. Pisha* 1.150–53; *'Abot R. Nat.* 1 A; 1.2B; *Pesiq Rab.* 51.2; Sir 46.1; 48.12; *T. Mos.* 1.7; 10.15; sometimes with diminution of authority [*Pesiq. Rab. Kah.* 24.18]).

After Jesus resurrected and met with the disciples, He encouraged them with both a commission and an enablement (John 20:21–23). Jesus blessed His disciples with peace. He next commissioned them to go; "As the Father has sent Me, I also send you." Jesus then breathed on the disciples, explaining that action as being their reception of the Holy Spirit. Either this is a temporary filling of the Spirit or John's orientation is more continuously an extension of Jesus' ministry without a break of a few days as Acts portrays. Enabled by the Spirit and sent by Jesus, the disciples are commissioned into a scribal ministry of forgiving sins to include others into Kingdom and retaining sins to exclude others from Kingdom.

The Great Commission

Jesus conveys the great commission to His disciples, sending them out to make disciples (Matt 28:17–20). Jesus claimed all authority in heaven and earth, commissioning the disciples with the coming Spirit empowerment to be witnesses proclaiming the Kingdom message of repentance for forgiveness of sins to all nations beginning in Jerusalem and to make disciples of all people groups, baptizing and teaching them to observe all that Jesus commanded them (Matt 28:18–20; Luke 24:47–53; John 20:21–23; Acts 1:5–8). This discipleship has more than conversion activities and communicating activities in view. Discipleship reproduces people who apply Jesus' teaching throughout their lives. Discipleship is thus a repetitive process multiplying more disciples for Christ. After reassuring them that He would be with them until the end of the age Jesus lifted His hands to bless them and then bodily ascended into heaven (Acts 1:9–11). Bodily He left, but spiritually He remained to empower their disciple-making of His disciples. Additionally, the Holy Spirit is given to the disciples to enable their disciple-making and witness (John 20:22; Act 1:5, 8, 2:4–18, 33, 38; 11:15–16).

Bestowal of the Spirit, Gentile Salvation and the Parting of the Ways

With the arrival of the Jewish Pentecost Feast (First Fruits), came the arrival of Jews and proselytes from all over the empire streaming back into Jerusalem. While the Pentateuch presented this as a feast of gratitude to Yahweh for the harvest, it also became recognized in Judaism as the celebration of the initial giving and renewal of the Law.[44] The crowds milled around speaking to one another in Greek and Aramaic. Many were devout, expectant of the events of the feast.

In a room nearby the believers waited for the coming of the Holy Spirit, prophesied by Jesus Christ just prior to His ascension (Acts 1:8; 2:15–21). They prayed and waited. Suddenly a powerful, forceful roar of wind filled (ἐπλήρωσεν) the house. The Holy Spirit came upon the believers, filling (πλήρεις) them for prophetic service.[45] An external sign of flames rested upon each believer's head signifying the Spirit's coming. All the believers then went out into the crowd and began proclaiming the gospel in a variety of languages. Those gathered from all over the empire were amazed to hear their native language spoken.[46] The message that they bore witness to was especially what identified Jesus as Lord.

Peter's witness began by identifying that phenomenon was what Joel 2:28–32 prophesied as coming upon all mankind to initiate the Kingdom (Acts 2:15–21). Peter also identified that Jesus as King had received the Holy Spirit from the Father so that the Lord Jesus could then pour out the Spirit upon them as well (Acts 2:33).[47] At the end of the sermon, Peter

---

44. Israel starts out on the exodus the day after Passover (the 14th day) of the first month (Exod 12:6, 31) and arrives at Mt. Sinai at the start of the third month (Exod 19:1 ḥdš/שׁדֹחַ is taken to be new moon so 45 days, rather than as *Jub.* 1:1 takes it to be the sixteenth day of the third month). Israel was to be prepared on the third day (48th day after Passover, Exod 19:15–16). Moses goes up the mountain and then back down and then back up so it is probably at least the fiftieth day after Passover or around Pentecost when the Covenant Decalogue is given to Moses (Exod 19:20, 25; 20:1; Pentecost became the celebration of the giving and yearly renewal of Mosaic Covenant (*Jub.* 6.17; 14.1, 10, 20; 15.1–14; 16.13–14; 22.15, 30); rabbinics identify Weeks as "the Giving of Torah" and read Exod 19 for the liturgy (*b. Meg.* 31a; *b. Šabb.* 23a, note 30; 86b; 129a); George Bush, *Notes, Critical and Practical, on the Book of Exodus*, 231; Sailhamer, *The Pentateuch as Narrative*, 281; Davis, "Acts 2," 13–18). Around 150 A.D. Rabbi Jose ben Chalaphtha redacted the *Seder Olam Rabba* to indicate that the Ten Commandments were given on the 6th of Siwan on the very day of the Feast of Weeks or Pentecost (Noack, "The Day of Pentecost," 79; Bruce, *Acts*, p. 53, n. 3). From 2 Chr 15:10–12 there is evidence of a connection between the Feast of Weeks and covenant renewal (*Jub.* 6.1[fused with Noahic Covenant], 10–11, 15–22; 15.1; 22.1–5; 29.7–8; 44.1–4; 1QS 1.18–2.25; 4Q266 11 16–18=4Q270 7 ii 11–12; 4Q286–290; Philo, *Contempl.* 8.65; VanderKam, "The Festival," 192–93; Park, *Pentecost*).

45. Prophetic filling of the Spirit can produce tongues which is a form of prophecy (1 Sam 10:5–13; 19:18–24; Acts 2:4–10, 17 and addition to quote in verse 18).

46. Such abundance of tongues is reminiscent of the rabbinic claim that all nations heard the Law spoken in their 70 languages from Mt. Sinai before all but Israel rejected the Law (*Šabb.* 88b).

47. Peter's gospel message focuses on Christ (Kennard, *Messiah Jesus*, 439–70).

offered the Spirit and forgiveness to those who would repent and align themselves with King Jesus (Acts 2:38). Many did, showing themselves to be of one mind and sharing property with each other (Acts 2:43–47; 4:32–37). Among such folk the Spirit fostered traits of boldness, generosity, wisdom, faith, and power (Acts 4:31–37; 6:3, 5, 8, 10).

Christianity begins to be shoved out of mainstream Judaism by the religious leaders, who were filled (ἐπλήσθησαν) with jealousy continued to persecute Christians like they had persecuted Jesus (Acts 4:1–22; 5:17–32; 6:9–8:3; 9:1–2, 23–30; 12:1–5; 13:45–46, 50; 14:2–6, 19; 17:5; 18:6, 12–16; 21:28–32, 35–36; 22:4–5, 22–23; 23:2, 12–21; 24:1–9; 25:2–3, 7, 24; 26:9–11, 21). Unlike most who develop the parting of Christianity from Judaism, it begins earlier than is often acknowledged, but a form of Jewish Christianity remained within Judaism for centuries.[48] Some of the Christians were martyred (Acts 7:60; 12:2). During these hearings before the Sanhedrin, Peter (after the pattern which Jesus promised) was filled (πλησθείς) with the Spirit and clarified that miracles and salvation are only accomplished in Jesus (Matt 10:16–20; Luke 12:12; Acts 4:8–12; 5:31–32). Additionally, the Council was unable to cope with the effective Spirit fostered wisdom of Stephen so they killed him (Acts 6:10; 7:51, 55). This killing motivated the Christians to scatter, proclaiming the gospel of the Kingdom as they went. Phillip is a good example of this witness as he was directed by the Spirit to Samaria, the Ethiopian eunuch, and the coastal cities (Acts 8:4–29–40). Wherever the gospel was received, the apostles followed providing believers with the Holy Spirit to powerfully confirm them in their faith (Acts 8:14–17).

One of the difficult adjustments Peter and Jewish Christians had to face was that of fully accepting Gentiles as equals before God. Most Jews did not have a problem if a Gentile would proselyte to become a Jew, but many considered Gentiles to be unclean and thus unacceptable to associate or eat with them (Acts 10:28; 11:2–3). Peter was staying with Simon the tanner; apparently, he had no problem staying with one of an unclean occupation.[49] In other respects, Simon must have still operated within the Jewish traditions. These included that the skins of the animals were soaked, scraped and hung to dry above the house roof where wind would blow the smell and moisture away. These skins hung under linen

---

48. Dunn, *Jesus, Jews and Christians*, and *Paul and the Mosaic Law*; Lieu, "The Parting of the Ways," 101–19; *Image*; Becker and Reed, *The Ways that Never Parted*; Häkkinen, "Ebionites," 247–78; Luomanen, "Nazarenes," 279–315.

49. *M. Ketub.* 7.10; *b. Pesaḥ* 65a; *Qidd.* 82b; Jeremias, *Jerusalem*, 310.

sheets which shaded them so that they would neither dry too quickly and become brittle nor too slowly and mildew. About noon, Peter was praying on the housetop, likely under these animal skins hung under sheets, and getting hungry. He had a vision of a large sheet lowered from heaven with all kinds of animals in it, clean and unclean. A voice announced to him, "Arise, Peter, kill and eat!" Peter responded, "By no means, Lord, for I have never eaten anything unholy and unclean." The first voice responded, "What God has cleansed, do not consider unholy." This interchange occurred three times and then the sheet was taken back up into heaven. This left Peter perplexed, wondering what the vision meant (Acts 9:43; 10:9–17).

As Peter reflected on the vision, the Spirit said to him, "Behold three men are looking for you, arise, go downstairs and accompany them without misgivings; for I have sent them Myself" (Acts 10; 11:6–12). Peter obeyed and on the next day went with the men to Caesarea. This vision and command was what Peter needed in order to convey the gospel to Gentiles without clothing it within Judaism. That is, when Jews go to Gentiles they must show authentic Christianity available to the Gentiles, without forcing them to become Jews first in order to be Christians.

Cornelius had assembled his relatives and close friends to hear Peter's message. Peter explained as he entered the house that Jews do not associate or visit Gentiles because it is illegal (ἀθέμιτόν, Acts 10:28),[50] considering Gentiles as unclean,[51] but God had shown Peter that he should not consider any man unclean, so he came without objection.[52] This provided an opportunity to explain the gospel to those in the house and so the Holy Spirit fell upon all listening. The Gentiles began to speak in tongues as the Christians had at Pentecost, showing that they were

---

50. The force of ἀθέμιτόν is frequently describing what is contrary to the Jewish Law (2 Macc 6:5; 7:1; Josephus, *J. W.* 1.650; 2.131; 4.99, 205; *C. Ap.* 2.119).

51. Jews believed it necessary to remain separate from Gentiles (Philo, *Spec. Leg.* 1.51; *Virt.* 175; *Migr. Abr.* 89-90; Josephus, *Ant.* 14.199-265; *C. Ap.* 2.190–219; *Sib. Or.* 3.592–593; Dio Cassius, *Hist.* 37.17.1–2; Tacitus, *Hist.* 5.5.4). This separation from the Gentiles especially included the separation from their food because it could render the Jew unclean he ate it (Lev 11:1–32; Dan 1:8; Jdt 12:1–4; Tob 1:10–11; *Jub.* 2:16–18; 2 Macc 6-7; Esth 4:17 (LXX); 3 Macc 3:4; 7:11; Josephus, *Ant.* 4.137).

52. This is not an allegorical interpretation of the vision. The vision identified that Gentile foods were clean and the Spirit commanded Peter to accompany the Gentiles without misgivings (Acts 10:20). Peter logically concludes that the Gentiles are clean since their food is clean and the Spirit orchestrated him to be there.

authentically saved with the repentance that leads to life (Acts 10:44-48; 11:15-18).

When Peter got back to Jerusalem, some circumcised believers took issue with Peter for eating with uncircumcised men (Acts 11:2-3). Peter explained the vision, the Spirit's command and that the Spirit fell upon them in the same manner as upon the Jewish Christians at Pentecost, authentically saving them (Acts 11:4-18). Upon hearing that God had accepted the Gentiles, the group of Jewish Christians quieted down and glorified God.

Peter found that while he knew the truth of the equality of Gentiles it was hard to consistently live it. Once in Gentile dominated Antioch he ate with uncircumcised believers until some believers arrived from James' Jewish Christianity. After their arrival, Peter withdrew, fearing the circumcised believers. Even Barnabus was carried away into hypocrisy. Paul confronted Peter before the believers, accusing him of adding a work so that they would be acceptable before God (Gal 2:11-21). Peter rejoined the believer's fellowship but with a new appreciation of living this loving unity more consistently.

Paul Called by Christ as Apostle to Gentiles

While Saul was on the way to Damascus to round up Christians, Christ met him on the road and called him to be His apostle to the Gentiles (Acts 9:3-19; 22:5-21; 26:12). Luke recorded this conversion event three times in Acts underscoring its significance for the issue of authentic Gentile salvation. Caught within Christ's blinding light, Paul fell to the ground. Christ demanded of him, "Saul, Saul, why are you persecuting Me? It is hard for you to kick against the goads." The speaker identified Himself as Jesus the Nazarene, whom Saul was persecuting (Acts 22:8; 26:15). Perhaps this statement, which reflects Jesus' teaching elsewhere (Matt 10:40; 25:35-40, 42-45), is the beginning of Paul's body of Christ metaphor because the persecution done to the Christians was as though it were done to Christ. The Lord Jesus informed Paul and Ananias that, Paul was an apostle chosen to communicate the gospel to the Gentiles (Acts 9:15; 22:15, 21; 26:17-18). Christ said, "I am sending you to the Gentiles, to open their eyes so that they may turn from darkness to light and from the dominion of Satan to God, in order that they may receive forgiveness of sins and an inheritance among those who have been sanctified by faith in Me" (Acts 26:17–18). The resurrected Christ explained that in this service Paul would need to suffer greatly for Christ's sake. Paul was filled with the Holy Spirit and healed of his blindness. He began to proclaim the gospel among the Jews and suffer for Christ's sake (Acts 9:20–30). As Jews repudiated this Christ-centered gospel, Paul shifted his focus of communicating it to the Gentiles (Acts 13:46–48; 14:2–3; 19:9; 26:20, 23; 28:24–28; Rom 1:16). He explained the move as fulfilling the prophesied Servant Song, "I have placed You as a light for the Gentiles, that You should bring salvation to the end of the earth" (Acts 13:47 quoting Isa 49:6). Paul continued to be empowered by the Spirit to proclaim the gospel to the Gentiles and confound the opposition (Acts 13:4, 9). Elect Gentiles believed in this gospel and were filled by the Spirit with joy and praised the word of the Lord (Acts 13:48–52). The Holy Spirit directed Paul to the Gentiles He wished to include as benefited in this ministry (Acts 16:6; 19:21). Likewise, the Spirit raised up elders among the churches (Acts 20:28). In this ministry to Gentiles, miracles confirmed to many that Paul was indeed empowered by God, but the Gentile context at times made it difficult to clarify that it was the Jewish God and not a pagan god that undergirded this ministry (Acts 13:8–12; 14:8–18; 16:16–18; 17:18; 19:11–12; 28:6–9). Paul was persecuted by Gentiles because some lost income with fewer idols being sold, others recognized the power and honor of pagan gods was overwhelmed by Christ (Acts 14:5, 19; 16:19–24; 17:5–9, 32; 19:23–34). Jesus Christ (to Paul while in a trance) and the Spirit (through prophets) warned Paul about some of the threats from these persecutions (Acts 21:11; 22:18, 21). The resurrected Christ appeared to Paul to reassure Paul that he would witness for Christ's cause in Rome because Jesus claimed to protect him from Jews and Gentiles (Acts 23:11; 26:17). Through all this, Gentiles continued to be saved throughout the Roman Empire. Additionally, Roman officials supported the innocence of Paul repeatedly, because the gospel proclaiming Jesus Christ actually did not violate Roman law, provided Christianity was viewed as a sect of Jewish Pharisaism (Acts 13:7–12; 16:35–39; 18:12–17; 19:35–41; 21:31–35; 23:6–9, 23–35; 24:21–26; 25:16–26; 26:8, 28–32). In spite of this Roman perception of Paul's innocence, Paul appealed to Caesar to prevent himself from having a trial in Jerusalem or being killed on the way (Acts 25:2–12). Wherever Paul went he "kept preaching the Kingdom of God, and teaching concerning the Lord Jesus Christ with all openness" (Acts 28:31).

Jerusalem Council Decision

Some Jewish Christians argued that Gentile Christians needed to embrace a Jewish way of life, including circumcision, kosher, and the keeping of Sabbath (Gal 2:14; Acts 15:1, 5).[53] Perhaps the issue was accentuated with the different presentations of James and Galatians, which were likely composed in 48 or 49 A.D. In fifty A.D., the Jerusalem Council took up this issue of authentic Gentile salvation and obligation in Christ (Acts 15:4-29).

Peter recounted that God saved the Gentiles in Cornelius' household by giving them the Holy Spirit as He had done with the Jewish Christians as well. Luke records this event three times in the book of Acts, indicating that Gentiles are authentically saved without becoming Jews. It is from this appeal that Peter urges, "Now therefore why do you put God to the test by placing upon the neck of the disciples a yoke which neither our fathers nor we have been able to bear? But we believe that we are saved through the grace of the Lord Jesus, in the same way as they also are" (Acts 15:10-11).

Paul and Barnabus recounted how the Spirit had performed signs and wonders among the Gentiles confirming that Gentiles obtained authentic salvation as well (Acts 15:12).

James, one of the three pillars of the Jerusalem Messianic Judaism along with Peter and John (Gal 2:9), called the council to encourage the Gentile Christians within their salvation (Acts 15:14-21). James shows he is Hebraically Jewish in referring to Peter by his Hebrew name, "Simeon." He recognized that the Spirit showed through Peter's ministry that Gentiles were authentically saved. Quoting Amos 9:11-12, which calls Gentiles to the Lord at God's coming and reconstruction of the Temple, James concludes that the Jewish Christians should not trouble the Gentiles who

---

53. Perhaps these Jewish Christians followed Matt and Jas arguments for affirming the Law and applied this Law life on to Gentiles through the lens of Jesus' commission in Matt 28:19-20. Namely, "make disciples of all nations . . . teaching them to observe all that Jesus had commanded you." Mark and Luke show Jesus' consistent discipleship teaching without the Jewish aspects included. Thus the Jerusalem council could be called to deal with Pharisaic Christians who are trying to apply to Gentiles Matthew and James teaching on the Law. Jewish ethics required Gentiles to reflect the core teachings in the Law (Jub 7.20; *Sib. Or.* 3.757-9,762-66; *Ps. Phoc.* 8-58, 86, 135-36, 147-154,177-83; *t. Abod. Zar.* 8.6, 45; *b. Sanh.* 56a, bar.; *Pesiq. Rab Kah.* 12.1 six Adamite commands; *Gen. Rab.* 34.8; Keener, *Acts*, 3:2266; Josephus, *J. W.* 2.17.10; 2.18.2; Plutarch, *Cic.* 7); however Jerome (*Isa.* 9.1) recounts that Paul's teaching prevailed over the Nazarenes' personal tradition for Christianity.

are turning to God and that if God did not require the Gentiles to keep the Law to be saved, then no one should require it of them (Acts 15:19). However, with James' commitment to the Law (Jas 2:8–12), he does not allow the Gentiles to be antinomian. James appropriated four of the features of proselytizing[54] to aid in keeping the Christians unified. The apostles and the elders of the church concurred with James conclusions and composed their decision to be sent to the Gentiles (Acts 15:22–29). Luke records this decision three times, indicating that the modest restrictions on Gentile Christians is significant reassurance of their acceptability in salvation (Acts 15:20, 29; 21:25). Stephen Wilson summarizes this view:

> For Jewish Christians, living according to the law, even doing so zealously (Acts 21), was a legitimate and useful expression of their piety and a natural expression of their Jewishness. Even though zeal for the law could not bring salvation, there is no doubt that Luke saw nothing incompatible between such zeal and being a Christian. This is already implicit in the birth narratives (Luke 1–2), in Jesus' emphasis upon doing the law (Luke 10:25f) and certain hints about his own practice in this regard, in the stories about the early Christian leaders in Acts and most especially in the firm defense of Stephen and Paul against the charge that they had undermined the authority of the law.[55]

Wilson records that James does not address the Law laden quality retained in Messianic Judaism, thus retaining them in Judaism[56], while he frees the Gentiles from being under a burden that they never had been and should not be.

James places a scribal ban on the Gentile Christians, binding them from practices as attempt for church unity. The first is to abstain from things contaminated by idols (Acts 15:20, 29; 21:25).[57] The contamina-

---

54. *B. Sanh.* 56b; *Gen. Rab.* 98.9.

55. Wilson, *Luke and the Law*, p. 105. Commentators sensitized on the Jewish side even before New Perspective recognize Jewish Christians will be keeping the Law while Gentile Christians are not (Schweitzer, *The Mysticism of Paul the Apostle*, 180, 187; Davies, *Paul and Rabbinic Judaism*, 71, 81–84, 136–45, 221–23; Stendahl, *Paul Among Jews*, 1–7, 80–81, 93; Tomson, *Paul and the Jewish Law*).

56. Jervell, *Luke and the People of God*, 190; Nanos, "Apostolic Decree," 166–238; Soulen, *The God of Israel*, 170–71; McKnight, "A Parting within the Way," 110; Bockmuehl, *Jewish Law*, 168–72; Kinzer, *Postmissionary*, 66–67, 158–60; Bauckham, "James and the Jerusalem Community," 75; Marguerat, "Paul and the Torah," 111–17; Rudolf, "Messianic Judaism," 23.

57. Rabbinics view that an idol defiles by touch (*Šabb.* 9.1, 11d; *t. Zav.* 5.6–7). On

tion referred to is probably the pollution of making the food ceremonially unclean through its involvement with idolatry. It is essentially an exclusion from any participation with idols. John and Jesus concur with this restriction (Rev 2:12, 14, 18, 20).[58]

James' second exclusion is from fornication (Acts 15:20, 29; 21:25).[59] Because the lists do not always retain this exclusion next to idolatry, it is clearly a ban from the immorality of fornication in order to maintain a pure life, rather than merely an exclusion of fornication as it relates to idolatry and temple prostitution. All the N.T. authors require such moral purity of Christians.

The other two exclusions always ride together, conveying that they are addressing flip sides of the same issue: abstain from strangled (therefore bloody) meat and from the blood itself (Acts 15:20, 29; 21:25).[60] This is a repeat of the restriction in the Noahic Covenant given when granting the privilege of eating meat (Gen 9:3).[61] Such killing of animals as food retains the force of the creation mandate to rule, for in this subduing the animals lose their lives, while humans obtain the spoils. However, in the midst of this domination of animals (for obtaining food) there is a

---

a different issue, Aune (*Revelation*, 1:186) assumes that the restriction about eating strangled meat is akin to the restriction of eating meat offered to idols, however these practices occur together only in the report of this Jerusalem council decision (Acts 15:20, 29; 21:25) contrary to Aune's claim.

58. Paul is freer, for he does not accept the rationale that idols would metaphysically make things unclean, but practically it works out the same way, that Gentiles should not eat meat sacrificed to idols when there is anyone with such scruples, in order to preserve unity of the Christian church (1 Cor 8:4–13; 10:7, 20).

59. There is no evidence for emending the text to read "pork" as excluded, as Neil (*Acts*, 174) proposes in an attempt to press kosher into these restrictions. The general tenure is to keep the Gentile Christians free from the Mosaic Covenant.

60. Those who claim the exclusion from blood is addressing marrying within blood family as Lev 18:6–18 demands or exclusion from murder (Exod 20:13; Deut 5:17) impose features of the Law that contextually would not fit because: 1) the strangled and blood restriction always hang together in these discussions, so they need to be defined in relation to each other, 2) this council is excluding the Mosaic Covenant from binding on Gentiles, which counters the intuition of both suggestions because those solutions are binding aspects of the Mosaic Covenant upon Gentiles counter to the council's decision, and 3) murder would be an unnecessary restriction since it is already universally mandated against throughout the Roman empire.

61. *Jub.* 6:6–7 discusses the privilege humans have of eating animal meat, but also mandates the restriction of not to intake their blood. *Jub.* 10–14 further develops that Noah and his son must swear not to eat this animal blood and holds over them curse that if they do eat animal blood then they will be uprooted from the land.

restriction (Gen 9:4). Living flesh (*'dbśr bnpśw*/אַךְ־בָּשָׂר בְּנַפְשׁוֹ) and blood (*dmw*/דָּמוֹ), which emblems this condition of life, are both excluded from human diet. This restriction also excludes from human diet meat that is still alive, such as swallowing goldfish and first kill celebrations where the animal begins to be devoured while still alive. This restriction also excludes blood from the diet, for it is a symbol of life. Ritual drinks of blood, German blood pudding or sausage, blood meal, and Filipino delicacies made from pig blood are all to be excluded from the human diet because such blood symbolizes life. These two sides of the restriction might also combine to exclude especially bloody meat from human diet which might happen if the animal were killed by strangulation. However, there is no development in Genesis or Acts of the more detailed stipulation of Lev 17:10–13, which discusses where the Israelite and resident alien can obtain their game animals. Furthermore, there is no restriction excluding rare meat from human diet. The blessings of eating meat (with this ethical restriction) continues to be in effect today because the Noahic Covenant is an everlasting covenant that continues to bless and restrict in this area of life, with the same persistence as the no-flood promise remains in effect. This continued restriction is not seen in the Mosaic Law because the Law bound a more restrictive obligation upon the Israelite and the resident alien (who lives in Israel) than did the Noahic covenant (Lev 17:10–13). However, the Apocryphal text of *Jub.* 6:6–7 and 10–14 mandates to not eat animal blood, and declares with the threat of a curse that any blood eater will be uprooted from the land. A latter Jewish tradition for proselytizing, called the "Noahic commands" as set out in *Sanh.* 56b, include among its seven restrictions: abstinence from blood and abstinence from meat cut from a living animal.[62] The N.T. continues to

---

62. Within *Sanh.* 56a-59a (and *M. M'lakhim* 9:1) the seven precepts of the Noahides are developed. *The Encyclopaedia Britannica: Micropaedia*, 8:737 in the article "Noachide Laws") describes that the Noachide precepts are "a Jewish Talmudic designation for seven biblical laws given to Adam and to Noah before the revelation to Moses on Mt. Sinai and consequently binding on all Mankind." Thus all humans are then "sons of Noah" (Gen 10; *Ned.* 31a; *Sanh.* 57b). Normally these seven precepts are listed as: prohibition of: idolatry, blasphemy, bloodshed, incest, robbery, eating a limb or flesh severed from a living animal, and the command to set up a just legal system. The 102nd United States Congress and President George Bush senior recognized that the Seven Noahide Laws are the "ethical values and principles [which] have been the bedrock of society from the dawn of civilization" (Public Law 102-14, a joint resolution for "Education Day, U.S.A., March 20, 1991" signed into law March 20, 1991. Some Jewish traditions, such as Rabbi Samuel ben Hofni develop this material within 30 precepts, for more detailed analysis. Some other Jewish traditions see the keeping

remind Christians that all animals are clean and therefore appropriate for food (Acts 10:12–16; Rom 14:14, 20). However, within this freedom, the N.T. reminds Gentile Christians that they should restrict from their diet meat that is strangled and blood (Acts 15:20, 29; 21:25; Rev 2:10, 14).[63]

James explains that these restrictions exist because, "Moses from ancient generations has in every city those who preach him, since he is read in the synagogues every Sabbath" (Acts 15:21). The emphasis on the longstanding practice of reading and preaching Moses in the synagogues has more to do with Jews being grounded in the Law already rather than the availability of the Law for future Gentile Christian study. Admittedly, some synagogues permitted interested Gentiles to come and study Law but that is not the past emphasis in the stated reason. In fact, the Gentiles outside of Israel had never been bound by the Mosaic Law. Rather, even the widely dispersed Jews had maintained their faith and identity on the Law for a long time, therefore Gentile Christians should abstain from these restrictions so that they would not drive Jews away from their Christianity, and could therefore join together in unified churches with Jewish Christians who would continue to practice the Law as their lifestyle. That is, the ban looks to provide Gentile Christians with the basic requirement they need to do in order to maintain peaceful relationships with Jewish Christians who continue to keep the Law.

Summarizing the Jerusalem Council: (1) Jewish and Gentile Christians are authentically saved in Christ, (2) Gentile Christians do not have to keep the Law, (3) Jewish Christians are not released from the Law, and (4) both have to live in harmony with each other in Christ. Each group should be sensitive to the context in which God has accepted the other. The authority of the ban is grounded in direct authority of God in accepting the Gentiles for salvation without the Law and circumcision (Acts 15:8, 19) and in the attempt of the apostles to release the tension between Jewish and Gentile Christians by commanding a few guidelines for the Gentiles to do (Acts 15:2, 19–20). This decision did not alter the established trajectory already laid down for the Jewish Christian. The direct authority for the decision comes from the Holy Spirit, apostles, and elders (Acts 15:23, 28) and is therefore binding on the Church.

---

of the Noahic Laws as the means of salvation for Gentiles (*Gen. Rab.* 98.9; anonymous, *Noahides & Their Seven Laws*).

63. Abstence from blood continued to be practiced by Gentile Christians (Eusebius, *Hist. eccl.* 5.1.26; Tertullian, *Apol.* 9.13; Augustine chides Christians who still abstain from blood [*Faust.* 32.13]).

Luke addresses these issues once more showing that he is consistent: Messianic Jews should keep the Law, Gentile Christians do not have to keep the Law but they need to keep the Jerusalem council ban. Paul came to the Jerusalem church and reported to James and the elders what God had done among the Gentiles (Acts 21:17–27). The Jerusalem church rejoiced over the impact of salvation among the Gentiles. James raised a concern on behalf of Messianic Judaism, some of whom had a false impression that Paul was urging Jewish Christians in the dispersion to forsake the Mosaic Law, circumcision and their traditions. These Messianic Jews were zealous for the Law and had heard or read some of the information that Paul told to Gentile Christians. Paul's teaching excluded circumcision, Law and Jewish customs from mandatory Gentile Christian practice. However, Paul had enabled the Jewish Christian Timothy to be circumcised (Acts 16:1–3) and had himself completed a Nazirite vow according to the Law, as modified only by the conditions of his ministry in the dispersion (Acts 18:18; Num 6:18). Paul was sensitive to Jewish Christians as weaker brothers and urged the church to be unified without judging each other (Rom 14–15; 1 Cor 8–10). So, Paul demonstrated that it was still appropriate for Jewish Christians to keep the Law, thus validating Messianic Jewish practice.[64] Therefore, James and the elders had Paul show his commitment to the Law and Jewish customs in Jerusalem by purifying himself in the *mikvot*[65] with four Jewish Christian men completing a Nazirite vow and thus paying for the four Messianic Jews' purification and burnt offerings (both of which atone),[66] according to the Law's demand, as they completed their Nazirite vows (Acts 21:23–24; Num 6:11–13).[67] So, Paul was in the process of accomplishing these Jewish practices and atoning sacrifices when the mob rushed him (Acts 21:26–27).

James then clarified that this did not change the previous decision which the Jerusalem council had decided concerning the Gentiles as not being bound by the Mosaic Law, nor by the Jewish traditions, but by only the four previous restrictions to aid in Jewish/Gentile unity in Christ

---

64. Rudolf, *A Jew to the Jews*, 53–73.

65. I.e., Ritual washing.

66. Purification offering atones: Lev 4:20, 26, 31, 35; 5:10, 13; Num 6:11; Guilt offering atones: Lev 6:7.

67. In Num 6:13 the statement about the sacrifices in the third person "one shall bring" indicates that another than the Nazirite should provide his completion sacrifices, and it was also Jewish custom to comply in this manner (Josephus, *Ant.* 19.6.1).

(Acts 21:25). God had accepted the Gentiles as authentically saved while neither becoming Jews nor complying with the Law, and that Gentile acceptability without the Law was the established operating order.

9

Conclusion

THE PREVIOUS VOLUME, BIBLICAL *Covenantalism in Torah* provides a basic orientation to this trilogy which this volume, *Biblical Covenantalism in Prophets, Psalms, Early Judaism, Gospels, and Acts*, extended further. The development in this volume will further be brought to an integrated Christian salvation, ethic and eschatological hope in the third volume: *Biblical Covenantalism in New Testament Epistles*.

Combining this and the previous volume, the basic covenant program was established for Israel. Each of the Biblical Covenants was initiated by God and continues forever. So instead of a multi-economy theology like Dispensationalism, or a Covenant Theology with a unified people of God for all time, or a supercession program under which the subsequent peoples of God only reflect part of the Biblical material, each of the respective peoples of God benefit from their respective covenants with which they are associated. Each additional covenant adds to the previous revelation so that the covenant program builds upon each other. However, once each of these Biblical covenants begins they continue as everlasting covenants from God describing another layer of divine governance. That is, the blessing and obligation continues from these covenants forever. This progressive revelation program can be charted as follows:

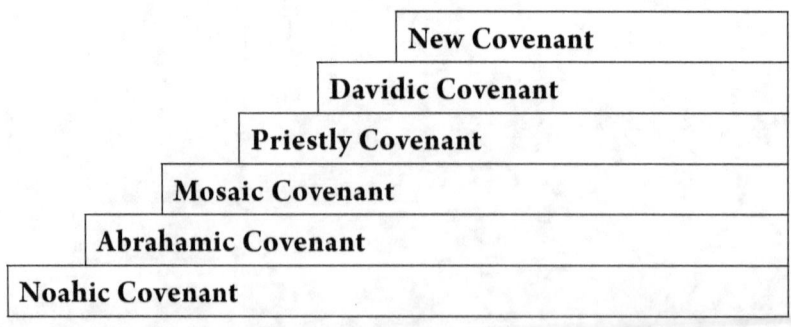

This volume also showed that the Church benefits from a number of these covenants. First, the Church is defined by the Davidic Covenant grounding that Jesus Christ is the Messiah King with whom Christians are identified. Second, the New Covenant empowers Christians in a transformed relationship with God and Christ. Both of these covenants establish that the Church is already in Kingdom and is heading toward a grander form of Kingdom in the new earth. These two covenants are grounded in blessing from the Abrahamic and Mosaic Covenants, even though the Church is not the focus of these covenants in the O.T.

Israel and the Church overlap, however, as distinct entities, so that some Jews are clearly also Christians. In this case the Abrahamic and Mosaic Covenants apply for Jewish Christians with a specific ethic so that these Jewish Christian contribute to Israel's blessings, while they as believers also share in blessings for both Israel and the Church. For Jewish Christians, the Abrahamic and the Mosaic Covenants contribute through the empowerment and framework of the New Covenant without losing their specificity.

If aspects of these covenants challenge or contradict each other then the subsequent covenantal revelation takes precedence for the intended audience. For example, the New Covenant governs the Christian, so that the Mosaic Covenant stipulations are not required for Gentile inclusion into Christianity (Acts 10:44–48; 11:15–18; 15:1–29). In the resolution for the inclusion of Gentiles within Christianity the everlasting universal unconditional Noahic Covenant was acknowledged to fund an ethic to facilitate the close proximity and love of Jews and Gentiles within Christianity (Acts 15:20, 29).

The election covenants (Abrahamic, Mosaic, and New) especially telescope out of each other and govern much of the same blessing. The previous volume laid a foundation in the first two of these covenants. The New Covenant was hinted at within the Mosaic Covenant. However, the New Covenant promises the divine Spirit to transform Israelites so that they may obey the Mosaic Covenant and continue with its covenant blessings even into an afterlife. In Luke-Acts and John, the New Covenant empowerment of the Spirit is extended to all Christians (including Gentile Christians) to transform their spiritual lives with God and others.

The Abrahamic Covenant is an everlasting unilateral covenant grant guaranteed by God for the nation of Israel but each individual male is conditionally included within the covenant based on his involvement with its sign of circumcision (Gen 12; 15; 17). The covenant primarily promises Israel's blessing (honor, blessed, blesser, nation, land). This covenant is especially important in defining Israel as a divinely elect ethnic people and nation continuing the genetic, national, and covenantal heritage of Abraham. Israel's eschatological future is grounded in this land promise. Political alignment and blessing of Israel provides other nations and peoples with the opportunity to be blessed by God. Some Abrahamic Covenant benefits are extended to the Church by blessing them with repentance and broad salvific blessing, and thus rendering the Church Abraham's spiritual seed (Acts 3:25–26; Gal 3:16–18). The Abrahamic Covenant telescopes into the Mosaic Covenant, since they are both everlasting covenants which elect the nation Israel and provide guidance for their relationship with Yahweh and His ethic, which Israel is to live.

The Mosaic Covenant is an everlasting suzerainty treaty binding Israel in a distinct relationship which for Israel extends God's Abrahamic Covenant blessings and land. God has elected Israel everlastingly as a people but this covenant is worked out in a conditional manner dependent upon each generation of Israel obeying the covenant stipulations (Exod-Lev; Deut; Josh 24; Neh 8; Jas 2:8–12). The loyalty issues and the call to love God are more reflected in the form of a suzerainty treaty. The remaining stipulations have more in common with ancient Near Eastern law codes because they are more concerned about the welfare of all subjects rather than primarily concerned about the Suzerain's rights.[1] Thus in its very makeup the Mosaic Covenant is a fusion of covenant and law or covenant nomism. This involves covenant nomism for Israel in blessing; Jewish faithfulness to God through the Mosaic Covenant contributes toward Yahweh's gracious national blessing. Such a Law governed life is a life of profound benefit (Ps 119). Unfortunately, the Bible is a record of Israel's rebellion and unwillingness to zealously live the Mosaic Covenant, so they repeatedly obtain curse. Jeremiah especially is exampled to show this impending curse through covenant lawsuit and oracle of judgment. Second Temple Judaism added a developed everlasting afterlife promising the faithful resurrection unto Kingdom. The measure of Jewish faithfulness was identified in Early Judaism through a love relationship with God as identified through obedience to the Mosaic Covenant. Since Yahweh graciously included Israel in the Mosaic Covenant and that there are gracious means of recovery imbedded within the Mosaic Covenant, the Jewish obedience to God through the Mosaic Covenant is not trying

---

1. Cross, *From Epic*, 3–21.

to earn salvation but trying to maintain Israel's place within covenant blessing. This covenant nomism theme is not the only theme within early Judaism, but it is a significant theme that governs Israel's continuing blessed relationship with God in this life and into everlasting resurrection life in Kingdom as well. The Mosaic Covenant sets a two ways framework within which Israel's relationship with Yahweh to show by her consistency of choosing to live within the narrow way of loving God and neighbor. Currently, Israel mostly in dispersion is under Mosaic Covenant curse for unfaithfulness to Yahweh and for rejecting their Messiah. Currently to politically bless and enable Israel while God has them under covenant curse is working at cross purposes with God's Deuteronmist and Messianic curses upon them. Those heading toward the Kingdom in a Jewish setting should live out the Mosaic Covenant in a zealous intrinsic manner (Deut 10:16; Matt 5:17-28). In the Matthew's gospel, the narrow way is also following Christ's ethic (which New Covenantaly embraces the Mosaic Covenant) and mimetic atonement.[2] Eventually Israel will be re-gathered into the land in Kingdom blessing and intrinsic obedience to Yahweh through the Mosaic Covenant (Deut 30:1-16; Rom 11:26). Historically, many Jewish Christians expressed their love of God through many of the details of the Law as well.[3] Within this perspective the phrase "works of the Law" in these contexts is best taken as the center of Jewish obedience to the Law.[4]

2. Pate and Kennard, *Deliverance Now and Not Yet*, 19-72, 301-334, 401-482.

3. Epiphanius, *Pan.* 2.3-5; 9.3.6; 15.3; 18.7-19.4; 21.1-6; 22.1-11; 30.7.1-7; 30.9.4; Justin Martyr, *Dial.* 47-48; Irenaeus, *Haer.* 1.26.2; Hyppelytus, *Refut.*; Clement of Alex., *Strom.* 2.9.45.5; Tertullian, *Marc.* 4.8; Origen, *Princ.* 4.3.8; Celsus statement in Origen, *Cels.* 2.1 and *Hom. Gen.* 3.5; Eusebius, *Hist. eccl.* 3.27.1-6; Chrysostom, *Homily* 32; Ignatius, *Magn.* 8-11; *Phld.* 6-9; Jerome, *Isaiah* 3.30 on Isa 9:1; Augustine, *Faust.* 19.7; Pseudo-*Clementines Recognitions* 1.28.1-2; 1.32.4; 1.37.1-4; Hippolytus, *Haer.* 8.18.1-2; *Ps.-Clementine Homilies* 7.8; 42.355-56; *Didascalia Apostolorum* 21; Rouwhorst, "Jewish Liturgical Traditions in Early Syriac Christianity," *VC* 51(1997): 82; These polemics against the Jewish-Christians are essentially the same polemics made against the Jews (for example, Aphrahat of Persia, Syriac *Demonstrations* 12-16); Klijn, "The Study of Jewish Christianity," 419-31; Taylor, "The Phenomenon," 313-34; Bagatti, *The Church from the Circumcision*; Velasco and Sabourin, "Jewish Christianity," 5-26; Klijn and Reinink, *Patristic Evidence*; Pritz, *Nazarene Jewish Christianity*; Skarsaune and Hvalvik, *Jewish Believers in Jesus*.

4. Several different Hebrew phrases translate as "works of the Law" (ἔργων νόμου) from either "works" (מַעֲשֵׂה) or "faithfulness" (עוֹלָם חַסְדֵי): Neh 13:14; 1QS 5.21, 23-24; 6.18; 1QpHab 7.11; 8.1; 12.4-5; CD 13.11; 4Q171 frgs. 1-2 ii 14; 4Q174 frgs. 1-3 ii 2; 4Q176 frg. 17 line 7; 4Q394 frag. 3-7 col. 1-2.1-3; 4Q398=4QMMT frag. 14 col. 2.3; C.23-28; 4QFlor. 1.1-7; 4Q470 frg. 1 line 4; 4QpPsa 1-2.2.14, 22; 11QT 56.3; *2 Bar*.

Daniel Block discusses the developing nature of the Law to be an evolution of Israel's Constitutional Tradition (see diagram below).[5]

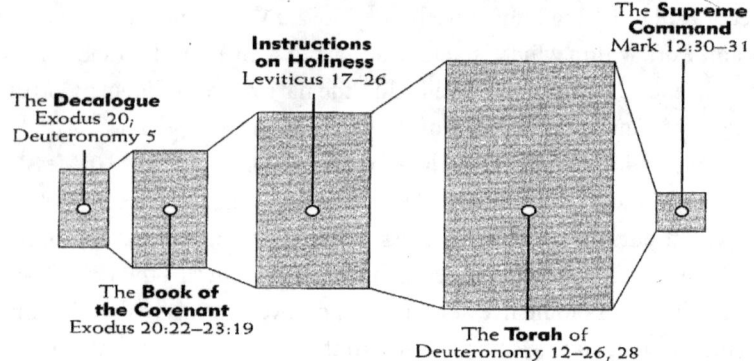

This development is similarly shown in the previous volume, *Biblical Covenantalism in Torah* provides a basic orientation from the discussion of the Ten Commandments, then the Book of the Covenant "YAHWEH Elects Israel to Exodus and to Mosaic Covenant Nomism." However, the development of the Law is most dramatic within Deuteronomy because the structure of the stipulation section of Deuteronomy intentionally expands and explains the Ten Commandments. The Leviticus Holiness code and laws in the book of Numbers primarily fit within the Deuteronomy treatment where the two overlap. However, much of Leviticus discussion extends the framework and practice of worship and recovery so that it receives special developed within the chapter on "Hebrew Metaphysic."

57.2; 4 Macc 7.9; cf. Lohmeyer, *Probleme paulinischer*, 31–74; Christianson, *The Covenant in Judaism*; Watson, *Paul and the Hermeneutics*, 334–35; Evans, "Paul and 'Works of Law,'" 201–26; Hofius, "Werke des Gesetzes," 271–310; Dunn, *The New Perspective on Paul*, especially chapters 1, 8, 10, 14, 17, 19 which were articles from 1992–2008 on works of the Law which nicely provides a trajectory for how the view grew; de Roo, "The Concept of 'Works of the Law,'" 116–47; "*Works of the Law*," 1–26; Cranfield, "The Works of the Law," 89–101; these contrast with Dunn, *Romans*, 1:159; Sanders, *Paul and Palestinian Judaism*, 118; for example, of reformation view: Moo, *Romans 1–8*, 216–17; "'Law', 'Works of the Law,'" 82; Bachmann, "Rechtfertigung," 1–33; "4QMMT," 91–113; *Anti-Judaism in Galatians?*, 15. In spite of Dunn's identification of the concept with the "palisades and iron walls to prevent mixing with any other peoples" *Letter of Aristeas* 139–42 (*The New Perspective on Paul*, 8–9), even though the phrase "works of the Law" is not in the *Letter of Aristeas*; Hogerterp, "4QMMT," 359–379.

5. Block, *Deuteronomy*, 169; *The Gospel*, 143.

All this development within the growing Mosaic Covenant, constitutes the same covenantal program. Within the available covenant atonement there is a recovery both of cleansing to holy and clean status, as well as a recovery to righteousness through forgiveness. In this volume, *Biblical Covenantalism in Prophets, Psalms, Early Judaism, Gospels, and Acts*, the New Covenant deepens the Mosaic Covenant into an internal inclination to obey and love God (Jer 31:31–34; Matt 5). Second Temple literature draws this narrow way of covenant nomism into an afterlife promise for the nation of Israel to have Kingdom hope. Likewise, Jesus frames this love for God in the synoptics and Acts as a mimetic atonement within the narrow way unto Kingdom. Within this narrow way to Kingdom, Jesus takes up a covenant nomism for Jews. Within His New Covenant teaching, Jesus simplifies the essence of the Law as rabbis had done to two concretized commands implying an internalized transformation of His disciples, which will be accomplished by the work of the Spirit (Matt 22:39; Mark 12:30–32; Luke 10:26–27; Rom 8:1–5).[6] This simplified expression of the Law internally prompted by the Spirit is a New Covenant spirituality and ethic appropriate for non- Jews to also motivate right practice to God and others.

These last paragraphs identify that I am an advocate for deepening both the Jewish perspective for Israel and the third quest for the historical Jesus. On the other hand I embrace only about one sixth of the new perspective for Paul, while I deeply position myself in the wake of pre-new Paul Jewish interpreters such as Albert Schweitzer and W. D. Davies. Such a position could also be identified as a post-new perspective one with more nuance than Douglas Campbell provided. However, the route through perspectives on Paul is provided especially within the next volume: *Biblical Covenantalism in New Testament Epistles*.

Additionally, there are covenants that ground ministries of service, like the Davidic and Priestly Covenants. The Davidic Covenant, developed in this volume, guarantees a continuing lineage for David's family being on the throne as king of Israel forever. Unfortunately, the sin of Davidic kings meant that they lost the throne for generations, leaving Judaism with the hope of a more ultimate Davidic King to come and

---

6. Greatest Command: *T. Iss.* 5.2; *T. Dan.* 5.3; *Jub.* 36.3–8; Josephus, *Ag. Ap.* 2.206; Philo, *Spec.* 2.63; *Decal.* 20.154; 108–10; *Abr.* 208; *m. Sanh.* 10.1; Rabbi Akiva in *Sifra Lev.* 19:18; *Sifre* on Deut 6:4; *b. Šabb.* 31a; *b. Ber.* 63a. Second Command: Rabbi Akiva considered love of neighbor in Lev 19:18 to be the great commandment (*Sifra Qed.* 4.200.3.7; *Sifra* on Lev. 19:18; *Gen. Rab.* 24.7; *b. Šabb.* 31A).

reign in the future. Many of the Abrahamic and Mosaic Covenant blessings are also enmeshed with the Davidic Covenant like fame, national protection, continuing in the land, peace, rest, blessing, and discipline in sin (2 Sam 7:4–17). This Davidic Covenant is an everlasting covenant that ultimately brings about the everlasting reign of the Messiah upon the earth (2 Sam 7:12–16; Pss 89:2, 4, 29, 36–37; 132:12, 14; Luke 1:32–33; Rev 1:5–6; 22:5).[7]

Jesus is born and honored by wise men, His disciples and God as this everlasting Messianic King of Israel (Matt 1–2:11; 3:17; 16:16–17).[8] Jesus dies as the King of the Jews (Matt 26:63–64; 27). However, as King, Jesus already has a growing Kingdom of disciples and the world as His Kingdom which will after judgment be combined to become an eschatological expression of Kingdom (Matt 5:3–11; 13:31–33, 38, 41–43). Jesus is proclaimed to be the Davidic King in the gospel on the basis that God raised him already from the dead and seated him at the right hand of God (Acts 2:29–36). On the basis of the Davidic Covenant, Jesus is already declared to be the Christ functioning in His reign by His titles, throne, anointing, place of honor, and Christ's pouring forth the New Covenant Holy Spirit for ministry in the Church (Acts 2:33; Heb 1:5–13). There is a grander eschatological expression of the Kingdom not yet realized in which Jesus Christ will reign forever (Matt 5:4–9; Luke 1:32–33; Heb 1:13; Rev 1:5–6; 19–22).

The Priestly Covenant developed in the earlier volume (*Biblical Covenantalism in Torah*) is a Covenant Grant of Peace resulting in the Levitical line in perpetual everlasting service as priests (Num 25:12–13). This promise is re-affirmed in the Davidic and New Covenants (Jer 33:14–22; Ezek 44:10, 15; 48:11).

The New Covenant emerges as an everlasting covenant grant to transform Israel into a responsive and *torah* obedient community in intimate relationship with Yahweh (Deut 30:3–6; Jer 31:27–37). Early Judaism recognizes that the New Covenant and the Mosaic Covenant fuse as the divine Spirit enables Israelites to obey and continue within

---

7. 4Q504 1–2 iv 4–8; cf. 4Q252 5.2–5; Abegg, "The Covenant of the Qumran," 82; 4Q161 frag. 7–10.iii.22; 4Q174 frag. 1–3.i.11–12; 4QpIsa. frag. 7–10 iii 22; 4QCommentary on Genesis A 5.3–4; 4Q252 frag. 1 v. 3–4; 4Q285 frag. 5.3–4; frag. 7 lines 3–4; 11Q14 lines 12–13; *Pss. Sol.* 17.4, 21, 27–36; 18.7; 4Q252 fragment 1, 5:1–5 translated by VanderKam and Flint, *The Meaning*, 266, and myself; a similar point is made by 4Q521 column 2, and 4Q521 frag. 7.3.

8. Kennard, *Messiah Jesus*, esp. 377–414.

the covenant blessings made available by these two covenants. This New Covenant is extended to all Christians, including Gentiles, highlighting that the believer in Christ is mystically in Christ in a New Covenantal manner in which the Holy Spirit is relationally present to transform the believer's life (Luke 22:20; Acts 2:16-21).

The Spirit's empowerment within the New Covenant will eschatologically transform the heart of Israel so that Israel will do the Law intrinsically and have all those Abrahamic, Mosaic, Priestly and Davidic promises like the land, kingship, peace, functioning Levitical priesthood, and Mosaic sacrifices (Jer 31:27-32:22; Ezek 40-46). Additionally, the New Covenant everlastingly brings resolution and peace for humankind and even animals in Kingdom (Isa 11:6-9; 54:9-10; Jer 32:40; Ezek 34:25-30; 37:26; Hos 2:18). As such, the New Covenant is already instituted for the Church by Christ's death in a weaker form than the eschatological Kingdom (of intrinsic Spirit motivation, Spirit produced righteousness and fruit, everlasting forgiveness, and cleansed conscience). Eventually, the transformation which the Spirit causes brings about Christian's immortal bodily resurrection unto eschatological Kingdom (Luke 22:20; 1 Cor 11:25; 2 Cor 3; Heb 9-10; Acts 2:17-21 as compared to Joel 2:28-29).

www.ingramcontent.com/pod-product-compliance
Lightning Source LLC
Chambersburg PA
CBHW051633230426
43669CB00013B/2290